CAPOEIRA

E aquest loch passen los mer
chaders q: entren en la terra del
negres de gineua lo qual passes
apellat vall de darha

tacorani

pasayota

sigilmessa

serra
clara: e se
moltes bor
baten los h
tava e sabu
fruytres:

Tota aquesta ytda tenen gens q: son
en bossats q: nols: neu hon sino los vyse
euan/entendes/e san caualcades ab
camels/e ay bisties qui han nom lemps
e daquel aiy v fan les bones carguess

sudam

ciutat de melly

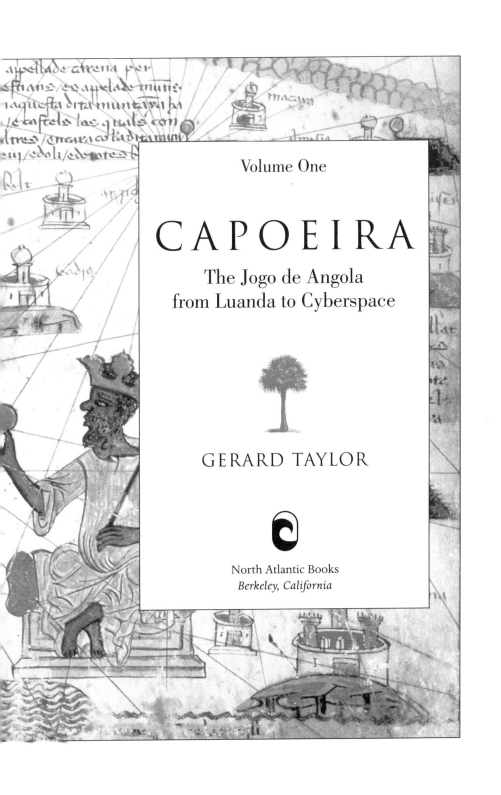

Volume One

CAPOEIRA

The Jogo de Angola
from Luanda to Cyberspace

GERARD TAYLOR

North Atlantic Books
Berkeley, California

Published by
North Atlantic Books
P.O. Box 12327
Berkeley, California 94712

Cover painting by unknown Brazilian artist
Cover and text design by Brad Greene
Printed in the United States of America
Distributed to the book trade
by Publishers Group West

Capoeira: The Jogo de Angola from Luanda to Cyberspace is sponsored by the Society for the Study of Native Arts and Sciences, a nonprofit educational corporation whose goals are to develop an educational and crosscultural perspective linking various scientific, social, and artistic fields; to nurture a holistic view of arts, sciences, humanities, and healing; and to publish and distribute literature on the relationship of mind, body, and nature.

Epigraph from Paulo Coelho, *Manual of the Warrior of Light*, HarperCollins Publishers, 2003. Reprinted by permission of the author.

North Atlantic Books' publications are available through most bookstores. For further information, call 800-337-2665 or visit our website at www.northatlanticbooks.com.

Substantial discounts on bulk quantities are available to corporations, professional associations, and other organizations. For details and discount information, contact our special sales department.

Library of Congress Cataloging-in-Publication Data
Taylor, Gerard, 1960–
    Capoeira : the Jogo de Angola from Luanda to cyberspace / by Gerard Taylor.
        p. cm.
    "Traces the social, cultural, and political history of this lively martial art and dance form. Volume I spans over four centuries, from the beginnings of slavery in the Americas, to the establishment of the Brazilian Republic in the early 20th century"—provided by the publisher.
    Includes bibliographical references and index.
    ISBN 1-55643-601-7 (pbk : v. 1)
    1. Capoeira (Dance) 2. Capoeira (Dance)—History.   I. Title.
GV1796.C145T39 2005
793.3'1981—dc22
                                                                    2005020917
                                                                    CIP

1 2 3 4 5 6 7 8 9 UNITED 10 09 08 07 06 05

DEDICATION

To Mestre Sombra of Associação de Capoeira Senzala de Santos,
and Mestre Sylvia Bazzarelli
and Contra Mestre Marcos Dos Santos
of the London School of Capoeira Herança.

And for Agnes, Hanna, Gerard, and Ameli.

The warrior of light sometimes behaves like water,
flowing around the obstacles he encounters.

Occasionally, resisting might mean being destroyed,
and so he adapts to circumstances . . . The waters of a river
adapt themselves to whatever route proves possible,
but the river never forgets its one objective: the sea.
So fragile at its source, it gradually gathers the strength
of the other rivers it encounters.

And, after a certain point, its power is absolute.

—PAULO COELHO

Contents

Table of Illustrations *xiii*

Permissions *xv*

Acknowledgments *xvii*

Introduction 1

Time Line 7

Chapter One

IN THE BEGINNING 31

Mandinga Gold Merchants 33

Islam's African Slaves 34

The Route of All Evil 35

The Colonial Era 39

Mwene Puto 42

"The rosy dawn of the era of capitalist production" 44

The Land of the True Cross 46

The Line of Tordesillas 50

The Triangular Trade 52

Chapter Two

SUGAR BLUES 57

Capture and the March to the Coast 65

Angolan Kilombos 67

A Cruel Era 70

Engenhos 72

Cutting the Cane 76

Barreado Sugar 79

Soca 80

Chapter Three
THE RISE OF THE QUILOMBO DOS PALMARES   83

The Dutch West India Company   85
Palmares   86
Imbangala   90
Laws of the Jaga   94
The Art of Deception: Kiluvia   95
Macaco   98
Caapuera   101
Inside the Quilombo dos Palmares   102
King of Congo   103
Kings Ganga Zumba and Zumbi dos Palmares   105
Johan Mauritz of Nassau and São Jorge   107
"Overflowing with slaves for sale"   110
"Rubbish heap of Portugal"   111
The War against Palmares   112
Imbangala Warriors   114
Santo Antônio é Protetor   123
Moradores   126
Bandeirantes   135
The End of an Era and the Birth of a Legend   141

Chapter Four
THE GOLD RUSH   149

Gold Mining   151
Tight Packing and the Middle Passage   157

CONTENTS

Chapter Five

FROM RIO TO THE GOLD MINES   169

Extracting the Gold   181
Africans and Amerindians in Quilombos   187
Cowboys, Indians, and Slaves   198
Amerindian and African Religious Cults in Quilombos   202
Crime and Punishment   203
Women in Colonial Brazil   208

Chapter Six

"BRAZILIAN BANTU LAND"   219

Ngolo, the Dance of the Zebra   221
The Bantu People   234
Agogô   240

Chapter Seven

ISLAMIC REVOLUTION
IN WEST AFRICA   245

Mandinga Magic   248
Gold Coast, Slave Coast, Fanti, and Ashanti   250
Islamic Jihad   254
Unannounced and Unplanned   255
The Sokoto Caliphate   256
Islam in Salvador, Bahia   257
Yoruba Culture in Bahia   260
Islam, the Fall of Old Oyo, and the Rise of Dahomey   262
Jeje and Nago   265

Chapter Eight
THE ST. DOMINGUE REVOLUTION 269

The Rights of Man 270

Fear Spreads to the USA and Brazil 274

Abolition 275

Engenho Santana 279

"We shall be able to play, relax and sing any time we wish" 282

Work Songs 283

Batuques Are Forbidden 287

Witchcraft and Feitiçaria 290

Sedan Chair Porters 292

Bad Night in Bahia: The 1835 Uprising 295

Chapter Nine
AN AWFUL LOT OF COFFEE
(AND CAPOEIRA) IN BRAZIL 303

Vadiagem 304

"United Kingdom of Portugal, Brazil and the Algarves" 305

Capoeiras, Spies, and Conspiracies 306

Fear and Loathing in Rio de Janeiro 307

Coffee and Capoeira 313

"Neither man nor his land rested" 315

Rio Coffee Carriers 317

Chapter Ten
O BERIMBAU 321

"O berimbau é o instrumento principal e indispensável" 322

Hundreds of Years of Tradition 324

Atabaques 325

Custom of the Black People 327

CONTENTS

"Nobody trusts you if you keep visiting around" 328

Orixá 328

"Berimbau bateu, angoleiro me chamou" 337

The San Hunting Bow 340

Caxixi 343

"Negroes fighting with their open hands" 346

Berimbau in Capoeira 348

Signs, Crosses, Circles, Rodas 351

"A canoa virou marinheiro, e no fundo do mar tem dinheiro" 352

"Look out sister, how you walk on the cross / Your foot
might slip and your soul get lost" 354

Chapter Eleven
THE EMPIRE OF BRAZIL 357

Major Nunes Vidigal 360

"There remains in the imperial palace but one silver spoon" 371

Cops and Capoeiristas 372

Paraguay 376

Paraná ê, Paraná ê, Paraná 377

"Club and Rope" Impressment 380

Capangagem 382

Nagôa and Guayamu 385

"A capoeirista . . . with his odd gait" 386

Malta Slang Names 388

"A special crime and punished with new penalties" 389

Rio de Janeiro Quilombos 391

The Beginning of the End of Empire 393

Abolition and the Brazilian Republic 396

The Law of the Free Womb 397

La Belle Époque 400

"Scientific" Racism 401

"In the pulverization of the earth, there was a long groan"   404
The Empire Strikes Back   405
Santos   406
Deodoro da Fonseca   407
"Slavery is declared abolished in Brazil"   410

Chapter Twelve
THE REPUBLIC   415

Vadiagem and Bens do Evento   416
"The exercise of agility and corporal dexterity known
by the term capoeiragem"   419
Old Portuguese Bantu-Land   424
Bahia and the End of the Beginning   426
Yoruba Magic   427
Besouro Mangangá   430
"Besouro quando morreu / Abriu a bôca e falô / Adeus
Maracangalha / Qui é terra de matadô"   433
Lampião   434
"The art form was slowly extinguished in Rio and Recife,
leaving capoeira only in Bahia"   441
"National representative symbol"   443
"Bahia de todos os santos, Bahia dos orixás, Bahia de Menininha,
Menininha do Gantois"   445

Appendices A–D   453
Notes   469
Glossary   493
Bibliography   521
Index   533
About the Author   539

Table of Illustrations

Unless otherwise indicated, all archival illustrations appear courtesy of the Mary Evans Picture Library.

Title page
King of Mali, from the Catalan Atlas, folio III, 1375. Courtesy of the Bibliothèque nationale de France.

Page 47
Bartolomeu Dias, Portugese navigator, sailing for the cape. Engraving by A. Fieg.

Page 74
Slaves working on a sugar plantation, circa 1870.

Pages 92–93
View of the roadstead and town of São Paulo de Luanda, circa 1875.

Page 155
Washing for gold in the Brazilian mountains, circa 1814.

Pages 192–193
Diamond washing.

Page 239
Great Zimbabwe, dated 1892. A plan of the site of the incredible ancient buildings at Great Zimbabwe, and a few of the many objects found at the site.

Page 258
Sokoto Market, Nigeria, during the 1850s.

Page 273
Saint Domingue revolution, dated 1802–1804. French and patriots in hand-to-hand combat.

Pages 308–309
Entrance to a Brazilian coffee plantation, dated 1879.

Page 330–331

Instrument photographs by Sue Parkhill and Anders Kjaergaard.

Pages 378–379

April 10, 1866. Brazilian colonel Willagram-Cabrita repels a Paraguayan attack at the island of Redempcion, in the Paraná River.

Pages 422–423

LEFT, Railroad in Brazilian tropics, dated 1864. RIGHT, A temporary rail bridge and the station of Rodeio on the Railway of Pedro II in Brazil. (Source: Engravings by Deroy and Cosson Smeeton from *L'Illustration, Journal Universal,* Paris, 1864.)

Permissions

Excerpts from Roderick J. Barman, *Citizen Emperor Pedro II and the Making of Brazil, 1825–91,* courtesy of the Stanford University Press. Robert Edgar Conrad, ed., *Children of God's Fire: A Documentary History of Black Slavery in Brazil,* pp. 66, 123, 125, 129, 135, 247, 249–250, 260–264, 304, 339, 369, 371, 373, 384, 391, 404–402, 404–411, 679. Copyright © 1994 by The Pennsylvania State University Press. Reproduced by permission of the publisher. Euclides da Cunha, *Rebellion in the Backlands.* Copyright © 1944 by The University of Chicago. Excerpts from Gilberto Freyre, *The Mansions and the Shanties, The Masters and the Slaves,* and *Order and Progress* courtesy of the Fundação Gilberto Freyre, Recife, Brazil. Excerpts from Peter Fryer, *Rhythms of Resistance: African Musical Heritage in Brazil,* reproduced by permission of the Pluto Press. Excerpts from John Hemmings, *Red Gold: The Conquest of the Brazilian Indians,* reproduced by permission of Macmillan, London, UK. Excerpts from Ruth Landes, *The City of Women,* reproduced by permission of the UNM Press. Excerpts from Joseph C. Miller, *Kings and Kinsmen: Early Mbundu States in Angola,* reproduced by permission of the Oxford University Press. Excerpts from Dennis Newsome, "Interview with Mestre Preto-Velho, Group Malandros-Touros," reproduced by permission of the author. Richard Price, ed., *Maroon Societies: Rebel Slave Communities in the Americas,* pp. 7, 8, 12, 26, 136, 152, 174, 180, 182, 184, 187, 196, 199, 214, 217, 219, 258. Copyright © 1979, 1996 by The Johns Hopkins University Press. Reprinted with permission of The Johns Hopkins University Press. João José Reis, *Slave Rebellion in Brazil: The Muslim Uprising of 1835 in Bahia,*

Acknowledgments

I wish to express my heartfelt thanks to the people and institutions who have helped me during the course of writing and publishing this book.

The staff at the Universitetsbiblioteket at Blindern campus in Oslo, and the Etnografisk Bibliotek in central Oslo, were helpful and efficient in securing books and manuscripts. The staff at the great Deichmanske Bibliotek in Oslo, and particularly at the Majorstua branch, were so pleasant during my many searches after books that needed ordering from out of town. I am indebted to Vanessa Taylor for occasional help supplying documents from the British Library and for her kind words of encouragement, which, coming from a better historian than I, were always greatly appreciated. I am indebted to the Liga e Tenda attached to Academia Senzala in Santos, São Paulo, for photocopying periodicals I requested and allowing me to view videos.

Thank you to Cesar Bargo Perez and Sandra Pires for professionalism and excellent translation work in Santos, São Paulo. I am grateful also to Volker Herrmann, "Ceará," of Associação de Capoeira Canigó, for help translating various pertinent questions for Professora Agnes Folkestad in Santos. On that point, special thanks to Agnes Folkestad for unwavering patience and more help than I can ever fully acknowledge with the years of multiple tasks necessary for completing the book. Thanks particularly to Agnes for moral support and assistance with various technical aspects of using a computer, and so many other things I couldn't add them up. Without her this book would likely never have been done.

I would like to sincerely thank many publishers for generously granting permission to quote from their publications. Included in this group are the Taylor & Francis Group LLC, Simon & Schuster, the Fundação Gilberto Freyre, the University of New Mexico Press, and the Pluto Press. Also thanks to Dennis Newsome (Mestre Preto Velho) for his permission to quote information regarding African-American fighting styles and related topics from his website. Thanks are due to HarperCollins and Paulo Coelho for the epigraph. Special thanks to Penn State University Press for the invaluable use of quotes from *Children of God's Fire,* Robert E. Conrad's masterful translation of documents from the Brazilian slave era. The University of Chicago Press and Duke University Press gave generous permission to quote from various books and articles. Thanks also to Routledge, Dover Publications, Oxford University Press, The John Hopkins University Press, the excellent Brazzil Magazine at www.brazzilmag.com, Cambridge University Press, Macmillan Publishers Ltd, and Stanford University Press.

Special thanks to Dr. John K. Thornton for granting permission to quote from his books and articles and for generously sending me a copy of his English translation of Cavazzi da Montecuccolo and Giovanni Antonio's *Istorica Descrizione de tre regni Congo, Matamba ed Angola*. I am grateful to Dido Sandler for allowing me to quote from material she researched for her unpublished dissertation, *Capoeira, Rio Past and Present,* written in 1987.

With gratitude I acknowledge Barth Niava of the Center for Afrikansk Kulturformidling (CAK) in Oslo for help and information and loan of the ngogo seen in this book. Also many thanks to Rud videregående skole for the use of their premises for photography, and to the London School of Capoeira for use of their premises for photography. Thanks to the Bibliothèque Nationale de France for use of the image from the Catalan Atlas, and to the Mary Evans Picture Library for the historical illustrations in this book. Thanks also to Mohamed El Hedi Habhab for his kind assistance communicating initially with the French National Library. Warm thanks to Sue Parkhill and Anders Kjaergaard for their friendship, to Sue for long hours spent in picture libraries seeking historical illustrations (even though she is a photographer) and to Anders for setting up and taking the photographs that introduce the twelve chapters of this volume.

Particular thanks are due to Mestre Sylvia Bazzarelli, who not only helped with translation work for the book, but introduced me initially to many of the subjects that later evolved into a general research map to follow. Much gratitude is also extended to Contra Mestre Marcos Dos Santos of the London School of Capoeira and Mestre Sombra of Associação Senzala de Santos.

Thank you very much to North Atlantic Books and Richard Grossinger for having enough faith to take on this project. Particular and special thanks to Yvonne Cárdenas, the project editor, who kept everything on track and patiently guided this team effort for many months, transforming the mess of an original manuscript into a readable book. True thanks also to Winn Kalmon for the daunting task of copyediting the whole lot. Yvonne and Winn have vastly improved the finished product by painstaking attention to detail and drawing attention to those areas that needed completion or clarification. Many thanks are also due to Brad Greene for creating the attractive design within the book and on the cover. Our gratitude also to the anonymous artist whose painting of capoeira in Salvador, Bahia illustrates the front cover.

Thanks to the board and the students of the Oslo Capoeira Klubb for being enthusiastic about playing capoeira and for being one of the best groups of people I've ever been fortunate enough to meet.

Introduction

In the 21st century we are seeing an unprecedented explosion of capoeira around the world. Capoeira groups and schools are to be found everywhere, from Brazil to the USA, Russia to Israel, Egypt to Poland, Mozambique to China, Australia to the Ukraine—and the list really could go on with new countries or cities added by the month. Clearly, many of the participants who have caught this "capoeira fever" have been moved by something deeply attractive in the art form to the human body and psyche, something that travels with ease across cultural and national borders. I know this because I was one of those who caught capoeira fever in Europe in the 1980s, and plainly many of us still haven't recovered completely.

Capoeira does travel lightly and yet many practitioners who are not Brazilian and have no roots in African Brazilian culture have from time to time struggled with concepts that are more than just foreign in terms of geography, but which also resonate from a different place at a deep cultural level. Studying northeastern Brazilian sugar plantations, Stuart Schwartz compared this predicament to that of a famous French historian who once sat in the British Museum staring at a Union Jack through a window, straining to understand what any English child in the street knew without giving it a second thought.

Capoeira: The Jogo de Angola from Luanda to Cyberspace focuses on 500 years of history, during which time Portuguese slave trade in

Africa created a colony in Brazil where for centuries the majority of the population of the towns and plantations were born in Africa. By chronologically matching events in regions as diverse as the Upper Guinea Coast, Benin/Nigeria, Central Africa, Congo, and Angola, this book attempts to clarify areas of particular interest concerning slave rebellion in Brazil, the formation of quilombos, and the interrelationship of these events to the art form capoeira. Particular attention is paid to African fighting forms, the use of certain types of military strategy, fortifications, weapons technique, and spiritual preparation for combat in warrior groups as diverse as the Ashanti, the Yoruba, the Oyo, the Imbangala, the Mbundu, and Congo forces. Attention is also paid to indigenous Amerindian groups that were regular collaborators with escaped slaves in the mocambos of Brazil's interior.

Books about capoeira are not uncommon. A quick search will reveal a long list of books and articles in Portuguese and English covering the history of the art form, summaries of capoeira music, reference to Capoeira Regional and Angola, and even courses and instruction in capoeira techniques and sequences. The aim of this book is to fill a knowledge gap that seemed to me vital for a greater understanding of the massive impact of the slave trade and its historic reverberations. As the book moves chronologically over events in Africa, Europe, and Brazil, as far as possible I have provided quotes and voices to give more contemporary reality to what might otherwise have become a dry academic exercise.

I came to the subject much as many other capoeira students have done. After hearing about capoeira in London, I tried some classes and found them incredibly difficult. After helping out with administration and writing short publicity pieces in a new capoeira school, I gradually became hooked and decided to find out more, so began reading some books. There was a sense of frustration that I could penetrate no further into the history than that capoeira seemed to be a mixture of Bantu and Yoruba components. As well as knowing no Portuguese, I had only a vague idea what was meant by the terms "Bantu" and "Yoruba," and with sadness realized I'd never learned a single thing about sub-Saharan or indeed any part of Africa other than biblical Egypt in school, and knew even less about how this weight of history might have affected the activity I was presuming to write publicity about.

Having trained in judo for years as a child, it struck me how much more emphasis there was on the past in capoeira than there had been in judo, and yet how much confusion there seemed to be about how these historical antecedents connected to each other to result in the art as we now know it.

The two volumes of the present study are the culmination of research I decided to carry out, once I began teaching capoeira myself in Norway after 1996. My method, if that isn`t too grandiose a term for the way I worked, was to put myself into the position of a capoeira student hungry for information about the history and development of this art form, within the context of the Atlantic slave trade and colonial era to which it is intrinsically linked. The aim was to answer the type of questions I'd heard asked many times by capoeira students, and create a kind of narrative that would follow capoeira through the often brutal history of colonial and post-colonial Brazil.

The difficulties in this approach were numerous. Paul Lovejoy eloquently pointed out that studies of slavery and ethnicity, and modern interpretation of causes and effects, present very definite problems. First, there is the requirement for knowledge of African history both by region and period, which for the non-specialist is a challenge. Even the most basic analysis necessitates a quite thorough knowledge of the diaspora, in this case particularly to Brazil, but also to other regions such as Saint Domingue (Haiti), Suriname (Dutch Guiana), Cuba, and so on. This is often as difficult to gain as the knowledge of African history. There is the problem of language, in my case Portuguese, but for scholars of slave trade and ethnicity and the diaspora, that would also include French, English, Spanish, Arabic, various Bantu languages, Hausa, Nupe, and Yoruba.

It was also necessary to avoid journalistic cliché and reiteration of phrases about "the horrors of the middle passage" or avaricious African middle men, evil European slave traders, and other hackneyed characterizations.

Not being a professional historian and having to resort often to the help of translators focused attention on achieving only what was possible, which made me eclectic in choosing the information I specifically wanted to supply. In this, the fact that I was actually training capoeira myself was an asset, as this gave an accurate clue to the kinds of areas that are relevant. It often led me to capoeira in literary places where I'd otherwise never have noticed it. It was also a revelation that a wealth of extremely good academic historians and anthropologists had trod much of this ground already and a main effort was keeping up with their footsteps.

This book makes no claim to being a definitive history; my hope is to answer, or at least raise, questions about how historical events affected capoeira. Hopefully, it will also inspire specialist students with their own expertise to build on this material and look further and deeper in the future.

The title "Luanda to Cyberspace" was chosen because today cyberspace actually is a powerful symbol and tool of 21st-century capoeira. In 0.57 seconds Yahoo and Google combined can give over 2 million hits, and not just about Eddie Gordo. Capoeira today exists in a world where the face-to-face invitation from one capoeirista to another to play in the roda is often replaced by a mailing list of thousands, an e-mail distribution, mass-membership associations, "mail-order master" franchises, and many new practices facilitated by the worldwide web. Capoeira exists in cyberspace.

This volume ends in the earliest years of the Brazilian Republic. Volume Two will explore many of the economic and cultural strands that link the violently repressed capoeira of Deodoro da Fonseca's Brazil, the neofascist years of Vargas's dictatorship, "national" recognition, and the present-day situation of runaway international acclaim. This will be achieved thankfully with the aid of in-depth interviews with capoeira students, teachers, and mestres, both in Brazil and Europe. The aim, as with the present volume, will be to show that the art form has never existed in a vacuum, but is the result of the people who practice it making sometimes very hard choices or adapting to the economic and social forces of the societies in which we live.

Capoeira isn't an academic, "book-learned" art. It is a living, breathing activity that is played in present time and maintained only by the people who do it in any given generation. Capoeira is a game; also it's healthy for the body, optimistic, fun, and, some would say, healing for the spirit.

Yet capoeira as a historical cultural phenomenon is becoming an ever more ripe subject for study by objective scholars who have no axe to grind when it comes to style or "association." Most would agree that some key questions of history and anthropology are presented by the riddle of capoeira. I hope that a youngster (or oldster) reading this book may find something in it that catches the imagination, informs, or is useful as a springboard for future study on his or her own. If this occurs, my efforts will not have been in vain.

—Gerard Taylor
Oslo, Norway
2005

Time Line

2000 BC

According to Bantu migration theory, the root Bantu language originated in Cameroon and Nigeria. By 1000 BC, Bantu speakers had spread to the savannas of Angola and east to Lake Victoria. By AD 500, the Bantu people had scattered throughout central and southern Africa, absorbing indigenous populations throughout the region.

570 AD

Birth of the prophet Muhammad in Mecca, Western Arabia.

700

Rise of the ancient empire of Ghana.

920–1050

Apogee of the Sarakole empire of Ghana.

1150

Beginnings of Yoruba city-states.

1200

Rise of the Mali empire.

1212

"Ghana is a great town to the south of the Maghrib, adjacent to the land of Sudan (the land of the blacks). Merchants meet in Ghana and from there one enters the arid wastes toward the land of Gold. Were it not for Ghana, this journey would be imposssible because the land of Gold is in a place isolated from the west in the land of Sudan. From Ghana, the merchants take provisions on the way to the land of Gold." (Yaqut) (Source: Carmichael, *African Eldorado,* p. 49. Yaqut is an Arab historian cited by Carmichael.)

1255

Mansa becomes an official title for the emperor in the Empire of Mali.

1300

Arab and Christian geographers are now regularly marking a fabled "River of Gold" on maps depicting the West African coastline west of the Cape of Bojador.

1312–1337

Reign of Mansa Musa.

1324

Mansa Musa makes a pilgrimage to Mecca via Cairo.

1350

An anonymous Spanish Franciscan writes a travelogue called *El Libro del Conocimiento* (The Book of Knowledge), relating tales of voyages around the world, including the coast of West Africa.

1350 (to 1450)

The late Middle Ages and early Renaissance in Europe.

1351

The Laurentian Portolan map gives an accurate outline of West Africa.

1352–1354

Half of Europe's population of 25 million people die due to Bubonic Plague or "Black Death."

1375

An atlas drawn by Abraham Cresques identifies Timbuktu, Taghazi, and Sijilmasa. At a pass in the Atlas mountains, he wrote, "Through this place pass the merchants who travel to the land of the blacks of Guinea, which place they call the valley of the Dra'a." The "Catalan Atlas" depicts the rule of Mali, the first European depiction of the region of West Africa.

1400

Portugal begins to develop a powerful commercial class, and simultaneously feels the effect of a gold bullion shortage. The Fante occupy the coast of Ghana.

1415

The Portuguese capture Ceuta, a Muslim entrepôt on the African coast, which they hope to use as a base to gain entry to the Saharan gold trade.

1420

Portugal colonizes Madeira and in 1427 colonizes the Azores.

1424

Henry the Navigator sends a flotilla of 120 ships and 2,500 men to occupy the Canary Islands.

1425

Florence, an Italian city with a population of 60,000, emerges as a center of change in art, writing, architecture, politics, and economy, and becomes a model of Renaissance culture.

1435

Gil Eanes rounds Cape Bojador in search of the "Rio Del Oro" described in *The Book of Knowledge.*

1440

The caravel is developed by Portuguese shipbuilders.

1441

The first African slaves and gold are exported from Africa for Lisbon.

1446

The Genoese House of Centurione forces a return to the gold standard, which begins a monopoly for companies with ample gold bullion reserves. Large banks begin to finance expeditions in search of gold in sub-Saharan Africa.

1450

The apogee of the Songhai empire is represented by the university at Timbuktu.

1454

Pope Nicholas V recognizes Portugal's sole rights to West African trade.

1460

Portugal colonizes Cape Verde. Henry the Navigator dies and Afonso V inherits all the rights to Portuguese African trade. A squadron of Portuguese push beyond Sierre Leone.

1461

Songhai becomes the imperial power on the Middle Niger.

1469

A union of the Spanish kingdoms is brought about by the marriage of King Ferdinand V of Aragón to Queen Isabella I of Castile.

1470

Portugal colonizes São Tomé. Afonso V grants the merchant Fernão Gomes a monopoly over the Guinea trade south of Sierre Leone for five years. For this deal Afonso receives 200,000 réis per year.

1474

Afonso V refuses to renew Gomes's contract and the lucrative Mina gold trade becomes a royal monopoly. The royal share of the gold was one-fifth of the total. Bullion supplies in Portugal are now restocked.

1478

Spanish Queen Isabella requests the Spanish Pope, Sextus IV, to establish an Inquisition to prosecute heresy. Sextus grants the crown powers to appoint bishops to complete the Inquisition, which continues until the early 1800s.

1481

Portugal creates the Casa da Mina, a special customs house for African trade.

1482

From 1482 onward Europeans demand the right to fortify their positions on the African coast. The fortress of São Jorge (Elmina Castle) was the first such structure. Each year, slave traffic at Elmina grows, so that by 1500, 500–600 captives a year were channeled through São Jorge. Gold obtained from Mina represents a significant addition to the Portuguese economy.

1483

Diogo Cão makes contact with the Kongo kingdom. He establishes links south with Ndongo, an African state less advanced than Kongo. Their leader, the ngola a kiluanje, was a tributory of the ManiKongo.

1492

A Spaniard, Christopher Columbus, discovers the "Indies" in the Caribbean Ocean.

1494

The Treaty of Tordesillas divides the "New World" between Spain and Portugal.

1498

Vasco da Gama makes the first sea voyage from western Europe around Africa to India.

1500

Pedro Alvares Cabral sails to Brazil and the colonial era commences in earnest. His men make contact with coastal Amerindians. At this time Brazilian Amerindians are divided into four main language groups: Gé, Tupi, Carib, and Aruak. Gé speakers inhabited the Atlantic littoral until they were ousted by Tupi tribes in the hundred years before Portugal's arrival. By 1500, Tupi-Guaraní speakers had moved north from Paraguay and Bolivia and inhabited most of the Brazilian seaboard. *Capuuera* is a Tupi-Guaraní word meaning extinct forest.

1510

Slave traffic between São Tomé and Mina reaches its height between 1510 and 1540. Six slaving vessels continually haul captives and sell to Mina merchants. Between 1500 and 1530 Brazil's main export is wood.

1517

Portugal develops a strong trading relationship with the Akan king, who supplies the purest 23-carat gold on the "Gold Coast."

The German monk, Martin Luther, nails his 95 Theses to a church door in Wittenberg, Germany, thus beginning a "Reformation" of the Church.

1530

Sugar overtakes lumber as the main export from Brazil, with Amerindian slaves doing the work on Brazilian plantations.

1533

In England, the child who will be crowned Elizabeth I is born to Henry VIII and Anne Boleyn.

1534

King João III creates fifteen captaincies in Brazil, to replace feitorias with permanent Portuguese settlements. Olinda is founded in 1537.

1540s

Jesuit missionaries arrive in Brazil. The "Society of Jesus" at this time was less than ten years old and was run in military fashion.

1543

Just nine months of gold trading produces 300 kg of gold for Portugal, and in this year a single caravel carries 170 kg of 22-carat gold from São Jorge castle to Lisbon.

1549

Tomé da Sousa establishes Salvador da Bahia as Brazil's capital.

1550

70 sugar engenhos are operating in Brazil. The Guinea cycle of slave imports from Africa to Brazil begins. Various Tupi-speaking tribes control much of the coast between Pernambuco and Bahia, and the banks of the São Fransisco River. Brazil becomes the first foreign province of the Jesuits in 1553, under the leadership of Manoel da Nóbrega.

1554

São Paulo de Piratininga is founded.

1556

The ManiKongo becomes angry that the Portuguese are trading with the ngola a kiluanje. He sends an army against Ndongo, but the Kongo army is defeated and the Ngola declares independence from Kongo, appealing to Portugal for support.

1561

Destruction of the Mali empire by Songhai. In the 1560s, Bubonic Plague hits Lisbon and is carried aboard ships to Brazil, where, along with small pox, it decimates Amerindian populations on the coast and in plantations and missions. By now 40,000 Amerindians are working on Bahian sugar plantations. Santidade religion begins to take hold in northeastern Brazil.

1565

Rio de Janeiro is founded.

The Imbangala are at war with the ngola a kiluanje in Angola. There are hostilities between Portugal and the Ndongo.

1570

As deadly diseases hit the Amerindian populations enslaved on Brazil's sugar plantations, planters are raising sufficient capital to purchase African slaves. Between 1570 and 1630, Africans begin to outnumber Amerindians on Brazilian sugar plantations.

1576

Paulo Dias carries out a bloody military campaign against the Ndongo, founding forts around Luanda, although never gaining total military control. He travels up the Kwanza River.

1580

Spain and Portugal establish the Iberian Union. Between 1580 and 1600, the Imbangala overrun the kingdom of Benguela and its surrounding provinces. In the 1580s, Portugal, using the military commander Mem de Sá, systematically attacks Amerindian tribes and the French (who also colonized areas of Brazil).

1590

The Dutch make occasional forays to the Guinea Gulf and become Portugal's main competitors for the coastal gold trade. The Portuguese king permits slaving operations in Mina.

1599

Aimoré Amerindians destroy all the sugar mills on the southern shore of the Bay of All Saints in Bahia, eating the slaves. Santo Amaro and its mills are abandoned. The Aimoré also take Ilhéus.

1600

The Angola cycle of slave imports to Brazil begins. At the same time, scores of Dutch ships financed by founders of the East India Company begin to trade in Mina even more efficiently than the Portuguese. There are by now 15,000 African people estimated to be in Brazil. The Imbangala make contact with the Portuguese for the first time.

1605

Escaped slaves from Pernambucan sugar plantations begin to enter Alagoas and establish the earliest mocambos of the Quilombo dos Palmares.

1612

Alexandre de Moura, captain of Pernambuco, petitions for the creation of a capitão do campo (bush captain) in each of the eight parishes of Pernambuco, to be aided by twenty Amerindians in each case.

1615

Portuguese negotiate a deal with the Imbangala to come north of the Kwanza to help in Portuguese wars.

1618–1621

Luis Mendes de Vasconcelos, allied with several Imbangala bands, attacks Ndongo and defeats them.

1621

The Dutch establish the West India Company. In Brazil, from the 1620s until the end of the century, bandeira flag expeditions begin to explore the Brazilian sertão, enslaving Amerindians as they march.

1624 (until 1663)

The rule of Queen Nzinga (Njinga Mbandi) in Angola. Between 1626 and 1629 she battles Portuguese forces and their Imbangala allies from within Ndongo but is defeated and moves east.

1625

The kingdom of Dahomey is established.

1630

The Dutch invade northeastern Brazil and capture Recife.

1631

Queen Nzinga captures Matamba, which becomes her power base.

1637

The São Jorge da Mina is handed over to the Dutch.

1639

Pope Urban VIII denounces trading in Amerindian slavery as punishable with excommunication.

1641

A Dutch expeditionary force arrives in Luanda. In 1642 an ambassador of the king of Kongo visits the Dutch captaincy of Recife in Brazil and performs "original dances, leaps and formidable swordplay."

1640s

Bandeirante Antônio Rapôso Tavares signs the act of acclamation, by which the Duke of Bragança becomes King João IV. The bandeirantes explore Paraná, Paraguay, Guaporé, Mamoré, Uruguay, and the Amazon. Their explorations demarcate the massive territory which the Portuguese claim as the country of Brazil, and which occupies half the South American continent.

1648

The Dutch are driven from Luanda by the Portuguese.

1650

The Gunpowder Revolution. Muskets are used increasingly by African armies on the Gold Coast.

1654

The Dutch withdraw from Brazil. In 1655 Queen Nzinga agrees to a peace deal and a status quo is established, thus ending the wars over the throne of Ndongo.

1655

Zumbi is born in the Quilombo dos Palmares in Alagoas, Brazil. Palmares at this point is ruled by King Ganga Zumba.

1656

"The . . . true purpose was to capture Indians: to draw from their veins the red gold which has always been the mine of that province!" Jesuit António Vieira said of the expeditions into central Brazil in search of gold.

1663

The first British machine-struck gold coin was produced. The gold came from Africa's Gold Coast, courtesy of the British "Africa Company," which used the symbol of the elephant. The coin was popularly called a "guinea," and after 1674 depicted an effigy of the king's head and an elephant and castle.

1665

The Battle of Mbwila. In one of the largest wars of Central African history, King Antonio I led an army into the Dembos Mountains between Angola and Kongo. Kongo forces are badly defeated. The "Great Plague" hits London, to end when the worst slum areas are destroyed by the "Great Fire of London" in 1666.

1670

The armies of Kongo and Soyo crush Portuguese forces at Kitombo, ending Portugal's ambitions in Kongo until mid-19th century. Zumbi is General of Arms in Palmares.

1678

The sack of São Salvador in Kongo.

1680

The total slave population of Brazil has reached approximately 150,000. The Ashanti state takes shape in Ghana's interior and rain forest.

1695

Palmares crushed in 1694 and King Zumbi executed on November 20, 1695.

First gold strike in Brazil in the River Velhos in Mina Gerais. This hails the gold boom, which lasts until around 1750. The gold boom coincides with the Mina Coast cycle of slave imports from Africa. It is estimated that 300,000 slaves, largely from Africa's Gold Coast, entered Mina Gerais alone between 1698 and 1770.

1699–1700

Ashanti at war with Denkyera. A rise of Ashanti power, with the Yoruba kingdom in decay.

1700

The Mina Coast cycle, 1700–1775. Between 1700 and 1709, 70,000 people are also transported from Kongo to the Americas.

1706

Dona Beatriz Kimpa Vita is burned at the stake in Kongo. She had gained a large and influential following in Kongo after claiming to be possessed by St. Anthony.

1709

From this year and for the following decade, members of Dona Beatriz's Antonian movement are exported to Brazil, North America, and the Caribbean in large numbers.

1720

Coffee introduced to Brazil.

1739

Stono slave rebellion in South Carolina.

1745

The approximate year of the birth of Toussaint L'Ouverture, one of the main leaders of the Haitian Revolution.

1750

Rise to power of the Marquis of Pombal, whose aim was to make the crown and his country rich by stimulating agricultural production in Brazil and tightening taxes. This is also a period of decline for both the sugar and gold industries in Brazil.

1754

The birth of Uthman Dan Fodio in northwest Hausaland. He was one of the early and main instigators of the Sokoto Caliphate, spreading Islamic jihad in Yorubaland.

1762

Jean-Jacques Rousseau writes *The Social Contract*. The 18th century is the period of philosophical trends that, taken together, are often called the "Age of Reason" or "The Enlightenment."

1763

Brazil's capital is transferred from Salvador to Rio de Janeiro.

1770

The Bight of Benin cycle of slave imports to Brazil begins. A Portuguese capoeirista nicknamed Amotinado was in this decade said to be bodyguard to the Marquis de Lavradio. At this time the Oyo empire is the principle supplier of slaves to the trading center at Abomey-Calavi, which supplied Lagos during the Bight of Benin cycle.

1776

On July 4th, political leaders in what becomes the United States of America publish the Declaration of Independence.

1789

On July 14th, members of the French populace storm the Bastille fortress. The French National Assembly publishes the Declaration of the Rights of Man. In Brazil, the Inconfidência Mineira (a plot to make Mina Gerais an independent republic). The first written reference to Capoeira: an arrest report of a slave named Adam.

1791

Slave rebellion in Saint Domingue (to become Haiti). This increases the international demand for sugar from Brazil, and the demand for African slaves. The Haitian Revolution was the only successful overthrow of slavery during the 18th century.

1792

Tiradentes is executed as a scapegoat for the Inconfidência Mineira.

1798

Revolt of the Tailors (Inconfidência Baiana). Among the revolutionary ideas handwritten on manifestos placed on walls in the city were: the abolition of slavery, an end to racial discrimination in employment, free trade with foreign countries, and confiscation of Church property.

1799

Napoleon Bonaparte seizes power in France.

1806

War between the Fante and Ashanti in Ghana is ended by a serious small pox and dysentery epidemic.

1807

Britain declares it illegal for British ships and merchants to engage in the Atlantic slave trade.

1808

The Portuguese royal family arrive in Brazil. João VI opens ports to world trade.

1809

Guarda Real de Polícia is established in Rio de Janeiro and led by Major Miguel Nunes Vidigal.

1810

A commercial treaty is signed between Britain and Brazil.

1814

Fante country becomes an Ashanti province. A citizens' council in Bahia petitions the Portuguese prince regent, Dom João, denouncing the weak policies of Bahia's governor, the Count dos Arcos, for allowing batuques and dances to the sound of a single stringed instrument in Salvador's town squares.

1815

Brazil is raised to the status of kingdom.

1820

The Austrian artist Rugendas visits Brazil and sketches the famous "Jogo de Capoeira" picture.

1821

João VI leaves Brazil for Portugal.

1822

Brazil breaks away from Portugal and becomes an empire under Pedro I.

1830

Brazil imposes a criminal code banning drumming, batuques, dancing, and shouting, and enforcing curfews.

1833

Abolition of slavery in the British empire. Coffee displaces sugar as Brazil's most valuable export.

1835

The Yoruba empire of Oyo falls, and many are taken prisoner and sent to Brazil, ending up in Salvador. Yoruba religion becomes strongly established in Salvador in the form of Candomblé. Nagô becomes the "lingua franca" of Bahian Africans. A major uprising of Nagô-led slaves in Salvador, Bahia occurs.

1840

Pedro II becomes emperor of Brazil.

1850

Declaration of the end of the Atlantic slave trade in Brazil.

1853–54

Major Nunes Vidigal dies and Manuel Antonio de Almeida writes a novel about Vidigal called *Memoirs of a Militia Sergeant*, in which capoeira features prominently.

1865–70

The Paraguayan War, in which many capoeiristas are press-ganged and sent to the front to fight. During this period, what's been dubbed the "breech loader revolution" takes Europe decisively ahead of Africa in armaments, speeding Europe's conquests during the scramble for African colonial control.

1870

Publication and distribution of a "Republican Manifesto" in Brazil. In 1871, the "Law of the Free Womb" is passed.

1873

The first recorded use of Gatling guns (machine guns) by European troops, in Africa by the British army during the Ashanti war of 1873–74.

1888

The "Golden Law" abolishes slavery in Brazil.

1889

A military coup overthrows the empire and establishes a Brazilian republic.

1889

Vincent Ferreira Pastinha is born.

1890

A federal statute is enacted officially outlawing capoeira. Ruy Barbosa orders all the papers in the ministry of the treasury relating to slavery or the slave trade to be burned.

1891

Mestre Siozinho born in Santos, São Paulo.

1895 or 1897

Birth of Manoel Henrique Pereira (Besouro Manganga).

1899

Manoel dos Reis Machado (Mestre Bimba) born on November 23 in Salvador, Bahia.

1906

Lieutenant Santo Porto writes a preface to a book on Japanese physical education recommending mixing jujitsu with capoeira as an effective self-defense system.

1909

At the Concerto Avenida I, capoeirista Macaco Velho knocks out the jujisu champion Sado Miako with a rabo-de-arraia.

1920

During 1920–26, Pedro de Azevedo Gordilho is chief of police in Salvador, Bahia. He prosecutes capoeira and capoeiristas with extreme force.

1922

In *Eu Sei Tudo*, Professor Mário Aleixo advocates mixing capoeira with other martial arts, including jujitsu, boxing, and wrestling.

1924

Besouro Manganga assasinated.

1926

Padre Cicero, Louis Carlos Prestes, and Lampião are all operating in northeastern Brazil.

1928

Aníbal Burlamáqui publishes *Ginástica (Capoeiragem) Metodizada e Regrada*. advocating capoeira in academies as a sport and influencing the development of capoeira in Rio de Janeiro. Both Aleixo's and Burlamáqui's ideas were later advocated during President Vargas's "Estado Novo," when the ministry of education produced subsidies for studying the methodology of *capoieragem*.

Chapter One
IN THE BEGINNING

The art of capoeira evolved during the colonial epoch, which spanned half a millennium from the 15th to the 20th century. After abolition of the Atlantic slave trade, capoeira was legally banned in Brazil until the 1930s. It's a beautiful art form but the conditions that made it what it is were cruel and frightening.

This history begins at the time when Africa received the first visits from Portuguese mariners and explorers. In fact, commerce and other contact had already taken place between Europe and Africa for centuries before (the Portuguese Prince) Henry the Navigator's ships first set sail down Africa's Atlantic coast searching for Guinea's legendary gold. Jews and Christians from Europe had long been trading with Muslims from North Africa. Crusades had taken Christian invaders into the lands of the Saracen. Wars of conquest fought between the Moors and Mediterranean states had been characteristic of the region.

During the medieval era many places in West Africa existed within the political sphere of Islamic civilization. Arab power lay primarily with people of rank. Mullahs dominated trade for hundreds of years before the arrival of ships carrying European traders, soldiers, and explorers. The trade was organized and busy, including that in slaves. To Arabs, Africa south of the Sahara was "the land of the blacks" (Bilad as Sudan); that included present-day Senegal, Mali, Upper Volta and Niger, areas of Mauritania, Guinea, and Nigeria.

> Gold and slaves traveled directly northward, from the successive Sudanic empires of West Africa to Morocco. . . . In the ninth century, there was a diagonal route from Ghana to Gao and then across the Sahara to Egypt . . . while another route, from Mali to upper Egypt rose to prominence in the fourteenth century, and in the sixteenth century, yet another one, from Timbuktu to Cairo.[1]

The Kingdoms of Ghana, Mali, and Songhai were "successor states" between the 9th and the 16th centuries. They came to prominence one after the other approximately every 200 years. The majority of the population of these trading states was involved in agriculture, cultivating various species of millet, rice, and cotton. Farmers used iron tools, which had been introduced in the millennium before the birth of Jesus Christ.

Horses and donkeys were reared in Western Sudan in areas free of tsetse flies. Specialist fishermen cast their nets on the river Niger. Agriculture increased food supplies, which led to greater population. The wealth thus created encouraged trade and industry. Luxury goods like cotton cloth enhanced internal trade. Western Sudanese pastoralism provided cattle hides and leather goods, while horses were vital for transport and military campaigns. Donkeys and mules carried the people, supplies, and products until the arrival of camels from North Africa. Camels were vital in trans-Saharan travel, which had been active since at least 1000 BC.

Particular royal clans were specialized blacksmiths and the desire to control iron, copper, and salt mines was the cause of wars. The rulers of Ghana, for example, pushed into Berber territory to take over mines in the 10th century. Mali and Songhai were involved in similar competition with Morocco over salt mines. Farther south were the gold sources of the Upper Senegal and Faleme tributory. In the 13th century gold mining began in Ghana's forest, which supplied the trans-Saharan gold trade.

Mandinga Gold Merchants

The early Portuguese who sailed to the river Gambia were dazzled by Mandinga gold merchants, skilled in weighing gold dust on solid silver scales dangling from finely twisted silk cords.[2] The Mandinga were travelers, trading middle men, often called *dioulas*. They traversed thousands of miles the length and breadth of Western Sudan. They weren't necessarily very rich merchants but their mobility was amazing. Arab literacy and language facilitated communication over very long distances and these men might be found anywhere from Sicily to Morocco or even China.

Some historians argue that the Mandinga crossed the Atlantic to America at least 150 years before Christopher Columbus. Harold G. Lawrence and Pathe Diagne write that Abubakari II of the Mali Kingdom employed Mandinga mariners to cross the Atlantic.

> Both Bakary II and Christopher Columbus learned from the African navigators of Senegambia and the Gulf of Guinea about ... trans-oceanic traffic and trade ... the existence of a corridor fed by North Equatorial winds and ... the existence of a current that was easy to navigate during the summer and fall and that led to the rich Maya, Olemeque, Aztec and Inca Kingdoms and civilizations. Neither Bakary II nor [later] Christopher Columbus were ready to share this geopolitical secret.[3]

The dioula merchants traded in salt, kola nuts, gold, leather, dried fish, cotton cloth, iron, shea butter, and, from North Africa, fabric and coral beads. The caravans that traversed the Sahara and the merchants who traded goods (from as far afield as Egypt, Maghreb, Guinea, upper Gambia, Hausaland, Ghana, Ivory Coast, and Liberia) spread Islamic culture. This accelerated the growth of famous cities like Timbuktu and Jenne. Trans-Saharan merchants didn't create the great kingdoms, however; this was achieved by the massive productivity of Western Sudan's population in a region that was very well suited to agriculture.

Islam's African Slaves

The financial capital for Saharan trade came largely from North Africa, where Islamic merchants controlled the proceedings. The balance of trade in dealings with lands to the south of the Atlas Mountains were tipped in North Africa's favor. A trans-Saharan trade in slaves from areas south of the desert flourished in the centuries prior to the arrival of the European trader and in fact continued during the era of Atlantic slave trade. The Mali and Songhai empires maintained powerful armies, wielding power over a large region. The Songhai monarchs had a ready supply of captives for use as a military guard, to harvest gum, to work in mines, and so forth. The Mali also used slaves in agriculture.

> Many of the black slaves exported from the central Sudan were destined for military service in North Africa. The trade also supplied eunuchs for employment in harems or in government service, and female slaves for sale as concubines. Ibn Battuta, who crossed the Sahara in the middle of the fourteenth century and traveled with a caravan of six hundred female slaves, wrote favorably of both the eunuchs and slave girls from Bornu. The trade supplied many other

slaves for more menial purposes. Still others were not provided to the trade but used as the currency of tribute or of gifts.[4]

Compared to the trade that would later develop over the Atlantic Ocean, the Songhai and Mali exported slaves in relatively small numbers. Zones that didn't control gold supplies (such as Kanem-Bornu) gave trans-Saharan slave trade higher priority, raiding as far south as Cameroon. For trans-Saharan merchants the slave and gold trades were closely connected, yet the gold trade boosted the forces of production in West Africa while the slave trade didn't. Slave labor's agricultural role in Western Sudan never reached the point where slavery became the mode of production. That was unknown in Africa before the arrival of the Portuguese; indeed, it was unknown to the Portuguese before their arrival in Africa.

Many of the Saharan trade routes had been used since the Middle Ages: traversing Berber and Arab territory over an area that today covers Mali, Mauritania, Morocco, Algeria, and Libya. The Portuguese were acutely aware that much of the gold that eventually reached Europe came across the Sahara from Bilad as Sudan ("the land of the blacks").

The Route of All Evil

Europe needed gold because the feudal system was transforming into a money economy based on capital. Gold for coin was needed in much greater quantity and Portugal was in the midst of a bullion shortage. It was the search for gold that inspired the very earliest Portuguese exploration of Africa's Atlantic coast.

Merchants and explorers spread stories that were widely known in Spain and Portugal, of kingdoms and monarchs in "the land of the blacks who possessed mines abounding in gold."[5] For two centuries before the Portuguese dominated the West African coast, Europeans hoped to bypass Muslim-controlled overland trade routes. The dream was to gain access to India via the West African coast. Fleets of galleys led by intrepid Europeans (Vivaldi in 1291 and Jaume Ferrer in 1346, for example) had set off in search of the shining riches, but they vanished without trace, presumably to the bottom of the Atlantic ocean.

In 1340 an expedition of Europeans sailed to West Africa, then captured and enslaved four *guanches* from the island of Tenerife. In the 14th century a by-product of European gold expeditions was the enslavement of the indigenous people of the Canary Islands, who were usually carried back to Portuguese and Spanish ports. At this time slavery was a familiar part of life in medieval West Africa. Slaves were proof of a ruler's or warlord's personal wealth and were one of the few forms of private property recognized in African custom. But the days were imminent of a new variety of slavery, previously unknown in West Africa. If one man could be said to have contributed to this development on an equal footing with Christopher Columbus, it would be the Portuguese prince, Henry the Navigator.

The Portuguese (including Henry the Navigator) thought that the area south of the Sahara was going to be a Christian monarchy. A myth that had persistently inspired explorers was that of the Christian monarch Prester John, popularly believed to live in a vast palace of crystal and precious stones. His retinue was said to include kings, giants, and centaurs. The optimistic hope was that Prester John would help his fellow Christians in their quest for gold and their pursuit of the legendary wealth of India.

Throughout the 1300s, Arab Muslim and European Christian geographers had begun to mark a fabled "River of Gold" on maps depicting the West African coast south of the Cape of Bojador. Ethiopia had been a European synonym for Africa. Was this the mythical Christian kingdom cut off from the Christian world by infidels? Ethiopian monarchs had become Christian more than a thousand years earlier, but in fact the area really envisaged as the lost Christian empire in Henry the Navigator's day was Mali. In 1375 the "Catalan Map" had depicted cities such as Timbuktu, and marked a pass in the Atlas Mountains with the legend, "Through here pass the merchants who come from the lands of the blacks of Guinea."[6]

In 1415 the Portuguese attacked and captured Ceuta, near Gibraltar. Via this entrepôt they expected to gain entry to the Saharan gold trade. Muslim traders had other ideas and shifted their routes and trade center elsewhere to deprive the Portuguese of any control over the Sahara desert. Henry the Navigator had no clue where the mythical gold fields of Guinea really lay, though he believed they could be reached by sea. He was based in Sagres in Portugal and although he never took to the waves himself, he had built an observatory there and established the first school for navigators in Europe. On Henry's orders, Portuguese mariners sailed in search of the Guinea treasure.

Portugal took the islands of Madeira and the Azores. Ships kept traveling farther south along the West African coast as far as Cape Juby. In 1434 Henry sent off one of his best navigators with a crew of fifteen to explore what Arabic sailors called the "Green Sea of Darkness." These were unexplored waters that had a terrifying reputation as the home of sea monsters and other phantoms of the medieval imagination. The sailor Gil Eannes from the Algarve found that the old myths weren't true. The fairly frequent Portuguese expeditions into the Green Sea of Darkness discovered no sea monsters,

CAPOEIRA

no cyclops or three-headed giants. Sailors didn't turn black when they rounded the cape, as Portuguese superstition supposed they might. By 1441 two Portuguese captains had reached Cabo Branco at the point of the coastal border between Morocco and Mauritania.

Nuno Tristão and Antão Gonçalves visited a market of Muslim traders where they received ostrich eggs and their first tantalizing small portion of gold dust. The commander ordered his men to capture twelve black Africans (Azanghi people). He said, "What a beautiful thing it would be . . . if we could capture some of the natives to lay before the face of our Prince."[7]

These were not the first Africans from Guinea to arrive in Portugal. In 1425 nearly sixty slaves from Guinea had been sold in Portugal after they'd been seized from a Moroccan slave ship. On that occasion Prince Henry had got a glimmer of the potential of selling African captives in Portugal. With that in mind in 1441, when the twelve new captives were presented at court, he was very interested when one of them, a chief named Adahu, communicated in Arabic that for his and a relative's release back to Cabo Branco, he would provide African slaves in return.

In 1442, the Portuguese captain Gonçalves returned to Cabo Branco and delivered to Portugal more gold dust and approximately ten Africans who'd been brought to Cabo Branco along one of the Arab caravan routes. The following year another Portuguese captain (Nuno Tristão) returned to the Bay of Arguin, just south of Cabo Branco, and took prisoner around thirty men, who were enslaved immediately. A chronicler reported that Tristão regretted, "Their boat was so small that they were not able to take such a cargo as they desired."[8] By this time, Henry's Lisbon shipbuilders had developed the hundred-foot caravel, which, though weighing less than seventy tons, was strong enough to withstand long periods at sea.

Its rigging was convenient for both coastal and river sailing, leading to its reputation as the handiest oceangoing vessel afloat.

Trade with Africa was then a royal monopoly after Pope Nicholas
V had recognized Portugal's sole rights to West African trade. In
1444 the first Portuguese company (de Freitas) sought a license
from the crown to travel along the African coast and trade. De Freitas traveled back into West African Atlantic waters with the first
Portuguese to have been there, Gil Eannes. The mood and motives
for the exploration had changed, for as the saying went, "The Portuguese served as setting dogs to spring the game."[9]

The African coastal explorations were highly expensive for Portugal. Afonso V cleverly granted the merchant Fernão Gomes a
monopoly of all Guinea trade from Sierra Leone southward for
five years in return for 200,000 *réis* to the crown. It was Gomes
who began pushing along the coast as it veered eastward. As he
navigated farther he noticed that villagers were now more heavily adorned with gold. In the 1470s Lisbon received word that at
last the "Gold Coast," soon to be called "Mina," had been reached,
and the nascent Portuguese slave trade had begun.

The Colonial Era

In 1482 Diogo Cão traveled farther south than any European before
him and came upon the mouth of a river: "For the space of 20
leagues [the river] preserves its fresh water unbroken by the briny
billows which encompass it on every side; as if this noble river had
determined to try its strength in pitched battle with the ocean itself,
and alone deny it the tribute which all other rivers in the world pay
without resistance."[10]

Cão ordered an iron cross to mark his "discovery" of the biggest river any European had ever laid eyes on: the river Congo. "In the year 6681 of the World and in that of 1482 since the birth of our Lord Jesus Christ, the most serene, the most excellent and potent prince, King João II of Portugal did order this land to be discovered and this pillar of stone to be erected by Diogo Cão, an esquire in his household."[11]

By 1487 Bartolomeu Dias had rounded the Cape of Good Hope. Having achieved navigation of the Indian Ocean, the Portuguese sailed to China and Japan. By now they'd established numerous *feitoras,* fortified trading posts along the West African coast. Portugal had colonized the islands of Madeira, the Azores, Cape Verde, and São Tomé. The royal monopoly had created the *Casa da Mina or Casa da Guine,* a customs house directly for African trade, specializing in gold dust, ivory, pimenta, and slaves for domestic service or urban labor in Portugal.

From the earliest days of Atlantic slavery, Africans were constrained by laws that became ever more numerous throughout the colonial era. By 1460 "representatives to the Cortes [the Portuguese parliament] . . . forty miles up the Tagus from Lisbon, complained that to serve the feasts which the slaves of the town organised to celebrate Sunday and other religious festivals, some chickens, ducks and even lambs had been stolen, and plans for escape had been hatched. So the Cortes forbade the slaves to hold such parties."[12]

A century later, in 1559, we find a similar law enacted: "The King, our Lord, orders that in the city of Lisbon, and one league around it, there might be no assembly of slaves or dances or playing of musical instruments performed in their [the African] manner, either at night or during the day. . . . And that the same prohibition be understood for free blacks."[13]

Farming on the islands that lay close to the coast of Africa, particularly São Tomé, became the model for the *engenhos* and plantations the Portuguese would establish elsewhere. There were wheat farms but far more profitable were the sugar plantations financed by Genoese and Jewish merchants in São Tomé. Increasing anti-Semitism in Spain and Portugal during the 1400s led to a massive increase in forced "conversions" of Jews and mass expulsion from Spain during the period of the *reqonquista*. The widespread arrival of *conversos* in Iberian colonies was closely connected to persecution of Jews in Europe, not only by the Inquisition, but also after the Reformation.

São Tomé sugar plantations relied solely on slave labor and, where there was slave labor, as night follows day, there was always slave revolt. A Jesuit father from Portugal wrote that the "foremost enemies of the colonizer are revolted Negroes from Guiné in some mountain areas, from where they raid and give much trouble, and the time may come when they will dare to attack and destroy farms as their relatives do on the island of São Tomé."[14]

Sugar cane had first been planted on the island of Madeira in 1452 at the behest of Prince Henry. African slaves were shipped to Madeira and soon Flanders and England were receiving sugar from the island. Farmers growing other crops were quickly bankrupted. Before the turn of the 16th century there were eighty sugar mills, making Madeira the primary sugar producer in the world. The planter-manager class on Madeira was mainly Portuguese and the slave laborers were African. This was the formula that would be reproduced in the Caribbean and Brazil a century later.

Voyages of discovery for gold involved kidnapping people by force and enslaving them as opportunity presented itself. Direct exchange of trade goods for human beings was emerging rapidly during the later 15th century.

The earliest merchants who dealt with the Portuguese were usually literate Muslims, often described as "Moorish" in historical accounts. They generally sold prisoners of war or people captured in raids, selling only those who weren't "people of the book."

Mwene Puto

Portugal was known in West Central Africa as Mwene Puto, whose people were believed to be followers of the "Lord of the Dead." Cooperation between West Central African rulers and Mwene Puto wasn't smooth and unbroken throughout the massive territory, which was eventually exploited by European nations for 15 million people transported over the ensuing four centuries, with twice as many killed in slave trade-related wars and forced marches to African coasts.

Traders spread unevenly and gradually into the West African interior. Portuguese administrative and military personnel started wars usually by encouraging or cynically exploiting existing local rivalries. Greater and greater debt was accrued against African rulers who were becoming steadily more dependent upon European import goods. The "New World" colonies producing sugar in the 16th and 17th centuries were also creating a mass market for slave labor. A transformation occurred from the exchange of commodities to repay debts, to the exchange of human beings as payment for goods.

The arrival of Mwene Puto wanting to trade goods for slaves on the Guinea coast didn't cause a great stir, as this was a place where slavery was well known. Yet in West Central Africa the population who constituted the dependents and subjects of a realm were a major signifier of wealth. People were not simply factors in a productive process leading to wealth via sale or export of a commodity. In West Africa people *were* the wealth. New arrivals could be assimilated into a kingdom as dependent subjects owing allegiance to a ruler of the realm; therefore, it was in a kingdom's interest to gain dependent subjects, not to shed them.

There was a strong preference among African traders to exchange export goods such as ivory and beeswax rather than people. The European traders arrived in numbers with cloth, alcohol, guns, and gunpowder. They used these highly valued goods to buy their way in. African monarchs wanted to keep their dependent subjects but the Europeans adopted the custom of extending credit, which naturally increased indebtedness on the African side. In the 15th century debts of this type continued to be paid by local exports wherever commerce had been strong prior to the arrival of the European slave ships. For instance at Benguela, local African traders were initially able to supply coastal salt, hides, feathers, copper, and cattle to cover their import debts. Trading human beings in exchange for goods from Portugal wasn't yet necessary.

Kongo and Mbundu chiefs near the mouth of the Kwanza River were reluctant to trade slaves with the Portuguese. They were able to hold back by covering their debts with salt and shells from Luanda Bay. The king of the Kongo (ManiKongo) envisaged mutual interchange of goods. It was inconceivable in the earliest years of contact with Europeans that they would so quickly make demands for the main commodity of human beings.

The Oba of Benin was extremely reluctant to sell African prisoners of war as these people could have been brought into Benin society as dependents representing greater riches to the Oba. These examples illustrate that the Atlantic slave trade in Africa was initiated by the Portuguese and not the African monarchs with whom they dealt.

Portuguese strategy was starkly demonstrated in Angola where they moved inland, ascending the Kwanza River. There they dealt with the Mbundu lords near its Lukala tributary who could no longer offer goods worth the high cost of transportation to the coast. The Portuguese bypassed the Mbunda chiefs near the coast and seized on the trading weaknesses of the inland Mbundu lords, particularly the *Ngola a Kiluanje,* manipulating them aggressively to their own advantage. Offering credit and goods hand in hand, they created a cycle of debt that could and would be paid back with slaves.

This process eventually interfered with the geopolitical structures of the whole of West Central Africa. Communities shifted and kinship ties were shattered by warlords' ruthless slave raids. Once Atlantic import goods became intrinsic to their power, local rulers became part of the process and joined the hunt for human cargo to finance the newly needed imports.

Many distrusted the Portuguese and resisted them for various reasons. The Songhai could capture a thousand slaves in a single day by raiding to the South. Sonni Ali, the Songhai emperor, saw no benefit in switching allegiance from his Arab trading partners in the Maghreb to the red-skinned, long-haired Portuguese in their "pretty boats," who couldn't at first shift as many slaves as the trans-Saharan trade.

"The rosy dawn of the era of capitalist production"

The Europeans didn't dominate the interior militarily. They established key trading posts and barracks on the coasts. Early colonizing efforts were made by Portuguese criminals transported to Africa. There was no pan-African economic or political structure to unite the rulers who wanted to fight the slave traders. It was rel-

atively easy for European powers to play off one ruler and his people against another. Sometimes they offered or sometimes they
gained military assistance from African armies as it suited their
needs. They were also able to strategically halt imports in a way
that could cripple an African ruler.

Instances abound of attempts to halt the slave trade when it was
clearly against African interests. The Angolan Queen Nzinga founded
Matamba on the Kwango directly to combat the Portuguese. The
leader of the Baga in Guinea made strong efforts against the slave
trade. In Dahomey, Agaja Trudo virtually managed to stop slaving
on the "Slave Coast." By looting and destroying *barracoons* (slave
camps) and forts, he waged war against the Europeans for years
until he was so deprived of the cowrie shells and guns Dahomey
needed that he was drawn back into slave trading.

African rulers and warlords branched out over greater distances
to capture prisoners who would be sold at slave markets deep in
the African interior. With supply lines and fields of hostility
stretched over a wide area, it became more difficult to control and
maintain armies or transport slaves. The erosion of traditional trading practices led to local subjects, even to members of the
monarch's own family, becoming potential "pieces" for sale. The
whole of West Central Africa became gradually drawn into the
Atlantic economy.

Walter Rodney described 15th-century West Central Africa,
where "co-resident communities shared among themselves on a
face to face basis. . . . Human relations obscured trade relations,
fabricated goods were inseparable from their fabricators, and a
consequent presumed directness of transactions between producer
and final consumer left utterly no logical space for the notion of
living from trade alone."[15]

But the world order under colonialism left little logical space for anything else. Karl Marx wrote: "The discovery of gold and silver in America, the extirpation, enslavement and entombment in mines of the aboriginal population, the turning of Africa into a commercial warren for the hunting of black skins signalled the rosy dawn of the era of capitalist production."[16]

The Land of the True Cross

When Pedro Alvarez Cabral's fleet of thirteen ships set sail from Lisbon, bound for India, in March of 1500, the awesome scale of the Diaspora that would take place was unimaginable.

Giving rise to this voyage had been those of Diogo Cão and Bartolemeu Dias. Cão, attempting to circumnavigate Africa, had reached Cabo de Santa Maria and returned to Portugal with slaves from an area south of Benguela. By 1491 the Portuguese arrived at Mbanza Kongo where they formed a relationship with Nzinga, the king of the Bantu state of Kongo. Nzinga was the richest king the Portuguese had encountered so far in their African explorations. His palace was at the center of a complex maze in the capital of Mbanza Kongo. Kongo had a politically sophisticated set of subdivisions serviced by a currency of nzimbu shells from the island of Luanda. Copper, iron, and salt were also products of the area. The ManiKongo was maintained by tribute from the realms dependents while Kongo kingdom was divided into provinces presided over by a civil service of local chiefs and judges.

This was a classic example of how the relationship between an African monarch and the Portuguese could turn poisonous very quickly. Nzinga (Affonso I) discovered that the Catholic missionaries, stonemasons, the exchange visits to Lisbon, emissaries and

Bartolomeu Dias set sail in 1487, attempting to round the southern tip of Africa in search of the mythical Christian African king known as Prester John. On this voyage, the two armed fifty-ton caravels became the first European vessels to reach the Cape of Good Hope. Thirteen years later, Dias commanded a ship in the fleet of Pedro Alvarez Cabral, which reached Brazil in April 1500. On that voyage, his ship was caught in a storm and Dias was lost at sea.

ambassadors, the coronations, the picturesque baptisms, and educational introduction to the Catholic saints were but prelude to a burgeoning and insatiable demand for his dependents as slaves. In Nzinga's letters to Portugal he complained hopelessly about the slave trade and clearly foresaw that it would be the destruction of the kingdom of Kongo. In 1526 he wrote to King João III:

Each day the traders are kidnapping our people—children of this country, sons of our nobles and vassals, even people of our own family. . . . This corruption and depravity are so widespread that our land is entirely depopulated. . . . We need in this Kingdom only priests and schoolteachers, and no merchandise, unless it is wine and flour for Mass. . . . It is our wish that this kingdom not be a place for the trade and transport of slaves.[17]

João III replied, "You . . . tell me that you want no slave-trading in your domains, because this trade is depopulating your country. . . . The Portuguese there, on the contrary, tell me how vast the Congo is, and how it is so thickly populated that it seems as if no slave has ever left."[18]

Diogo Cão died soon after his Kongo voyages and it was Bartolemeu Dias who sailed the famous voyage from Lisbon to find India. Five years before Christopher Columbus journeyed to the Caribbean, the Portuguese had already rounded the Cape of Good Hope and attained access to the Indian Ocean, leaving columns of men in Mozambique and East Africa. In 1500 Pedro Cabral was supposed to be bound for the Indian Ocean, but instead of rounding the various capes as Dias had done, Cabral's fleet sailed west after passing Cape Verde.

There are theories that Portuguese navigators had sighted the New World mainland on earlier voyages, so Cabral had secretly been heading there all along. Others speculate that high winds and ocean currents blew the fleet too far west until they realized by accident that they were approaching land after sighting a mountain. Whatever the truth, on April 22, 1500, the fleet anchored a mile from the mouth of a river surrounded by forest at Porto Seguro on the coast of Bahia. Cabral's crew only stayed for about a week and a half, sailing along the coastline where Cabral's men made contact with some Tupi-Guaraní Amerindians living on the coast. (There were approximately 5 million tribal Amerindians living in Brazil in 1500, while today there are less than 200,000.)

King Dom Manuel called the land "Vera Cruz" (Land of the True Cross). In 1503 the name "Brazil" was first coined, after the tropical wood (*caesalpinia echinata*) that was abundant in forests along the coast. This redwood was exported for its deep red wine-colored dye for the next 350 years.

Cloth was a primary commodity used by the earliest European traders to inveigle themselves into African commerce, while in Brazil, as the indigenous people were still in the Stone Age, knives, axes, and other tools were very successfully used to win over a populace who hadn't seen metal before.

The earliest reaction of Cabral to the Amerindian was predictable: He sent some back to Portugal so that the court could marvel. The next consideration was trade, and the first three decades of Portuguese and French contact with Brazilian Amerindians mainly involved collecting brazilwood, using European metal tools for felling the trees. Amerindian laborers chopped them down and carried them up to ten miles to the ships that transported the wood to Europe. The Amerindians could be induced to work for the French and Portuguese by guile. Amerindian people whose lifestyle involved felling trees with stone tools, suddenly in possession of metal axes and knives, were naturally deeply impressed.

The development from coercion to slavery took only a few decades. The influential Jesuit friar Manoel da Nóbrega wrote to the colony's first governor, Tomé da Souza, in 1559 that "the Christians teach the heathens to kidnap their own people and sell them as slaves."[19]

Nóbrega had seen enslavement of the Amerindians in Rio de Janeiro; it also happened in Pernambuco and Bahia. The enslavement of Amerindians in the Americas had begun at the beginning of the 16th century. Genocide through disease of Caribs, Arawaks, and others in the Spanish Caribbean was dealt with by the Spanish by shipping Amerindian slaves from the region today called Nicaragua and also from parts of Brazil.

The Line of Tordesillas

Ferdinand of Spain appreciated that the king of Portugal had recently made 2 million réis in a single year from taxes and duties derived from the West African slave trade. In 1510 he granted permission for African slaves to be sent to Hispaniola for work in the mines. He also gave royal approval for mass seizures of Amerindians around the islands of the Caribbean to labor in the Spanish colonies of Cuba and Puerto Rico.

The unforeseen collapse of the indigenous populations of the Caribbean transformed the African slave trade to the Americas into an international business enterprise involving the whole European commercial sector.

By 1515 it was apparent that sugar could be grown very successfully in the Caribbean. It was soon mass produced at a network of mills on the island colonies of Santo Domingo, Puerto Rico, Barbados, and Jamaica. The Church of Rome was also actively petitioning for Africans to work in gold mines to raise money for major cathedral building projects. In 1524, Spain gave allowance for 300 African slaves to be imported to Cuba for labor in the gold mines at Jagua.

In the earliest years of colonization Brazil was not as important or commercially productive as the islands of the Spanish Caribbean. The first large shipments of people from Guinea went to these islands. The Portuguese were the only nation capable of supplying slaves in large numbers, so they were responsible for shipping. Spain, under the terms of agreements made with Portugal, could not legally send ships to Guinea. This arrangement between Spain and Portugal was decreed by the Spanish Pope Alexander VI in pre-Reformation Europe at the time when the power for such action lay in the hands of the Church.

After papal bulls in 1493 and 1494 the Portuguese retained legally decreed possession of the entire West African coastline and the lands facing the South Atlantic (soon to include Brazil). The New World, or "Kingdom of the Sun," was thus annexed by Spain and Portugal. Iberian self-confidence was striking, and the world had effectively been split into two hemispheres on either side of the invisible Line of Tordesillas. This laid 370 leagues west of the Cape Verde islands and caused many problems as there was as yet no reliable method for measuring longitude.

The Portuguese were more threatened by French than Spanish power in mid-16th-century Brazil. The French had no interest in the Tordesillas line, nor had they signed any treaties with either Portugal or Spain. The French wanted the redwood of the littoral forests just as much as their European rivals.

A French Protestant pastor wrote, "That some interpreters from Normandy who have lived eight or nine years in [Brazil] accommodated themselves to the savages and led the lives of atheists. They not only polluted themselves with all sorts of lewdness and villainy among the women and girls . . . but surpassed the savages in inhumanity."[20]

The French generally sent interpreters from Normandy into the forest to live among the Amerindians and organize the wood collection. By contrast, the Portuguese established warehouses mainly on the coast, trading with the local tribes who collected the wood.

Even though there was now a colonial administration and a general governor, it was impossible for Portugal to defend the whole Brazilian coastline from French ships. In the 1550s, this wasn't particularly important because King João III of Portugal only received approximately 2.5 percent of his crown income from Brazil, as opposed to 25 percent coming through trade with India.

There was by now trade between the Portuguese and China and Japan. Jesuits followed on the heels of the first sailors blown onto Japanese shores in a Chinese junk during a typhoon in the 1540s and began a notably unsuccessful quest to convert the Japanese to Christianity. One provincial lord noted, "I don't know whether they have a proper system of ceremonial etiquette. They eat with their fingers instead of with chopsticks such as we use. They show their feelings without any self control. . . . They are people who spend their lives roving hither and yon. They have no fixed abode and barter things that they have for those they do not, but withal they are a harmless sort of people."[21]

They weren't as harmless as they seemed. After waves of Jesuit missionaries and traders began interfering in Japanese feudal politics, Japan expelled all but a small number of Dutch traders in the mid 17th century. The only trace left of the Portuguese in Japan were the deep fried foods ("tempura" after *Quatour Tempora*) cooked on Catholic ember days when they ate only fish, often fried shrimp.

The Triangular Trade

The earliest Portuguese slave trade in Brazil was an export market. A slave "factory" organized the sale of Tupi Amerindians, mostly for labor in cutting redwood in Brazil and for small-scale export to slave markets in Portugal.

The Portuguese were already transporting Africans to Portugal and the North Atlantic islands. In the first twenty-five years of the 16th century it's estimated that 12,000 African slaves were shipped to Portugal and 5,000 to Madeira, the Azores, and Canaries. Portugal was also transporting slaves from one part of the African coast to another.

By the 1480s, Portugal had begun demanding its right to fortify its positions on the African coast. In 1482 they built São Jorge (Elmina castle) on the Gold Coast. Captives were transported from Arguin and Benin to Elmina and sold to African gold merchants who paid a higher price than merchants in Lisbon. Decades before Cabral had sailed to Brazil, Portugal was already channeling 500–600 slaves a year through São Jorge.

In the early 1500s the Portuguese found it very difficult to meet the Spanish demand for slaves in the Caribbean. Portuguese traders died very quickly at the trading post at Ughoton on the Benin River. Mortality rates were extremely high there for Europeans who often caught deadly fever as soon as they arrived.

The center of operations was switched to São Tomé and its neighbor, Príncipe. Both these plantation island's governors had won monopolies to send ships to the rivers of Benin and supply Elmina and their own islands with slaves. The increased demand for labor from Benin to work at the scores of sugar mills on São Tomé and Príncipe undermined Portugal's ability to supply sufficient numbers of captives to Elmina. If slaves didn't reach Elmina, gold supplies fell off to Portugal, which needed the bullion more than ever. This situation prompted the Portuguese crown to get directly involved in slave trade through a royal official based in São Tomé, empowered to do business in the whole region of West and Central Africa.

The Oba of Benin didn't want to sell slaves to the Portuguese, particularly the male prisoners of war in their prime who were mostly sought by the buyers. The Oba banned the sale of male slaves at Benin eventually and successfully blocked Portuguese exports of male slaves from his territory. They then established a new center for trading in the Kongo, with a trading post at Mpindi at the mouth of the Congo River.

A little over a decade after Cabral had first arrived on Brazilian shores, it was the São Tomé demand for slaves that began more significant upheavals in West Central Africa's hinterlands because of the new patterns of commerce the slave trade brought there. The São Tomé market was largely supplied by sale and gifts of Kongo's people to the Portuguese; by the latter half of the 16th century, slaves were also supplied by Mbundu kings in Angola.

For the next centuries the Portuguese built on these foundations, although it wasn't until the 19th century that they physically and militarily "conquered" Angola. Even then, as late as 1846, there were still only six white men recorded actually residing in Angola's backlands.[22] The "Kingdoms of Angola and Benguella" were maintained from a steadily increasing, though always limited, number of forts. Even in the 20th century large areas of the country remained out of reach, particularly in the East and South. It was an extractive system, relying on military alliances with African forces and the freelance efforts of colonists, which trapped Angola's people inside Portugal's colonial grip. Venancio Guimarães wrote in 1923, "The colonization of Angola was carried out in the early centuries almost exclusively by convicted criminals."[23] As Miller describes it, "The Atlantic zone also advanced eastward from . . . Benguela. From there Euro-Africans, joined by an assortment of immigrant renegades from Lisbon and Luanda, often settled on the higher elevations leading to the interior plateau. They married into the emerging elites of neighboring African states, surrounded themselves with retinues of slaves and became commercial brokers."[24]

In the Kongo the demand for slaves outstripped the ManiKongo's ability to supply from his own "disposable" dependents, so Kongo set about raiding their neighbors (the Mbundu), but still the supply was inadequate to meet demand coming from the Portuguese slave ships.

This raiding of neighbors spread contagiously, so that the Pangu a Lungu started raiding on the north coast of the river Congo. The King of Kongo wrote in 1526, "There are many traders in all parts of the country. They bring ruin. . . . Every day people are kidnapped and enslaved, even members of the King's family."[25]

The solution was to establish slave markets far inland, where captives were purchased by merchants called *pombeiros*. Pombeiros were Africans or Luso-African (mixed-race African-Portuguese) caravan leaders who were prepared to travel where no "pure blood" European would ever set foot. Slave caravans had to pass through Mbanza Kongo where the king levied a tax on any who passed through the kingdom. Currency in the form of nzimbu shells was given to the Tio people who controlled the commerce at the markets that supplied captives to the pombeiros. This currency was paid by the Portuguese, who purchased it from the King of Kongo with Atlantic goods. He was better satisfied with this arrangement as he benefited from the goods, the tax, and the decreased pressure on Kongo's population.

In the era of the Renaissance and latter half of the 16th century, the Atlantic slave trade finally surpassed the trans-Saharan trade that had continued to supply North Africa and parts of Europe from Nigeria (Yorubaland).

Chapter Two

SUGAR BLUES

Now Brazil came into its own as a sugar producer. Epidemic waves of European illnesses—measles, smallpox, the common cold—were attacking the Amerindian population by the tens of thousands. In the year 1562, an estimated 60,000 coastal Tupi Amerindians died as a result of these illnesses.

The Jesuits baptized Amerindians and then put them to work. They were "reduced" to towns and villages called *aldeias*. The imported culture of these aldeias was based on the Christian family model with an inherent ethic of producing to create excess profit. Excess profit beyond present need was a meaningless concept to the Amerindians and these experiments were complete failures. Many perished or fled from the littoral to the *sertão* (interior).

Brazil, or "The Brazils" as they were commonly referred to, had been divided into fifteen hereditary "captaincies." These were sections of land running flush with the equator and toward the Line of Tordesillas. They were awarded to individuals in one way or another closely connected to the King of Portugal. By 1550 the captaincy of São Vicente (near present-day Santos) had a large, working engenho (sugar mill), and the northeastern captaincy of Pernambuco had five engenhos up and running. Work in the sugar cane fields was done by Amerindian slaves.

After twenty years the "captains" were growing dissatisfied with the Tupi-Guaraní workers' output and longevity. The enslaved labor force was weak and died rapidly on the plantations. They were also harder to isolate than Africans, as their familiarity with the terrain and knowledge of local language made escape from plantations easier. There were only two to three thousand African slaves in Brazil at this time, but the Portuguese realized that African workers might more successfully survive the hardships of field labor than the Amerindian labor force. The turning point came in 1570, when people from West Africa were suddenly imported into Brazil en masse, and the reason for this was undoubtedly sugar.

Sugar had been brought to the New World originally by Christopher Columbus. In northeastern Brazil there was a long coastal band of dark, rich, clay soil (*massapé*) that was perfectly suited to sugar cane cultivation. Moist plains ran from Rio de Janeiro to the coast north of Pernambuco. In Maranhão, Pernambuco, Bahia, and southern Rio de Janeiro, sugar cane thrived.

The cane was an ancient reed with origins in the South Pacific. By 800 BC it had been dispersed via New Guinea and Hawaii to China and India. In India it was described by early conquerors as "a reed that makes honey without bees."[1] The Prophet Mohammed's armies found sugar cane in Persia and carried it to Egypt. The cane progressed westward across North Africa, through Morocco to the Mediterranean, Sicily, and southern Spain. Via the Mediterranean route, the cane reached Madeira, the Canary Islands, and, farther south, São Tomé.

The refined product crushed out of the cane, in Arabic *al zucar,* in Spanish *azúcar* (both words deriving from Sanskrit *sarkar* for grain) was so precious it could be traded for its weight in gold. Centuries earlier the Chinese had developed a refining technique to boil the crushed cane juice to reduce it and sun dry the crystals to produce "stone honey." It was the Sicilians who developed the grinding stone, in Sicily turned by men, and elsewhere millstones turned by mules or oxen.

An early account of a Mediterranean sugar mill described "the men who worked there being blackened by the smoke from the fires, dirty, sweaty and scorched, more like demons than men."[2]

This is similar to Padre Antônio Vieira's 1633 description of a Brazilian mill:

> Who sees in the blackness of night those tremendous furnaces per-petually burning; the flames leaping from the [apertures] of each through the two mouths or nostrils by which the fire breaths; the Ethiopians . . . bathed in sweat, as black as they are strong, feeding the hard and heavy fuel into the fire, and the tools they use to mix and stir them; the cauldrons, or boiling lakes, continually stirred or restirred, now vomiting froth, exhaling clouds of steam, more of heat than of smoke . . . the noise of the wheels and the chains, peo-ples the colour of the very night working intensely and moaning together without a moment of peace or rest; who sees all the con-fused and tumultuous machinery and apparatus of that Babylon can not doubt though they may have seen Vesuvias or Mount Etna that this is the same as hell.[3]

The earliest sugar trade between the Middle East and Europe was primarily conducted by Venetians. Sugar was incredibly expen-sive; fifty tons of it was purchased in England from Venetian mer-chants in 1319 for £3000, equivalent to around £11 million (nearly $21 million) today. By the 16th century, a single teaspoon of white sugar would have cost £2.60 ($5.00) at today's prices. Not surprisingly, it was a product used only by the very rich in Europe as a status symbol or for medicinal purposes (it reputedly rotted the first Queen Elizabeth's teeth).

In early 16th-century Brazil the know-how to produce sugar was conspicuously lacking, so skilled sugar masters and artisans capable of building mills were sought from Madeira and São Tomé, where the plantation system had already been perfected. The first law of that system was the total reliance on slave labor.

By 1572, Amerindian slaves in Brazil cost 9 reis, whereas African slaves cost 25 reis. Despite this, Brazilian planters grew ever more reliant on an uninterrupted supply of the latter. The heavy work on the sugar plantation fell for the most part to field slaves. A colonial contemporary wrote a report about a plantation inspection in Brazil:

> [He] came to a fazenda where he was not looked for, and there beheld what he did not expect—a Negro about to be boiled to death for some act of insubordination. His owner had incited, according to custom in such cases, neighbouring proprietors to witness the tragedy. . . . I should suppose the country slaves are the worst off. Every morning, while nature was enshrouded in the blackness of darkness, did I hear them driving wagons through the thick mist, and as late as ten at night were they shouting at the oxen as the jolting and groaning wheels rolled by. . . . On large estates, a few days' rest are given them every three or four weeks during the sugar season, but on smaller ones, where owners commonly have difficulty keeping out of debt, they fare badly and are worked to death. Staggering into their huts, or dropping where their labours close, hardly do their aching bones allow the angel of sleep to drive away the memory of their sorrows, than two demons, lurking in the bell and lash, awaken them to fresh tortures.[4]

The population of the plantation was not self-sustaining. The deaths of both the European owner-managers and the African labor force far outnumbered the births on the engenhos. The life expectancy of an African sugar plantation field slave newly arrived in Brazil in the prime of life would be anywhere between six to ten years, maximum. The Portuguese had no interest in raising slaves from infancy on the plantations, or in any long-term care for their health or physical well-being.

There were greater numbers of African men than women going into Brazil in the late 16th and early 17th centuries. A ratio of 80 percent male to 20 percent female were the norm and the sound of babies crying was not often heard in the *senzalas*. It was common for women to abort themselves rather than bring a baby into the world under slavery in Brazil. Many more were infertile or miscarried due to the heavy labor they were forced to do every day.

Women didn't only abort their babies, they also often committed suicide. Among both men and women, suicide was very common. In 1695, for example, the Capuchin Father Luca recorded an incident in Kongo where a pombeiro was negotiating the cost of a female slave for transport to Brazil: "When she realized from what she overheard in her master's conversation that she and the child were to be sold overseas, she went into a terrible rage, and she took up her son and furiously threw him against a stone, and then she grabbed some arrows from the hands of a man and angrily pierced her breast, thus killing both herself and her child."[5]

Slave mortality was factored into the plantation economy: "All I ever understood was that purchasing slaves was much the cheapest method of keeping up their numbers; for . . . the mother of a bred slave was taken from the field labour for three years, which labour was of more value than the cost of a prime slave or new Negro."[6]

In the last quarter of the 16th century, when the initial sugar boom peaked, the cycle of Africans imported to Pernambuco and Bahia reached approximately 50,000, mainly from Guinea. What was called Guinea included the staging post of the Cape Verde islands, Senegal (Bissau and Cacheu), Gambia, the Mina Coast, and various ports along the Dahomey littoral. In this period, the coast of Senegal was particularly favored by Portuguese slave traders.

As 50,000 Africans reached Brazil between 1576 and 1591, and there were only 20,000 slaves in Brazil by the end of the century, approximately 30,000 Africans working in the sugar fields died during the first twenty-five years of the sugar boom, not to mention Amerindians in a similarly desperate situation.

J. Lewis cites Verger's cyclical model of slave imports to Bahia throughout the colonial era.

The Guinea cycle during the second half of the 16th century.

The Angola cycle in the 17th century.

The Mina Coast cycle during the first three quarters of the 18th century.

The Bight of Benin cycle between 1770 and 1851, to be precise.[7]

The Angola cycle also included tens of thousands from Kongo. The Mina Coast and Bight of Benin cycles referred to slaves from those coasts, including Ghana, Togo, Dahomey, and Nigeria.

In the 16th century, the Jesuits and the Governor of Brazil and Maranhão had agreed that only Tupi Amerindians taken in a "just war" or who had been absent from their aldeia for over twelve months could be enslaved. The Church and the Jesuits enjoyed highbrow debates on the justice of enslaving Amerindians or whether fully human characteristics could be attributed to them. With the exception of one or two virtually unread pamphlets, these debates never extended to Africans, who the Jesuits considered fair game for enslavement.

From 1580 to 1640, during a dual Spanish and Portuguese monarchy, the Portuguese not only supplied all the slaves to Bahia but also the Spanish Caribbean and North American colonies. Slaves from Senegal and Guinea were shipped all over South America. They were the "Mohammedanized Guinea-Sudanese group of Malesian and Hausa peoples" referred to by Bira Almeida. It was not only in the 19th century that Muslims were shipped to Brazil; they arrived in Bahia in the 16th century too. Many were taken as prisoners of war or as refugees and they accepted neither slavery nor baptism. In fact, the Spanish issued decrees banning imports of Guinea-Sudanese slaves because of violent slave revolts all over South America during this period. The Spaniards began to consider these slaves (many of whom had been members of the armies and cavalries of the African Savannah) too dangerous.

It was the predominance of the slave trade that drove the people of the Senegal valley to support Islamic (anti-slavery) purification movements, such as that of Nasr al-Din in 1673–77. The Guinea cycle of slave trade to northeast Brazil coincided with the break-up of the kingdom of Jolof, which had been predominant on the lower Senegal River and the coast since the early 16th century. The Fulbe of the middle Senegal were branching out both east and west so that by the 1600s, after the decline of the Jolof and Songhai, the Fulbe ruled in Senegal and established the Empire of the "Great Fulo."

The Spanish were well educated in the military challenges posed by slaves who had been captured as a result of the civil wars (for example, the Songhai civil war of 1588) during the Guinea cycle. In Brazil too, the first recorded *quilombo* dates back to 1575. In 1597,

Père Rodrigues wrote, "The colonists' principal enemies are the rebellious Guinea Negroes who live in the mountains from which they make periodic raids."[8] Bahia is known for "Nago" (Islamic and Yoruba) uprisings in the early 19th century which involved slaves from Nigeria and Benin, although even in 1607 the Count of Ponde wrote to the King of Portugal about a Hausa rebellion in Bahia.

Maroon towns, or quilombos, were built by escaped Africans; they existed from the earliest days of the colonization of northeast Brazil. These (often small) quilombos existed on the periphery of the plantations.

Slaves were mainly young adults when they arrived in Brazil, and the majority of their life was spent in Africa. It was not always the case that hugely diverse groups of people from different "tribes" arrived and lived together totally randomly. The African identity from the mother country, constantly reinforced by new arrivals on the plantations, gave a measure of cultural cohesion to plantation life. Captives who'd survived as far as Brazil had already shared harrowing experiences and formed powerful bonds. In Brazil, the term *malungo* was used by those who'd been transported on the same slave ship.

James Giblin writes: "Perhaps no idea about the African past is as persistent and misleading as the idea that Africans traditionally lived in isolated and homogenous 'tribes.' This idea implies that connections among different societies, language groups and regions were unimportant."[9]

Giblin cites instances where interrelated culture, religion, and commerce was spread over thousands of kilometers, even in regions of dense equatorial forest where the tribal model is most popularly described. The river systems were the highways and shared languages, tribute systems, religious organization, trade, and other factors were the means of complex and far-reaching contact between population groups; this included institutions like the "Drum of Affliction," which associated people over great distances.

Capture and the March to the Coast

The conditions of captives taken in the interior of Africa until their disembarkation in Salvador or Rio de Janeiro were appalling. Inadequate food and water, disease, and naked exposure to the elements night and day added to the deadly nature of the ordeal. Floods, drought, and warfare had often led to the initial vulnerability and had been the reason for people's capture in the first place. Those in the "coffles" marching to the coast were already weakened. Many had been raided by stronger neighbors and may already have been on the run, suffering from malnutrition before the march began. The weak, the elderly, women, and children were captured first. Soldiers captured as prisoners of war were also prominent numerically.

After kidnap came a long journey to the nearest slave market in the interior. Immunity to foreign disease was compromised by *mal de Loanda,* or scurvy. Captives marched eating only low-quality starch, devoid of vitamin C and protein. Water supplies along the caravan trails were overused and contaminated by excrement from dense concentrations of people who stopped to drink at water holes. Dysentery and amoebic stomach bugs (*câmaras*) were epidemic. Fever increased dehydration among those deprived of clean drinking water.

At the markets were hundreds, sometimes thousands, of slaves closely bound in chains and penned together in barracoons. Awaiting them were the pombeiros, the sons of Portuguese merchants (*lançados*) who'd married African chiefs' daughters or sisters. Only very occasionally Portuguese *degrados* (European criminal exiles) survived the deadly fevers of the well-trodden slave routes and acted as pombeiros.

In 17th-century Angola, at these slave "fairs," typhoid, typhus, and smallpox reached their apex after being carried in from many trails where caravans passed. The barracoons offered no shelter in highland areas when it was extremely cold and wet at night. As the march progressed toward the coast, the coffles were funneled into greater concentration along the ridges and paths leading to Luanda, Benguela, and other ports on the African coast.

The tendency of the slave trade to move inland to the center of Africa meant long, painfully slow marches. Pombeiros in Angola representing merchants in Luanda or Benguela might be gone for a year before returning with trains of 100–600 slaves carrying ivory or copper. By the late 18th century, caravans of 1,000 were arriving at Luanda from Kongo. Marches from markets in the central highlands or Kwango valley could take six months, during which time half of the captives had died along the way. People were bound by the right wrist and the neck in chains called *libambos* (a term also used to describe a coffle of slaves, as was *conduta* in Portuguese or *kibuka* in Congo). The main caravan was split into sub-groups of men, women, and children. Those who fell along the way were dragged by the main group or, if they were too sick to recover, they were cut loose and left to die alone.

Mungo Park, writing for the African Association, traveled with a caravan and said that the captives were bound by placing the right leg of one and left leg of another in the same fetters so they could walk slowly. Groups of four were bound by the neck with a rope and their hands were chained at night. Any who argued would receive a heavy piece of wood bolted to an iron ring around their ankle. A group of six musicians traveled with the caravan to sing and keep up spirits or gain a welcome in new villages. Park said that many of the captives had been in irons "for years" and were consequently crippled.

Loads of heavy goods were a further burden; a single elephant's tusk might weigh 100 kilograms or more. Food was bought in villages and carried, though they rarely carried water. Slave drivers were very wary of the large groups under their command. They knew the captives would certainly attack them and escape, given the first opportunity. It was only incentives paid by the pombeiros to the slave drivers (who were often slaves themselves) that kept them at their task. Slave drivers ran no financial risks from a slave's death. They also knew that exhausted people were less dangerous and they had many strategies, including depriving captives of sleep. All delays were potentially lethal. Stopping and starting, bartering for small numbers of slaves at minor trading posts, attacks by bandits en route, rumors of attack—all these things could halt the march. And the longer it took, the more people died.

Surrounded by enemies at every turn, captives did what they could to help each other survive. There was theft of food and water from the weakened during the march, yet there were countless instances of sharing and kindness too. People rationed inadequate lumps of rotting meat and spoiled manioc among themselves, offering encouragement to perform the miracle of reaching their unknown destination alive.

Angolan Kilombos

The trading frontier in Angola was mobile. Slaving moved cyclically from one coast to another at different periods throughout the colonial era. During Brazil's first sugar years, many slaves came from Luanda and Benguela's direct hinterland and north as far as the Zaire (Congo) River. This area included the Kwango River, the Kwanza River, and the central plateau directly to the east of Benguela.

The political face of Angola changed as the Ngola a Kiluanje halfway up the Kwanza River began to trade. The 960-kilometer Kwanza River became "the largest slave route in the history of the world."[10] Between 1575 and 1630 the Portuguese took possession of the Ngola a Kiluanje's land as a Portuguese crown colony and it was from this title that they named the colony "Angola." In 1623 Queen Nzinga became ngola of the region and her realm acted as a large-scale *kilombo* (the Kimbundu word for an Imbangala-fortified military camp, evolving to *quilombo* in Brazil).

Slaves were constantly and desperately trying to flee from the death-trap coffles, but the odds were heavily stacked against them. Shackled and under constant guard, they moved through sparsely populated or hostile areas. Escape often led to starvation. They clambered up sandy ridges between rivers, forded them or crossed in canoes, traversing both forest and savannah. The coffles walked high, narrow trails toward the central plateau before a steep, rocky descent took them to the vast Atlantic Ocean. Individuals who escaped in the interior near the slave markets would be surrounded by the very people who'd just sold them; if they escaped near the sea, at the northern edge of the plateau, they'd have been lost in forests or to the south in barren terrain.

As late as 1904, journalist Henry Nevinson, on a writing job in Angola for *Harper's Monthly,* wrote:

The Cuanza [river] is just in front, and behind them lies the long stretch of the Hungry Country, which they could never get through alive if they tried to run back to their homes. So it is that the trees of the Hungry Country bear shackles in profusion—shackles for the hands, shackles for the feet, shackles for three or four slaves who are clamped together at night. The drivers hang them up with the idea of using them again when they return for the next consignment of human merchandise.[11]

On both sides of Luanda, south of the Kwanza River and also north of the Dande, there were kilombos deep inside the Portuguese colony. A kilombo with agriculture, hundreds of fugitives, and extensive fortifications and buildings was situated on the periphery of Luanda for a hundred years at the height of the colonial era.

As in Brazil, the people who inhabited the kilombos sustained themselves by smuggling supplies and food from the *fazendas* that Portuguese settlers had planted in the river valleys of Luanda. A kilombo in Kisama, south of the Kwanza River, was protected by chiefs who were enemies to Portuguese colonials in the 1600s to 1700s.

The fugitives generally hid out beyond rivers, in deep forests, and on inaccessible mountaintops, but individuals also found refuge in the churches of the town and on missionary-run estates . . . exempt from intrusions by civilian authorities. Slaves who fled the Portuguese after years of experience in Luanda found a particular welcome among the lords of Kisama, who used them as spies who could return undetected to the city, dressed like its other African residents, and report back on Portuguese military capacities and manoeuvres.[12]

Kilombo fugitives formed bandit guerrilla units that specialized in ambushing and hijacking trade caravans moving in the opposite flow to the slaves. These caravans carried guns, liquor, cloth, tobacco, and other goods eastward. The Portuguese feared the threat from kilombos and they were hostile to the chiefs who harbored them. They declared war on Queen Nzinga for that reason and set up a puppet ngola, who paid them for his title with slaves, opening his territory to Jesuit missionaries.

Queen Nzinga overshadowed the puppet ngola and became the most powerful military leader in Southern Angola. The Portuguese engaged in a long war with her because her forces aimed to shut down the supply of slaves coming from this region. It was only in 1656 that Nzinga allowed Christian missionaries into her territory at Matamba. Nzinga's heirs did eventually go on to supply slaves to the Portuguese at Luanda. They were defeated by a regime called "Jinga," which opposed the Portuguese slave trade at Matamba and fought to conduct the trade themselves. Jinga territory eventually became a kilombo stronghold after captives fled there during the slump in Angola's economy in the mid-19th century.

A Cruel Era

For those who survived the march from their homelands to the coast, worse lay ahead. Luanda and Benguela, the pleasant coastal bays that had been transformed into mercantile hell holes, were built upon the bones of tens of thousands of dead human beings. It was there that captives embarked in the suffocating holds of the "floating tombs" (*tombeiros*) for the middle passage.

These were cruel times in Europe; the colonial experience and Atlantic trade reflected this. In Europe, children could be hung for petty theft and mass executions were popular carnivals. Jacob

Sprenger's "Malleus Malaficarum" (Hammer of Witches) was said "to have caused the death of more human beings than any other book."[13] Many of those killed were women falling afoul of Pope Innocent VIII's bull against witchcraft; some 200,000 heretics, Muslims, and "witches" were burned at the stake. Countless more were broken on the rack, whipped, crushed to death, drowned, garrotted, or imprisoned throughout the 16th and 17th centuries in Europe.

Jews had long been subject to expulsions, and during the 15th and 16th centuries, Spanish Jews were expelled to the Maghreb, Portuguese Jews to Holland and Brazil, while Jews from Germany, Austria, and Hungary were expelled to Poland and Russia.

The whole court of Spain enjoyed an Inquisition *auto-da-fé* in Madrid in 1682, holding a party as they watched scores of victims burned or flogged. Voltaire wrote, "An Asiatic arriving in Madrid on the day of an auto-da-fé would doubt whether here was a festival, a religious celebration, a sacrifice, or a massacre."[14] Europeans marveled at the human sacrifices on behalf of the African kings of Dahomey while the Catholic Church engaged in similarly bloodthirsty conduct under the auspices of the Inquisition.

If life was merciless on the religious front, in commerce and business it was scarcely better. Capitalist production was operating in its most naked form, undisguised by any intermediate pretension to decorum. Europe's peasants were on the threshold of leaving feudalism behind to become the raw working-class fodder for the "Satanic mills" of the industrial revolution. Chattel slavery had been transformed into a racial covenant. Not all black Africans and indigenous people of the New World were slaves, but all New World slaves were black Africans or indigenous people.

Engenhos

Plantation life was agriculturally based on an economy of scale. The enterprise required 100–200 field slaves with a fluctuating group of European and some "mulatto" managers, which included the owner and his family who possessed a number of domestic slaves, cooks, wet-nurses, seamstresses, and so on.

Most of the mill owners were Catholics, although of the first forty mills in Bahia, twelve were owned by New Christians, Jewish conversos. Naturally, the ever-vigilant Holy Office sought to expose them by any means, "If there was no smoke rising from their chimneys on a Saturday (thus implying they were observing the Jewish Sabbath), if they ate meat in Lent, gave a party before leaving on a long journey (the Jewish Ruega), changed their sheets or underwear on a Saturday, cut the fat off meat, or if any of their relations while dying had turned their faces to the wall."[15]

During the time of the Spanish-Portuguese dual monarchy and *asienti,* Jewish merchants dominated the slave trade in Spain and Portugal. The asienti was the Church of Rome's recognized contract to supply slaves to the Americas and Spanish Indies. It was held at different times by the Spanish, the Portuguese, the French, and the British. Many Jewish slave-trading families in Seville and Lisbon were forced into conversion and emigration, explaining why over a quarter of the early sugar mills and plantations in Brazil were converso owned.

Most of the plantations were concentrated on the coast where the well-irrigated massapé suited sugar cane. The first important towns in Brazil were in Bahia, Pernambuco, and Rio de Janeiro. The engenho included the sugar fields, a great house and attached offices, a still, a sugar mill, boiling house, a chapel, slave quarters, and attached land where the slaves grew crops. The sugar plantation also needed cattle and pasture land, as well as equipment like carts and a lot of specialized semi-industrial machinery.

Aside from the field workers were the sugar masters, purgers, blacksmiths, kettlemen, and sugar craters. They worked at the end of the harvest (*safra*) while the sugar was made in the boiling house. A sugar master was a skilled worker, sometimes a slave who'd risen to the position of free black. As the final arbiter of sugar quality at the end of production, his word was law. "Bankers" were the sugar master's assistants, enjoying a better life up the slave hierarchy. The work around the ovens and copper kettles was so terrible that it was often assigned as a punishment to men in chains. Only men worked at the kettles and they were, paradoxically in view of the hardship, elite among skilled workers. There could be many kettles, with specific regulations of temperature. The different sizes required different handling, so men often specialized in certain kettle sizes.

The work was extremely hot and smoky. The boiling liquid in the open kettles caused regular accidents. Rolling stone grinders called *moendas* crushed the juice from the sugar and were very hazardous to the women who fed the sugar cane into them, as a momentary loss of concentration might lead to a crushed hand or amputation of an arm.

Setting up a mill was complex, expensive, and financially risky. Some were run using a system similar to sharecropping, wherein the mill owner leased his land to smaller planters, *lavradors de cana*, who paid him with a percentage of the sugar they produced. Because of the need to stick to strict deadlines so that the cut sugar wouldn't deteriorate, the plantation owner used every conceivable means of bribing or punishing the workforce. Foremen (*feitors*) used a whip (*chicote*) to make slaves work faster in the cane fields.

Field slaves cutting cane during the harvest on a sugar plantation. The ever-present feitors, wielding their chicote, are seen in the background.

In the mill itself, incentives like alcohol and free time were the favored form of coercion.

Relations between the field slaves barracked in the senzalas and the *senhor de engenho* who owned the mill were not warm and paternalistic, as has been suggested by some Brazilian historians. The aim of many slaves was escape, while the aim of the owner was to work the slaves to the productive maximum during the few years their health and strength held out. He relied on total control of the slaves for his lifestyle, so no act of rebellion was trivial to the master.

> You had some field Negroes, who lived in huts, had nothing to lose. They wore the worst kind of clothes. They ate the worst food. And they caught hell. They felt the sting of the lash. They hated this land. You know what they did? If the master got sick, they'd pray that the master'd die. If the master's house caught afire, they'd pray for a strong wind to come along.[16]

The plantation was the forerunner of the factory production line, employing the kind of heavy machinery more characteristic of the industrial era together with agriculture and punishing manual labor.

Like a feudal lord, the senhor de engenho owned the bodies and controlled the lives of his slaves. Law was in the hands of the mill owner, who could wield "justice" as it suited him. Owners who tortured or killed their slaves were hardly ever prosecuted in courts in Brazil and the enterprise was essentially to create profit at the optimum rate until an individual worker died of exhaustion and had to be replaced.

Cutting the Cane

The first work involved preparing the ground for sugar cane. This was usually done by the strongest field slaves as it was heavy work and covered a large area. The size of plantations varied but the fields might extend for 750 acres. In Brazil there were small-scale sugar planters who were often financially strapped European share-croppers who owned just two or three slaves; if they were more affluent, thirty or forty. A true fazenda had at least 300 acres covered by the cane fields; often, fazendas were twice that size.

Herds of oxen and other livestock were reared for food on the fazenda. Oxen also hauled carts and turned the grinding wheels. Slaves with experience of raising cattle in Africa were given the task of looking after the forty to fifty head on the plantation. The colonial authorities eventually banned cattle ranching anywhere within 80 kilometers of the coast because it was destroying the sugar fields. Cattle ranching then spread inland to the sertão in the 18th and 19th centuries, and at that time there were farmers who owned ranches that were larger than Portugal itself.

The cane fields were laid out in a grid pattern by gangs of slaves who cleared the land ready for cultivation.

> In a large fallow, in the midst of this green amphitheatre were from eighty to one hundred negroes of both sexes; some with infants strapped on their backs, in a rank, breaking up the ground for fresh crops with hoes. . . . they all struck with the regularity of soldiers drilling for the manual exercise, and cut the ground into square blocks about twice the size of bricks. Over them presided a tawny-coloured driver, in a cotton jacquet and a large straw hat, with a long rod in his hand by which he directed their industry and punished the idle.[17]

An eighteen- to twenty-hour workday was normal for a field slave. They used iron tools: axes, hoes, and chisel-headed pickaxes to clear weeds and break up the soil for planting. Holes were dug like trenches. Two canes to each hole were laid horizontally on the earth. After a fortnight, small shoots grew up from the soil. It took fourteen to eighteen months of weeding before the small flowers signaling safra (harvest) appeared. This weeding wasn't like tending rose beds, as the fight against weeds taking hold of the cane fields was a constant process. The blades of the sugar cane were strong and sharp, and made weeding painful. The fields had to be completely cleared of weeds at least three times between planting and harvest, by which time the cane were around 2 inches thick and 6 or 7 feet tall.

The choice of when exactly to harvest cane was a complex process involving considerations of weather, maturation of the cane, and the type of land it was planted on. As Englishman Henry Koster wrote, "Everything in Brazil . . . is done by the eye."[18]

Cane fields were harvested whenever possible in rotation, so that cutting, transporting, and extracting the sugar could happen in an uninterrupted sequence.

Field slaves cut the cane at the base with a machete (fouce de cortar cana), leaving a stump for the following season's crop (as this harvest cycle could be repeated three or four times). After the cane was cut they stripped it of leaves and sliced it into 30-inch spears that were piled in bundles and heaved onto oxcarts for transport to the mill. Younger boys generally drove the carts and tended the animals that turned the wheel in the mill house. This work was massively labor-intensive and done rigidly with no breaks. Saccharine quality in cut cane spoils rapidly so the necessity of having it ready for the crusher, or "animal round," within twenty-four hours was urgent. Work gangs were three or four dozen strong and the slaves worked in pairs, often where a man cut the cane and stripped it down and a woman bound it up in its own leaves, heaving bundles onto the cart or a boat waiting at the riverbank. Many engenhos were on rivers and sugar cane was often transported directly to the sugar house by water.

Slaves worked to quotas. When they achieved the daily quota of cutting and carting the cane, there was always the further work of weeding, repairs, and collecting firewood for the ever-burning mill furnaces, which added to the workday.

Usually the cane was crushed through three rollers powered either by water mill, blindfolded animals, or, very occasionally, windmill. Water mills, or *engenhos de real* ("royal mills"), were the biggest and most productive, although animal-powered mills were the most common in Bahia and Pernambuco.

The animal mill had three iron rollers within a wooden frame. The central roller was attached to beams that were harnessed to horses, mules, or oxen. Via cogs, the central roller turned the other two. A work gang of slaves brought the sugar cane to the women called *moedeiras,* who fed it into the rollers, passing it back and forth twice to squash out the cane sap into a wooden tank. The full tank was channeled to a holding cistern or run straight into open copper vats in the boiling house. Sometimes a slave called a *guindadeira* would hoist the liquid to the boiling house. The purpose of boiling was to reduce the juice to a syrupy consistency in enormous vats. Any solid residue and cane pith floating in the liquid had to be scooped away by a kettleman after it rose to the surface. As the juice neared perfect consistency it was transferred from one vat to another and more residues were discarded.

This process gave rise to the word *bagaceira* (a life built around cane waste) to describe the life lived in the engenhos. The cane waste was used for fuel for the furnaces. Further along the reduction process in the final two or three vats, the waste called *molasses* was collected and used for *gerebita*, a cheap rum that became a mainstay product traded by Brazilian and Portuguese merchants in Africa.

Gerebita was virtually cost-free as it came from waste by-products of the sugar-making process. It was different to the white rum called *cachaça* (whose name was taken from the Malawi and northern Mozambique, *kachasu*). Cachaça was distilled from pure cane juice of the first crush; gerebita was always from molasses and was the Angolan name for cane brandy.

Gerebita traveled on the outbound voyage of slave ships. It was sold to subsidize costs on the African coast without much trouble, even though it was low quality and often watered down to cheat the Luso-African buyers. It was transported in 500-liter wooden hogsheads called *pipas,* which were re-used to store the stagnant water that slaves drank on the return journey to Brazil.

Barreado Sugar

The molasses was removed after the cane juice went to the second copper and the remaining liquid continued simmering as it was treated with an alkaline lye and water solution. By the time the liquid was in the third copper, it was beginning to solidify, at which stage it was poured into the smallest and hottest kettle of all.

The slaves stoking the furnaces were called *metedors.* The slaves who worked in the boiling house itself were usually *mulattos* or *crioulos* (slaves born in Brazil). It was specialized work and they were trained in the job from an early age. Kettlemen, called *caldereiros,* often specialized in a particular kettle size. They worked in shifts and were expected to clarify a quota of liquid per shift—for instance, three kettles, which would take around four hours. A woman called the *calcanha* kept the whale oil lamps lit and returned scum from the latter kettles to the first for further clarification.

During the final phase of this monumental process of production, the sugar master decided exactly when the sugar solution was ready to be hand-ladled or run off through a conduit into cooling pans, where it would be stirred constantly to help final solidification. During purging the sugar was transferred into barrels and any last vestige of molasses was drained away. Male slaves carried the forms full of solidified sugar to the purging house, where women took over. *Purgadeiras* added clay, and a dozen women, led by *mães de balcão* (mothers of the platform) made the sugar ready for the craters, *caixeiros,* who were often field slaves doing shifts at the mill. After purging, high-quality white sugar called *barreado* fetched a high price in Europe, and brown *muscavo* sugar was also sold at a lower price.

Soca

Tobacco was another product connected to the sugar industry. By the 17th century tobacco had overtaken redwood as Brazil's second most important export product after sugar. It was largely grown in the Bahian *recôncavo* by Portuguese immigrants with insufficient capital to set them up in the sugar business. There were also some mulatto small-holding farmers who'd previously grown manioc to compensate for the food shortages that had been caused by so much sugar monoculture. Some of the Brazilian tobacco destined for European markets was high quality, but the majority was coarse, crumbly stuff the Portuguese called *soca*. Molasses-sweetened soca was a staple export to Africa throughout the colonial era and was authorized as a Brazilian export outside Lisbon's control.

In 1699, a letter from one Captain Dampier explained, "Bahia had tobacco, and wanted slaves, the coast of Mina had slaves and wanted tobacco . . . in rolls, not in leaf."[19] The tobacco that went to African ports from Brazil had a sweet flavor as it had been treated with molasses to stop it from crumbling to dust. The sweet flavor reputedly made it more popular among African buyers and smokers so the Mina Coast remained a major market for this Brazilian tobacco for well over a hundred years. So great was the market for Brazilian tobacco on the Mina Coast that the governor of Bahia collaborated with Lisbon politicians to take precautions against soca causing a monopoly of slaves from Mina reaching Bahia. The white citizens were terrified of receiving so many (often Muslim) Africans who were often soldiers and closely related by language, religion, and politics.

Chapter Three

THE RISE OF THE QUILOMBO DOS PALMARES

The Portuguese didn't have an unbroken run of success in the new colony. Two European nations might announce the division of the world between them, but there was nothing in the contract forcing the rest of Europe to follow the program. There were plenty of contenders watching the Portuguese ascent on the West African coast with envy. One in particular had a strong interest in Brazil.

> Instead of the sibilant Portuguese tongue, to which the free Africans and the domestic slaves at Elmina had been for generations accustomed, the hideous language of the Netherlands now rent the soft tropical air—the abrasive consonants, the booming, oblong vowels of Plattdeutsch. . . . this rapid switch of masters, the clang and din of conquest, the stamping of the oiled leather thigh boots, the glint of swords and muskets, the cannon balls hissing over the huddled rooftops. . . . and the hulking red-faced Netherlanders and German mercenaries, their fair hair hanging to their shoulders beneath wide-brimmed hats with drooping plumes.[1]

Thus was the transition from Portuguese to Dutch power on

the Gold Coast achieved, in the rather colorful words of James Pope-Hennessey. Dutch ambition in Brazil was quickened by the disintegration of the dual monarchy of Spain and Portugal, which lasted from 1580 until 1640. The Portuguese nobility and bourgeoisie had put Philip II of Spain on the Portuguese throne to gain access to the silver being mined in Spanish America. In return for silver, Lisbon supplied Spain with slaves from Angola and the Guinea coast. On the other hand, the alliance between Spain and Portugal made all of Spain's enemies Portugal's enemies too. Among others, one of those enemies was the United Provinces, which included Holland.

West Indische Compagnie (the Dutch West India Company) was formed by charter and was a mixture of state and private capital. It was founded in 1621 at the end of a truce between Holland and Spain. The Company's intention was no less than to conquer Portugal's sugar estates in Brazil and to completely control the supply of slaves entering Brazil from Africa.

In December 1623, a fleet of twenty-six ships carrying more than 3,000 Dutch soldiers and 450 cannon began preparing for an assault on Salvador da Bahia. This assault was to be coordinated with an invasion by the Dutch of the Portuguese *conquista* colony in Angola. They took Benguela first and in May 1624 entered the town of Salvador. "When we entered Bahia, we only met blacks, for everyone else had fled from the city."[2]

They planned to send the fleet across the Atlantic to meet another sailing from Holland to add Luanda to Benguela as a new Dutch province.

The Dutch rounded up all the Africans they found in Salvador and formed a company to fight with them against the Portuguese. The Portuguese governor of Salvador and the townsmen who'd fled were putting together a resistance movement consisting of European colonial, African, and Indian combatants. A fleet of fifty-two Portuguese ships carrying more than 12,000 men and a thousand cannon soon appeared off the coast and a series of bloody, violent battles left the Dutch forces depleted, exhausted, and defeated. The Portuguese retook Salvador on May 1, 1625, after just one year of Dutch occupation.

The Portuguese tortured and hung any recaptured Africans who'd been fighting with the Dutch and moved back into their former residences. They'd held on in Luanda but the Atlantic Ocean had become a vast arena of sea battles with the Dutch for control of slave ships crossing to Brazil. When the Dutch West India Company captured a ship, it sold the slaves for 250 guilders "a piece"; indeed, most slaves imported for work in Brazil by the Dutch were captured at sea from Portuguese slavers.

During the first quarter of the 17th century, 200,000 men and women were taken from Africa; of those, 100,000 went to Brazil. Holland, having lost Salvador, was consolidating its fortunes elsewhere. They disembarked their first cargo of slaves at Manhattan Island (New Amsterdam) in 1625 and, although they were temporarily interrupted, they had no intention of giving up the ghost in Brazil. By the beginning of the 17th century, the Dutch had half the carrying trade between Brazil and European ports. The raw sugar they carried from Brazil was refined in Holland. Dutch capital was heavily invested in Brazilian plantations and they supplied the Italian-manufactured kettles and equipment for Brazilian mills.

The Dutch West India Company

The Dutch were definitely a force to be reckoned with, possessing the biggest merchant marine in the world and the largest standing army in Europe alongside Spain. Many of the Jews who'd previously been in Seville and Lisbon had escaped to Amsterdam, by now the financial and insurance capital of the world. These merchants knew the vast profits to be gained in Brazil. During the very brief time when the directors of the Dutch West India Company were opposed to slavery for economic reasons, independent merchants in Amsterdam, such as Diogo Dias Querido, kept up slaving operations on the Guinea coast anyway.

In 1630, Dutch sails were again seen above the horizon at Pernambuco. Sixty-seven ships laden with heavy artillery and 7,000 soldiers anchored off the coast. They attacked with a heavy bombardment of cannon to soften up the Portuguese forces before the infantry moved in. By the evening of the second day's assault, the Dutch had taken the town of Olinda, and marched to take Recife.

There followed seven long years of guerrilla fighting centred on forts along the sugar littoral. A highly skilled Luso-Brazilian military strategist by the name of Domingos Fernandez Calabar defected to the Dutch side, spreading victories along the coast from Cabo de Santo Agostinho to Rio Grande.

Palmares

The military confrontation increased the opportunities for slaves to escape from plantations in Pernambuco. Like the defector Calabar, there were many Pernambucans, slaves and free blacks, poor mulatto farmers, outsiders like Tupi Indians, Jews in fear of the Inquisition, and others with no stake in Portuguese society who preferred to fight with the Dutch.

African people had already been fleeing into mountainous and inhospitable regions of Pernambuco for three decades. In 1612, Alexandre de Moura, the captain of Pernambuco, had petitioned for a *capitão do campo* with a force of twenty Amerindians for each of Pernambuco's eight parishes. By the 1630s the stream of fugitives from the plantations was gaining impetus. The following description of their destination was written at the time:

> Extending through the upper reaches of the Rio São Fransisco is a chord of untamed forest that bounds the sertão of Cabo de Santo Agostinho, running almost north to south, paralleling the coast. The *palmares agrestes* are the principle trees and gave the region its name. . . . The area is naturally rugged, mountainous and wild, supporting all varieties of known and unknown trees with such thickness and entangled branches that, in many places, it is impenetrable by light. A diversity of thorns and creeping, harmful plants and intertwined trunks impedes passage.[3]

Most information about Palmares comes from Dutch and Portuguese officers who fought against the quilombo. Palmares's growth during the 1630s precipitated three major attacks, in 1640, 1643, and 1645 (all during the Dutch occupation of Pernambuco). In 1640 it was reported that there were two large *mocambos* (quilombos) in the region. In 1645 the invaders found one large mocambo and another that had been abandoned. (In the early 17th century, the term quilombo wasn't used in Brazil, and references to Palmares mention mocambos, which is the Mbundu term for a "hideout"—*mu-kambo*.)

Abandoning the quilombo to evade the enemy by disappearing farther into the forest was a favorite strategy of the *palmarinos*. There were no fronts or set battle lines, but fluid and sporadic combat over an extensive area. Sabotage, booby traps, attacks against supply lines, and the use of spies in the settlements and plantations nearest Palmares were all regularly applied tactics. Fighting fugitives who lived in quilombos was a very dangerous operation.

The authorities hated Palmares not only as a physical threat but also as a symbol of revolt having a destabilizing effect on the whole region. The Europeans who wanted to keep tight control of the colony were very aware of being outnumbered by Amerindians and Africans. An anonymous governor's report of the late 17th century said:

> Today they use all types of arms. They make bows and arrows, but steal and purchase firearms. Our assaults have made them wary and experienced. They do not all live in the same place, so that one defeat will not wipe them out. . . . They wage all forms of war, with all the superior commanders and inferiors, as much for victory in battle as for assistance to the King (Ganga Zumba). . . . This is the enemy who lasted for so many years within these captaincies, who defended the area, who perseveres. Our injuries from this enemy are innumerable because they endanger the crown and destroy the settlers. . . . they demolish property and rob slaves. As for honour, women and daughters are irreverently treated. As for life, vassals are always exposed to sudden assaults. Furthermore the roads are not free and journeys not safe, so that one only travels with troops who can repel the enemy.[4]

The Portuguese military concluded that the fighters of Palmares were a tougher enemy than the world's leading military power, the Dutch. "Our weapons are powerful enough to beat that enemy [the Dutch] who oppressed us for so many years, but were never effective in destroying the opposite enemy who infested us internally and who inflicted losses just as great."[5]

The governor of Pernambuco knew that skilled commanders and battle-tested soldiers had been employed in the armed raids against Palmares, but they always returned with little to show for their efforts. This war continued throughout the 17th century and it was incumbent upon every successive governor in Recife to provide funds for fresh campaigns against the quilombo.

The failure to crush Palmares was attributed to the rugged terrain and treacherous roads, which made transportation of troops and supplies virtually impossible. The military also acknowledged the discipline and military prowess of the palmarinos, who used the inhospitable terrain to great advantage.

John Stedman, who led many attacks against quilombos in Dutch territory, wrote of some of the hardships of this type of warfare.

> Innumerable, indeed, are the many plagues and dangers one is hourly exposed to in the woods of this tropical climate. . . . I only make mention of such few . . . the mosquitoes, mompieras, patat- and scrapat lice, chigoes, cockroaches, common ants, fire ants, horseflies, wild bees, and spiders. Besides the prickly heat, ringworm, dry gripes, putrid fevers, boils, consaca, bloody flux, thorns, briars, alligators, snakes, and jaguars . . . the bush worms, large ants, locusts, centipedes, scorpions, bats and flying lice, the crassy-crassy, yaws, lethargy, leprosy, and dropsy . . . it will ever be my opinion that one of these free Negroes was preferable to half a dozen white men in the woods.[6]

When Stedman referred to "free Negroes," he was writing about the African Rangers who accompanied his European Marines in attacks against quilombos, in much the same way the Portuguese used Amerindian *bandeirante* irregulars in attacking Palmares. In this regard Stedman also observed, "However little [a Dutch colonel] affected to care for these black soldiers at other times, he seemed very far from displeased with their company at this time, when he knew he was fast approaching an enemy, whom certainly the Rangers knew better how to engage than Marines."[7]

Imbangala

Kilombo is a Bantu (Kimbundu) word for settlement and many kilombos existed on the central plateau, south of the Kwanza River and east of Benguela. "A late 16th Century military cult . . . the 'Jaga' . . . Imbangala, had spilled down in every direction over the flanks of the plateau."[8]

The Jaga (Imbangala) had a fearsome reputation for their nomadic-warrior lifestyle. During the collapse of the kingdom of Kongo, the Imbangala movement developed in response to the Angolan wars of the 17th century. They were a lineageless coalition of warlords who existed on a permanent war footing. Imbangala lords like the Muzumbo a Kalunga had their greatest power in the 17th century and retained their awe-inspiring reputation hundreds of miles north until well into the 18th century.[9]

The Jaga were not a "tribe" and their existence was essentially due to the slave trade: "The constant raids of the Lunda on their neighbours, those of the Jagas on theirs, and the Angolan troops, white, mulatto or black, on the borders of their dominions, [were] to be explained largely by the demand for slaves."[10]

Some writers describe the Jaga as a "savage" and "cannibalistic" people.[11] Besides slave raiding wars there were long droughts and the threat of starvation was constant in Central Africa. On the periphery of the war and famine zones:

> Marauders [preyed] callously on one another in order to survive. . . . Mobility, which farmers reluctantly accepted in normal times only as a necessary retreat . . . became an end in itself and formed the basis of new kinds of social and political organisation. . . . People caught in such straits raised cannibalism, prohibitions against reproduction, infanticide, murder, and destruction . . . to the level of philosophical ideals.[12]

Infanticide gave mobility to nomadic warriors because children were of no use to soldiers with very limited options for survival. Babies were killed and replaced by adolescents caught in raids. Imbangala bands in the Kwango Valley supplied slaves to Luanda and adapted cannibalism and infanticide learned from the Lunda (whose power base was to the east). The Imbangala were extending their power throughout the period of the Dutch-Portuguese wars, especially in areas most prone to slave raiding, on the central plateau and around the areas protected by Ovimbundu warlords.

Kilombos were typical Imbangala institutions in the mid-17th century and are described by Schwartz as male initiation camps in a male military society.[13]

> Since these communities existed in a time and place of military conflict and political upheaval, they found in the institution of the kilombo a unifying structure suitable for a people under constant military alert. . . . the flexibility of the institution of the kilombo as a mechanism for integrating a lineage less community engaged in warfare and self defence . . . explains why some adaptation of the Imbangala institution would thrive in Brazil.[14]

The origins of the Angolan kilombo can be traced back to a band of people who were called *kinguri* after the title of their rulers. There are numerous Imbangala traditions that tell of the kinguri's departure from Lunda. Armed with a battery of charms he had gained from the Luba, he traveled west, using magic to part rivers and overcome poisonous snakes and supernatural wild animals on the journey.

Among other symbols of power with Lunda origins that the kinguri took were the *lubembe,* a clapperless double bell, the talking drum called *mondo,* and a drum called *ngoma ya mukamba.*[15] The move west was very slow, and the kinguri band spent many years

This Portuguese colonial town on the northwest coast of Angola
was christened São Paulo de Luanda by explorer Paulo Dias Novias in
1575. It eventually gained independence from Portugal four centuries
later, in 1975.

passing through the region of Cokwe, moving over the Kasai, through Itengo, Mona Kimbundo, crossing the Kwango, aided always by the powerful magic gained from the Luba, particularly charmed daggers called *mukwale*. Their terrifying legend was confirmed by Cokwe oral tradition hundreds of years later. An image that epitomized the power of the kinguri was a custom that required two slaves to kneel at his side whenever he rose or lowered himself, resting his weight on daggers stabbed into their backs.[16]

As it moved through Cokwe states, the band was always assimilating outsiders from various lineage descents. In a society where matrilineal descent titles were paramount, this was the source of tremendous discord. In the 16th century, reaching the upper Kwango, the kinguri eventually converged with other migrating Lunda titles onto the area of Songo where, for the first time, they faced powerful kingdoms and titles such as the Ngola a Kiluanje.

At the upper Kwanza River, the kinguri band made the acquaintance of the Ovimbundu kilombo. The kinguri kingdom in upper Songo was situated where the land was drained by the Luhando and Jombo rivers. Miller depicts a general narrative of the way Lunda titles came to be in the Ovimbundu highlands: "War between members of a migrating band over the issue of their leader's cruel domination, movement south-west by a part of the band, and gradual fragmentation which resulted in the settlement of kings."[17]

Many Lunda reverted to living a settled life while the rest who were fragmented under the kinguri used the kilombo to solve the problems inherent when many strangers bereft of genealogical connections were drawn together in need of effective military, political, and social cohesion.

Laws of the Jaga

The kilombo was made up of Cokwe and Ovimbundu institutions. The rites of the kilombo were sometimes called the "laws of the Jagas."[18] These focused on the mythical figure of Temba Andumba, a warrior queen who achieved many military victories and introduced the worst ceremonies ever seen among the Mbundu people. The basis of these ceremonies involved preparing an ointment of various herbs and the pounded flesh of the queen's baby daughter boiled into a solution called *maji a samba*. The Imbangala eventually used the rituals of the maji a samba to gain supernatural invincibility in battle and to compensate for their lack of lineage. The maji a samba isn't necessarily to be understood literally. The killing of infants, like the kinguri's ritual stabbing of slaves, was often a mythological metaphor for power over a king's or queen's subjects. Yet Imbangala infanticide and strict laws against sexual intercourse within the kilombo (*yijila* laws) did cut lineage ties and ensured that no new ones developed.

The myth told that Queen Temba Andumba married an evil warrior named Kulembe, who eventually poisoned her and took her kingdom for himself. This part of the myth probably refers to a union of those peoples who practiced the maji a samba rituals with Ovimbundu people in the Kulembe region on the Benguela plateau. The Ovimbundu of Kulembe were the pure warrior society called the kilombo. Miller has shown that the word kilombo's root comes from the Umbundu word for circumcision, and "the word kilombo . . . indicated the origin of the kulembe's warrior society as an Ovimbundu circumcision camp."[19]

The Art of Deception: Kiluvia

Many Imbangala myths describe the way the kinguri leader was eventually defeated by another band called the makota. All of these myths emphasize the use of deception and entrapment to overcome the kinguri. In some he is entrapped in a circular stake enclosure and left to starve; in others, he is suffocated after entrapment, or lured into a pit trap and buried alive. These Imbangala myths all conformed to a kilombo ritual called *kiluvia,* in which prisoners of the kilombo were deceived about their fate through false honor shown to them until the very moment of their execution.

Chronologically, the historical period when the makota (Lunda) Imbangala were at war against the Ngola a Kiluanje was in the 1560s. Having defeated the original kilombo state of Kulembe, they had taken over leadership of the kilombo themselves. The Imbangala traveled north along Angola's coast for two decades from 1580. In the region of the Kuvo River around 1600 they finally made contact with the Portuguese. It was this vital meeting of Portuguese traders and Imbangala outsiders, only recently established at the Kwanza, which set the stage for an Imbangala-Portuguese partnership in the early decades of the 1600s.

This military partnership coincided with a São Tomé and Pernambuco demand for slaves by the thousands for sugar plantations. Portuguese military personnel only controlled a base on Luanda Bay and some few barracks on the lower Kwanza, yet after meeting the Imbangala at the Kuvo River in 1601, they formed a trading agreement after assisting the latter in crossing the Kuvo to attack enemies. The Imbangala provided their new allies with slaves and were paid with trade goods. Imbangala captured in war on the mobile slaving frontiers of Angola were certainly cutting sugar cane on the plantations of Pernambuco by the mid 1600s and were highly likely contributing to, if not leading, the organization of quilombos in Alagoas during the same period.

The Quilombo dos Palmares was unlikely to have been founded by Imbangala (Jaga). Palmares's original establishment between 1600 and 1605 was too early for Imbangala to have been shipped to Pernambuco. The earliest official report of the quilombo dates from 1612. The first Imbangala didn't arrive in Brazil until 1616 after being transported there on the orders of Luis Mendes de Vascocellos, who became Angolan governor the following year. He used Imbangala auxiliaries to fight against the Ngola. Many Imbangala were sold into Brazilian slavery after battles in Kasanje in 1624.

The Portuguese wrote that the first leader of Palmares was Ganga Zumba. This name is believed to derive from *nganga a nzumbi*, which was a Kimbundo religious title among the Imbangala,[20] though believed to mean Great Lord by the Portuguese. It was a title rather than a personal name, as one of the functions of the nganga a nzumbi was to "relieve the sufferings caused by an unhappy spirit of a lineage ancestor."[21]

There were different types of nganga in Angola. Campbell recorded several in the early 20th century:

> nganga ya mawesa (doctor of the boiling pot ordeal), nganga ya chilumbu (diviner about sickness and trouble), nganga ya chishimba (witch doctor who uses crystal gazing (ngulu), nganga ya kapale (seed-gourd-rattling doctor and diviner), nganga ya Mupini (doctor who divines with axe on a skin), nganga ya kamimbi (rain doctor, or the "swallow doctor"), nganga ya chipungu (pot and basket diviner), nganga ya musashi (clairvoyant, who professes to see in a gourd of oil sickness and trouble, etc.), nganga ya chikupo (doctor who does not divine, but treats those who have already been diagnosed. He has cures for barreness and serious ailments), nganga ya mukove (smeller out of witches and wizards . . . he is called the "spear doctor"), nganga ya mwafi (poison cup doctor).[22]

In 1882, traveling from Benguela to the territory of Yacca, Capello and Ivens wrote that in the valley of Dombe Grande, the Bandombes, "When drinking aguardente . . . pour a small portion on the ground, as a libation . . . to the zumbi or nzumbi of the other world, by and with whom they always deem themselves surrounded and connected."[23]

Lineage ties had been cut by war in Angola and by membership of the Imbangala. Mbundu who were not Imbangala had also experienced their ancestral and land ties abruptly severed by transportation to Brazil. The Ganga Zumba could mediate supernatural reconciliation between disconnected ancestral spirits to descendents who were unable to appease them themselves. The nganga a nzumbi who dealt with spirits of dead kinsmen (plural jinzumbi, and singular nzumbi) were vital in Mbundu society. Imbangala nganga a nzumbi were priests and specialist necromancers able to control potentially dangerous jinzumbi who could psychically or physically attack their own descendents.

Macaco

Ganga Zumba lived in a royal city called Macaco. The name of the Palmares royal city was a name for death, associated with the monkey (*macaco*). As in West Central Africa, the King, Ganga Zumba, was awarded tribute by his subjects: "He enjoys everything produced in Palmares in addition to imported goods."[24]

When not defending against attack, the palmarinos traded with their neighbors in Pernambuco. Palmares produced crops, palm oil, palm rope, straw goods, gourds, and ceramics. The Imbangala of Angola were leading producers and consumers of palm wine and in Palmares they are likely to have continued this custom. What the palmarinos sought from trade were mainly firearms, ammunition, and salt. Salt was a commodity always in short supply in "maroon towns" throughout the New World.

African quilombolas were adept producers of palm products for survival.

> Salt they make with the ashes of the palm trees. . . . We even discovered, concealed near the trunk of an old tree, a case-bottle with excellent butter, which . . . they made by melting and clarifying the fat of the palm-tree worms. . . . The palm tree wine they are never in want of, which they make by cutting deep incisions of a foot square in the fallen tree trunk, where the juice being gathered, it soon ferments by the heat of the sun, when it is not only a cool and agreeable beverage but strong sufficient to intoxicate.[25]

Ganga Zumba had "a palace and a royal cloak, and is attended to by guards and officers who are accustomed to royal houses. In all respects, he receives a King's treatment and the ceremonies proper for a lord. People immediately kneel in his presence, applaud him and affirm his excellence. They speak to him as His Majesty and obey him out of admiration."[26]

Commanders of the raid on Palmares of 1645 said that the largest mocambo was "surrounded by a double palisade with a spike-lined trough inside. This quilombo was half a mile long, its street six feet wide. There was a swamp on the north side and large felled trees on the south."[27]

Trees were cut down to cultivate crops and for defensive purposes. Forest clearance, using a slash-and-burn method, was an old Amerindian technique in Brazil. Euclides da Cunha describes it in *Os Sertões* (*Rebellion in the Backlands*):

> Having trimmed the trees with their sharp-edged dgis, fashioned out of diorite, they would make a pile of dry boughs and then would stew them, crackling, over the tops of the tree trunks. They then would lay out, in the neighborhood of the burned stumps, an area that once

was luxuriant forest, now in ashes, and would proceed to cultivate it. They would repeat this same process the following season, until this spot of earth had been completely exhausted and, henceforth untillable, had been abandoned as caapuera—"extinct forest," in the Tupi language. . . . the vegetable families which subsequently sprang up on the burned-over patch were invariably types of scraggy shrubs wholly distinct from the vegetation of the primitive forest.[28]

Also note, from Miller:

The Imbangala made extensive and prodigious use of palm wine in their rituals, cutting down the trees (*elaeis Guineensis,* or ndende in Kimbundu) . . . to obtain the fruit, which they ate, and the wine, which they drank. Their requirements were so enormous that they devastated the palm groves wherever they passed, pouring the wine over the graves of their ancestors and using it in attempts to contact the dead through intoxification, trances and spirit possession. The importance of palm wine probably derived from the Lunda tubungu chief's close association with the drink.[29]

John Stedman wrote: "This stratagem of the enemy of surrounding and interspersing the field with the large trunks and the roots of fallen trees made our advancing very different and dangerous, and at the back of which fortifications they lay lurking and firing upon us, without themselves could be materially hurt, and over numbers of which timbers we had to scramble before we could come to the [maroon] town."[30]

Archaeologists who have excavated Palmares have concluded there were Amerindian women in the quilombo. In Tupi society men cleared the forest and hunted, while agriculture was practiced by women. Unlike many makeshift Imbangala fortress kilombos in Angola, Palmares was a long-term settlement—it lasted nearly a century, so slash-and-burn techniques were practiced there to clear ground for agriculture. Because of this, *caapuera* must have characterized the immediate terrain surrounding the mocambos.

Caapuera

"Beyond the narrow strip of canebrake along the coast, [was] a full-fledged pastoral regime. From the beginning of the seventeenth century, in our abusively parceled back lands, huge tracts were opened up, common grazing lands without boundaries, stretching away across the uplands: [opened up] by the free use of fire . . . which swept across the vast spaces, borne on the gusts of the north-east wind."[31]

Fugitive slaves escaping into the backlands were forced to move away from the sugar littoral over these areas of caapuera to get to the forest where their protection lay. Much of the evasive action to escape the slave hunters (who chased with dogs and on horse-back) naturally occurred in the caapuera. The Portuguese often complained that the cattle ranches linked to plantations helped slaves to escape. This was precisely because of the caapuera, created by colonizers using the Amerindian slash-and-burn technique for forest clearance.

It is interesting that caapuera was so often characterized by felled trees, when one considers that these were a major part of quilombo defense systems. Holloway notes that "Capoeira . . . [was] an old name for defensive military bulwarks made of interwoven sticks (as in the technique for coarse baskets) and packed with earth, with slits through which archers or musketeers could fire."[32]

Palmares's royal city of Macaco had fortifications made "entirely by a wall of wattle and daub, with openings aimed so that the combatants might harm your safety. The area outside the wall is entirely planted with iron spikes, and such clever traps that even the most vigilant will be imperiled."[33]

Central Africans used just such fortifications in many wars for which there are records prior to 1800. The Kongo armies, the Ndongo, and the Imbangala used field fortifications of this type. The Ndongo built quickly constructed "wood and straw" forts a day's journey apart in retreat during a 1558 battle with the Portuguese. Thornton records instances of interwoven stick fortifications in Central African wars; among them, "The Imbangala of the early 17th century [who] entrenched themselves behind palisades at every stop, complete with gates for each commander and a separately entrenched section for the overall commander." The town of Mbamba was "protected by pit traps covered with grass and ditches." The Portuguese forces in Mbanza Kina in 1794 were amazed by "the complex fortifications of redoubts, hidden roads and mutually supporting bulwarks as well as naturally occurring but carefully used features such as hills and especially dense forests."[34] And in 1685, the Portuguese said that the Jaga Caconda "was entrenched in a fortress . . . behind his customary line of sharpened stakes."[35] A Central African trick of using forts to exhaust enemy forces, while in reality the armies were retreating into the forest or preparing for an ambush, was also evidenced in the regularly abandoned mocambos of the Brazilian quilombo.

Inside the Quilombo dos Palmares

The palmarinos were adept with bow and arrow and excellent marksmen with firearms. They had many spies in the towns and plantations who warned them about attacks in advance. Thus, approaching the quilombo was famously treacherous, and launching a surprise attack was virtually impossible. Indeed, the ingenious traps and hidden pits lined with sharp spikes killed many before they'd even reached the outer wall of the main enclosure. The element of surprise always belonged to the residents of the quilombo.

The size of the city of Macaco is illustrated by the fact that it was said to contain 1,500 houses (although other translations have it as 1,500 inhabitants). At different periods in its history, colonial forces reported that Palmares had 220 main buildings, including a chapel. The nominally Catholic chapel was filled with images in the tradition of the cult of saints. At the chapel entrance was an image of the baby Jesus, with Our Lady of Conception and Saint Bras. A contemporary reported that the priest who carried out the baptisms and marriages at Palmares followed the church-decreed form with modifications. Polygamy was permitted, as Ganga Zumba was said to have had three wives.

There were four blacksmith shops for ironworking and weapons manufacture, plus a Government House used by "ministers of justice for the necessary execution of laws. They imitate everything found in a republic."[36]

King of Congo

The political and judicial infrastructure in Palmares was well developed and reflected the practice of electing kings and queens of Congo through Rosary Brotherhoods that became popular in Brazil in the second half of the 17th century. In 1642 an ambassador of the King of Congo visited Recife, impressing the Dutchman, Gaspar Barlaeus, who said the Congolese group performed for the Brazilians with "original dances, leaps, formidable swordplay, [and] the dazzle of eyes simulating anger against an enemy."[37] As we'll see, this demonstration of martial dexterity represented *sangar,* a common type of Central African military review that was often performed to the drum.

Rosary Brotherhoods had been founded in Brazil by 1654 and membership was often restricted to Angolans or crioulos, who ". . . elected members . . . to be kings, queens, and male and female judges, and the positions were held by both slaves and free men and women."[38]

Laws against coronations of kings and queens (fashioned after monarchs in Central Africa) within brotherhoods of Our Lady of the Rosary were eventually passed in the early 1700s, although they continued secretly in towns and quilombos for hundreds of years. In 1818 Von Martius "recorded the election, coronation, and visits not only of a King of Congo, but also of a Queen Xinga—the first such documentary record of a Queen Xinga in Brazil. The famous [Jaga-Imbangala] Queen Njinga ruled the Central African kingdom of Matamba in the mid-seventeenth century."[39]

Incidentally, the name of this queen is also spelled Nzinga, Zinga, Jinga, and Ginga in Portuguese documents, or Njinga and Anna Njinga in African documents. "She herself spelled the name 'Ginga' in her extant letters."[40] The term for capoeira's famous swaying dance step is often reckoned to be called *ginga* after the verb *gingar,* which means to sway, swing, or roll in Portuguese. It shouldn't be forgotten that Angola's most famous colonial-era queen also spelled her name Ginga. The lords who followed Queen Nzinga in the area of Matamba in the late 17th and 18th century retained the title Jinga.[41]

Kings Ganga Zumba and Zumbi Dos Palmares

King Ganga Zumba and King Zumbi are sometimes said to have been kings in Africa who were enslaved and brought to Brazil. Although members of royal families were sometimes enslaved, it is possible that Ganga Zumba was born in Angola, from an Imbangala background, and was elected to his position in Brazil after the manner of the election of Kings of Congo by the Angolan inhabitants of Palmares. This is conjecture, of course, and there is really no way of knowing for certain how Ganga Zumba came to be the leader of Palmares at this time. The anonymous author of one 17th-century account of the defeat of Ganga Zumba wrote that the king's mother lived in the mocambo of Acainene; if this is true, it is somewhat unlikely that mother and son both traveled from Angola together.

Zumbi is believed to have been born in the Quilombo dos Palmares. The election of judges was frequent in Rosary Brotherhoods and there were many laws and a well-defined division of labor inside the large quilombos. In Palmares there were strict punishments for sorcery and any attempts to escape. Slaves were sometimes captured and taken to the quilombos, where they remained slaves until they themselves captured new recruits. Palmares was on a constant war footing for more than sixty years, with attacks against its mocambos averaging at least one a year or even more frequently after the Dutch were defeated in the Northeast. War was a way of life, yet Palmares was still an improvement on Pernumbuco sugar plantations. A contemporary wrote that palmarinos "felt more secure where they could be more at risk."

Of the 3,000 Europeans living in Pernambuco in 1645, half were Sephardic Jews who'd found a niche in Recife's local economy, aided by the fact that they often spoke Hebrew, Dutch, and Portuguese. It would be a misrepresentation to say that the Jewish merchants of northeast Brazil were rich and powerful. They were often living on the poverty line. Many had come from Amsterdam with the Dutch and were wary of the Portuguese military struggle, siding with the more religiously tolerant Dutch. Many Jews died in battle and scores died of starvation during the nine years of the Portuguese fight for reclamation. Some Sephardim headed for New Amsterdam and founded the first Jewish community of New York; others sought their fortune on the sugar-producing island of Jamaica.

In the starvation years, some who'd been financially ruined in Pernambuco made their way into the dense palm-covered territory straddling the Serra da Barriga in Alagoas. Palmares comprised runaway African slaves, crioulos born in Palmares, free people captured in raids, and Amerindians. In a similar way to Angolan kilombos, Palmares provided for diverse inhabitants brought together in coexistence on a war footing. But when people wanted to leave, they faced the quilombo's laws. Palmares needed fighters as well as farmers and artisans to maintain itself.

To describe Palmares as a single entity is misleading. A 17th-century author wrote:

> These Palmares do not run so uniformly. . . . to the northwest, sixteen leagues from Porto Calvo, is the mucambo of Zambi (Zumbi), five leagues north of that is Arotireui; a little east of that are the two mucambos of the Tabocas; fourteen leagues northwest of these is Dambrabanga; eight leagues to the north is the walled city of Subupira; six more leagues to the north, the royal walled city of Macaco; five leagues to the west is the mucambo of Osenga; nine leagues northwest from our settlement of Serinhaem, the city of Amaro; and twenty-five leagues northwest from Alagoas is the Palmares of Andalaquituxe. These are the largest and most defendable."[42]

One league is approximately 3 miles, so the area of Palmares was vast. The Portuguese knew the population were sustained by farming, using the land between the separate towns to hunt and grow vegetables, fruit, and corn. Palmarinos were careful to preserve and store food for sieges. "Distinct functions exist in Palmares as much for sustenance as security,"[43] said one governor's report.

Johan Mauritz of Nassau and São Jorge

In 1637, eighteen years before Zumbi's birth, Prince Johan Mauritz of Nassau became governor-general of Brazil. He understood no African or Amerindian languages and was said to become tongue-tied when he tried to speak Portuguese. His first task was to make sense of the colony. Mauritz was followed into Pernambuco and Recife by a wave of Dutch immigrants and he immediately sold off plantations on credit after the previous owners fled to Bahia.

Today, Prince Mauritz has a good reputation as an influence on the colony. He is commonly described as an "enlightened" lover of art and letters who civilized Recife, landscaping the streets like a New World Amsterdam. While he was enlightened, he was no Jean-Jacques Rousseau. He wrote to faint-hearted West India Company directors in Holland, "It is not possible to effect anything in Brazil without slaves . . . and they cannot be dispensed with upon any occasion whatsoever; if anyone feels this is wrong, it is a futile scruple."[44]

He's credited with "trying to improve the lamentable relations of the Europeans with the Indians."[45] High on his agenda was recruitment of Amerindians by the thousands to fight alongside Dutch regulars in the battle for the fort at Porto Calvo.

He also had to deal with the food shortages in the colony. Mauritz offered incentives for manioc farming. Recurrent famine in the

Northeast was caused by the increasing population and dominance of the sugar and tobacco crops. Landowners were in the habit of planting manioc only according to the number of slaves they owned. The Northeast needed a crop to provide staple food in times of famine, and manioc fitted the bill. It was an easily grown, high-carbohydrate food made from the versatile cassava root. Amerindians had been refining it for generations, by compressing the pulp away from the poisonous juice and roasting it. This made coarse flour called *farinha de mandioca*. Starch was also heated until the grains popped into clusters of tapioca.

In addition to domestic, military, food, and landscaping projects, Mauritz ordered off a 1637 expedition to attack the castle of São Jorge at the gateway to slaving on the Gold Coast. Although Elmina had declined as a center for gold, it still had its uses and the Dutch were aware that it would be a useful base to collect slaves to send to Brazil.

The battle for São Jorge (El Mina Castle) had really begun in 1625 when the Dutch had sent 1,200 soldiers in fifteen ships and blockaded the harbor, attacking with a heavy naval bombardment. They knew that the Elmina garrison was defended by just fifty-six Portuguese. The Fante nation signed a trade agreement with the Dutch, who also expected Commany and Efutu chiefs to join their cause (which didn't happen). When they began marching along the coastal road to São Jorge they seriously underestimated the possibility of an African force attacking them. The Portuguese garrison's African allies from Elmina were waiting in the brush on the side of the road and the Dutch were decimated; according to the Portuguese governor, Sotomayor, only forty-five of them survived the slaughter.

In 1637 the Dutch were careful not to fall into another ambush and decided to attack the fortress from the heights of St. Iago Hill.

The Elminan forces were massed at the foot of the hill and initially defeated four companies of Dutch troops. Yet after the African forces returned to the village to celebrate victory, another Dutch unit took the hill and defeated the few Portuguese on the summit. When the Hollanders hauled their guns up the hill of St. Iago at El Mina, they blasted their cannonballs over the river into the court-yard of the castle.

The Dutch invented the iron cannonball. Twenty-four pounds of solid iron howling through the air for 3,000 yards could cause immense damage to people and buildings. By now São Jorge had been well reinforced, and accurate fire from St. Iago Hill wasn't possible. But the Dutch were very effective with cannon. Their navy used these weapons successfully in the Atlantic. Barbell-shaped, double-headed cannonballs were hurled into the rigging of fleeing ships, slicing up sails and anything else in their path or pounding through the hull and flooding the ship. Partridge shot packed with lead musket balls could also be blasted onto an enemy ship's deck to maim the crew. The new cannon were far more accurate than they had been in the era of the Spanish Armada a generation earlier, when a powerful powder charge often did more damage to press-ganged convict gun crews than their intended targets.

At Elmina, the Dutch commander sent his main troops out onto the peninsula so that his batteries could bombard the fort from point-blank range. The determined gun crew wrought total havoc in a matter of hours. In some accounts it's written that the Por-tuguese troops were troubled by alcoholism in the ranks, and in fact each Portuguese soldier barracked at Elmina was issued two liters of wine every day and they weren't in fighting shape. After 160 years of occupation, the Portuguese at Elmina surrendered to the Dutch.

"Overflowing with slaves for sale"

Johan Mauritz was indefatigable in his colonial designs. Although he remained governor in Brazil for only seven years, his next plan was for the Dutch fleet to capture Luanda from the Portuguese. He and the West India Company were in disagreement over this—one of a series of disagreements that led to Mauritz's return to Holland in 1644.

After the cessation of the "Iberian Union" in 1640, relations between Portugal and Holland did not return to their former friendliness, which is hardly surprising considering Johan Maurtiz's mission in life was to dismantle Portuguese power piece by piece. The West India Company's "supreme authority," the Heeren XIX, were told, "Without negroes and oxen nothing can be expected from Pernambuco."[46] Categorical statements of this kind were standard fare; the Portuguese commentator, Frei António Vieira, wrote, "Without blacks there is no Pernambuco and, without Angola, there are no blacks."[47]

There was a brief truce between Holland and Portugal, which Johan Mauritz immediately broke. The Dutch captured Luanda in August, São Tomé in October, and Benguela in December of 1641. In Luanda they were trading with redwood, Swedish iron bars, nzimbu shells, Dutch textiles, and good quality cloth collected from the Loango coast. The King of Congo and Queen Nzinga were willing to trade slaves for these goods.

Nzinga was the ruler of Matamba by now and a contender for the title Ngola a Kiluanje. By the 1620s she had undergone the rites of the kilombo and was a fully fledged Imbangala. She differed fundamentally from other northern Imbangala rulers because of the Mbundu system of titles that existed in Matamba. These indigenous titles were considered authentic in comparison to Lunda titles.

This allowed Nzinga:

> to command her own people with marginally more security than the alien Imbangala bands and thus to behave more independently. . . . the trade route which developed during the 1630s from Matamba through ndemba toward the Dutch on the coast ensured her access to European trade goods regardless of her relations with governors in Luanda. . . . the Dutch occupation of Angola cleared the way for large-scale exports of slaves from Matamba and fuelled Nzinga's rise to the stature of the most powerful ruler in the interior during the 1640s. She established a virtual monopoly over the slave trade from the interior during that decade.[48]

A new Dutch director in Luanda said that the town was now "overflowing with slaves for sale."[49]

"Rubbish heap of Portugal"

In the Luanda hinterland an anonymous 17th-century Portuguese poet wrote:

> There is in this turbulent land a storehouse of pain and trouble, confused mother of fear, Hell in life. Land of oppressed peoples, rubbish heap of Portugal, where she purges her evil and her scum.

> Where the lie and falsehood, theft and malevolence, selfishness, represent vain glory. Where justice perishes, for want of men to understand it, where God must be sought to achieve salvation.

> From his throne God casts upon us, with cruel and bloody war, with the power of the land and pestilence, hot and malignant fever, which in three to seven days places beneath the ground the most robust.[50]

It was down the trail from Matamba through Ndemba that the vast majority of slaves taken from Angola during the Dutch occupation passed. The Portuguese, the Dutch, and the African allies of both sides fought relentlessly to control the trail.

The Dutch empire and West India Company were at their zenith, controlling virtually the whole West African coast, Recife, Pernambuco, and Maranão. They possessed islands in the Caribbean and off West Africa, not to mention the Dutch East India Company, which drove the British and Portuguese from Indonesia, Malaya, and Ceylon (Sri Lanka). This company also won control of the Spice Islands, established a Dutch Colony at the Cape of Good Hope, and many forts and settlements in Newfoundland and North America.

Yet everything wasn't quite as rosy as it seemed for the Hollanders. In reality, the return of Mauritz of Nassau to Holland marked the beginning of the end for the Dutch in Brazil. The period of reconquest between 1645 and 1654 brought nothing but defeat after defeat to the Dutch West India Company in Brazil and Africa. They succumbed to the age-old malady of would-be rulers of the world and overextended themselves. The final nail in the coffin came in 1652 after war with Britain, another seafaring nation not averse to dreams of world domination. Resources for the Dutch Brazilian garrisons were almost nonexistent. In December of the following year, a Portuguese fleet of seventy-seven warships appeared off the coast of Recife. The Dutch soldiers and some Amerindian allies were unable to offer any meaningful resistance and by mid-January 1654 it was all over. After thirty years the Dutch surrendered their Brazilian territories to Portugal.

The War against Palmares

The end of the war with the Dutch in northeast Brazil signaled the beginning of an intensified war against the Quilombo dos Palmares. In 1655 Brás da Rocha Cordosa led the first attack of the new era, capturing many prisoners. Zumbi's life story begins with this attack, according to the biography *Palmares, A Guerra Dos Escravos* by Décio Freitas.[51] Zumbi dos Palmares is a legend in Brazil. In the manner of legends, his history begins and ends differently according to who's telling it. One beginning has it that Zumbi was an African king sold into slavery in Brazil, where he escaped and resumed his royal and military functions after serving as *general das armas* in Palmares for many years.

Another theory is that Zumbi was born in Palmares in 1655. After the attack by Cordosa, he was captured while still a baby and carried away to Porto Calvo. Here he was adopted by a priest, Antonio Melo, who baptized him Francisco and raised him as a son, teaching him Latin and Portuguese. In 1670, still only fifteen years old, Zumbi fled to the place of his birth after Antonio Melo told him it was Palmares.[52]

As the General of Arms, Zumbi was responsible for training the palmarinos to fight the Portuguese. Sergeant Major Manuel Lopez Galvão, who led an attack against the quilombo in the 1670s (when Zumbi was twenty), wrote that their strength lay in "military practice made warlike in the discipline of their captain and general, Zumbi, who made them very handy in the use of all arms, of which they have many and in great quantity—firearms, as well as swords, lances and arrows."[53]

He was described as "a black man of singular valour, great spirit, and rare constancy. He is overseer of the rest, because his industry, judgement and strength to our people serve as an obstacle, to his an example."[54]

Sometimes the Portuguese referred to him as Zambi, which would be equivalent to Nzambi in Angolan Kimbundo, meaning

Supreme Being. Recall also the Imbangala religious title Nganga a nzumbi (doctor of the ancestral spirit), and that the nzumbi was the ancestral spirit demanding appeasement. To gain an idea of the type of warfare Zumbi may have trained his comrades in, it is useful to consider both the Imbangala and 17th-century Angolan military techniques generally.

Imbangala Warriors

The Imbangala kilombo was dedicated first and foremost to the art of war. Its main advantage was the ability to absorb genealogically unconnected warriors into a well-organized, highly trained armed force with a strong and centralized political structure. In this way the Imbangala kilombo was identical to the Quilombo dos Palmares.

In Angola, warfare was fought on both the material and supernatural planes. The Imbangala north of the Kwanza used extremely intense rituals to convince their Mbundu enemies that they were supernatural beings. This so lowered the morale of the Mbundu that battles were often won before any meaningful physical combat had occurred. To the Mbundu, human beings possessed three things: land, lineage, and agriculture. The Imbangala, on the contrary, deliberately transformed themselves into supernatural beings because they didn't settle to cultivate crops and they radically cut all lineage ties. The Mbundu had no methods or soldiers ready to deal with assault from "non-humans" and were thus rendered extremely vulnerable to the Imbangala. In itself, this was enough to instill terror in the hearts of their foes, both Mbundu and Portuguese alike. Many of the European terms of abuse referring to "savages" and "devils" stem from this period.

The kilombo was a sacred place dedicated to extremely tough military training and weapons. In addition, there were the supernatural rules called yijila and the use of the potion known as maji a samba already referred to in connection with the Queen Temba Andumba. The yijila laws excluded women from the kilombo and forbade the birth of children to the Imbangala within its confines. There was flexibility in these areas outside, but any flouting of the rules inside was a very serious matter and ended in the death of both mother and child. The Imbangala also excluded menstruating women from all rituals within the kilombo. In the 17th century, it was said that Imbangala warriors sometimes gave up battles because a warrior's woman began menstruating during the course of the fighting. Any function that suggested fertility and the creation of matrilineage was absolutely forbidden by the yijila laws. Even in rites involving cannibalism, female flesh was never eaten. Maji a samba was used by the warriors to gain invulnerability to the enemy's weapons. When going to battle, the Imbangala were convinced of victory while the enemy were almost always convinced of defeat. Because Imbangala could expand their membership by kidnap and ritual ceremonies, as opposed to lineage, they also had an advantage over the Mbundu groups who could only swell their numbers at the local birth rate.

In contradiction to the original function of the kilombo, only uncircumcised youths were inducted into the Imbangala band. The king of the kilombo was married to a *tembanza* (named after the original Temba Andumba). Fully initiated Imbangala fighters assembled before the king and showed off their prowess in mock battle. This mock battle was essential to the function of the kilombo. Angolan warriors, both Imbangala and the full-time soldiers of other states, possessed skills:

that could be acquired only through long practice and were not to be found among the ordinary population. These included facility in hand-to-hand combat with sword, club, battle axe, and stabbing spear, and in some cases the use of the shield. Although one could reasonably expect the average central African adult male to be fairly adept in archery, since he would have needed such skill to hunt, most warfare was in fact waged in close, hand-to-hand fighting. . . . Thus the important skill was, above all, the ability to twist, leap, and dodge to avoid arrows or the blows of opponents: "All their defence," wrote one European observer of late sixteenth century Ndongo, "consists of sanguar, which is to leap from one side to another with a thousand twists and such agility that they can dodge arrows and spears" . . . and Cavazzi describes the arduous physical training as one of the requirements of the Imbangala, mercenary soldiers who served in all the armies of seventeenth-century Angola. Dutch observers resident in Brazil were astonished at the skill with which members of the Kongolese delegation, which passed Brazil on its way to the Low Countries in 1642, handled the broadsword and their skill at leaping and parrying with this weapon. . . . the attitude of most African soldiers is clearly revealed in the boast of Queen Njinga, who often personally led her forces against the Portuguese. When Cavazzi saw and praised her performance at a military review in 1662, noting her agility despite her age (nearly 80) and sex, she replied, "Excuse me Father, for I am old, but when I was young I yielded nothing in agility or ability to wound any Jaga, and I was not afraid to face twenty-five armed men."[55]

In Angola it was customary for fighters to indulge in mock hand-to-hand battle involving the twisting, leaping, and dodging referred to by Cavazzi in the 1660s. The factor of ritual battle was essential in Imbangala initiation ceremonies. After the mock battle by the adult Imbangala inside the kilombo, symbolic "mothers" would bring the previously hidden new recruits up to the gates.

The Imbangala soldiers confronted the initiates at the gates of the enclosure with drawn bows, as if to defend the kilombo from attack. But then, instead of assaulting the boys, they touched them lightly on the chest with arrows to signify a ritual slaying, or capture as prisoners of war. On the following night, the soldiers finally anointed the youths' bodies with maji a samba, the ointment which the tembanza made from human fat, and brought them inside the kilombo.[56]

The role of the Imbangala kings differed from that of non-Imbangala Mbundu kings. This is relevant in considering the role of the two kings of Palmares, who both had names (Ganga Zumba and Zumbi) associated with supernatural rather than temporal or purely political functions. The Ngola a Kiluanje and other Mbundu kings were temporal, while Imbangala kings had a temporal and supernatural role, closer to priests than traditional kings. Recall that nganga a zumbi was a priestly function.

The Imbangala military trained its recruits to a very high level of fitness for battle. Troops were divided into squadrons under the command of *musungos,* who were closely controlled by the king. An individual musungo's fitness as a field commander didn't have anything to do with hereditary rights—only with military ability. This gave the Imbangala an immediate advantage over Mbundu armies. The Imbangala's large armies were adaptable and able to reform and recover from defeat or capture by assimilating yet more recruits.

Zumbi was said by his opponents to be an expert in all kinds of weapons. What kind of weapons were African warriors in Angola using in the 17th century? Bows and arrows were a certainty, and sometimes these arrows were tipped with poison. Lances, axes, hatchets, broadswords, and spears were all used in this period. Different Imbangala groups specialized in particular weapons, and they tended to adapt fighting techniques to their choice of weapon.

Miller reported that in the 1640s the Imbangala who fought the Portuguese at Kisama, were deadly with a war hatchet, while farther south there were Imbangala who specialized using a longbow that had one end planted in the ground and an arrowhead shaped like a spear and battleaxe (a halberd).

The Imbangala north of the Kwanza, and at Lukala and the Kwango, were basically allied to the Portuguese and fought for them as mercenaries from the mid-17th century until the latter half of the 19th century. During the early colonial era the Portuguese never managed to physically conquer the most important ruling group of Ndongo in Angola. It wasn't until the 19th century and the era of the Maxim gun that European technical superiority could reliably overwhelm African armies. As Thornton has pointed out, in Africa, European armies had to adapt their manner of waging war. In Angola and Kongo, European techniques also influenced the traditional military strategies of local armies from the 15th century onward. Portugal couldn't overwhelm Angola, but it proved "successful" by choosing the most effective African mercenaries to fight on its side.

The kingdoms of Kongo and Ndongo went to war in 1579, largely due to competition for trade with the Portuguese. Capuchins and Jesuits who witnessed the way these armies fought have given some indication of the differences between African and European fighting techniques. We learn that most fighting was close, one-on-one, hand-to-hand combat using the array of weapons previously mentioned. There were no horses in Central Africa, and cavalry played no part in these wars. Arrow strikes also played only a limited role at the very beginning of a battle, possibly only one volley. In fact, the fewer arrows a warrior carried, the more valiant he was considered.

In the case of the Imbangala, warriors sometimes killed their enemies with individual "trademarks"—a pattern of wounding that would indicate which soldier had done the killing. In Central Africa, unless a slain enemy was buried in accordance with traditional rites of land and lineage, the spirits of the dead would remain on earth, causing trouble for the living. Imbangala wounded their enemies individually so they could retrieve the body and return it to the kilombo, where certain body parts would be eaten to avoid potential haunting.

Friars and priests observing the Kongo army noted that only the nobility carried shields. As we have seen, armor and shields were not an important factor of defense. It was an individual's ability to dodge and twist to avoid stabbing spears, hatchets, swords, and arrows that gave superiority in the field. Capoeira inherited the absence of shielding (blocking) techniques and the ability to deliver attack techniques at close range while simultaneously performing dodging *esquiva* techniques. "Cavazzi related that Kongo's defeat at Mbwila in 1665 was presaged by the appearance in the sky of a spectral combat between two soldiers, one equipped as a Kongo with a shield, the other as an Imbangala . . . without arms, in which the Imbangala won."[57]

Thornton has illustrated that the Central African reliance on sangar, speed, individual agility, and hand-to-hand fighting meant that armies spread into what he termed "open order" formations, wherein soldiers ranged out into a wide, open line, giving each combatant plenty of room to use fighting techniques. Many Europeans interpreted this open-order fighting as chaotic, although what looked to the uninformed like hundreds of individual fighters dashing at each other in total disorder was in reality more organized.

Each fighting unit or squadron of the Ndongo armies had their own standards and flags, and in the case of Imbangala, they were usually identified by individual insignia. Soldiers in the units were controlled by drums and horns of different sizes, which signaled to the soldiers over the roar of the battle. These musical instruments had specific pitches that were understood by the fighters, and they interacted in a complex pattern, so that one set of orders might override another, or reinforce orders coming from a central command.

The Imbangala had an advantage over regular Mbundu forces here, as their musungo squadron leaders were far more able to carry out direct orders from the king quickly. These musungos were tried and tested veterans, selected by *vunga* war leaders known as *ngola a mbole* (political officials subject to the kilombo king).

Central African warriors were professional in the sense that it was not the general population of males who did the fighting, but a limited number of people who were specially trained for the task. There were also scouts called *pumbo* or *pombo*. Portuguese knew them as *gente escoteria* or *gente de bom pe,* selected for being very fast runners. The Capuchin Cavazzi wrote of the gente de bom pe. He referred to them in relation to a *Tandala*, which he described as holding "the place of the viceroy or viceduke among Europeans, who is situated in the rearguard which they call Iquoque, that is the main road to the royal court. . . . he is normally an elder and a good soldier and much respected by all." Continuing:

> These and other officials behave as is customary in Europe, except for the cavalry, as they all go on foot but the sum of war consists in the above officials who are those who make the advance or retreat or go right or left as they think expedient. These do not fight in military order as the Europeans do, but spread out over the field and the bravest soldier is he who is the fastest runner, most skillful in leaping or twisting his body. The boldest, the most barbarous and the cru-

elest are the good and brave soldiers and the most esteemed. Each of the officials has his subalterns as for example Samba Colambola which means vice-lieutenant general, Samba Tandala vice Tandala, vice governor and so on for the others. Each of these has his soldiers with their captains [and] lieutenants in their black fashions. . . . The war scouts they call Pombos who make up a company of good soldiers with their captain who strike out in front of everyone to find out the enemies' movements and give continual reports on how many of the enemy they hear and see and secure the roads. When the king attacks the enemy in person all the lieutenants accompany him with their insignia, making various demonstrating with them and shouting in their barbarous way.[58]

In Ndongo, among the Mbundu, specially trained soldiers were called *quimbares* (*kimbare,* plural *imbare*).[59] Their training for the position of kimbare prepared them in the use of weapons, sangar (or *sanguar-esquivas*), and the understanding of the signals of drums and horns that determined the fighting strategy on the field of battle. In the case of the Mbundu, the central part played by magic in their fighting strategy often put them at a disadvantage to the Imbangala, who used their own yijila laws secretly within the kilombo and maji a samba to give them a strong supernatural advantage. They didn't need to spend days on end drumming, dancing, and chanting, as did the Mbundu before a battle, which warned enemies of their intention. Having said this, the similarities in fighting strategy between Imbangala, Mbundu, and Kongo armies outweighed the differences. Weaponry, hand-to-hand combat, and open-order fighting were common to all armies in Central Africa.

The Central African war drum, the horn, and the agile fighting style of the kimbares are found in various contexts wherever prisoners from Angola and Kongo were transported during this period.

Of all slaves entering South Carolina prior to 1740, 40 percent to 60 percent were from Angola/Kongo coast. R. C. Rath cites the case of one "Thomas Butler," who was sought by plantation owner Vander Dussen via a notice in the *South Carolina Gazette* in 1733. Thomas was an escaped slave noted as "the famous pushing and dancing master." As Rath points out, for a slave to be referred to as a "famous master" in an antebellum southern newspaper was unusual, and even more intriguing is that his mastery was of "pushing and dancing." As Herbert Aptheker also related, "Evidence of the existence of at least fifty [quilombos or maroon towns] in various places and at various times, from 1672 to 1864 has been found. The mountainous, forested, or swampy regions of South Carolina, North Carolina, Virginia, Louisiana, Florida, Georgia, Mississipi, and Alabama (in order of importance) appear to have been the favorite haunts of these black Robin Hoods."[60]

Rath writes that in 1740:

South Carolina planters' worst nightmare came true. . . . about 20 slaves . . . "Surpriz'd a warehouse belonging to Mr. Hutchenson, at a place called [Stono]; they there killed Mr. Robert bathurst and Mr. Gibbs, plunder'd the House, and took a pretty many small Arms and Powder" . . . after thus arming themselves, the slaves marched southward with "Colours displayed and two Drums beating." When their ranks had swollen to between sixty and one hundred slave defectors, they stopped, still not far from Charleston, and "set to Dancing, Singing and beating Drums" for the purpose of calling more slaves to join them. . . . In 1740, the new slave code was rushed through the assembly. At the same time, South Carolinians stepped up hostilities toward the Spanish in St. Augustine, who offered freedom to any slaves who could escape there. Among its strictures, the new slave code prohibited "wooden swords and other dangerous weapons, or using or keeping of drums, horns, or other loud instruments which may call together, or give sign or notice to one another of their wicked designs or purposes."[61]

This was the biggest slave rebellion that America had ever seen and was led by a Kongolese slave named "Jemmy." It is reliably argued by Thornton that most of the participants were likely to have been captured as prisoners of war from Mbamba in Kongo some years previously.[62]

Many traditions and varieties of stick fighting come from Africa: from Donga in Ethiopia, using long staffs, and Dula Maketa, Nuba stick fighting, Trinidad *kalenda* or *kalinda* and in Brazil, *jogo de bastões, bate-pau,* and *maculelê,* widely practiced today and said to have been most popular in the Bahian Recôncavo at Santo Amaro de Purificação. These are surely just a small variety of styles that exist.

Dennis Newsome has referred to a stick-fighting art in the southern states of America also known by the generic term Kalenda. Says Newsome, "The oldest name in reference to Kalenda I know of is *mousondi*. Mousondi is from the Kongo Africa."[63]

Santo Antônio é Protetor

Thornton has related that many of the slaves participating in the Stono rebellion shouted *"lukanga,"* which means liberty in Kikongo, and comes from a root word, *kanga,* which also meant salvation to a Kongolese Christian.[64] Slaves had been arriving in Brazil and South Carolina from Kongo in large numbers ever since the wars that had started for control of the fallen Kongolese capital of São Salvador after the burning at the stake of Dona Beatriz Kimpa Vita in 1706. Dona Beatriz was a minor member of the Kongolese nobility who had gained a very wide following in Kongo after she had become possessed by St. Anthony. Dona Beatriz and members of her "Antonian Movement" had wanted to bring about reunification of the Kingdom of Kongo, to end corrupt politics and the exploitation of Kongo people through the slave trade.

From 1707, after battles in 1714–15, and up to 1740, hundreds of thousands of Kongolese, many of them members of the Antonian Movement, were shipped to Brazil from Luanda and to South Carolina from Cabinda for work on rice and indigo plantations. St. Anthony has traditionally been an important saint for protecting West Central Africans in Brazil. Thornton points out that during the Haitian revolution at the end of the 1700s, the same word, kanga, was shouted in the chant used by the revolutionaries of Santo Domingo: "Kanga bafiote, Kanga mundele, Kanga ndoki la, Kanga Li." This word Kanga was the first word of Dona Beatriz's "Salve Antonia" in Kongo.[65]

The armies of the Imbangala, the Mbundu, and the Kongo had many strategic and tactical characteristics in common—qualities that would have been imported with captured soldiers to the Quilombo dos Palmares and Stono in South Carolina. When the Stono rebels "set to dancing," for example, it wasn't a party but a military exercise. In Angola and Kongo:

> Dancing was a form of training to quicken reflexes and develop parrying skills. Those soldiers in Kongo and in the neighbouring regions that did not carry defensive arms instead developed great skill in fencing and in dodging lance thrusts, arrows, or javelins. . . . the physical agility of central African soldiers was notable . . . and required arduous physical training that was constantly renewed, especially in military reviews and dances where virtuosity was displayed. The Imbangala, who were wholly devoted to fighting were particularly adept at this mode of warfare, but it could be found everywhere.[66]

Another example of Central African military techniques refers to the Haitian revolution, yet could just as easily describe the open-order retreat and reformation tactics of Kongo, Mbundu, and Imbangala armed forces. In Haiti the revolution was led mainly by "creole" slaves born on the Island, but the soldiers of the revolution in its early phases were African fighters from Dahomey, Oyo, and Kongo. The Dahomey and particularly the Oyo provided cavalry experience, but the Kongolese slaves used experience gained in Kongo civil wars to great advantage.

> The pattern of attacks with small scale harassing manoeuvres, short, sustained battles and then rapid withdrawals are also reminiscent of the campaign diaries of the Portuguese field commanders in Angola. Felix Carteau, an early observer of the war in the north of St. Domingue noted that the [slave revolutionaries] harassed French forces day and night. Usually, he commented, they were repelled, but each time, they dispersed so quickly, so completely in ditches, hedges and other areas of natural cover that real pursuit was impossible. However, rebel casualties were light in these attacks, so that the next day they reappeared with great numbers of people. They never mass in the open, wrote another witness, or wait in line to charge, but advance dispersed, so that they appear to be six times as numerous as they really are. Yet they were disciplined, since they might advance with great clamor and then suddenly and simultaneously fall silent.[67]

Kongolese and Angolan soldiers were also able to combine smaller bodies of fighters speedily to form larger units when the situation required it. This was reported of 17th- and 18th-century Kongo forces and Queen Nzinga's army at different battles. Angolan forces, like the fighters of Palmares, didn't have to contend with cavalry, so after many skirmishing attacks carried out by their light infantry, Central African armies simply ran away if defeat seemed imminent. Portuguese commanders were sometimes tricked by this, as the "defeated" armies often reformed elsewhere sometime later and attacked again at a moment when the enemy were mistakenly enjoying the spoils of victory.[68]

Stedman related an ingenious retreat by quilombo rebels in Dutch Suriname:

> The mystery again was unraveled of why the rebels had kept shouting, singing, and firing round us the whole night . . . not only to cover the retreat of their friends by cutting off the pass, but by their unremitting noise preventing us from hearing them, who were the whole night employed—men, women and children—in preparing hampers . . . with the finest rice, yams, cassava . . . for their subsistence during their escape, and of which they only left us the chaff and dregs for our contemplation, to our great and inconceivable astonishment. This most certainly was such a piece of generalship in a savage people, whom we affect to despise, as would have done honour to a European prince, and even Frederick the Great himself needed not to have been ashamed of it.[69]

Retreat, reformation, and subsequent surprise attack was a signature of Central African fighting strategy.

Moradores

Although Palmares was a self-defensive institution in an aggressive society, offensive operations were carried out. Palmarinos ambushed "vassals" traveling the roads as servants of colonial authorities. They sabotaged and destroyed property and liberated slaves, helping others to escape by providing military cover as they fled Pernambuco's plantations. They also attacked armed *capitaes da mata* who chased fugitives over the caapueras.

As in the kilombos of Luanda, the palmarinos robbed travelers and traders on the roads. Settlers traveled in convoys accompanied by troops for protection. Palmarinos had a fair amount of geographical mobility and they maintained a level of local trade with settlers, which won support for Palmares among some free traders as well as the slaves of the *fazendas de cana*. Palmarinos could enter plantations undetected and they had friends and informants there. This two-way traffic and the underground grapevine of information coming from the towns and plantations informed Palmares of imminent military activities.

When Lieutenant Jürgens Reijmbach led a Dutch expedition against Palmares in 1645, his forces captured a few palmarinos in the bush. They told Reijmbach that Palmares "knew of the expedition for some time because [they] had been forewarned from Alagoas."[70]

Destroying Palmares became as important to the Portuguese as defeating the Dutch had been. The troop numbers that accompanied some invasions of Palmares surpassed those that it had taken to reconquer Recife, Salvador, and Pernambuco from the Dutch. "The army's best fighters, the most experienced leaders of the war against the Dutch, were at once employed for this purpose, with immense effort and suffering, but very little achieved."[71] Deprived of their heavy artillery, which was impossible to lug into the bush, the Portuguese were unable to outmaneuver the brilliant strategist Zumbi.

The war against Palmares intensified after 1672. The period after Reijmbach's expedition had been relatively peaceful by comparison. One of the reasons for this intensification was the expansion of planter society inland from the coast. *Moradores* (agricultural workers) who lived on sugar estates and the residents of small towns were getting geographically closer to the palmarinos, and this was causing conflict. Palmares as a whole, including all its mocambos, covered about 3,300 square miles (1,100 leagues). By the 1660s, Bahia, Sergipe, Espirito Santo, and Pernambuco were all undergoing an *expansão pequena*. "The Negroes . . . had good relations with moradores, as long as the latter kept their slave huts and plantations away from the free lands of Palmares."[72]

The expansion of morador settlements was encroaching on Palmares. There were strict laws against townsfolk or plantation residents maintaining any kind of commercial relationship with the quilombo. Palmares had both gold and silver seized in raids, and agricultural products from its farms. In times of famine, these were very welcome to moradores, while palmarinos purchased both guns and information about military activity with gold.

In the 1660s, the price of slaves was rising steeply in Brazil. Plantation owners were more inclined to hire professional capitaes da mata to pursue escaped slaves into the bush. Palmares lands were considered a mini-Africa—a source of slaves for whom engenho owners, or even moradores hoping to better their standing, wouldn't have to pay a single reis. They banded together into private armies and launched raids into Palmares. Crushing the quilombo wasn't the aim of these raids. They were undertaken to capture palmarinos and enslave them for profit. The deaths of moradores on the roads that the Portuguese complained about were usually the deaths of moradores slave raiding in Palmares territory.

In the 1670s, Zumbi led his own mocambo (said to be 16 leagues northeast of Porto Calvo). Subupuira was "ruled by the king's brother (Gana) Zona. . . . It has 800 casas and occupies a site one square league in size, right along the river Cachingi. It is here that Negroes are trained to fight [against] our assaults (and weapons are forged there)."[73] *Subusupu hara vura* meant "forged weapon of war" in Zande Angolan. A 17th-century author wrote about this mocambo: "Sucupira, the war command centre where the confederation's defence forces and sentinels were trained, was also fortified, but with stone and wood. Nearly a league in length, it contained within its boundaries three lofty mountains and a river called Cachingi, meaning 'an abundance of water.'"[74]

More than twenty years after the end of the Portuguese-Dutch wars in Pernambuco, the population of Palmares was high in people who, like Zumbi, had never been slaves because they'd been born in the quilombo and lived there all their lives. Kent cites Pitta, who maintained that:

> The only slaves in Palmares were those captured in razzias [raids]. . . .
> But they had the option of going out on raids to secure freedom by
> returning with a substitute. This is confirmed by Nieuhof, who wrote
> that the main "business" of palmaristas "is to rob the Portuguese of
> their slaves, who remain in slavery among them, until they have
> redeemed themselves by stealing another; but such slaves as run over
> to them, are as free as the rest."[75]

A large number of women also lived in Palmares, acquired from raids on Pernambuco engenhos. Nobody was allowed to leave voluntarily and the punishment for escape from Palmares was death.

The 1676–77 *entradas* of Fernão Carrilho were executed with extreme force. *Capitão-mor* Carrilho was experienced in war against quilombos. He'd successfully destroyed a number in Sergipe del Rey by the time he led the attacks against Palmares. He was aware of the special defenses at Palmares, the mud and wattle parapets full of caltrops, a kind of spiked ball that could be heaved at the enemy. He was wary, knowing that even when his forces had detected these fortifications, they remained a big danger.

An eyewitness account of the quilombo dos Palmares described that:

> The line of defence was very strong, of 2,470 fathoms, with parapets of two fires at each fathom, complete with flanks, redoubts, redans, faces, sentry-boxes, . . . and the exterior terrain so full of caltrops (pointed stakes) and of pits full of them, at all levels—some at the feet, others at the groin, others at the throat—that it was absolutely impossible for anyone to come close to the said line of defense at all from any angle. . . . Nor was it possible for them to make approaches, such was the density and the thickness of the underbrush in the woods; and indeed this factor had made it impossible for them to dig trenches.[76]

This stockade at Palmares was clearly the work of individuals with military training. The traps showed an Amerindian influence although the pointed stake pit trap was in use in African warfare too. The inaccessibility of the stockade was a common quilombo feature, and seems to have been universal in maroon communities throughout America, the Caribbean, and islands off the African coast.

The governor, Dom Pedro de Almeida, had learned a lot about Palmares from previous expeditions: "Taking great precautions, he told Fernão Carrilho that his most successful strategy would be to maintain a fortified camp inside Palmares . . . ordering the needed provisions to be supplied from nearby towns, so that nothing would be lacking."[77] Carrilho met his forces in Porto Calvo. They consisted of whites, mestizos, and Amerindians, including warriors of a famous Amerindian commander of the Dutch wars named Camarão.

The first mocambo to be attacked by Carrilho's forces was Acainene, where Ganga Zumba's mother lived. Captain D. Pedro de Almeida had become governor of Pernambuco in January 1674. He sent Carrilho to attack Acainene in October 1677. This mocambo was 25 leagues from Porto Calvo. The quilombolas of Palmares still hadn't fully recovered from a major attack nearly two years earlier that had been led by Major Manoel Lopes. Lopes had burned a large mocambo (reputedly of more than 2,000 houses) down and had left many palmarinos dead or wounded and without homes. With the memory of this violent attack still fresh, when Carrilho's force of 200 armed men arrived at Acainene, the inhabitants fled quickly deeper into the forest. Carrilho's soldiers hunted them down and killed as many as they could, also taking nine prisoners.

They used these prisoners to find out where other mocambos were and, more important, where Ganga Zumba and members of his immediate family were located. Ganga Zumba was in the fortified mocambo of Sucupira. He had received word from palmarinos who had fled Carrilho's men that the mocambo would soon be attacked, and had ordered that the inhabitants retreat and burn Sucupira, to leave nothing for Carrilho to use for sustenance or resupply. Carrilho established Sucupira as his own camp, renaming it Bom Jesus e a Cruz. Carrilho's forces had now marched through forest trails 45 leagues (135 miles, or 217 km) from Porto Calvo. The march from Acainene to Sucupira had been 20 leagues (60 miles or 96km). At Sucupira, Carrilho erected field fortifications, including batteries of cannon. The quilombolas attacked the captured stockade but a Palmares commander named Gangamuiza was captured and executed, along with many of his fighters. Ganga Zumba once again escaped and retreated with as many of his people as he could to a place of relative safety.

The operation had now become more a hunt than a war. Carrilho sent a force of fifty fresh soldiers to find Ganga Zumba and the escaped quilombolas. After three weeks they heard that the king was with an independent Palmares leader by name of Amaro, who had a mocambo named after him. The November 1677 attack on the quilombo of Amaro turned into an intense battle and only fierce fighting stopped the Portuguese from overrunning the territory.

A writer of the day described Amaro himself as being:

> Celebrated for his bravery, impudence, and insulting behavior, was also greatly feared by our men, and he had made himself known by incursions into the surrounding towns. He lived separated from the others as an independent ruler. His mocambo, which was known by his name, was fortified by high, thick palisades extending the length of a league and containing more than a thousand inhabited houses."[78]

Ganga Zumba himself was seriously wounded during the attack on Amaro, while his sons, nephews, and grandchildren were captured—a fate that could mean being sold back into slavery in a distant captaincy, Rio de Janeiro or Spanish America.

In 1678 Governor de Almeida sent a mission of lieutenants into Palmares. They returned with three of Ganga Zumba's sons and twelve other palmarinos.

> They brought the king's request for fealty, asking for peace which was desired, stating that only peace could end the difficulties of Palmares, peace which so many governors and leaders had proffered but never stuck to; that they have come to ask for his good offices; that they have never desired war; that they have only fought to save their own lives; that they were being left without cidades, without supplies, without wives. . . . The king had sent them to seek peace with no other desires but to trade with moradores, to have a treaty to serve his Highness in whatever capacity; it is only the liberty of those born in Palmares that is now being sought, while those who fled from other

people will be returned; Palmares will be no more as long as a site is provided where they will be able to live.[79]

An account eventually published in the *Revista do Instituto Histórico e Geográfico Brasileiro* in 1876 was originally written by an anonymous author in the late 17th century and discovered in the Biblioteca Pública in Evora, Portugal. It said of this meeting:

> The appearance of those barbarians caused amazement, because they came naked, and with their natural parts alone covered. Some wore their beards in braids, others wore false beards and moustaches, and others were shaved, and nothing more. All were husky and powerful, armed with bows and arrows, and carrying only one firearm. One of the king's sons rode a horse, because he still bore an open bullet wound which he had received during the fighting.[80]

The Portuguese smelled victory. It is plain from reports written at the time that the Portuguese knew that their main enemy in Palmares was the General of Arms, Zumbi, and not the weakened Ganga Zumba. To the latter, via the new governor of Pernambuco, Aires de Souza Castro, they offered a peace deal. It was couched in the beautiful language of diplomacy and was full of generous promises, as if from one sovereign state to another. It ensured Ganga Zumba's continued sovereignty over his people.

But there were conditions. First, Ganga Zumba had to return fugitive slaves living in Palmares to their "owners." Ganga Zumba was expected also to move the whole operation to the Cucaú Valley, into another palm forest in the region of the headwaters of the rivers Serinhaem and Formoso. This deprived the quilombo of its single greatest strength: isolated geography.

Why Ganga Zumba would have trusted the Portuguese now after all their double-dealing in the past is not known, and clearly the leopard hadn't changed its spots, for even after the treaty was ratified the troops that had been attacking Palmares throughout 1677 and 1678 were not demobilized. De Souza issued vast tracts of Palmares land to combatants on the Portuguese side. Carrilho was given 60 square miles of land just for himself, and more than 500 square miles were distributed among fifteen other individuals.

When Ganga Zumba agreed to the move to Cucaú in 1678–79, Zumbi and a faction of hardline rebels who supported him staged a "palace revolt." Kent cites Carneiro, who wrote that Zumbi, along with "João mulato, Canhonga, Gaspar, [and] Amaro," poisoned Ganga Zumba. This was an act of "sanctioned regicide," an accepted response in West Africa, and indeed Europe, being "the ultimate check on royal weakness or abuse."[81]

Kent has pointed out that both Zumbi, whose mocambo was less than 50 miles from Porto Calvo, and Amaro, with a mocambo a mere 27 miles from Surinhaem, possibly had populations with a greater proportion of escaped slaves born in Africa than the mocambo of Ganga Zumba, which was hidden deeper (135 miles) into the forest. We know the peace deal included the clause that all these liberated slaves would be returned to their owners, and Ganga Zumba, via his son, gave assurances that he had the power to assist in this process and crush any rebellion among his followers. His son, speaking for Ganga Zumba at a council meeting in the presence of both the previous governor, Dom Pedro, and the new one, Aires de Souza, also claimed that Ganga Zumba would provide guides to help the morador/Portuguese faction in defeating any rebels who didn't accept Ganga Zumba's authority.

The quilombo king was no longer a young man. He'd been attacked so many times and seen so many deaths, it must have been a heavy burden to carry. Given these circumstances, it is not difficult to interpret why Zumbi and his allies decided that Ganga Zumba had to go.

In 1680 Sergeant-Major Manuel Lopez ordered "Captain" Zumbi to honor the terms of Ganga Zumba's treaty with the governor of Pernambuco and quit the uprising in Palmares. He also ordered Zumbi to go to his uncle, Gana Zona, who appears to have moved to Cucaú also.

"Captain" Zumbi had no more intention of adhering to the treaty than had the Portuguese. Even had he wanted to, the governor of Pernambuco was in no position to guarantee independent sovereignty to a quilombo in Brazil; it was a political impossibility.

Zumbi was now the chief of Palmares, residing in the capital city of Macaco, where he would remain for the next fourteen years. He was a military genius in the art of guerrilla war. He possessed the leadership qualities to pass his knowledge on to others. Carrilho, until now, had been used as a threat to beat the old guard of Palmares into signing the treaty. Given the new circumstances, what the Portuguese needed was a military leader and a force of men who played by different rules. If Palmares fighters used the forest to their advantage, using unconventional methods, then those who fought them had to do the same thing. If they were to defeat Zumbi and his soldiers, the Portuguese needed to employ a military commander who was a little bit special. They found their man at last in the singular figure of Domingos Jorge Velho.

Bandeirantes

Domingos Jorge Velho was a bandeirante. The bandeirantes derived their name from the *bandeiras,* or "flag" expeditions. According to Amerindian custom, a flag bearer led their columns. The bandeirantes originated in the region of the Piratininga Plateau, where a little over a century earlier the Jesuits had founded São Paulo. São Paulo was inhabited by Amerindians and by the late 17th century their presence attracted Portuguese settlers and Jesuits, who variously wished to convert, control, or enslave the indigenous population wherever they found the opportunity. Cut off from the coast, São Paulo developed autonomously. There was scarcely any currency, trade was conducted by barter, and Tupi Indian culture and language were dominant there through the 17th century.

Portuguese men who settled in the region usually had sexual relationships with Amerindian women, so that a mixed-race population of people they called *caboclos* grew rapidly in São Paulo. Tupi ways of hunting and surviving predominated in these early years—for instance, the use of bow and arrow as well as firearms in hunting and defense.

There's no written record of a single Catholic or Protestant preacher speaking out publicly against the Atlantic slave trade in Europe in the 17th century. On the other hand, Amerindian slavery was a live issue. The Catholic Church was very active in condemning Amerindian slavery, especially in 1639 when Pope Urban VIII denounced it completely as punishable by excommunication. He was reacting to Spanish Jesuit representations in Rome, which had strongly condemned the activities of São Paulo bandeirantes in Brazil.

Because of pressure from the paulistas, the Jesuits were expelled from Rio de Janeiro and São Paulo after Pope Urban's proclamation (although by mid-century they'd returned). The paulista bandeirantes, whose number included Domingos Jorge Velho, were frontiersmen. The minority were white, who led a majority of enslaved Amerindians, with a medium group of *mamelucos* or caboclos. These expeditions, 2,000 to 3,000 strong, would march from São Paulo in huge convoys, exploring, cutting, burning, and taming the sertão as they went.

They covered many thousands of kilometers, destroying Indian villages as they discovered them. It made no difference whether these were Jesuit-run aldeias or not. The bandeirantes marched through the backlands, sacking and enslaving whole communities of Amerindians in their path. On one journey, bandeirante Raposo Tavares traveled as far as the foothills of the Andes. His bandeira cut back to the Amazon River, which it followed as far as Belém. This was a 12,000-kilometer journey through some of the toughest terrain on earth. By the time the trip was over, Tavares was said to be physically unrecognizable as the man who'd set off from São Paulo four years earlier.

The crown had a loosely paternal relationship with the bandeirante expeditions. Their marches had the useful function of pushing back the Spanish American borders beyond those originally agreed upon by the Line of Tordesillas. They collected Amerindian slaves and located areas of mineral and precious metal wealth. The Portuguese colonial authorities were generally well disposed toward them. The bandeirantes' heyday was during the war against the Dutch, when Portuguese access to Angola and the Mina Coast was disrupted. This reduced slave imports for the sugar plantations in Rio de Janeiro and Bahia. Even those slaves they did ship were regularly hijacked by Dutch warships, and put to work in Pernambuco and Recife instead. The Portuguese needed Amerindian labor to subsidize the shortfall. Jesuits calculated that as many as 300,000 Amerindians were captured by the bandeirantes from Jesuit missions in Paraguay alone. Sugar plantations in Rio were using a quarter to half Amerindian labor during the Dutch occupation of Brazil.

Amerindians were also put to work in wheat farming. The demand for wheat was created to feed Dutch, German, Portuguese, Spanish, and Neapolitan mercenaries and troops, though it was a short-lived experiment because of the difficulty of growing wheat compared to corn or manioc.

Amerindians were also needed for the bandeiras themselves. They constituted the majority of the force. Paulista ranching and agriculture opened vast swathes of the Brazilian hinterland to commerce and settlement. Minas Gerais, Mato Grosso, and Paraná were all breached by the paulista expansion.

In the Northeast, the bandeirante field commander, or "bush captain," Domingos Jorge Velho, had been selected by Governor João da Cunha, "for the conquest and destruction of the Negroes of Palmares."[82] Velho had a track record for putting down Amerindian insurrection. The Bishop of Pernambuco said of him:

> This man is one of the worst savages I have ever met. When he came to see me he brought an interpreter, for he cannot even speak correctly. He is no different from the most barbarous Tapuia, except in calling himself a Christian. And although recently married, seven Indian concubines attend him—from which one can infer his other habits. Until now, ever since he first had the use of reason—if, that is, he ever possessed it, for if he did he has lost it and I venture that he will not easily regain it—he has roamed the forests hunting Indian men and women, the latter to exercise his lusts and the former to work on the fields he owns.[83]

Using Amerindian fighters to destroy quilombos wasn't a new strategy. Roelox Baro had taken a large force of Tapuia and a contingent of Dutch regulars into Alagoas to "put the large Palmares through 'fire and sword' [and] devastate the small Palmares."[84] Baro's force had killed a hundred "Negro" quilombolas and captured thirty-seven (including seven Amerindian quilombolas) and "mulatto children." In 1674 there was also a plan to send the Tupi of Dom Diogo Pinheiro Camarão into Palmares. The six expeditions that entered the interior and attacked Palmares while it was under Zumbi's command between 1680 and 1686 cost Pernambuco 1 million cruzados. Some 400,000 cruzados of this expense were directly covered by the Portuguese crown, which now had exactly nothing to show for it. (A cruzado was a Portuguese currency unit, a gold coin, reported by Miller to be worth approximately 400 réis or 400$000 milréis in the 18th century.)

So in 1687, the governor of Pernambuco, Sotto-Maior (also written Sotomayor), wrote to Lisbon, reporting that he'd agreed to Velho's 1685 request for "commissions as commander-in-chief and captains in order to subdue . . . [Palmares]"[85] Sotto-Maior reassured the Portuguese king that hiring Velho and his men would be merely "a small expense to the treasury of Your Majesty."[86]

Domingos Velho had himself already told the king:

> Our militia, Sire, is unlike the regular one found anywhere else. First, our troops, with whom we undertook the conquest of the savage heathen of this very vast sertão are not made up of people registered in Your Majesty's muster books, nor are they obligated by wages or rations. They are in groups which some of us assemble: each of us joins with the servants he possesses under arms, and together we enter the sertão of this continent—not to enslave (as some hypochondracs [sic] would have Your Majesty believe), but to acquire Tapuia (a fierce people who eat human flesh) to domesticate them to the knowledge of civilised life and human society and association and rational commerce. In this way they will come to have the light of God and of the mysteries of the Catholic faith which is necessary for their salvation—for anyone who would make them angels before making them men labours in vain. We enlarge our troops from those

thus acquired and brought into settlements. And with them we wage war on those who are obstinate and refractory to settlement. If we later use them in our fields we do them no injustice, for this is to support them and their children as much to support us and ours. Far from enslaving them, we render them a gratuitous service by teaching them to till, plant, harvest and work for their livelihood—something they do not know until the whites teach them. Do you understand this, Sire?[87]

Velho had enlisted some of the most fierce and warlike Amerindian fighters in Brazil: Tobajara, Orua, and Cupinharuen. He pushed his men to extremes, showing no mercy to anyone for any reason. A thousand Amerindian bowmen set off to Pernambuco on the march for Palmares. They covered many hundreds of miles of arid backland, red earth, and scrub. Two hundred had guns. Eighty-four whites and mulattos also joined the march, which was described as "made under the worst conditions of toil, hunger, thirst, and destitution that have yet been known in this sertão."[88] By all accounts the march was made in agony and misery. Two hundred deserted, more than 130 starved to death, more than 60 died of disease. Between 500 and 600 half-starved men eventually arrived in Pernambuco. Incredibly, they postponed attacking Palmares to march to Rio Grande do Norte, where Janduin Amerindians were fighting the Portuguese in one of the bloodiest wars in Brazil's history (the so-called "Barbarians' War").

In the Barbarians' War the Janduin had virtually cleared settlers out of the captaincy of Rio Grande. Rio Grande's treasury was completely empty, so Domingos Jorge Velho was paid with any Amerindians he captured. The governor-general warned him:

Your honour must be sure not to permit any quarter being given to the barbarians during the fighting. Do not let a desire to take captive slaves mean that they are left alive. . . . Your Honour is to slaughter [the Indian enemy] and continue until you finally destroy them, giving such punishment that it will lodge in the memory of other tribes and fill them with fear.[89]

In four days, thirty-five of Velho's men were dead and seventy wounded. Other bandeirante commanders turned up, all of them paulistas with their private armies.

Domingos Jorge Velho and Matias Cardosa de Almeida had reputations as men who were "accustomed to penetrating the sertão [to endure] hunger, thirst, and inclements of climate and weather. The regular infantry have no experience whatsoever of such conditions; nor do the militia, who lack discipline and endurance."[90] The governor-general wrote to Velho, "I congratulate Your Honour . . . on having slaughtered 260 Tapuia."[91] By 1692, after two years of fighting, the Janduin signed a treaty promising to be "humble vassals" and "accept Christian baptism." After intervention by the king of Portugal they were awarded a land treaty not dissimilar to the type Ganga Zumba had gained in 1680. Uniquely, Portugal recognized the Janduin as a kingdom. The crown bought them from the paulistas, and "freed" them into Jesuit aldeias as far afield as Rio de Janeiro. Naturally, the unique treaty was broken by the Portuguese who redistributed the land to Portuguese cattlemen and small planters.

The End of an Era and the Birth of a Legend

Domingos Jorge Velho and his men marched once again toward Pernambuco for the final battles of the ninety-year-old "Central African State" in Brazil. The first attack on Palmares by Velho and his men came in 1692. His fighters were joined by Portuguese regulars from Pernambuco and Bahia. The palmarinos won the battle, just as Velho had expected. He'd taken the opportunity to reconnoiter the terrain and locate sources of food for a longer siege next time. In 1693 his forces once again gathered in Porto Calvo for a major offensive. Velho's strategy was to clear the mocambos one by one and to concentrate Zumbi's forces in a single fortified position, which would then be besieged. This process took approximately two years.

For the final offensive the governor provided Velho's forces (which with auxiliaries now numbered 6,000 men) with 200 kilograms of gunpowder and lead, as well as food stocks, military supplies, firearms, and 1,000 cruzados from the public treasury. Firearms in the 17th century had only a brief useful life without constant maintenance and they were useless without dry gunpowder. The guns used by the palmarinos and the Portuguese forces were long-barreled flintlock muskets. These were relatively inexpensive and efficient. They'd replaced the complicated wheel-locks that had been in use during the Dutch campaigns. They were also the main weapon used for military campaigns and slave trading in Africa where the British dubbed them the "Angola gun."

Velho and his forces were at a distinct advantage over Zumbi's fighters, who were not being resupplied by the captaincy. Velho and his officers were promised land grants in the whole territory of Palmares, in addition to the spoils, including any jewels and tax revenues in Palmares that belonged to the crown.

As a final condition, once in control of Palmares, Velho agreed to hunt down and return any escaping slaves to plantation owners in the future and stop slaves thus returned from escaping again, "since the Governor does not want . . . the Negroes, in any manner, to become free from captivity."[92]

Velho's army attacked Macaco, Zumbi's stronghold. The siege continued for three weeks, after which the state of Pernambuco supplied 3,000 more fighters to continue for another three weeks. The quilombo was defended by an iron-spiked outer wall, traps, ditches, and many vantage points from which to fire on the invaders. Velho sought to cut off Macaco by building a counter-fortification and deprive the quilombo of food, military supplies, or a path of retreat. After six weeks of siege, Zumbi ordered his fighters to abandon their positions and escape through gaps in Velho's counter-fortification, attacking from the rear while making their escape.

Accounts say that 6,000–9,000 men lay siege to the quilombo. The final battle on the night of 5th–6th February, 1694 was extremely bloody. Three hundred of Zumbi's soldiers were killed and 400 taken prisoner. The eventual total of prisoners came to 500; 200 of the quilombo's inhabitants were forced to hurl themselves over the precipice that lay to the rear of Macaco's fortress. (The details of how so many palmarinos came to throw themselves over the cliff has been a subject of long debate. Kent recommends Ennes's summary of the final days of Palmares, drawn from a collection of ninety-five documents in Ennes's collection.) Some of these deaths may have been suicides by palmarinos who would rather have died than face capture and enslavement. Others may have been forced to jump by the invaders. Some accounts of Zumbi's own death recall that he threw himself from the cliff edge.

In his book, *Capoeira: A Brazilian Art Form*, Mestre Accordeon writes, "Zumbi took up arms against the quilombo invaders, and after a tremendous resistance, plunged to his death from a cliff rather than to be captured. Zumbi . . . is honorarily considered for all of us capoeiristas, the number one artist of capoeira."[93]

Zumbi's legend is closely linked to capoeira: "Indication that capoeira was used by the people of Palmares was its diffusion throughout large parts of Brazil. When the quilombos were destroyed, the watchful warriors, no longer able to stay together, were scattered throughout several states, even as far as Rio Grande do Sul, and with them went their fight, traced to them through studies in the following centuries." The author of this, Augusto Ferreira in *Historia da Capoeira,* doesn't explain which specific studies link capoeira to Palmares warriors diffused throughout Brazil, yet his view reflects a legend, echoed many times in songs and histories of the art. From another source: "Zumbi is considered by many Masters of Capoeira and students as the first capoeirista and by inference he is regarded as the Patron Saint of Capoeira."[94]

The story of Zumbi's suicide reputedly originated with Sebastião da Rocha Pitta. The chronology and subsequent events don't add up to this conclusion, however. If he hurled himself from a precipice in February 1694, how was he executed by decapitation on November 20, 1695? Military records suggest that Zumbi didn't jump during battle. He escaped and carried on fighting for another year alongside groups of armed palmarinos who were still hiding out in the forest. Velho's men captured a fighter named Antonio Soares, who under torture led them to Zumbi's hiding place. Here the Palmares leader, now forty years old, was ambushed and killed. His body was identified in Porto Calvo, the same place he was born, and after he'd been decapitated, his head was taken to Recife to display as proof of his death. Another account reads:

> Some two hundred palmaristas fell or hurled themselves—the point has been long debated—"from a rock so high that they were broken to pieces." Hand-to-hand combat took another two hundred Palmarista lives, and over five hundred "of both sexes and all ages" were captured and sold outside Pernambuco. Zambi, taken alive and

wounded, was decapitated on November 20, 1695. The head was exhibited in public "to kill the legend of his immortality."[95]

The death of Zumbi marked the end of the era of Palmares. According to the conditions agreed between Velho and Pernambuco's governor:

> After suppressing the said Negroes, they cannot use their services in these captaincies, and he, Domingos Jorge, will be obliged to have all the prisoners put in the plaza in Recife, from there to sell them to Rio de Janeiro or Buenos Aires . . . and only the Negro children of Palmares from seven to twelve years of age can stay in these captaincies, some who will be sold according to their value for the account of the said colonel and his people.[96]

This strategy ensured that the fame of the Quilombo dos Palmares was spread far and wide by recaptured slaves exiled into slavery in distant captaincies or locations. The historical silence from the vanquished is inevitable. Oral history passed on by the palmarinos themselves wasn't lost altogether. The legend of Zumbi, in the end, proved far more powerful than the deeds of the Portuguese, Dutch, or paulista commanders. After the destruction of the quilombo, capitães do mata were employed very extensively, ensuring that no more federations of diverse mocambos developed into kingdoms in the backlands. The Portuguese created laws against royal coronations among Africans in Brazil. They were mindful that Ganga Zumba was an elected king whose family held vital offices of state in Palmares. There was also a new policy at the ports of Salvador, Recife, and Rio de Janeiro, which "sought to prevent . . . an over concentration of African slaves from the same ethnic group or ship."[97]

Though no evidence exists of capoeira as it's known today being played or fought in Palmares, the quilombo soldiers were adept in the use of all weapons, from guns, to swords, bow and arrow, and lance. Zumbi trained them.

The palmarinos were "tillers of land," who planted "every kind of vegetable." In the overgrown forests of Alagoas, this had to mean caapueras on a wide scale. It took twenty to thirty years before extinct land could be reused. The generations who lived in Palmares were tilling the land for nearly a hundred years. Tupi Amerindians, who used the term caapuera, were among them throughout the whole 17th century. The wattle-and-daub fortifications surrounding Palmares main settlements were also known as capoeiras.

It is also the case that Luanda was a main embarkation port for slaves who were shipped to Pernambuco throughout the 17th century. As many of these slaves were prisoners of war, with the specialist military training of the Mbundu, Imbangala, and Kongolese forces described by Cavazzi and others in Angola, we can reliably say that the art of sanguar, the speed and agility, the jumping and twisting of the central African warrior were used by these same people once they escaped Pernambuco's sugar plantations and took up residence in the macambos of Palmares.

Was the Tupi word then endowed with significance beyond its original meaning? Was the function of the quilombo as an institution of resistance to slavery absorbed into the meaning of the word so that capoeira came to signify the Central African way of fighting or resistance to slavery itself? Did the word travel with the captured prisoners of Palmares to the captaincies of Rio de Janeiro and elsewhere, or remain in the language of the scores of seven- to twelve-year-old children who were resold as slaves in Bahia and Pernambuco? We shall sadly probably never know the answers to these questions.

What we do know is that all the governors of Pernambuco and the military commanders of the Dutch and Portuguese armies who tried to destroy Palmares have been long forgotten, while Zumbi dos Palmares has lived on in Brazil until now, more than three centuries later, his memory is honored and respected all over the world.

Chapter Four
THE GOLD RUSH

Sugar was by now very big business indeed. It had completely over-taken honey as a sweetener, particularly since the discovery of its preservative properties in jam, marmalade, and chutney. When the Dutch left Brazil, they took their investment capital with them. In the Caribbean they joined the British, French, and Spanish in plant-ing sugar large-scale. Jamaica, Barbados, Suriname, and Saint Domingue had better access to capital and merchant fleets than Brazil and they enjoyed a smoother commercial passage to the markets of northern Europe.

Due to the Dutch retreat from Brazil to the Caribbean and because of falling sugar prices in Northern Europe, the Northeast's sugar industry was stagnating. The provinces were always reliant on one or two export commodities, leaving them vulnerable to world market competition and price fluctuations. Many slaves were sold from Bahia to Rio de Janeiro.

The sugar crisis was the downside of economic boom and bust that characterized Brazil throughout the colonial era. Now half of northern Europe was fighting for a piece of the action. Portuguese merchants and colonial producers no longer set the prices, which subsequently dropped dramatically. The decades of Brazil's sugar boom and monopoly were over, but a new commodity was soon to be dug out of Brazilian soil by African hands in such huge quantity that it is sometimes claimed to have financed the Industrial Revolution.

The discovery of gold in Brazil has been credited to Manuel Borba Gato in Minas Gerais in 1695. The Brazilian gold rush happened a century and a half before California's. It not only financed industrial development in England but had a huge impact on the slaving frontiers of the Ovimbundo-controlled southern highlands of early 18th-century Angola.

For fifty years it was a bonanza of opportunity for all kinds of people. Baroque churches laden with gold leaf were built all over Minas Gerais. Casks overflowing with gold and diamonds were hauled overland to the port at Rio de Janeiro. The precious minerals were exchanged for European import goods and slaves from Angola. Brazilian gold was shipped to Lisbon and from there it made an immediate departure to England in exchange for manufactured textiles in loads by the ton.

Slavers, merchants, prospectors, architects, financiers, and textile mill owners all hit paydirt. But the slaves in Brazil, the gold miners themselves, and the English working class in the textile mills were not invited to the profit party. Mining work was said to be even worse than plantation labor. The gold boom also coincided with a further deterioration of physical conditions on the middle passage as customarily overloaded slave ships made the voyage from Luanda and Benguela to Rio de Janeiro.

The first gold may have been discovered and kept secret by bandeirantes before 1695. They realized their discovery would attract a gold rush; indeed, Minas Gerais did act as a magnet for vast numbers of treasure hunters from all corners of the globe. The first sightings were between the Serra de Mantiqueira and the headwaters of the Rio São Francisco. The rumors spread of other places in Minas Gerais, particularly the Serra do Espinhaço, where every small stream, river, and brook was said to glitter with gold.

Within a decade of those first discoveries, the Vale São Francisco had "become a lawless region filled with the dregs of the Portuguese world."[1] The historian Charles Boxer described life in the mining towns as "nasty, brutish and short." There were not enough provisions to support the growing population of European immigrants and the even greater numbers of slaves from Angola and the Mina Coast. It wasn't until the 1720s that hogs and poultry arrived to adequately supply Minas Gerais with protein. Corn and wheat flour were very rare and expensive. A flask of salt sold for half a pound of gold and the manioc was often spoiled.

Cholera, typhoid, dysentery, malaria, and pulmonary infections threatened the inhabitants of the mining districts. Wading in water for long hours at a time made for arduous and very unhealthy work. Slave mortality in the mines ran at 50 percent of the workforce within the first ten years. The mining year was also disturbed by seasonal changes and slaves were less productive at some times than others. They became redundant when particular mines petered out or slave owners couldn't afford to hold them any longer. "Self ownership" (manumission) created larger numbers of free blacks, who made up 34 percent of all the people in Minas Gerais by the end of the mining boom.

Gold Mining

Placer mining or "panning" occurred when the gold was a riverbed deposit. The work was done by chain gangs (*lavras*). This was open-pit mining where the earth was dug with a pick and shovel to locate underground gold deposits near the surface, then the rock was smashed and the gold extracted using a sluice box.

The panner, *faiscador,* might sometimes work unsupervised. The exchange of the fazenda fouce (a short scythe) for the mine's pan, pick, and shovel sometimes increased opportunities for escape to the many quilombos that grew on the periphery of the mining communities. For those tens of thousands who didn't escape, weekly quotas of gold had to be delivered to the mine owners very strictly.

Mine owners feared that slaves stole gold from the mines. This fear traveled upward to the Portuguese authority and crown, who suspected the mine owners just as strongly. The crown bought the gold at fixed prices, and taxed the movement of slaves as well as the import of the basic mining equipment and tools. The mining boom drove the price of slaves to the highest ever. Buyers made endless distinctions among different nations. Captives from Guinca were considered stronger than those taken in Angola. Slaves imported from Whydah (on the Slave Coast) were believed to have a magic propensity for discovering new gold deposits.[2]

The gold rush doubled the price of slaves coming into Brazil through the port of Rio de Janeiro, which had overtaken Salvador to supply the mines at Minas Gerais. A slave in Bahia was saleable at 200 reis, while in Minas Gerais the price was 400 reis.

The currency called *real* (meaning royal) was originally printed in 1654 by the Dutch in northeast Brazil. The real (plural réis) became official currency in 1690 and remained the official Portuguese currency of account in the 18th century.

It was counted in "thousand réis" (*milréis*). The milréis is a now obsolete Portuguese unit of currency that was widely used in Brazil.

The $ symbol was used to depict the number of thousands, so that 1,000 réis is written 1$000 or 1 milréis. It is difficult to convert this into US dollars, as the equivalence of values varied so widely from place to place and period to period. In 1775, in North Carolina, for example, seventeen different forms of money were being used as legal tender, though their common accounting basis was still the British pound. Benjamin Franklin had tried to persuade the British parliament of an urgent need to issue colonial paper money in 1766, but to no avail. In fact, the conflict over the right to issue paper money was a pivotal factor in the American Revolution.

The *dollar* is older than the American unit of currency. It was originally an Anglicized version of the word *thaler* (pronounced with a long "a" and no "h" sound). "Taler" had come from coins minted in 1519 from a silver mine in Joachimsthal in Bohemia.

The English version ("dollar") was given to coins similar in weight, such as the Spanish peso and the Portuguese eight-real piece. When old pirates talked of "pieces of eight," they were referring to this coin. Those coins, particularly the Spanish peso or dollar, were well known in Britain's North American colonies, especially due to a chronic lack of official British coins. After the United States gained independence, the name "dollar" was retained in preference to the pound.[3]

In terms of prices, one can see that during the Brazilian gold rush, the price of slaves was double in Minas Gerais to that in Bahia. Hugh Thomas converts an 1811 figure of 150 milréis (or 150$000) to £45 and an 1848 figure of 400 milréis (or 400$000) also to £45–50. Other relative values given by Thomas are for 1657: The cost of one slave was 22,000 "reals" in Brazil, and cites Spaniards offering Dutch 200 "reals (pieces of eight) per slave."[4]

At the height of the mining boom, the government officials in

Bahia were afraid that Brazil (meaning them) was going to be ruined by the rising price of slaves. In 1742, the Bahian viceroy complained to Pernambuco's governor about the slave trade: "Unless we find a good means of reorganizing it, I am afraid it may finish altogether. The consequence would be the ruin of Brazil, which cannot subsist without the service of slaves. . . . The mining people here who come and look for blacks which they need ruin themselves by paying prices both exorbitant and intolerable."

In the1730s, approximately 160,000 Africans were imported into Brazil; 100,000 embarked on slave ships in Luanda or Benguela, while 60,000 came from the Mina Coast of Ghana and Benin. It wasn't a magical gift for discovering gold deposits that made Mina Coast slaves more adept at the mines, but rather that mine owners knew nothing about gold mining, while many slaves hailed from regions of Africa with centuries of tradition. Some Mina slaves were experts in gold mining, refining, gold working, and debasing, and they were prominent as goldsmiths and blacksmiths.

The economics of the trade meant that mine owners still preferred to replace slaves after a short working life. There was no medical care and life expectancy for a miner was still less than a decade after beginning at the mines. The Portuguese crown and English mercantile business community were in reality offshore pimps of the African women slaving in Minas Gerais. Slave women were put to work as faiscadoras, with the same weekly quota of gold to be delivered as the men. They were not issued pans or picks, and it was understood that prostitution was their only means to produce the quota.

Britain, the recipient of much of the Brazilian gold, by now outstripped all the other trading nations as a carrier of slaves, both on its own account in the West Indies and as transporters for the others.

After gold was discovered in Minas Gerais in 1695, the Vale São Fransisco became "a lawless region filled with the dregs of the Portuguese world." Hundreds of thousands of people were shipped from the Mina Coast of Ghana and Benin to work in the gold mines, while there was also an increase in people being transported from Luanda and Benguela to Rio de Janeiro.

Brazilian demand for slaves adversely affected development in early 18th-century Ghana and Benin.

In the 17th century, the Portuguese and Dutch actually discouraged slave trade on the "Gold Coast" for they recognized that it would be incompatible with gold trade. However, by the end of that century, gold had been discovered in Brazil, and the importance of gold supplies from Africa was lessened. Within the total Atlantic pattern,

African slaves became more important than gold, and Brazilian gold was offered for African captives at Whydah (Dahomey) and Accra. At that point, slaving began to undermine the "Gold Coast" economy and destroying the gold trade. Slave-raiding and kidnapping made it unsafe to mine and travel with gold; and raiding for captives proved more profitable than gold-mining. One European on the scene noted . . . [they] . . . "exert themselves rather in war, robbery and plunder than their old business of digging and collecting gold."[5]

In Brazil it was different. Commerce expanded during the gold boom in the fields of ranching, manufacture, and north-south trade. This created boomtowns like Ouro Prêto, Mariana, and Sabara. The city of Rio de Janeiro was also a winner from the far greater sea traffic using its port.

The mine owners of Minas Gerais didn't have the close relationships with shippers enjoyed by the senhors de engenho of Bahia and Pernambuco. The high prices realized for slaves in Minas Gerais meant that Northeasterners tried to bolster their economies by gaining cheaper slaves on the Mina Coast (the Gold Coast) than they were getting from Luanda. They sold some of these slaves in the Rio de Janeiro market (for gold); they kept others for work in the sugar fields. This opened up the new trade route between Salvador and Rio de Janeiro. Rio was the nearest port to the mines and prior to the gold rush it had been without merchant wealth or an African network. Now it took over from Salvador as the center of the Brazilian slave trade and that sector of the shipping industry began to flourish.

There was a specialized fleet of fast slave ships in Rio de Janeiro with captains only concerned to transport slaves owned by merchants in Angola. A horizontal trade between Brazil and Africa eclipsed the triangular trade that had included Lisbon. It also cut

Bahia and Pernambuco planters out of the picture, adding much to their grief at the time.

By the first half of the 18th century, Brazil was the world's leading supplier of precious metals, producing 16.5 tons of gold a year. Minas Gerais alone covered an area the size of France. Eventually, 1,000 tons of Minas Gerais and Mato Grosso gold went to Lisbon via Rio de Janeiro. Lisbon merchants purchased slaves in Luanda with Asian and European (British) textiles and other goods they'd been able to purchase with Brazilian gold.

Tight Packing and the Middle Passage

As the Brazilians didn't own the slaves aboard their ships, they made efforts to pack as many as possible between decks. There were legal carrying capacities given to slave ships, called *arqueaçóes*, but the Brazilian shippers earned money by transporting maximum numbers over the Atlantic. They stowed away many extra slaves for private deals in Brazil. If those slaves died onboard, they could shift the losses to consignments of slaves owned by Luso-Africans or Portuguese merchants who wouldn't know any different.

From one report: "Our schooner was loaded beyond capacity and the deck had to be fitted with temporary platforms or shelves, as high as the taffrail, above which stiff netting was drawn to prevent the shackled slaves from leaping overboard. In walking the deck we frequently trod on a hand or foot sticking out from the lower tier."[6]

But Lisbon merchants hadn't that much to lose from deaths onboard ship, as their concern was selling the highest amount of trade goods for bills of exchange payable with slaves. Colonial revenues depended partly on slave export duties. These increased the more slaves were exported. As they were paid before embarkation, they were not affected by how many captives reached Brazil alive. The captains of the ships had little financial stake in reducing mortality, unless epidemics onboard threatened to wipe out the crew as well as the slaves—which happened not infrequently. The bonus to captains of 1–2 percent of sale price for every slave delivered alive was overcome by the greater profits derived from smuggling slaves to trade privately. It was only when Lisbon merchants began to settle in Rio at the end of the 18th century and actually owned those onboard ship that it began to matter to them how many reached Brazil alive. The results were described many times:

> The living, the dying, and the dead, huddled together in one mass. Some unfortunates in the most disgusting state of smallpox, distressingly ill with opthalmia, a few perfectly blind, others living skeletons, with difficulty crawled from below, unable to bear the weight of their miserable bodies. Mothers with young infants hanging at their breasts, unable to give a drop of nourishment. How they had brought them thus far appeared astonishing: all were perfectly naked. Their limbs were excoriated from lying on the hard plank for so long a period. On going below, the stench was insupportable. How beings could breathe such an atmosphere, and live, appeared incredible. Several were under the soughing, which was called the deck, dying—one dead.[7]

Often ships carried too little food and water to adequately feed the captives. Space that barrels of water and trunks of food should have taken up was filled by more slaves, creating a critical situation onboard. The heat below decks was intense by day, or on some journeys, particularly the long voyage round the Cape of Good Hope from Mozambique, very cold at night. Dehydration and pneumonia were constant enemies.

The effect of lying in one spot for weeks and months, unable to move, was also described by a ship's doctor:

> One would naturally suppose that an attention to their own interest would prompt the owners of the Guinea ships not to permit their captains to take on board greater numbers of negroes than the ship would allow room sufficient for them to lie with ease to themselves or, at least, without rubbing against each other . . . [However] . . . The place allotted for the sick negroes is under the half deck, where they lie on bare planks. By this means those who are emaciated frequently have their skin and even their flesh entirely rubbed off, by the motion of the ship, from the prominent parts of the shoulders, elbows and hips so as to render the bones quite bare. And some of them, by constantly lying in the blood and mucus that had flowed from those afflicted with the flux and which is generally so violent as to prevent their being kept clean, have their flesh much sooner rubbed off than those who have only to contend with the mere friction of the ship. . . . The loss of slaves, through mortality . . . is frequently very considerable. One half, sometimes two thirds and even beyond that have been known to perish.[8]

The journey from Angola to Rio de Janeiro took an average of fifty days. To Bahia and Pernambuco it took approximately thirty-five to forty days. Each ship was required to carry a legal minimum of water according to the number of slaves onboard. But the carriers were always trying to pack on 10–20 percent extra slaves, and if that extra group of people (which could mean another forty to 100 onboard) were then delayed by another week or two on the journey, it could reduce the amount of drinking water by as much as a third. A 1684 law only allowed for just under a liter and a half of water per person per day. If the ship was delayed, as they commonly were, disaster was inevitable.

A logbook from one ship recorded: "A group of . . . [slaves] . . . lay stretched, many in the last stages of exhaustion . . . several of these, I noticed, had crawled to the spot where the water had been served out, in the hope of procuring a mouthful of the precious liquid; but unable to return to their proper places, lay prostrate around the empty tub."[9]

Fresh water was virtually unknown in Luanda and was never available in Benguela. When the ships purchased it, the water was filled with dirt and, if it lasted the two-month journey, it remained warm in the heat below deck, maximizing bacteria.

The captains knew the danger of taking on too many slaves for the journey. They hoped to collect fresh rainwater en route, but the amount of rainwater they could expect was highly variable. The crew also had to drink the same supplies of filthy liquid from the old geribita casks, so dysentery was rife on the ships. Whether the water would last the journey was a life-and-death gamble that Rio's ten regular slave ships played over and over again.

> Among the slavers sailing out of old Calabar [Nigeria to Brazil], at that time, was the Brazilian brig Gloria. . . . Once off the coast the ship became half bedlam and half brothel. Ruiz, our captain, and his two mates set an example of reckless wickedness. . . . Meanwhile our slaves crammed in hold, cabin and peak and packed like herrings on shelves around our vessel's sides, were kept down by gratings fully half the time. The shrieks and groans of the stifling wretches below echoed our orgies above. . . . Hardly were we out a fortnight when it was discovered that our roystering crew had neglected to change the sea-water in the lower casks, which had served as ballast and which ought to have been replaced with fresh water in Africa. . . . the horror of the situation sobered Captain Ruiz . . . it was decided, in order to save our cargo, that we should allow the slaves a half-gill and the crew

a gill each day. Then began a torture worse than death for the blacks. They suffered continual torment. Instead of lowering buckets of water to them, as was customary, it became necessary to pour the water in half-pint measures. Those farthest from the gratings never got a drop and soon became raving mad for drink. Fevers and fluxs soon added to their misery and deaths followed so fast that in a short time at least a hundred slaves were shackled to dead partners. . . . Captain Ruiz ordered the hatches down and swore to make the run on our regular rations and take the chances with his stock. That night we caroused and satisfied our thirst, while the negroes suffocated below. . . . I began to notice a strange, fetid smell pervading the vessel and a low, heavy fog on deck, almost like steam, and then the horrid truth became apparent. Our rotting Negroes under hatches had generated the plague and it was this death-mist that I saw rising.[10]

Laws set in 1684 gave instructions for the amount of manioc, salt beef, limes, and so on that should be stored, but Brazilian slavers from Rio bribed officials in Angola to use the room for more slaves instead. Malnutrition verging on starvation was commonplace; hence the need for "refreshing" slaves before their final sale. The Portuguese had a word (*banzo*) to describe the state of depression they saw among the starving, who'd most often been sick and hungry even before beginning the voyage.

At the height of the gold rush, Rio shippers became confident enough to try to collect Mina Coast slaves themselves, to beat off the Bahian monopoly there. When that failed, they sailed all the way round to Mozambique to collect the Asian textiles they'd need to buy slaves in Luanda. The Portuguese had begun slave trading in Mozambique when their access to Mina, Congo, and Angola was blocked during the Dutch occupation. Mozambique remained important to the Brazilian traders. The following passage describes one of these Mozambique-Brazil journeys (which had the worst survival rates for those onboard):

> Suddenly the weather closes in, and the seas rise so high and so strongly that the ships must obey the waves, sailing at the mercy of the winds without true course or control. It is then that the din from the slaves, bound to one another, becomes horrible. The clanking of the irons, the moans, the weeping, the cries, the waves breaking over one side of the ship and then the other, the shouting of the sailors, the whistling of the winds, and the continuous roar of the waves. The tempo of the storm increases, and with it the danger. A portion of food provisions is heaved overboard, and also other objects to save the cargo and the crew. Many slaves break legs and arms, others die of suffocation. One ship or another will break apart from the fury of the storm, and sink. Another drifts on, dismasted, its rigging ruined by the will of the ocean, unable to heed the helm, on the verge of capsizing.[11]

On Brazilian slave ships, a high proportion of crew were free blacks or slaves who were rented out as crew by their European masters. The Portuguese had always crewed their Atlantic trade ships with African sailors—for instance, when transporting slaves between Guinea and São Tomé. When the crew was mostly African, the captains avoided combat with other ships, for fear of arming Africans and risking an onboard rebellion. Often captains used one group of Africans to subdue the majority and act as spies. "We have some 30 or 40 Gold Coast negroes, which we buy, and are procur'd us there by our factors, to make guardians and over-seers of the Whidaw negroes. . . . when we constitute a guardian, we give him a cat of nine tails as a badge of his office, which he is not a little proud of, and will exercise with great authority."[12]

The Europeans onboard were conscious of their own weakness

in numbers and the possibility of armed rebellion. "It is nearly time, too, that the negroes were disposed of, for it does not require a very bright pair of eyes to see that they have not quite so much fear of the white man as they had when first brought on board. The kroomen [slave overseers], also, have become bolder and sometimes an order given to them has to be accompanied with a crack of the whip, so little inclination do they show to move."[13]

By the end of the 18th century, half of the ships had some slaves among the crew. These might become free blacks and rise to the level of able seaman, but they never became officers. Crews pledged oaths of allegiance to captains, as in war, because the chances of survival weren't much better than they would have been in war. Crews often jumped ship to escape voyages they'd been tricked or pressed into. The captains, who had access to the best provisions, died at the rate of one every ten voyages, according to the Dutch West India Company. Most captains attempted only three or four journeys to Africa and hoped to accumulate enough wealth to become investors or ship owners without having to be present during the hazardous journey.

Slave ship crews were notoriously badly treated and they died at a proportionally higher rate than the slaves as they spent longer onboard. Free men were tricked onboard while they were drunk and debtors were sometimes given the choice of imprisonment or an Atlantic voyage. They were kept disciplined using the ubiquitous lash and they slept on deck. "They lie on deck and they die on deck."[14] Once the ship was out of sight of the African mainland, on Portuguese and indeed most slave ships, the crew took groups of slaves out of shackles and on deck to eat or get air. At least this was the ideal (although it was often impossible due to tight packing). They'd be given tobacco and alcohol and were told to dance and sing. "We had tambourines aboard, which some of the younger darkies fought for regularly, and every evening we enjoyed the novelty of African war songs and ring dances, fore and aft, with the satisfaction of knowing that these pleasant exercises were keeping our stock in good condition and of course enhancing our prospects of making a profitable voyage."[15]

Relations between the crew and captives were always underpinned by violence. For many who arrived at the coast from the interior, the ports and slave ships were not only their first sight of the ocean, but also of white men. A firsthand account from one man, Eloudah Equiano in the 1760s, expressed feelings that were common:

> The first object which saluted my eyes . . . was the sea, and a slave ship, which was then riding at anchor. . . . These filled me with astonishment, which was then converted into terror, when I was carried on board. I was immediately handled and tossed up, to see if I were sound, by some of the crew, and I was now persuaded that I had got into a world of bad spirits and that they were going to kill me. Their complexions too, differing so much from ours, their long hair and the language they spoke . . . united to confirm me in this belief. Indeed, such were the horrors of my views and fears at that moment that, if ten thousand worlds had been my own, I would have freely parted with them all to have exchanged my condition with that of the meanest slave in my own country. . . . When I looked round the ship . . . and saw a large . . . copper boiling . . . I no longer doubted my fate. . . . I fell motionless on the deck and fainted. When I recovered I found some black people about me who, I believed, were some of those who had brought me on board. . . . I asked them if we were not to be eaten by those white men, with horrible looks, red faces and loose hair. They told me I was not, and one of the crew brought me a small portion of spiritous liquor in a wine glass . . . which . . . threw me

into the greatest consternation, at the strange feeling it produced, having never tasted any such liquor before.[16]

Some believed white men's cheese was made from black people's brains, red wine from their blood, and olive oil pressed from their bodies. Mwene Puto, the Portuguese, were said to emerge from beneath the horizon, appearing to rise from the sea, living aboard ships with no women, and they were sometimes mistaken for evil spirits. Equiano continued:

> The stench of the hold while we were on the coast was so intolerably loathsome that it was dangerous to remain there for any time, and some of us had been permitted to stay on deck for the fresh air; but now that the whole ship's cargo were confined together, it became absolutely pestilential. The closeness of the place, and the heat of the climate, added to the number in the ship, which was so crowded that each had hardly room to turn himself, almost suffocated us. This produced constant perspirations, so that the air soon became unfit for respiration . . . and brought on a sickness among the slaves, of which many died, thus falling victims to the improvident avarice, as I may call it, of their purchasers. This wretched situation was again aggravated by the galling of the chains, now become insupportable; and the filth of the tubs, into which children often fell, and were almost suffocated. The shrieks of the women, and the groans of the dying, rendered a scene of horror almost inconceivable.[17]

There were also children on slave ships although records are distorted by the trick of registering adults as children (*moleques*). This false registration was done because captains were allowed to carry five children per ton of the ship's weight, as opposed to two-and-a-half adults.

Uprisings were recorded at a rate of at least one every eight voyages. The rebellions onboard slave ships were mostly before setting sail or during the earliest stages of the voyage, while the ships were still within sight of Africa's coast. There were some successful slave rebellions, although the vast majority ended in severe punishment for the rebels. If they took place in open sea, the rebels were drowned. For this reason male slaves were usually kept chained beneath the deck until the ship was out of sight of land.

Sickness among crew members was an opportunity for many escape attempts. For instance, a ship's captain reported in 1765:

> Soon after he left the coast, the number of his men being reduced by sickness, he was obliged to let some of the slaves come upon deck to assist the people: these slaves contrived to release the others, and the whole rose upon the people and endeavoured to get possession of the vessel; but was . . . prevented by the captain, who killed, wounded, and forced overboard eighty of them which obliged the rest to submit.[18]

Many Africans threw themselves overboard deliberately, believing their spirit would return to the land of the ancestors. In eyewitness accounts, slavers were commonly preoccupied with making it difficult for captives to commit suicide, which to many slaves was a better fate than being carried away to Mwene Puto, a land of bad spirits. The slavers sometimes resorted to beheading the leaders of uprisings. "For many of the blacks believe that, if they are put to death and not dismembered, they shall return again to their own country after they are thrown overboard."[19]

Ships during the early 18th-century gold rush were often named after saints or the Virgin Mary—Nossa Senhora, San Antônio, and so on. The port at Rio de Janeiro was alerted to their arrival by a rotting smell that filled the whole town. The Brazilian João Dunshee de Abrantes wrote: "Removed from the ship into barges, they came in neck chains, or libambos, leashed to one another to stop them running away or throwing themselves into the water. Often, they had already been divided into lots before leaving the ship. And they were delivered in bunches to the merchants or the bush captains. . . . The traffickers did everything they could to land those horrible cargoes at once."[20]

From initial embarkation to the point of final sale was always a rush by the sellers to get the "cargo" or "pieces" off their hands as quickly as possible, as every delay increased the death toll. The aim was to shunt mortality losses onto somebody else further along the line. Merchants and captains had many strategies for making mortally sick or old people look healthy just long enough to make a sale. Port authorities and customs houses knew all the tricks, and they knew how important it was for captains to unload cargoes of slaves quickly. Corrupt officials could extract kickbacks by interrupting the slave ship unloading its cargo or perhaps falsifying an epidemic, so the ship remained in quarantine until the officials had gained the inflated bribes they required. Other than these orchestrated delays, once the ship had arrived in port, the actual sale of slaves was usually carried out speedily and efficiently.

Chapter Five
FROM RIO TO THE GOLD MINES

One of the first indignities suffered was branding. Arriving in Brazil from Luanda, captives had already been branded twice, first with the design of the merchant who owned them, and then with the Royal Arms on their right breast to show they were under the dominion of the Portuguese crown. Amerindian slaves captured in Brazil were also branded as an identifying punishment for escape attempts: "Those who bought them used to brand them on the face at their first (attempted) flight or fault: they claimed that they cost money and were their slaves. The preachers used to pound their pulpit about this but they might as well have been preaching in the desert."[1]

Brandings were performed with a red-hot iron. The third one, in Brazil, often was done with a silver iron to show that the captives were legally imported. Yet other brands were inflicted when the slaves were sold to new owners in Brazil. The Portuguese had introduced laws that made it illegal to import any slave to Portuguese territory who had not been baptized. This made a mockery of Pope Pius II's edict that no baptized Christian could be enslaved, when this system ensured it was only the baptized who were enslaved. The Jesuits shared some the intellectual sophistry of their countrymen, because in their opposition to the enslavement and branding of Amerindians they remained blind to the evil of enslaving Africans.

Baptism itself was a beaurocratic piece of trickery taking place in one of the small churches in Luanda, Cabinda, or Benguela. A slave catechist would inform captives of their Christian transformation in Kimbundu and a priest would give each of the slaves a "Christian" name while sprinkling salt and holy water on their tongues.

A Kimbundu-speaking interpreter would then translate the priest's final words and the ritual *batizado* would be complete. The priest solemnly told the captives en route to the waiting ships: "Consider that you are now children of Christ. You are going to set off for Portuguese territory, where you will learn matters of the faith. Never think anymore of your place of origin. Do not eat dogs, nor rats, nor horses. Be content."[2]

In Rio de Janeiro, as the 18th century progressed, slave dealers lived in huge houses that lined the Rua Vallongo (today Rua Camerino) to the beach. The family of the merchants lived on the balconied upper stories. The lower stories contained storehouses for goods, barrels, bales, crates, and slaves. These were built like the houses in Luanda, where storage areas opened onto the street. In Angola, Kimbundu and Kikongo pombeiros could deal directly with the merchant's bilingual wives and younger family members.

In Rio too, each townhouse had two or three stories, where upstairs the Luso-Brazilian merchants lived their lives, barely separated from the ware rooms in which hundreds of slaves were displayed for sale like any other form of livestock. The Luso-Brazilian slave dealers and their Luso-African counterparts in Luanda shared similar aspirations. Fernão Cardim, a Jesuit, said of the Brazilians:

> In their abundance they seem like counts and spend lavishly. . . . Some of them are heavily in debt, because of the great losses they have had with slaves from Guinea, many of whom die on them, and because of the excesses and heavy expenditure they incur in their style of life. They and their wives and children dress in all sorts of velvets, and other silks, and show great excess in this. The women behave as great ladies but are not very devout and do not frequent mass, sermons, confession, etc. . . . They are very addicted to parties. If a girl of good family marries an (eligible) man the friends and relatives come dressed in crimson velvet, others in green, and others damasks and other silks of various colours, and the pennants and saddlecloths of their horses are the same silks that they are wearing. . . . They each entertain in turn, and spend all they have. Every year they commonly drink 50,000 cruzados worth of wines from Portugal.[3]

In 1817, the slave trader Captain Drake consigned 850 slaves to a Mr. Floss, and was entertained on the latter's estate in Rio de Janeiro. He wrote that Floss "lived in grand style and gave concerts and balls to the neighboring gentry. That evening there was a sumptuous entertainment, the Dons and Donnas wearing their richest clothing. The men shone in all colors and the ladies' taffeta petticoats were fringed with gold lace and their tight velvet jackets were laced and buttoned with pearl tassels."[4]

A comparable account of life in Luanda:

> The wealthy Luso-African minority in Luanda affected an aristocratic style of living, putting a highly visible portion of their profits into luxury imports—fine silks, velvets, and other costly textiles, as well as silver furnishings for their houses, for the churches of the town, and for ornate decorations on their tombstones. . . . Aside from frenetically

conspicuous consumption, the Luso-Africans also invested in colonial real estate. Large multistoried townhouses known as sobrados became virtual symbols of local aristocratic pretensions at Luanda. Some . . . lived with their families on the second stories of the sobrados in the upper part of the city, where large balconied windows opened on the sea and brought a measure of comfort and, it was fondly but vainly assumed, also of health from onshore daytime breezes.[5]

After the middle passage, the aim in Rio was to "refresh" the slaves for sale. After the near starvation of the voyage, Africans were fed with *pirão* and *angu de fubá* to try to fatten them up to look healthy at the point of sale. There were also (before the 18th century) many thousands of Amerindian slaves being sold in Rio de Janeiro. Said Don Pedro Estevan Dávila: "Before my very eyes they were selling Indians brought to [Rio de Janeiro] by the citizens of São Paulo, as if they were slaves and considered as such by Your Majesty."

Up until the mid-17th century there were still many Amerindian slaves on sugar plantations. African and Amerindian people had their first experience of each other in the slave markets of Rio de Janeiro and Salvador. It was then still less than a century since a fleet of settlers had landed at the foot of the Sugar Loaf Mountain and subdued the Tamoio Indians around Botafogo and Guanabara Bays. "Everyone worked at felling trees and carrying logs. They fortified the camp with trenches, stockades, artillery redoubts and even tile roofs on their huts as protection against fire arrows."[6]

By the 18th century, it was mainly people born in Central Africa being sold in Rio. In the slave markets there, buyers felt limbs and made the captives show their teeth and tongues. They examined their eyes and genitals. They had to move around and jump up and down to prove their health and strength. Sometimes the slaves were auctioned in the showrooms of the townhouses; other times they'd be hawked around in their chains and sold in the city from door to door.

Scurvy, dysentery, buboes, and scabies all caused deaths in the overcrowded warehouses in Rio.[7] The bubonic plague that hit Europe in the late 17th century spread to Rio's port on ships leaving European cities. There were so many deaths from the diseases, heat, and chronic overcrowding in Rio's showrooms that colonists constantly feared epidemics in the town and complained of the smell of death that hung in the air, as it also did in Benguela. Slave pens were built in the swamps on the shoreline to distance the sick from the Luso-Brazilians and Europeans, who hated and feared but needed slaves to maintain their luxurious lifestyle.

The same Marquis of Lavradio who retained the bodyguard Amotinado, reputed to be the "first representative of Capoeira in Rio de Janeiro,"[8] wrote that the slaves:

> Had done everything which nature suggested in the middle of the street where they were seated on some boards that had laid there, not only causing the worst kind of stench on those streets, and their vicinity, but even providing the most terrible spectacle that the human eye can witness. Decent people did not dare go to the windows, [and] the inexperienced learned there what they had not known.[9]

After surviving the march to the barracoons of Africa's coast, the middle passage, and then sale in Rio de Janeiro, those who'd miraculously survived up to this point still had the arduous journey to the gold mines of Brazil's interior ahead of them. The mines were spread over a wide region: Minas Gerais, Mato Grosso, and Goiás. There was no easy route to Brazil's interior and great physical distances were traveled. The coastal plains, sertão, and central highland possessed daunting natural barriers, including torrential rivers, mountain ranges, and densely wooded valleys or arid areas devoid of food. Caravans traveling to the mines faced extreme hardship because of hostile Amerindians, natural fauna, cold, heat, drought and rain, malarial mosquitoes, wild animals, jaguars, poisonous insects, and venomous snakes.

There were three main routes from Rio de Janeiro to Minas Gerais. The journey from the coast at Santos or Rio de Janeiro took four to six weeks. At the end of the 17th century, the governor of Rio de Janeiro commissioned the opening of a direct route to the general mines, as those existing were too difficult. The resulting *caminho novo* was still beset with outcrops and perilous ravines, as well as almost impenetrable undergrowth and mountains. Work progressed on a road between Rio and São Paulo in the early 18th century.

The annual groups of gold prospectors who flocked to the gold fields were dubbed *monções* ("monsoons"). Around the same time work started on the Rio-to-São Paulo road (1725), a monsoon of twenty canoes, with 200 people, set off on the dangerous journey to the Paraguay River. A war party of Paiaguá Amerindians attacked the canoes and killed every member of the convoy save for one Portuguese and one African. Such attacks were frequent and one of the worst risks of the journey between the coast and the mines.

Minas Gerais could be reached from both Bahia and São Paulo, while Mato Grosso was more accessible from Rio de Janeiro and São Paulo. Voyages by river from São Paulo to Cuiabá took six or seven months on the outbound journey. Canoes laden with tools, food, slaves, and colonists shot more than a hundred rapids. The larger monsoons consisted of thousands of people carried in hundreds of canoes.

In the early 18th century, the Paiaguá Amerindians were the greatest obstacle for the bandeirantes and gold miners passing through their territory in search of slaves and minerals. The bandeirante Anhangüera had for years fanatically searched Goiás for the Cuiabá gold. He eventually found it by capturing Goiás women and holding them hostage until the men showed him where the ornamental gold came from.

The mining camps that were set up at Vila Boa brought nothing but death, slavery, and destruction to the region's Amerindians. The towns that sprung up where mining was at its peak were anarchic places where men roamed armed with clubs, knives, swords, and guns. They congregated from all corners of the empire—Portugal, Maderia, the Azores, the coasts of Brazil, and many from São Paulo and Bahia. They were joined by adventurers and treasure hunters from England, Ireland, Holland, and France, as well as soldiers who'd fled from the garrisons of Salvador and Rio. Planters whose fortunes had been affected by the rising costs of African slaves on sugar plantations also headed for the prospecting areas. Black free men as well as African and Amerindian slaves were transported to the mines by the thousand. They either worked digging or acted as scouts and paddlers on the canoes.

Costa da Mina slaves (from the Mina Coast) were numerous. The Portuguese were informed in all aspects of mining and metalwork by African slaves. In 1818, a Swedish mining engineer who worked in central Brazil wrote, "The captaincy of Minas Geráis seems to have been the last in which the use of iron ore and the extraction of iron was learnt from African negro slaves."[10] Akanspeaking Mina slaves from wars in the region that is today Ghana have featured prominently in slave revolts from Hispaniola to Jamaica to New York. The Mina slaves (called Coromantee in

English-speaking colonies) were in fact arriving in Brazil via wars fought in the interior forests of the Gold Coast region.

Interestingly, after the slave trader Captain Drake was entertained in grand style by slave owner Mr. Floss in Rio de Janeiro, Floss's mansion was burned to the ground during a mass uprising of slaves led by "Quobah," an "Ashantee [who] it afterwards turned out, was the head of the conspiracy. He had lately been brought from Africa and sold to Mr. Floss and by his order, flogged several times, to break him in. This had been Floss's usual custom with high-strung darkies."[11] Drake's life was spared in Rio de Janeiro because he had met Quobah before, in Dahomey, when the chief had defeated two lions in a sacrificial fight, armed with a spear, a sword, and a carbine.

In Rio de Janeiro, Drake watched the Ashanti chief beating Mr. Floss to death with a club. Quobah and many of his followers, who were also likely to be Ashanti soldiers, also killed a well-known local racist, a Dr. Maxwell, whose catchphrase was "Niggers must be treated like niggers." Drake related that:

> Quobah struck the Doctor a blow with his club, which dashed his skull open, and this was a signal to the blacks to finish their work. They scattered the burning cane and tore the charred bodies of their victims into a thousand pieces, as they danced and trampled on the embers. . . . Chief Quobah told Drake, "Go and tell the white King how Quobah has avenged himself on these dead brutes. . . . Quobah is ready to die, but he will be a slave no more." . . . Quobah, the Ashantee, was never taken by the Brazilians. He fled to the wild plains, with a few followers, and was either killed or adopted by the Indians.

Drake, an English captain who always had his mind on slave trading, continued: "It was noticed at the time, that both Brazilian and West Indian insurgents adopted flags and were apparently organized and there was little doubt that some plan had been concocted for a general uprising of the slaves. . . . All this enhanced the price of negroes and improved the market and . . . predicted more than average luck for us in the next twelve months."[12]

Drake wrote a description of Quobah as he had been in Yallaba, when they'd both been taken prisoner during the Ashanti war with Dahomey: "The head man of the Ashantee soldiers . . . was a giant in height. He carried a spear and had a powder horn and pouch strapped to his neck. Three slaves bore his arms—one carrying a heavy, curved broadsword, another his club and a third his musket."[13] This description rings true, as Ashanti were mainly heavy infantry soldiers, usually armed with a double-edged sword, lances, and bows. Increasingly in the 19th century they also used muskets. Weapons were specialized according to the class to which the soldier belonged. Nobility and their specially trained, professional elite, who led Akan towns, would have been using the whole array of weapons, including the sword, while the lower-class soldiers carried spears (javelins) and often bow and arrow. Vandevort has also noted that "forest zone soldiers tended to favour clubs and swords."[14] Thornton points out that double-edged swords, throwing javelins, and shields had no non-military uses and so professional Ashanti soldiers such as Quobah would have required "considerable skill and training, especially [in] the throwing of javelins and fighting hand to hand with sword and shield."[15]

It is noteworthy that in the mining districts, slaves armed with swords and clubs were a common sight. The club (in 19th-century Rio, nicknamed *petropolis*) was also a main weapon carried by capoeiristas; recall the bodyguard Amotinado, "extremely strong and skillful in the use of his legs, head, clubs, knives, and swords." Certainly the slave-owning class in Rio de Janeiro, the likes of Mr.

Floss and Dr. Maxwell, who were both clubbed to death by Quobah, seriously misjudged whom they were dealing with when they ordered him repeatedly whipped as a "high-strung darkie." Quobah was an Ashanti commander-in-chief. The Ashanti were one of the most well-disciplined and trained of the African armies, with elite corps (Afunasuafo) and a medical corps (Esumankwafo). Like the Imbangala, they took with them to battle a powerful magic (Ju Ju) that made them invisible to bullets and other weapons. Chief Quobah's skill with his weapons is described in detail by the slaver Drake, who saw him in action in Yallaba, where King Mammee of Dahomey allowed him to choose the manner of his sacrifice.

Before long Quobah was brought out from his hut. He was armed with a long spear, his own huge sword, and with my carbine, the only really serviceable firearm in the town. He alone appeared to be unmoved as he marched to the south gate. Scarcely had he got beyond the heavy stone that secured the log door, before a terrific roar sounded from the fields and an enormous lion came cantering toward the approaching man. The priests and women began to howl and the men pounded their war drums to frighten the lion, but he only lashed his tail the fiercer and crouched for a spring. Quobah sunk on one knee and the next moment the lion leaped and came down on the sharp point of Quobah's spear which the crafty warrior had suddenly raised, the butt resting on the ground. The Ashantee jumped aside and left the brute floundering with the lance through his shoulder.

At this instant another loud roar was heard from the forest and soon a lioness came crashing through the corn followed by two half-grown cubs. Then, indeed, it seemed that all was over with the Ashantee, for the wounded lion had broken the spear to fragments in his struggle and was crouching for another spring, though evidently severely wounded. Quobah lifted the carbine and then as the lion made his second leap, the Ashantee sprang nimbly aside and as the beast fell heavily on its wounded shoulder he ran close to him and fired the carbine into his jaws. When the smoke cleared we could see the lion writhing in his death agony and the lioness snuffing the ground about a dozen feet from Quobah. An instant later she gave a frightful roar and rose with a flying leap, directly for the warrior, who awaited her attack and as she fell, with all his giant strength drove his sword-blade straight into the animal's mouth.[16]

At the height of the gold rush, powerful states such as Denkyira, Akwamu, Axim, and Ashanti were fighting for control of Ghana's interior. The conflicts grew so that in 1730 and 1742, full-on wars were fought, which by 1750 had been won by the Ashanti kingdom. The Ashanti and coastal Fante were also at loggerheads. Many of the slaves working in the gold mines were men captured and sold as prisoners of war in these battles. The conflicts that began in Africa during the gold-mining era in Brazil (1700–1750) spread and intensified during Brazil's coffee boom, the so-called Bight of Benin cycle, a hundred years later.

Again, Captain Drake wrote in his autobiography:

We shaped our course for Badagry, in the Bight of Benin, which at the time (1828–9) was doing a thriving business in slaves as the market was generally well stocked by kaffles arriving through the Kingdom of Dahomey. From the Rio Volta, south to the Niger and north to the Gambia, the intervening country was then engaged in internal slave wars of the fiercest kind. Dahomans, Asahntees, Foulahs, Mandingoes, Sherbross, Fellatahs and Bambarras were preying on each other like wild beasts and kept the slave market constantly supplied.[17]

It is not a surprise that Minas Gerais and the gold-mining regions were the location of quilombos on a scale almost as large as Palmares. The quilombos at Minas in Brazil were said to have a population of 20,000. Additionally, "the entire region of Campo Grande and São Francisco was overrun with fugitive Negroes, who posed a constant problem to the settlers. In 1741, Jean Ferreira had organized an expedition against them, but they managed to escape, regroup and begin to ambush people traveling along the Goyas road in search of gold."(18) If these quilombolas were men previously from armies of Ghana's interior, they were well used to warfare in thick forest with narrow roads. Here combat entailed constant raiding and skirmishing, where "their principle tactic . . . [was] to cut off the enemy's passage: to this end they encamp along the roads and in the bushes by which the enemy must inevitably pass."[19]

The wars that supplied Gold Coast slaves to Brazil involved armies of tens of thousands of troops stretched out in columns covering up to 3 kilometers on the march and which could stretch for as far as 15 kilometers when they advanced in a single column. In 1741, when Ashanti and Akyem went to war, the major battle wasn't fought until they had skirmished for a whole year. A battlefield for a major pitched fight needed to be literally cut out of the surrounding forests, and involved up to 10,000 people felling trees to create a clear battlefield such as that when Akyem's army were defeated by Ashanti in 1742.[20] After defeating an enemy, the victorious army rounded up the local population and enemy troops, who were then despatched to the coast for transportation to Brazil, North America, and the Caribbean.

A very skillful force could withstand Ashanti if they commanded the forest to their advantage. Ntsiful was an early 1700s war leader of Wasa, who was able to move his entire army around the heavy rainforests as a shifting population and to retain control of the military situation by occupying vital positions with a mere 2,000 men. The military advantage in the Gold Coast wars went to the force that occupied key positions and could cut off food supplies to the enemy. A conclusion of the way Ashanti eventually ruled the region is suggested by Thornton: "The nature of the forest of the Gold Coast imposed significant restrictions on the way war could be waged. It banned horses and, for much of the region, also naval forces. Moreover, it created opportunities for certain types of tactics, and particularly for the use of clearings and roads that lay behind Ashanti's ultimate success in the region."[21]

Extracting the Gold

"The most ignorant miner of Minas Gerais was better informed than the best of Goiás, and the most ignorant miner of Goiás was infinitely more skilled than the best of Mato Grosso."[22]

Gold panning involved standing waist-high in cold water under a blazing sun all day long. This led to sun stroke, dysentery, pleurisy, and pneumonia. Malarial mosquitoes were another hazard. Where gold lay in veins, some slaves worked in underground mines where bad ventilation caused pulmonary illnesses or occasional cave-ins made the work extremely dangerous. The prospectors in placer mines (faiscadores) panned rivers and streams using a wooden or metal pan (bateia). Whole riverbed works were known as taboleiros. When the workings were on the banks of rivers or surrounding hillsides they were called grupiaras. The mineshafts dug into hillside were called catas. Eyewitness reflections from the slaves themselves don't exist but the diary of a pan miner in 1849 gives an outline of the work:

Here we are . . . in the gold diggings. Seated around us . . . are a group of wild Indians. . . . We have spent the day in "prospecting." . . . In order to find the gold the ground must be prospected. . . . The stones and loose upper soil . . . almost down to the primitive rock, are removed. Upon or near this rock most of the gold is found and it is the object in every mining operation, to reach this rock, however great the labour. . . . Some of the dirt is then put into a pan, taken to the water and washed out with great care. The miner stoops down by the stream and dipping a quantity of water into the pan with the dirt, stirs it about with his hands, washing and throwing out the large pebbles, till the dirt is thoroughly wet. More water is then taken into the pan, the whole mass well stirred and shaken and the top gravel thrown off with the fingers while the gold, being heavier, sinks deeper into the pan. It is then shaken about, more water being continually added, and thrown off with a sideways motion which carries with it the dirt at the top, while the gold settles yet lower down.

When the dirt is nearly washed out great care is requisite to prevent the lighter scales of gold from being washed out with the sand. At length a ridge of gold scales, mixed with a little sand, remains in the pan, from the quantity of which some estimates may be formed of the richness of the place. If there are five to eight grains it is considered that it will pay. If less, the miner digs deeper or opens a new hole, until he finds a place affording a good prospect. When this is done he sets his cradle by the side of the stream and proceeds to wash all the dirt. Thus have we been employed the whole of this day, digging one hole after another, washing out many test pans, hoping at every new attempt to find that which would reward our toil. . . . For several hours I have been seated by the river side rocking a heavy cradle filled with dirt and stones. . . . The dirt is gradually washed out, the mud being carried of in the stream . . . twenty five buckets of dirt are usually washed through, the residue being drawn off through holes at the bottom of the cradle, and "panned" out or washed in the same manner as in prospecting. . . . More dirt is thrown in the hopper and again the grating, scraping sounds are heard which are peculiar to the rocking of the cradle—which, years hence, will accompany our dreams of the mines. . . .

This life of hardships and exposure has affected my health. Our feet are wet all day, while a hot sun shines down upon our heads and the very air parches the skin like the hot air of an oven. Our drinking water comes down to us thoroughly impregnated with the mineral substances washed through the thousand cradles above us. After our days of labor, exhausted and faint, we retire—if this word may be applied to the simple act of lying down in our clothes. . . . The feet and the hands of a novice in this business become blistered and lame, and the limbs are stiff. Besides all these causes of sickness, the anxieties and cares which wear away the lives of so many men who . . . come to this land of gold, contribute, in no small degree, to the same result.[23]

The chain gangs, lavras, needed special skills to use the pans and sluices effectively. They were overseen by armed foremen to deter escape or theft of the gold. Faiscador slaves weren't under direct control but returned each week with an agreed amount of gold. This was a system later used by the Belgians in the Congo for collecting rubber. The faiscador system led to higher levels of manumission as some slaves bought their own freedom. This naturally led to gold contraband and illegal trafficking. Contraband was also smuggled by mine owners wishing to avoid the "fifth" tax on their gold required by the Portuguese crown. Everyone wanted to maximize their investment. Slaves were sometimes skilled in coin counterfeiting, debasement, and smelting. Knowing this, the Portuguese made sure harsh laws were introduced prohibiting Africans, crioulos, and mulattos from entering the trade of goldsmith. But contraband flowed from the mining areas, and cattle drovers or backwoodsmen with knowledge of hidden trails to the coast were well placed to charge for their services.

Quilombos abounded in the remote regions of the mines. Among the free population, violence and lawlessness were everywhere. Militias were an essential branch of the law during the gold cycle, between 1690 and 1750. During this time capoeira had emerged as a recognized fighting form.

Written references to capoeira date from 1789. Almeida cites a 19th-century description written by Melo de Morais Filho:

> The fighters set themselves in combat position, moving close to each other with eyes shining. The lips murmur phrases that can be threat or disdain. There is an almost imperceptible undulation that comes to life in a snake-like crescendo during the course of the fight; there is a swinging of bodies and arms, but the heads and necks are immobile. The contenders analyze one another. Suddenly like lightning they close in, flank to flank, and one being held is turned upside down, falling behind the back of the other. So there lies the opponent prostrate and inert, cold as a cadaver.[24]

Rio de Janeiro journalist Joaquim Manuel de Macedo tells of a militia lieutenant and bodyguard, a Portuguese by name of Amotinado, who was a ferocious and skilled fighter and famous capoeirista who, according to Almeida, was "a loyal bodyguard of the Vice-Rei Marques de Lavradio." Lavradio was viceroy in the decade from 1760 onward. As well as being a nocturnal Don Juan, he staked a claim to fame as the man who introduced rice to Brazil. (See Appendix C.)

In Luanda and Benguela at this time, the whites felt anxiety that blacks (who outnumbered them greatly) roamed the towns' back streets armed with knives, clubs, and short swords. The same situation prevailed in Brazil's cities. Many references to capoeiristas noted their dexterity with knives and other weapons, including clubs, straight razors, and sharpened throwing coins. In the 18th century, Amotinado was an all-round capoeirista, "extremely strong and skillful in the use of his legs, head, clubs, knives, and swords."[25] The tradition of knife and sword fighting was equally strong in Central and West Africa, as was the custom of training and military activity to the rhythm of music.

The reverend Robert Walsh, C.E., traveled to Brazil in 1828–1829. His account, published in 1830, noted that:

Some of the blacks and mulattos are the most vigorous and athletic looking persons that it is possible to contemplate, and who would be models for a Farnesian Hercules. Their natural muscular frame is hardened and improved by exercise; and when the fibres are swelled out in any laborious action, they exhibit a magnificent picture of strength and activity. Their faka, or long knife, they use with tremendous effect. They sometimes hurl it, as an Indian does his tomahawk, with irresistible force, and drive the blade, at a considerable distance, through a thick deal board. In this respect, they are strongly contrasted with the flabby Brazilians of Portuguese descent, who look the very personification of indolence and inactivity; and should they ever unhappily come into contact with their vigorous opponents in the field, it would seem as if they would be crushed at once, under the mere physical weight of their antagonists.[26]

A ban on weapons was issued in Minas Gerais in 1732 and is typical of the period:

Be it known to all those who receive this proclamation that, because I have been informed and received repeated complaints that the blacks of the district of Serro do Frio are going about fully armed committing murder and many other offenses. . . . I order by this my proclamation that no black or mulatto, either free or captive, may carry a defensive weapon of any sort whatever, not even the staffs which the blacks customarily carry under, under penalty of two hundred lashes which will be given to them in the most public place in the [mining] camp or town.[27]

This was reinforced to include the whole of Brazil in 1756:

Dom José, by the grace of God King of Portugal and the Algarves, etc. Be it known to those who receive this my law that having been informed that in the State of Brazil the mulatto and black slaves continue to use knives and other prohibited weapons. . . . I hold that it is beneficial that instead of the punishment of 10 years in the galley service . . . the said black and mulatto slaves . . . should receive 100 lashes, administered on the pillory, and repeated for ten alternating days.[28]

West Africans had a long tradition of wrestling. It had been recorded as part of warfare there since the 16th century. Early lore of Yoruba towns characterized "war" as wrestling matches between the primary antagonists. A warlord in Yorubaland was expected to show martial prowess in wrestling. Prince Faboro of Ido-Ekiti, for example, who was born at the same time that the aforementioned Robert Walsh was traveling in Brazil, was famous for his bravery and physical strength. Before he ever went to war he was locally renowned in Ido-Ekiti as a champion grappler. Wrestling was one of the main forms of exercise Yoruba youth trained in to be in condition for a military career.

Kubik points out that "the large Yoruba lamellophone called agidigbo . . . was used long ago as an instrument to accompany a wrestling game called gidigbo. So there is a Yoruba tradition of accompanying wrestling games with 'melodic' instruments."[29] In Angola too, by 1687, "Cavazzi . . . described and depicted musical instruments used in war dances in what is now northern Angola."[30]

The weapons of capoeira, the club and the knife, were also well known in African warfare. By the late 19th century, Yoruban wars had been transformed by the introduction of firearms, but prior to that, warriors trained mostly with blades and clubs. In some towns, youths were said to roam about wearing "aprons" of knives and swords.

A warrior named Isola Fabunmi who waged war on Ibadan, was claimed in his praise poem to be a very strong fighter who was able to outsmart his opponents and an "adroit dancer who refuses to disclose his dancing techniques. . . . who petrifies spectators with amazement."[31]

Ibadan was a Yoruban city of warriors, where the inhabitants devoted their lives to the art of war and martial arts. No young man ever went out without arms. It was a fundamental expectation that Ibadan's male population would be equipped with a bladed weapon—a sword or, more usually, a knife strapped to the wrist—and a club, specially reinforced with iron rings. Guns were banned in Ibadan in the 19th century, but in the town, fighting was an everyday occurrence and to go out and return without the marks of a brawl just wasn't good form.

Africans and Amerindians in Quilombos

In northeastern Brazil, Portuguese, African, and Amerindian fighters participated in the Dutch wars in Recife and Bahia. Their fighting traditions blended into effective guerrilla fighting for which Brazilians became noted, particularly the São Paulo caboclo forces and their "dreaded bandeira." These were waging war on missions in the Tape and upper Uruguay. The Tape, a province in southeast Brazil (Rio Grande do Sul), was home to a number of missions.

The main area of the missions was 175 miles east of the River Uruguay and approximately 200 miles west of the town of Pôrto Alegre.

Some Jesuits were ex-soldiers and they trained mission Indians to try to resist the bandeirante slaving invasions. A Jesuit report noted that the mission Indians "attend to the military exercises, under the direction of our Brother Bernal, with great enthusiasm. They march out to the fields every day in a troop to train in attacks and counter attacks, in gymnastics, shooting and fencing."[32]

The Jesuits trained Amerindians to defend themselves, yet more frequently Amerindians were trained for militia activities against quilombos. Private militias in the mining areas replaced garrisons. They settled mining disputes and guarded monsoons loaded with gold. They acted as police or enforcers in taverns and ensured that slaves kept to curfews. They intervened in fights between paulistas and outsiders traveling into the mining areas from the Northeast, Portugal, or elsewhere.

Among the militias in the mining regions in the early 18th century were professional Portuguese "dragoons" who were veterans of European and North African wars; they suppressed revolts in Minas Gerais and Goiás. There were also companies of free blacks and free mulattos. These militias were called *terços. Pardos e bastardos fôrros* were mulatto companies, *prêtos e pardos fôrros* were black and mulatto, *indios e bastardos* were Amerindian and "half-caste." The colonial governors tried to keep an ethnic mix in the terços to avoid their becoming ethnically based forces of revolt in themselves.

Black militia regiments were known as "Henriques," after Henrique Dias, who had been the leader of a 300-strong African regiment on the Portuguese side against the Dutch. In 1648 he reported that his regiment consisted of "Angolas" and "crioulos," with a minority of "Minas" and "Ardras." In some units, only crioulos could rise to the rank of officer.

It was not unusual for militia members to escape into the very quilombos they were deployed to destroy. "How many times mulattos fleeing from slavery or deserting military service, have been proclaimed captains of tribes of Indians with whom they had taken refuge," d'Assier complained in 1867.[33]

During the Dutch wars in Bahia, the Marques of Montalvão suggested that Henrique Dias go to an intractable Bahia quilombo to offer a peace deal if the runaway slaves would join the militia. Using quilombolas as soldiers would have been a very Brazilian strategy, as was witnessed later when capoeiristas fought in local and international military conflicts. The town council of Salvador told Montalvão, "Under no circumstances is it proper to attempt reconciliation nor to give way to the slaves who might be conciliated in this matter. That which is proper is only to extinguish them and conquer them so that those who are still domesticated will not join them and those who are in rebellion will not aspire to greater misdeeds."[34]

It was impossible for the colonizers to control African slaves and quilombos without the militias or without Amerindians. One mission inspector of Cuiabá wrote in 1752:

This settlement was nothing more than a lair of bandits attacking the lives, honour and property of the Indians, on whom they declared war with no motive or authority other than greed. Fifty or a hundred men would arm themselves and, leaving guards on the sandbank, would plunge into the sertão and attack the first Indian village they encountered. They would kill all who seized their bows in just defence. They would put the rest who did not escape into chains and shackle, destroy

or burn the houses, ravage the fields, kill the animals and return tri-
umphantly. . . . they would divide the vanquished among the victors
and send them to Cuiabá and Mato Grosso under contract of sale. . . .
Many Indians perished here like beasts, felled by an axe or as targets for
arrows and guns, and a great multitude from ill-treatment and illness.
The women paid with their lives and honour in the same way.[35]

Even though Palmares, Alagoas, and Bahia have entered folklore as the centers of quilombo resistance during the 17th century,
it was the mining areas in which the quilombos were concentrated
in the 18th century. The word "quilombo" for hideouts of fugitive
slaves was mainly used in Minas Gerais, while "mocambo" was the
customary term in Bahia. Famous quilombos in Minas Gerais, such
as Ambrósio and Quilombo Grande, were the object of extraordinary military and judicial efforts by the authorities. Conde de
Assumar, who was governor of Minas Gerais from 1717 until 1721,
pinned his whole governorship on the absolute need to control the
region's slaves. Men like Conde de Assumar were occupied with
the very recent memory of Palmares. He wrote in 1719 that "the
blacks [of Minas] may be tempted to repeat the acts of the Palmares of Pernambuco, emboldened by their multitude."[36] Minas
Gerais was filled with tough African slaves from military back-
grounds in both Angola and the hinterland of the Gold Coast.
These were the *calhambolas* who inhabited the quilombos. Slave
owners and mining entrepreneurs were often from São Paulo.
Paulistas, with their tradition of bandeira expeditions, were the
same aggressors already referred to who plunged into the sertão
of the mining regions in search of Amerindian slaves.

The early paulista prospectors resented the later waves of "foreigners" and the government officials who turned up to enforce
taxes. Father André João Antonil wrote in 1711:

Every year great numbers of Portuguese and foreigners come in the fleets bound for the mines. From the cities, villages, inlets, and hinterland of Brazil there go whites, browns, blacks, and many Indians who are in the service of the paulistas. The mixture is of every kind and condition of person: men and women, young and old, rich and poor, nobles and commoners, laymen and priests, and monks of all orders, many of whom have neither convent nor chapter in Brazil.[37]

Slave owners took to arming their African slaves and this conflagrated into an actual war from 1708 to 1709, called the "War of the Emboabas." In this war, armed slaves fought government soldiers on behalf of slave owners wanting to avoid paying tax on their gold.

The War of the Emboabas gave Portugal all the reasons it needed to impose greater colonial control on the mining areas, and even more so when diamonds were discovered. The Portuguese Marquis of Pombal made tax collection of "the fifth" (owed to the crown) and greater power to Lisbon politicians in Brazilian affairs the cornerstones of Portuguese economic policy in Brazil. This reflected just how important revenues from Brazil had become to the Portguese. The growth of quilombos in Minas Gerais and the physical situation on the ground became so unstable that royal officials and municipal councils were very jittery.

It was in this context that racists like Conde de Assumar flourished. Laws and town council resolutions hardened. The town council of Vila Rica proclaimed that the punishment for an escaped slave should be amputation of a hand, and the town council of Mariana ordered that fugitives should have their Achilles tendon sliced through so they would only be able to limp to work. In 1744, royal judicial authorities were finally able to collect taxes in gold to finance Amerindian militias and capitães do mato. Their initial

establishment in Minas Gerais had been organized by Conde de Assumar twenty years earlier, along with laws giving anyone the right to attack a quilombo and carry whatever arms they needed for that purpose.

Militias and capitãos do campo were paid commission for every slave they recaptured. Specially trained mulatto militias or bands

Slaves washing for diamonds were carefully watched by the overseers. The English traveler George Gardner wrote, "The privilege of diamond washing, formerly a monopoly of the government, is now accessible to any individual who chooses. . . . The greater portion of the inhabitants of the Cidade Diamantina who possess a few slaves employ them in the washings. . . . The persons engaged in these adventures are generally a very improvident race, for even those who carry on the most extensive Serviços, as the workings are called, often run deeply in debt after a rich washing has been exhausted. . . . I was assured by one of the most extensive miners in the district that the excitement produced by this kind of life is like that of a gambler; whoever enters on it, never renounces it."(Source: Levine and Crocitti, eds., *The Brazil Reader: History, Culture, Politics*, pp. 52–53 [Gardner, "Smuggling in the Diamond District"].)

A slave who found a diamond weighing "one dram," or one-eighth of an ounce, was awarded freedom. Because of this, it was said that slaves preferred extracting diamonds to working directly for their masters. (Source: Auguste de Sainte-Hilaire, in Conrad, *Children of God's Fire*, p. 141.)

of Amerindians pursued escapees into the bush. Amerindian fighters were almost always used to defeat quilombos. One colonist of Parahiba wrote:

There is no doubt that without Indians in Brazil there can be no negroes of Guinea, or better said, there can be no Brazil, for without [Negroes] nothing can be done and they are ten times more numerous than the whites, and if today it is costly to dominate them with the Indians whom they greatly fear . . . what will happen without Indians. The next day they will revolt and it is a great task to resist domestic enemies.[38]

An enduring myth was (and is) that African slaves were peculiarly well adapted to living life in inaccessible areas of the American and Caribbean interior. The African homelands were not necessarily similar to the Brazilian sertão, and fugitives suffered shortages of basics like salt, gunpowder, metal tools, utensils, and firearms. Not only trained militias, but hostile Amerindian tribes could also be highly dangerous to runaway Africans. Massacres of quilombolas or slaves on sugar plantations or in transit to the mines also occurred.

Four hundred people were carrying 900 kilograms of gold to the coast by river in 1730, when they were attacked by Paiaguá Indians. The Africans were rowing the canoes, and the passengers "were almost ecstatic with terror." Many of the slaves dove into the water. Whites, armed with guns, threatened the rest of the paddlers that if they didn't keep going they'd shoot them. "Paiaguá glided up and killed the panic stricken with their arrows, lances and clubs. . . . In the heat of battle they calmly felt the pulses of blacks who surrendered, keeping the strongest and killing the weaker."[39]

Despite all the risks, African quilombos penetrated deep into the sertão. Roquette Pinto wrote, "It is a big mistake to believe that in the great central sertáo and the Amazonian lowlands the sertanejo is exclusively the caboclo. In the rolling highlands of the northeast as in the rubber forests . . . there are cafusos or caborés, of part-Negro descent. . . . Many slaves fled to the quilombos in the forests, in the vicinity of the Indian tribes."[40]

Recall that the Ashanti Quobah had led a large force of escaped slaves in Rio de Janeiro. Quobah's rebels had fought a battle with Brazilian troops but they dispersed to the hills and then made "sallies and burned several country houses . . . setting fire to cane fields, devastating crops and smashing machinery in the ingenios. . . . Quobah, the Ashantee, was never taken by the Brazilians. He fled to the wild plains, with a few followers, and was either killed or adopted by the Indians."[41]

Freyre reported that Pinto had published archives from the Brazilian Historical Institute:

> Concerning the caborés of the Serra do Norte, in the very heart of Brazil, showing that they were the hybrid offspring of Negro fugitives from the mines and Indian women. . . . In travelling recently through lower Cuminá, Gastão Cruls came upon various remains of the old mucambos or quilombos. . . . What is more . . . these slave refuges were to be found along nearly all the rivers of the Amazon region; and even on the upper Içá, Crevaux discovered the thatched hut of an old black woman. . . . Wherever one turns, even in places where it is supposed that Amerindian blood or that of the Portuguese-Indian hybrid is preserved in its purest state, it will be found that the African has been there: in the very heart of the Amazon region, on the Serra do Norte, and in the back lands. . . . For this activity of the fugitive Negroes in the back lands regions and along the Amazon River represents an impulse that is almost equal to that of the São Paulo bandeirantes or the settlers of Ceará.[42]

There was also a great deal of cooperation between Africans and Amerindians. Discriminatory laws were continually created to thwart physical, material, or even spiritual values that might unite the enslaved of Brazil. In 1621 it was decreed that no Amerindian, black African, crioulo, or mulatto could become a goldsmith. Laws were also passed in 1696 and 1709 that no slave, free black, or mulatto could wear either silk or gold clothing or jewelry. Slaves were forbidden to wear shoes. Black people were excluded from joining influential lay brotherhoods like the Third Order of St. Francis. In 1726 the town council of Bahia voted to exclude mulattos from its membership. Blacks were prohibited from carrying arms after a law of 1626. A freed slave's liberty could be reversed if he disrespected a former owner, and in many cases a free black also had to serve a compulsory period of labor for his previous master, even after manumission.

To create networks of their own, outside of the whites' sphere of influence, blacks and mulattos sometimes united in alternative, lay solidarities. Bahia in the 18th century was home to six African and five mulatto brotherhoods dedicated to Nossa Senhora. Some of these brotherhoods had membership limited to a particular African nation of origin. These provided alms and social services, dowries, funerals, and organized religious ceremonies. Such brotherhoods were common in Brazilian cities and less often though sometimes on engenhos.[43]

In the cities, *escravos de ganho* were self-employed slaves who paid part of their earnings to the master. Escravos de ganho sold goods or provided services to earn extra money to supplement slave work. They were laborers, prostitutes, barbers, tradesmen and women, and sometimes beggars. There were also *pardo* mulatto artisans who could gain freedom more easily than dark-skinned blacks. "Free" was a nominal term and, though artisans formed trade guilds and brotherhoods, they weren't allowed to sit on town councils, so trade guilds weren't a stepping stone to social, economic, or political empowerment.

The most effective resistance to slavery was still the quilombo.

It was there that the fusion of African and Amerindian culture developed. In 1706, "the crown ordered that 'blacks, mixed bloods and slaves' be prevented from penetrating the back lands, where they might join with hostile Indians."[44]

Here, in a report about quilombos of the Amazon Valley to the British Foreign Office, a Mr. Vine wrote:

> Another detachment of forty soldiers, under the command of a Captain, left Pará to destroy the quilombo of Trombetas, a famous settlement, over 50 years old, and which hitherto had been deemed inaccessible to military enterprise, and looked upon by the slave population as a sort of enchanted land. . . . a captured negro gave such an account of the difficulties and dangers of the journey to this settlement, that thirty-three out of forty soldiers, refused to accompany their captain, and he and seven soldiers proceeded in search of it; after nine days wandering through dense forests, they reached the settlement, which they found deserted and burned by the negroes, who had broken up their ovens and utensils for making farinha and mandioca. About three leagues from the quilombo of Trombetas exists a tribe of white Indians, of the Uariquena nation, who being on friendly terms with the fugitive slaves, are supposed to have given them notice of the intended attack.[45]

In the 1750s, a new and aggressive foreign minister in Portugal, the Marquis of Pombal, sought to regulate the mining industry in Brazil. He aimed to stop smuggling, make the colony of Brazil more subordinate to Portugal and Portugal less subordinate to Britain. Pombal also shifted power from Salvador to Rio de Janeiro. He ensured that the State of Maranhão was incorporated into Brazil and introduced the "Law of Liberties," which freed Amerindian slaves.

The governor of Maranhão-Pará introduced African slaves to

Maranhão to replace the Amerindians. More than 25,000 Africans were shipped to Maranhão over the next twenty years. The governor wrote to Pombal: "I consider it inevitable that these Indians—being barbaric, rustic and also lazy—as soon as they realize that they are completely free, and that no one can force them to live in the fazendas. . . . I am convinced that they will totally abandon the work in that same instant, and run off to mocambos. This will leave everything in confusion and disorder—for they will admit no half measure."[46]

But Amerindians had been fleeing slavery long before Pombal's law. Tupinamba had migrated all the way across South America. Sixty thousand people had traveled 3,500 miles in one of the biggest mass migrations in history. Finding Spaniards on the other side of the continent, they fled to an island in the Amazon river where no white man saw them until Pedro Teixeira's bandeira came across them in the 1630s.

Cowboys, Indians, and Slaves

Africans and Amerindians shared much common ground. In São Paulo, the Tupi language was dominant until the 18th century. On sugar plantations in Bahia and Pernambuco, Tupi was spoken by two-thirds of the slaves up until the mid-17th century. Africans and Indians worked side by side on the plantations and often escaped and fought side by side in quilombos. The Imbangala and Jaga mercenary slaves who'd been captured in the Kwango valley and Mbundu regions were familiar with the "mobile war" tactics that were effectively used defending quilombos. In Brazil, easily surrounded quilombos and Amerindian tribes who stayed in one place didn't last very long.

At Palmares it had taken two years to gradually reduce the perimeter of the main mocambos, during which time the palmarinos moved around as they fought to avoid being surrounded. It was only when the main force was finally pinned down in a siege that the quilombo succumbed to the paulista and Amerindian irregulars who attacked them.

The Jaga of Angola practiced infanticide to maximize their mobility. The warrior tribe of Amerindian horsemen, the Guaicurú, used a similar approach. Their women self-aborted and kidnapped youths from other tribes. A Guaicurú woman said, "There is nothing more tedious for us than to raise children and take them on our various journeys, during which we are often short of food. This is what decides us to arrange an abortion as soon as we feel pregnant."[47]

The bandeirantes (paulistas) were the only force capable of going to war successfully with Amerindians in the sertão. But when the Portuguese first penetrated the mining area of Cuiabá:

> With their horses [the Guaicurú] terrorised . . . even the paulistas, who ventured into the bush only in great bands, and were frightened to meet them on an open plain because of the way they attacked. As soon as Guaicurú saw [paulistas] they would join their horses, with ox hides to cover their flanks, and attacked them in such a way that they broke. They trampled their enemy with the violence of their charge and killed with their lances any they caught in their path.[48]

Other nomadic tribes who fought with great mobility, like the Aimore, Nheegaiba, or Marajo, defended more successfully against the Portuguese attacks because they were scattered and kept on the move, making it impossible to surround them in an ambush. An eyewitness account of the Aimore said:

> They are excessively strong and carry very long bows that are thick

in proportion to their strength and with arrows to match. . . . [They fight with] treacherous assaults and ambushes without any order, and they hide themselves easily under the little leaves. . . . they are extraordinarily agile and great runners . . . afraid of no sort of people or weapons . . . as swift of foot as any horse. These cannibals . . . are so desperate that five or six of them will set upon a sugar house, where there are at least one hundred persons.[49]

Additionally: "Without being seen they shoot arrows at people and kill them. They run away so agilely and disappear into the forest as if they were wild goats, often running on hands and feet with their bows and arrows on their backs. . . . our men cannot see them except when they feel themselves hit by their arrows."[50]

The *casa grande* (big house) of Brazilian sugar plantations was typically a heavily defended fortress. Diogo Dias, a powerful Goiana planter, built his stone house inside a stockade, guarded by hundreds of African slaves and Amerindian archers.

Bandeirantes wore heavy cotton padded armor to defend themselves against Indian arrows. "These arrows might appear ludicrous, but they are a cruel weapon that can pierce cotton cuirasses . . . or sometimes pass clean through a man and plunge into the ground behind him. They practice with these weapons from a very young age and are great archers, so accurate that no bird escapes them, however small."[51]

The Waitaca people went to war with great skill against the Portuguese for a hundred years. They were also nomadic and renowned for their speed and agility as runners, making them hard to entrap. Andre Thevet wrote:

They train their children to manoeuvre agilely, to resist and elude the flight of arrows, at first using little stunning arrows, then to train them better they shoot more dangerous arrows at them. If they sometimes wound some of them, they tell them: I prefer that you should die at my hand than my enemies. . . . They are more expert at war than any other tribe, added to which they are in an almost impregnable place because of the rivers and swamps that surround it.[52]

Africans and Amerindians at the mines and sugar plantations of Brazil pooled skills to maximize the effectiveness of the quilombo, not least in the area of military strategy. Portuguese records of certain Amerindian tribes note the use of traps and ambush to draw the enemy in and kill them. In the 16th century, when the Portuguese commander Martím Leitão went after the Potiguar Indians in Pernambuco, his column of men, which was two miles long, had to "remove the pits and traps with which the Potiguar had mined the jungle trails."[53] At the Potiguar stockade, Leitão had to contend with a barrage of ingenious log obstacles: "Great trees had been arranged in traps which, if a bird touched them, would crash down and crush twenty men."

Historian Richard Price suggests:

A good deal of maroon (quilombo) technology must have been developed on the plantations during slavery. Throughout Afro-America, Indians interacted with slaves, whether as fellow sufferers, as trading partners, or in other capacities. Indian technologies—from pottery making and hammock weaving to fish drugging and manioc processing—were taken over and, often, further developed by the slaves, who were often responsible for supplying the bulk of their daily needs. . . . it was on a base of technical knowledge developed in the interaction between indians and blacks on plantations that most of the remarkable maroon adaptations were built.[54]

Also:

In many areas, maroons used bows and arrows extensively as weapons, as well as home-made spears and Amerindian war clubs, and even, in some cases, "crooked sticks shaped something like a musket" to frighten the whites by their apparent force of arms.[55]

Amerindian and African Religious Cults in Quilombos

It wasn't only in the practical fields that African and Amerindian culture fused. Centuries before the religion known as Caboclo blended Yoruba and Amerindian gods in Brazil, religion already played a unifying part in quilombos composed of different nations and cultures.

Early in the colonial era, the Brazilian authorities became alarmed by a network of quilombos based around the Jaguaripe River. These developed after Amerindian escapes from plantations and missions in Bahia. Disease epidemics had disillusioned the Amerindians in the Jesuit God, who was clearly unable or unwilling to protect them from the measles, flu, and smallpox that attacked the mission communities.

The Tupi who fled into Jaguaripe practiced a syncretic, messianic religion called *Santidade*. This had become popular in Bahia. Among the tenets of Santidade was the belief that "white people would be turned into game for them [the Indians] to eat."(56) African slaves fled into the wild interior of Jaguaripe and joined Santidade communities. Raids were organized from the quilombos to free slaves from the city of Salvador. Many raids for food were launched into settlers' farms outside the city. The planters were losing their investment to the forest, and the church was losing souls to a religion that told its congregations that "their god would free them from slavery and make them masters of the white people, who would become their slaves." The Paraguaçu River, up from the Bay of All Saints, was home to Amerindian and African Santidade quilombos. In 1627, "colonists in Jaguaripe were still suffering from attacks of the Santidade villages."[57] The religion was essentially an imitation of Catholicism with an emphasis on beads and rosaries with some idol worship thrown in. Yet in its basic premise it provided common possibilities for the Amerindians and Africans who lived together in the quilombo. Both the Inquisition and the governor became focused on crushing the Santidade quilombos.

The Portuguese took this so seriously that King Philip III wrote to the governor-general of Brazil, ordering him to destroy the quilombos with whatever force necessary, to return all African slaves to their owners and imprison the Amerindians. Predictably, the king of Portugal recommended a mameluco backwoodsman named Afonso Rodrigues Adorno for the task of crushing the Santidade quilombo. He used an Amerindian militia to do it. As King Philip put it: "He has some heathen whom his ancestors gathered together in times past, and continues to possess their administration. When necessary he rallies with 200 bowmen."[58]

Crime and Punishment

It was no easy thing to defeat a quilombo once it was well established. The fiercely reactionary colonial governors and slave owners believed that the only solution to the problem was harsh punishment to deter others by example. "The traveller passing through the ancient towns of Minas Gerais was struck by the omnipresence of prisons with fortress-thick walls, which had become their architectural centers. These prisons were testimony to the brutal repression of fugitive slaves."[59]

Punishment was handed out privately by individual slave owners and their foremen. Men like Jorge Velho and Tomacauna (who attacked Santidade quilombos) acted as freelancers in the pay of individual governors. Freyre agrees with Ruediger Bilden, that "in Brazil it was private colonizing effort to a far greater extent than official action that promoted . . . a latifundiary agriculture and slavery."[60]

In colonial Brazil punishment was dished out with medieval overkill, not only to satisfy the sadism of the individuals involved but to terrorize African workers into submission. It always involved corporal punishment and some kind of torture. This process began in Africa, continued during the middle passage, and was inherent to the process of slave labor. Drake reported on a trip to Havana:

The Napoleon [his ship] had trouble before her departure. The men slaves composing her freight were some of the fiercest warriors of the Kassaos, the Fi nation, and the Sherbroo Buttom people, who had been provoked by a cruel war by the traders. It was only with difficulty that they were got on board the clipper, though secured by one foot chains round the neck as well as their ankle irons. On reaching the boats a rush was made by several for the purpose of leaping into the sea and thumb screws had to be clapped on them before they would be quiet.[61]

In the mid-1800s the American Thomas Ewbank wrote a first-hand account of his travels in Brazil:

The mask is the reputed ordinary punishment and preventative of drunkenness. As the barrel is often chained to the slave that bears it, to prevent him from selling it for rum, so the mask is to hinder him or her from conveying the liquor to the mouth, below which the metal is continued, and opposite to which there is no opening.

Observing one day masks hanging out for sale at a tin and sheet iron store, I stopped to examine them, and subsequently borrowed one. . . . Except a projecting piece for the nose, the metal is simply bent cylinderwise. Minute holes are punched to admit air to the nostrils, and similar ones in front of the eyes. A jointed strap (of metal) on each side goes round below the ears (sometimes two) and meets one that passes over the crown of the head. A staple unites and a padlock secures them.

At most of the smiths shops, collars are exposed. . . . at one shop in Rua das Violas, there was quite a variety, with gyves, chains, etc. Most of the collars were of five-eighths-inch-round iron, some with one prong, others with two, and some with none except a short upright tubular lock. Here, too, were the heaviest and cruellest instruments of torture—shackles for binding the ankles and wrists close together, and consequently doubling the bodies of the victims into the most painful and unnatural positions. Had I not seen them, I could hardly have thought such things were [possible]. . . . A black man in his shirt sleeves, came from the rear, and handling them, spoke by way of rec-ommending them, supposing I was a customer. They were made of bar iron, three inches wide and three-eighths of an inch thick! Each consisted of three pieces, bent, jointed, and fastened. The large open-ings were for the legs, the smaller for the wrists. A screw bolt drew the straight parts close together. . . . The distance from joint to joint was two feet.

Such are the tortures that slaves privately endure in the cellars, garrets, and outhouses of their masters. . . . A native merchant says another common punishment is to enclose the legs in wooden shackles or stocks. Some owners fasten their slaves' hands in similar devices, and some again, retain relics of the old thumbscrews to lock those mem-bers together. In northern provinces, he says, the slaves are much worse used than in Rio; that it is no uncommon thing to tie their hands and feet together, hoist them off the ground, and then, beat them as near to death as possible. A heavy log fastened by a chain to the neck or leg of a slave who has absconded, or who is supposed to be inclined to run away, is a usual punishment and precaution. He is compelled to labour with it, laying it on the ground when at work, and bearing it under his arm or on his shoulder when he moves.

I observed one day a slave wearing a collar, the largest and roughest of hundreds I have seen . . . of inch round iron, with a hinge in the middle, made by bending the metal of its full size into loops, the open ends flattened and connected by a half-inch rivet. The upright bar terminated in a deaths head, which reached above that of the wearer, and to it another piece, in the form of the letter S, was welded. The joint galled him, for he kept gathering portions of his canvas shirt under it. Rest or sleep would seem impossible.[62]

Recaptured fugitive slaves were often tortured. There were occasional royal orders, such as one in 1688, to try and curb "excessive" cruelty. Slaves could make formal complaints about this to judicial authorities, but such cases were very rare and virtually never guaranteed a prosecution. The fact that Ewbank saw torture devices openly on sale in a blacksmith's shop more than 150 years after 1688 shows that laws safeguarding slaves against cruelty were completely ineffective.

In 1741, fugitives who were captured after a battle for a quilombo were thrown into jail in Salvador. Thirty-one of them were branded with the letter F, denoting *Fugido*.

Certain of the slaves . . . were singled out for special punishment. . . . Antonio de Sousa, war captain of the quilombo, was sentenced to a public flogging and life in the galleys. His friend Miguel Cosme . . . received a sentence of flogging and six years as a galley slave. Theodoro and José Lopez both were publicly whipped and sent to ten years in the galleys. José Piahuy . . . received two hundred lashes and a four year term at the oars, while crioulu Leonardo received a like number of stripes.[63]

Despite the punishments, escape was still a popular goal and quilombos were part of the Brazilian landscape. Most quilombos traded with moradores. On the periphery of the gold fields, the Minas quilombos became centers of contraband gold, which was traded for arms and food supplies like salt or manioc. In almost all cases in Minas Gerais, the quilombos were occupied by both Africans and Amerindians.

Roger Bastide argues:

Each time such a fusion took place, it was the Negroes who took charge of the new community, whether by reducing the Indians to slavery, as in Bahia in 1704, or by becoming the military or religious leader of the community, as in Mato Grosso in 1795. There must have been a religious syncretism, with the dominant influence coming from African civilization, which supplied both the liturgy and the mythology for the Negro priest and the procedures for magical cures for the Negro "doctor." . . . This syncretism encompassed elements of white culture as well, and the Negro became an instrument for the diffusion of Portuguese Catholicism, albeit in a modified and corrupt form, among the Indians. . . . Thus there was created . . . a social system that combined the dual organization of the Indian tribes (the two sections or camps of the quilombos of Mato Grosso) with the African tribal federation under the rule of a monarch-priest.[64]

The names of those recaptured in Brazil's mocambos are reminiscent of capoeira nicknames. A famous mocambo called Buraco de Tatú ("Armadillo's Hole") existed in Bahia in the 1740s. One of its members was documented as Mandingueiro. One of the captured and executed leaders of a quilombo (*palenque*) in 18th-century Cuba was named Mariano Mandinga. Another quilombo was led by a man known as Malunguinho, this being a diminutive form of the African name for comrade. In the quilombo of Marcel Congo, destroyed near Petropolis in 1839, recaptured slaves were listed as Justino Benguela, Antonio Nâgo, Canuto Maçambique, Afonse Angola, Miguel Crioulo, and Maria Crioula.[65]

Women in Colonial Brazil

Monogamy and polygamy were practiced in different quilombos. In the quilombo of Buraco de Tatú, the houses were small, built only for two people living in a monogamous relationship. In many quilombos, women were in the minority. Where a woman had more than one man, there were often polygamy rules. Days were assigned to each "husband" separately to avoid potentially explosive conflicts that could occur in these secluded environments. In other cases, a person's rank in the quilombo determined marital status. Ganga Zumba of Palmares was said to have three wives. Bastide reports that in Brazil, there were two documented cases where the "captain" or leader of the quilombo was a woman. After 100 years of existence, not a single piece of written material came out of Palmares from any of its inhabitants and even among the colonial European classes, women were especially silent. "I do not believe that in Brazil there has ever been a single diary written by a woman," said Gilberto Freyre, after searching the historical archives in vain.

Women in roles as spiritual leaders were more numerous in African religions than in the Catholic society of male religious orders like those of Saint Benedict, the Franciscans, or Jesuits. Women played a leading role in Candomblé, for example: "According to oral tradition, three priestesses of the Orixá Xangô; Iyá Kalá, Iyá Detá, Iyá Nassó, were transported by slave ships from Africa (Nigeria) to Bahia in 1830 and founded the first real Candomblé terreiro, The White House of the Old Mill. From it were born all the great Candomblé houses of the city of Salvador, Bahia."[66]

Slave imports into Brazil were largely male and, because many quilombos were close to Amerindian tribes, most of the women living in quilombos were Amerindian. In that culture women were responsible for agriculture, and this was true in quilombos. The charge of rape was common from moradores, who claimed quilombolas kidnapped and dishonored their wives and daughters. Kent writes:

> Women were a rarity in Palmares and were actively sought during razzias (raids). But female relatives of the morador did not constitute the main target, and those occasionally taken were returned unmolested for ransom. . . . Checking the "rape of Sabines" tales, Edison Carneiro [discovered they were simply not true]. . . . he found [only] one exception to the ransom rule, reported by a Pernambucan soldier in 1682.[67]

Schwartz writes of the raids made by fugitives of the Bahian quilombo, Buraco de Tatú:

> The principle victims . . . were not white sugar-planters but rather the Negroes who "came every day to the city to sell the food stuffs they grow on their plots." Aside from being despoiled of their produce and possessions, as was traditionally the case, the most appealing women were forced to return to the quilombos. Runaway communities seemed to suffer from a chronic lack of females, and escaped male slaves seemed to prefer black or mulatto women. Instances of the capture of European women are extremely rare, and in the case of the Buraco de Tatú, no such charge was made.[68]

The implicit assumption that female slaves entering quilombos would always have been victims of coercion is unfounded. Why would women rather have worked on sugar plantations than escape to a quilombo? At the plantation she was no better protected from a male majority than in a quilombo. Slaveholders had an absolute legal right to possess female slaves. There was an ineffective legal theory that masters could not force slaves to commit "immoral" acts, but in reality, gaining a prosecution against a master (or mistress) for physical or sexual violence against slaves was virtually impossible.

Subsequently, there were countless physical and sexual attacks against women. Female slaves were as likely to be punished and tortured in Brazil as men. Of the four cases where Thomas Ewbank saw slaves in padlocked metal face masks, all were women. At every phase of the sugar production process, women were involved— during the twenty-hour working day of the harvest, to preparing the pots for draining molasses and the eventual separating of the sugar-loaves. Female slaves were hired out as prostitutes in the mining regions and the cities of Brazil and coastal areas of Angola. In Luanda, which by the 1750s onward was suffering a decline in prosperity, female slaves were used in this way. "Slave masters in Luanda had been reduced to using their slave women as prostitutes, partly as favors to friends and business associates, but also . . . to increase the quantity and value of labor they could control under the prevailing manpower shortage, through the mulatto slave children they expected to result."[69]

In 1871, Rio de Janeiro's police chief reported, "There has been an increase in the public protests in this city against the immoral scandal of slave women prostituting themselves either by order or with the express consent of their masters, from which the latter gain exorbitant profits."[70]

A woman's lot was not an easy one in Brazil, whatever her origin. European girls were considered to have become marriageable by age twelve and began giving birth by the age of thirteen, often dying during delivery. Few Portuguese women were attracted by the prospect of climbing aboard ships filled with Portuguese convicts to begin a new life in the colonies. Women were very vulnerable under Portuguese law at the time. During the era of the Inquisition, the Portuguese could extract a man's tongue and burn him alive for heresy, but would fine him one chicken if he raped his daughter.

In the moradores family, "a rigid double standard of female chastity and constancy and male promiscuity was condoned to the point of the law's permitting an offended husband to kill his wife caught in an act of adultery."[71]

Given the limited scope for a satisfactory life for men or women under the yolk of slavery, the quilombo offered a way out for both sexes. What was described as kidnap could with only a slight adjustment be interpreted as facilitation of escape and protection from pursuit by slave hunters.

Women not only worked in the sugar fields but were often employed as wet nurses. To have a black wet nurse was a status symbol among the white planter class, and sometimes owners who were close to bankruptcy would acquire one to hide the true state of their finances. There were guides written for white mothers hoping to choose black wet nurses:

> Let us recognize in the first place that white wet nurses would be preferable in every respect, if in this climate they offered the same advantages as those of the African race. The latter, organically formed to live in hot regions, in which their health prospers . . . acquire in this climate an ability to suckle babies which the same climate generally denies to white women. . . . This fact being sufficiently obvious, our

choice must therefore fall upon a black wet nurse, but we require that she be . . . young, strong, and robust, that is between twenty and twenty-four years of age, and physically well constituted. [72]

Free and slave African women ran the small-scale, mobile street trade in colonial cities, which gave them some room to maneuver. These women were called *ganhadeiras*.

> Vilhena observed . . . that for all intents and purposes, the ganhadeiras monopolized the sale of fish, vegetables, and contraband. They gathered in open air markets (at the time called *quitandas*) and . . . got together to sell all they had, be it fish, half-cooked meat (which they call *moqueada*), salt pork, whale meat . . . greens, what have you. . . . Using ingenious systems of market speculation and smuggling— which they called *carambola* . . . or *cacheteira* . . . ["somersault" or "mockery"] ganhadeiras, often in cahoots with their former or current mistresses, controlled the supply of basic foodstuffs in the city. Some forty years after Vilhena's observations, the situation had not changed, according to an American missionary.[73]

Marriages and monogamous unions on plantations were common. They were often determined by cultural ties between partners, particularly West African Nâgos. Angolans were more ready to marry outside of their nation.

Historical evidence leads to the conclusion that it was mainly men who were successful in escaping the plantations and mines (it was mainly men who worked in the mines). This says little about the level of coercion necessary to supply women to quilombos, because some women must have escaped with their men. In quilombos there were records of female leaders. Even in Angola, the most famous and powerful of the Imbangala leaders of the mid-17th century was Queen Nzinga of Matamba. In West Africa too, women were effective combatants. In Dahomey in the 18th century, the monarchs employed a court of female soldiers as a personal bodyguard for the king.

In Angola, women were mainly captured in war as camp followers and were not normally combatants. But Queen Nzinga was an Imbangala of great fighting prowess and it would be a fruitful field of study to determine whether girls were taught the skills of sangar in Central Africa.

Women's role in Brazilian society is relevant to the study of capoeira. At a seminar of Capoeira Angola mestres, Mestre Moraes drew attention to the fact that in Africa there is a clear distinction between male and female roles in many activities. He said that before jumping to conclusions as to why so few women participated in traditional capoeira, this must be taken into account.

In traditional Candomblé, in contrast to the more recent religions of Caboclo, Macumba or Umbanda, the women were exclusively the priests and held the power. In the 1930s Edison Carneiro explained that "it is almost as difficult for a man to become great in Candomblé as it is for him to have a baby. And for the same reason: it is believed to be against his nature."[74]

Carneiro, who was a friend or acquaintance of most of the influential Candomblé practitioners in Bahia in the 1920s and '30s, told Ruth Landes, an American anthropologist:

> A great difference between Candomblé and Catholic practices is that the Africans try to bring their gods down to earth where they can see and hear them. And this is the most sensational job of the women who are priestesses of a temple. A temple woman becomes possessed by a saint or god who is her patron and guardian; they say he—or she—"descends into her head and rides her," and then through her body he dances and talks. Sometimes they call a priestess the wife of

a god and sometimes she is his horse. The god gives advice and places demands, but sometimes he just mounts and plays.

So you can see why the priestesses develop great influence among the people. They are the pathway to the gods, but no upright man will allow himself to be ridden by a god, unless he does not care about losing his manhood. His mind should always be sober, never dizzy or "tonto" from invasion by a god.

Now, here's the loophole. Some men do let themselves be ridden, and they become priests with the women; but they are known to be homosexuals. In the temple they put on the skirts and mannerisms of the women, and they dance like the women. Sometimes they are much better looking than the women.

But this could not happen in the great Yoruba temples.[75]

Men generally supported the Candomblé *terreiro* financially, acted as *ogans*, which was an honorary position in the religion for laymen; they played the drums and musical instruments at ceremonies, slaughtered sacrificial animals, and collected herbs necessary for various rites. If men danced, which they could, it was without being "ridden," and they had to dance in a sober way and not with the women.

According to Edison Carneiro, it wasn't always easy for the men to remain sober:

Some men really have the urge to become priests, and they set up cult organizations according to traditions of the Angola nation or of the Congo nation. There is one Angola priest who conducts his own temple. He is Father Bernadino, and the cult people respect him because his work is good. He is a big powerful man who dances wonderfully, but in the style of the women. There is a handsome young Congo father named João who knows almost nothing and is taken seriously by nobody, not even by his own "daughters in the saint-hood"—as they call the body of the priestesses; he is a wonderful dancer, and he has a certain charm. People know he is a homosexual because he straightens his long thick hair, and that is blasphemous. "What! How can one let a hot iron touch the head where a saint resides!" the women cry.[76]

Although this observation came after slavery was abolished in Brazil, so running ahead of our history chronologically, Ruth Landes comments that in Bahia:

> Most of the men who visit [the Candomblé] are too poor to have homes or to afford commercial entertainment. They seldom know their fathers and have often lived on the streets. They are hangers-on and stability is provided by the black women. And the women have everything: they have the temples, the religion, the priestly offices, the bearing and rearing of children, and opportunities for self-support through domestic work and related fields. If the temples did not welcome the men, they would be left permanently to the streets, where they would become as ruffianly as they have long been in Rio.[77]

Landes points out that the temple women and priestesses usually didn't marry in a way recognized by the church. First, under Brazilian law they would have lost too much. After marriage, everything a woman owned was automatically transferred to her husband. Most black men couldn't afford the cost of a church wedding either, and the matriarchal trend in African-Bahian society was strong. "Women submit solely to the gods," observes Landes, and their duties to the gods took precedence over everything else.

She felt that the Bahian women were ambivalent to many of the men. In Rio, ruffians were "called 'malandros,'" writes Landes. "The women do not voice their fears in this conscious way, but their awareness of it is clear when mention is made of capoeiristas—the street wrestlers whom they hate for their denial of Candomblé."[78]

Edison Carneiro thought that women didn't like capoeira because they were excluded from it.

> It is true . . . that capoeiristas do not care about Candomblé. Maybe they like more roughhouse than they find in the temple, and of course there is little that most men can do among all those possessed women. Feeling is so high between them, you would think they were enemies. Maybe they are still carrying on an old fight between Yoruba Candomblé from the northern west coast and Angola capoeira from the southern. . . . Brazil was always close to Africa, especially between her plantation areas and the slave markets of Africa.[79]

Another factor that excluded women from capoeira was the dress code in Brazil, which was particularly strong in Bahia. Mestre Pastinha said that in the old days of Bahia capoeira there were some women, but he named only two and one of them was named Maria Homen ("Maria Man"). Even in the 20th century, "Bahia life was laden with regulations about women's wear, and during my stay the Archbishop issued new pronunciamentos concerning the length of women's skirts and of the skirts and pants of their bathing suits."[80] Prior to the 1930s, capoeira was almost exclusively in the domain of African-Brazilian men in Bahia, and African-Brazilian women were often involved in Candomblé and the Catholic Church simultaneously.

This digression strayed from the subject of quilombos, to which we now return with a brief conclusion. Amerindians and Africans pooled their skills in quilombos. The high proportion of Amerindian women played a prominent role in agriculture.

By the era of the gold boom, slave-driven industries were up and running all along the Brazilian coast and over large areas of the sertão. The fusion of varied Amerindian and African military, agricultural, and manufacturing methods was extensive, finding expression on plantations, though as the indigenous people of Brazil were scarcely present on plantations by then, the fusion found fullest expression in quilombos.

In the cities there was a mix of West African and Angolan slaves, many acting as slave-wage earners on the weekly quota system. Capoeira was already recorded and it is likely that Candomblé was being practiced in the Northeast long before the often given date of 1830. In Bahia, African women held a niche running the markets for food and Candomblé terreiros. In quilombos and on the periphery of sugar, manioc, tobacco, and rice plantations, the traditional Amerindian farming methods had created caapuera (extinct forest), a landscape feature that became closely associated with fugitive slaves and their fight against capitães do mata.

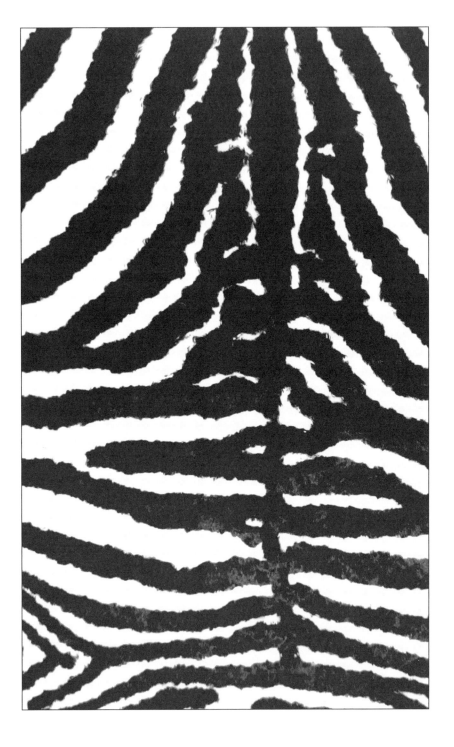

Chapter Six
"BRAZILIAN BANTU LAND"

Brazil's original capital city of Salvador, founded by Tomé de Sousa in 1549, relinquished the title to Rio de Janeiro in 1763. This event epitomized a shift of economic and political power from the northeast coast to Brazil's highlands, a shift that had begun after the first gold strikes seven decades earlier.

By the 1760s, Rio de Janeiro was the star commercial entrepôt of the colony. Sugar was still the main profit earner and remained so even during the so-called sugar slump of the gold era. The late 18th century brought a rising demand for slave labor. Brazil was diversifying with tobacco fields, sugar plantations, forest clearance, cotton, and mining. Benguela in Southern Angola emerged as an extraordinarily efficient port for supplying slaves. For the next fifty years after Rio became the capital, slaving to Brazil increased from Benguela and the East African coast, Mozambique, the mouth of the Zambezi River, Inhambane, and along the Loango Coast at the mouth of the Zaire River.

At the turn of the 18th/19th century, with the development of coffee estates, the region north of Luanda became vital as an exporter of slaves to ensure that Brazilian economic expansion continued. Exports of slaves increased annually. Only the Mina trade declined after it was internationally outlawed in 1815.

Rio's main export to Angola was gerebita—sugar cane brandy. Some of this came from the big engenhos, but much of it was produced in the several hundred small stills that littered the city. Luanda and Benguela were both packed with rum houses and taverns, which consumed approximately 2,500 hogsheads of gerebita per year by the 1780s. A hogshead was a unit of measurement equal to approximately 286 liters or 504 pints of liquid. To indicate just how much rum was imported into Luanda and Benguela, we see that 2,500 hogsheads was 1,260,000 pints or 716,000 liters of gerebita entering Angola via these ports each year. Other units of measurement regularly seen in Portuguese colonial import and export accounts include: *pipa* (500 liters), *barril* (85 liters), *almude* (20 liters), *canada* (1.4 liters), and *tonel* or plural *toneis,* which was a term for any huge water cask.

Two-thirds of Brazilian gerebita was exported to Angola. From the coast it was transported to the interior to be traded for slaves. It constituted at least six times the combined volume of all other Brazilian imports arriving in Angola through the ports of Luanda or Benguela. Competition among European nations to import other products to Angola was intense, though when it came to rum, Angolan traders preferred Brazilian gerebita. The Portuguese had no competition in this department, even from British suppliers of Jamaican rum.

Rio traders exported everything from cheese, to hides, manioc, dried meats, rice, beans, furniture, wood, and building materials like roof tiles. It was the Rio de Janeiro traders who put Benguela fully on the map as a slaving town. Benguela's climate and geography made it quite dependent on the food that Brazil could provide and 90 percent of slaves leaving Benguela were on ships bound for Rio de Janeiro.

Benguela was infamous as a death-trap in the 18th century. Southwesterly onshore breezes and a powerful northerly current flowing along the coast made it very difficult for ships to reach. It was easier to get at from southern Brazil than from Lisbon or even other Portuguese territories to its north on the West African coast, including Luanda.

Ngolo, the Dance of the Zebra

In "Capoeiragem—Arte and Malandragem," Jair Moura quotes Albano de Neves e Souza's influential theory that bandits in Benguela, *muxilingues,* used the steps of an Angolan folk dance as a fight.

> Among the Mucupe in Southern Angola, there is a zebra dance, the *n'golo,* that takes place during the *efundula,* the celebration of the puberty of young girls, when they stop being *muficuemes,* or girls, and pass to the role of women, ready for marriage and childrearing. The boy who wins the n'golo is directed to choose a wife from among the new initiates, without paying the dowry. The n'golo is *capoeira.* The slaves from the south that went there (to Brazil) through the trade port of Benguela took with them the tradition of fighting with their feet. Over time, that which was principally a tribal tradition was transformed into a weapon of attack and defense which helped them to make themselves felt in a hostile environment. . . . The worst bandits of Benguela in general were *muxilingues,* who, in the city, used the steps of the n'golo as a weapon.[1] (See Appendix A.)

For readers of books about capoeira, this quote is nothing new, and it won't be a surprise to see it here. The "n'golo" described seems to have become the pivot in an argument between those who say that capoeira comes from Africa, and those who say it was developed by African-Brazilians in Brazil. Writers like Nestor Capoeira agree with Waldeloir Rego, who believed that this idea of capoeira coming from the ngolo was a "bizarre thesis." The anthropologist J. Lowell Lewis says he hasn't been able to find any reference to the "Mucope" [sic] in anthropological literature, and nobody has yet provided any reference to the ngolo from primary sources preceding the ngolo-capoeira debate. Although Mestre Pastinha is reputed to have said he was told of the ngolo zebra dance through an oral tradition from his mestre, he did not mention the ngolo dance in his 1964 book.

Other mestres from the Angola tradition say that not only does capoeira have origins in the ngolo dance, but that they've visited Angola and met and talked with elders of the ngola tradition. There are also academic writers such as T. J. Desch Obi who have been to Angola and describe dances that are virtually mirror images of capoeira. When one studies the notes, one finds they relate to T. J. Desch Obi's own Angola field journal and other manuscripts of his. This is not to undermine the importance of his observation, but rather simply to assert that it doesn't represent definitive evidence of the ngolo as the original form of capoeira.

Field trips to Angola and Congo that use a participant-observer method and interview technique such as applied by Joseph C. Miller, in his study of early Mbundu states in Angola (*Kings and Kinsmen*), would be very helpful with regard to capoeira. Film, photography, region names, dates, and other verifiable data are the means to move the study ahead. Painstaking debate about a single engraving by Rugendas or hearsay evidence based on ideological bias is not going to get any closer to the origins.

It does become evident from historical documents and police reports, which we will read later, that capoeira was a fight practiced by a great number of young men captured in Angola, and shipped to Rio de Janeiro during the 18th and 19th centuries. As these men only had a short life expectancy once they arrived in Brazil, and precious little leisure time, it is apparent there was something they brought with them from Angola that culminated in an entity the police and judiciary called "capoeira" in Brazil.

Some argue that this certain something was emerging as *lagya* (Martinique), as Pushing and Dancing (South Carolina), as *soesa* (Suriname), as Knocking and Kicking (Georgia and South Carolina), as *batuque* (Brazil), as *danmyé* (Martinique), as *mani* (Cuba), as capoeira.

The ngolo dance described by Albano de Neves e Souza may well have had a link to capoeira, though as the original form of the art it remains spectacularly unproven. The issue became important at a time in Brazil when there were no doubt many antagonistic forces and ill-informed people who tried to deny African roots to the art form. In the 21st century it is time to grant that there is no contradiction between the reality that capoeira comes from Africa and is also "Brazilian."

In the 1960s the distinction between Brazilian nationality and African identity may have been so pronounced that the zebra dance was honorably seized upon in what appeared to be a vital struggle between antagonistic ideas. The ngolo was a potent symbol for Capoeira Angola and remains so today.

But why was there this contradictory antagonism? Originally because in a society built upon universal racism there was a problem between a thing being both African and Brazilian at the same time. We will see that a great number of people came up with many strategies to construct a "national" identity for Brazil that assimilated the African into a homogenous cultural vortex represented by the Green and Yellow, the "Nation," by Order and Progress.

The ngolo represented an antidote of sorts. But not everything is as black and white as the zebra. To spend much more time debating the ngolo without visiting the *mucupe* of southern Angola and accurately recording the encounter will become the capoeira equivalent of pondering how many angels are able to dance on a pinhead. No one denies that angels dance, but there is no reason why the surface area of the debated dance floor can't be widened

A way of fighting, sometimes resembling a dance, at others a game, was emerging out of Kongo-Angola wherever Bantu people were dispersed. Take, for example, the case of Esteban Montejo, a Cuban slave born in 1860, who escaped his plantation and lived as a solitary fugitive in the mountains for a number of years at the close of the 19th century. In his oral testimony to Cuban anthropologist and novelist Miguel Barnet in the 1940s, he spoke of life on Cuban barracoons:

> Sundays were the noisiest days on the plantation. I don't know where the slaves found the energy. The biggest fiestas during slavery took place on that day of the week. There were plantations where the drum began at noon or at one. . . . it started very early. At sunrise the noise began, and the games, the children started to spin around. The barracoon came to life in a flash. . . . folks just went on with their dances. The one I remember best is the yuka. . . . there was another more complicated dance. I don't know if it was a dance or a game because the punches given out were serious. That dance was called the mani. The mani dancers made a circle of forty or fifty men. . . . they wore ordinary work clothes and put red kerchiefs with drawings on them around their heads and waists. . . . So that the licks of the mani would

be of the most painful kind, their wrists were charged up with any old kind of witchcraft. The women didn't dance but made a hand-clapping chorus. They would shout from the scare they got because sometimes a black would fall down and never get up again. The mani was a cruel game. The dancers didn't bet on the challenges. At some plantations, the masters themselves bet, but at Flor de Sagua I don't remember them doing it. What the masters did do was to prohibit the blacks from hitting each other too much because sometimes they got so beaten up they couldn't work. Boys couldn't play, but they took it all in. Take me for example, I will never forget it.[2]

Then there is the narrative of John Stedman, describing a dance he saw in Suriname (Dutch Guiana) in the 1770s. Stedman is describing dances of the "Loangos" of Suriname. Loango was an independent kingdom extending from the mouth of the Kwilou to that of the River Congo. Portuguese power held sway in Loango, and from Cabinda, Loango slaves were shipped to both Brazil and Suriname in large numbers.

No people can more esteem or have greater friendship for each other than the Negro slaves, who enjoy each other's company with an unbounded pleasure, during which they are not destitute of diversions such as soesa, which consists of dancing opposite each other and clapping their hands on their sides to keep in time, when each with pleasure throws out one foot. If they meet across, the party wins one point, if sides, it is for the other, till one or the other has got twelve, sometimes twenty points, who gets the game. So very eager are they at this play, in which sometimes six or eight couples are engaged at once, that the violent exercise having killed some of the Negroes, it is forbidden by the magistrates at Paramaribo.[3]

Elsewhere, Stedman writes, "Never did I see greater feats of activity in the water, the Negroes fighting a sham battle by plunging, or rather tumbling like porpoises, when they strike each other with their legs at a wonderful rate but never use their hands."[4]

The Irish clergyman, Robert Walsh, doing a term as vicar to the British Embassy in Rio de Janeiro in the 1820s, wrote about African musicians and dances he saw in Brazil: "The minstrel is generally surrounded by a group sitting in a circle, who all unite their voices as accompaniments to the music." Walsh listed instruments these musicians used, including, "a single string stretched on a bamboo, such as I have described to you before at Chapado do Mato, in the Minas Geraes."[5]

He described also dances he saw on his travels:

The dances begin with a slow movement of two persons, who approach each other with a shy and diffident air, and then recede bashful and embarrassed; by degrees, the time of the music increases, the diffidence wears off, and the dance concludes with indecencies not fit to be seen or described. Sometimes it is of a different character, attended with jumping, shouting, and throwing their arms over each other's heads, and assuming the most fierce and stern aspects. The first is a dance of love, and the latter of war. Dancing seems the great passion of the negro, and the great consolation.[6]

It would be an untenable proposition that these varied examples of kicking, hitting, and fighting dances and games from the 18th and early 19th centuries spread throughout the Carolinas, Cuba, Suriname, and Brazil, appeared suddenly in the bodies of the African population as if by magic only on the New World side of the Atlantic Ocean.

What were the two colonial towns Luanda and Benguela like when muxilingues—the "worst bandits of Benguela"—were transported to Brazil in the 18th century? In the 17th century, the main slaving frontiers in Angola were near Luanda. By the mid-18th century, the whole country to the east of the Kwango was up in arms. Portuguese encouraged the wars that were fought so bitterly there. In southern Angola, bands of very hungry and desperate people moved nomadically to avoid the worst areas of violence. They built makeshift, temporary fortresses of upright pointed stakes for self-protection. These were near farming communities they could raid for food. Angolan kilombos of the same "palisaded" type, described by Father Cavazzi in Angola in 1688, differed from the well-established Brazilian quilombos. In mid-18th-century Angolan kilombos east of the Kwango, there was no attempt to grow crops. The brigands who inhabited these palisaded forts, driven to the very edge of starvation by drought and war, survived by eating anything available. They were heavily involved in cattle rustling in areas southeast of Benguela where cattle were raised. Taboo foods like lizards, snakes, and monkeys were consumed to fend off starvation. Any crops or food that could be stolen, even the flesh of prisoners who were too old to be exchanged or sold for food, were eaten in those desperate times. The brigands were far too poor to be able to afford firearms and always fought with the traditional weapons of bow and arrow or spear and club.

The slave business in Brazil completely changed the character of Benguela. In the mid-17th century, it had been mainly a port for the traditional trade of salt. Nearby Lobito had been a source of marine salt since before European involvement at Benguela Bay. Copper and cattle were also traded there.

Being so difficult to reach, Benguela remained cut off from the Portuguese colonial authority. It became the favorite base for any Brazilian, Portuguese, or Luso-African outlaw wanting to avoid prosecution, bureaucratic troubles, toll, or taxation. By the 1770s, at the time when it's known for sure that capoeira already existed in Brazil, tens of thousands boarded Brazilian slave ships in Benguela every year. In 1771 alone, 13,000 Central Africans were exported from Luanda and Benguela.

Talking of "bandits" and "merchants" in Luanda and Benguela is often a fine distinction. Bandits were major suppliers of slaves to the towns. They brought in the weakened and vulnerable people who'd been separated from their kin and homelands as a result of war and famine. Many merchants were debtors or criminals exiled from Portugal or Brazil. They'd often burned their last bridges and arrived in Luanda and Benguela broke, desperate, and striving for one final opportunity to scratch a parasitic living from the Atlantic Ocean trade.

There were very few first-generation Portuguese merchants who called Luanda or Benguela "home." Luso-African traders, a minority, were sometimes content to live there in the absence of anything better. But as even the more "upmarket" Luanda was a glorified graveyard, a hotbed of rum houses, violence, misery, and disease wedged between hostile kilombos, even a "merchant" who survived financially rarely lasted more than a few months before succumbing to the fevers that earned Luanda its nickname, "the white man's grave."[7]

If, after the failures that had already placed them in shackles on the shoreline, the exiled Europeans were inspired by any dreams— perhaps to raise enough money to escape back to Portugal in financial triumph, or to "marry up" with a well-placed African woman—those dreams never included putting down roots in Luanda's upper city. Even though the upper city's churches, governor's palace, and fortress were the pride of the town, residence in Luanda or Benguela for a single day longer than necessary was more the nightmare than the dream of the European immigrant.

Luanda "was a place where every variety of flotsam and jetsam from three continents washed up on the shore, including not only people but also merchandise, spoiled wines, bad rum, flimsy textiles, faulty guns, and other goods unsalable elsewhere in the world but sent to Angola for dumping on the African markets."[8]

By the 1770s, there were a dozen major slave merchants in Luanda, and four or five in Benguela. At Benguela they'd perfected a practice that the losers in the game sought to emulate. Portugal's secretary of state wrote, "One could not without great sorrow see how our Brazilian colonies have absorbed commerce and shipping on the African coast to the total exclusion of Portugal."[9]

The Angolan end merchants bought goods in Rio de Janeiro and Bahia with money made selling slaves. The goods, imported to Angola, bought more slaves. This kind of direct exchange of people for trade goods prospered in Benguela where Portuguese politicians rarely (never if they could avoid it) showed their faces. The bigger Lisbon ships also didn't go there. This meant Benguela wasn't flooded with goods offered on credit, as was the case in Luanda. "Rio merchants at Benguela . . . could command the trade by selling cane brandies for slaves they acquired on the spot from the rather less well-heeled traders of the town."[10]

By 1730, Rio traders had secured royal permission to import slaves directly from Benguela without having to deal with inspectors at Luanda. Captives were marched from Luanda to Benguela to join the mass coffles arriving from deep in Central Africa. Rio merchants, left to themselves, preferred to buy their slaves at Benguela and they were the main buyers until the end of the legal era of slave trade.

The Brazilian buyers settled the price in a buyers' market. Slaves were delivered in excess of demand. At the huge Valongo market in Rio, people were sold in lots, creating a class of specialist merchant called *comissários*. Comissários took over responsibility for feeding and clothing, sheltering, and finally selling the slaves in Rio for owners in Angola. The merchants in Benguela and Luanda needed to use these miserable men, as it was only after they made the sale that they covered themselves financially. The slave trade was often referred to as more a game of roulette than a legitimate business enterprise. Generally, if merchants built up assets, they wanted to invest them in Portugal, not reinvest them owning and embarking yet more slaves in Angola, thus multiplying their risks.

João Victor da Silva wrote in 1792:

> We . . . live in a country most unsuited to our nature. We are disturbed by the threat to life brought by continual and devastating diseases, and we become wanton with our sights set on the Fatherland, to which we do not expect to return as poor as we left it. The absence of more gratifying pleasures turns us to the love of money, which we still cannot acquire in quantities sufficient for the great expenses that we must here sustain, especially with the European imports on which we depend, and particularly with the drugs and physics of which we are in daily need. If this sole object of our desires did not quiet our spirits, we would be men worth nothing. Indolence would possess us, and misery would overwhelm our lives, because our wages and salaries come to only a small part of what it costs us to live.[11]

Many merchants bailed out and fled when they owed money in Luanda. They tried to reverse their losses in the slave markets of the interior, very dangerous places physically and financially, though because their mercantile bridges had been torched they had nothing left to lose. At this stage, they mostly disappeared without trace. Others, under siege with Portuguese creditors on one side and

Angolan wars on the other, seemed to posses nine lives. In the strange world of the Angolan slaving frontier, they were a weird variety of the rags-to-riches success story. These rogue slave traders and the pombeiros who represented merchants from the coast weren't "respectable" people, but neither were they bandits by the standards of the day.

There were, however, many bandits in Benguela and along the trails of its hinterland. Their methods of attack and defense were shaped by their access to arms and by the fact that many lived in kilombos in Angola, with the advantages and limitations that this implied.

Guns had changed the balance of power in Angola as they started to spread in certain regions. Traditionally, it had been followers and dependents that determined the power of kings and lords. The gun put power into the hands of ruthless warlords with few followers. These men generally made their camps in mountainous, rocky forts or unreachable sites in dense forests. They raided settled people and traded slaves for guns. Without musket, gunpowder, and lead shot, they would have been powerless. The opportunities opened to them by the slave trade made this type of brigand a distinct force in 17th-century Angola and onward. But the role of the gun in Central Africa shouldn't be overestimated and it was no wonder that capoeiristas in Brazil were renowned for their use of knives. "Even in Kasanje, the premier slave-selling state of the middle Kwango valley . . . and notoriously well armed by local standards, the reportedly huge army of the king still preferred to fight with bows, arrows, spears, and swords of local manufacture in the 1750s. The Lunda . . . fought only with daggers and spears, forging the barrels of enemy muskets they captured in their wars into the bladed weapons they preferred."[12]

On the Angolan central highlands, the Ovimbundu warlords maintained hostilities with each other throughout the slaving era. They had access to guns but used the services of their masses of dependents as spear throwers. They kept captives to populate their territories and traded them for gerebita, cotton, and guns. "Outright bandits and 'maroon' colonies of fugitive slaves thrived on the fringes of this chaos. . . . flights, seizures, and killings thus drove off the populations of the war zones. . . . Empty expanses in between the compact settlements were abandoned to all but outlaw bands and heavily defended trading caravans."[13]

The lower Kwanza region was a massive source of captives for Brazil via the port of Benguela. Fugitives here and at Kisama had formed large kilombos. The populations of these kilombos grew strong enough to mount attacks against the Portuguese. They took to highway robbery, targeting the goods carried by eastbound caravans. In fact, the trails leading to the interior had a terrible reputation because there were so many bandits ready to attack the caravans, using traditional methods—traps and ambushes, often armed only with spears, swords, and daggers.

These bandits converged in the towns of Luanda and Benguela and mingled with the slave traders, Luso-Africans, slaves, pombeiros, and others. They couldn't conceal muskets, but they could hide the long daggers with which many were adept. If these were the muxulingues, they were knife and sword fighters, and the fighting tradition to which they belonged was one of close combat without armor. It was the same fighting tradition to which Imbangala and Mbundu warriors belonged, based on attack and defense using sangar. There were other places in Angola and Kongo that used the same methods; in fact, these martial skills were used all over Central Africa.

The Ngola a Kiluanje kings and later Mbundu warlords had already begun to shed their Portuguese mercenary allies and train their own warriors (mostly slaves) in the use of the Angola gun against the Portuguese. Bandits who hijacked trade goods transported by caravans through the interior started using guns for their raids. Border raids by the Ngola a Kiluanje caused Ovimbundu people to seek military protection from warlords encamped on the north face of the central plateau above Benguela, or as far as Huila to the south.

It was the Lunda, attacking large, vulnerable communities in the easily conquered valleys on the edges of forests north of Mussumba, who largely controlled slave supplies during the 18th century, opening up a "channel of tribute . . . for slaves from the heart of Africa."[14] Many came from Kongo, Zambia, and even Mozambique—overland! (In 1787, Captain Louis Grandpré met a woman in Angola who must have traveled overland from Tanzania or Mozambique because she told him she remembered "seeing the sun rising over the [sea] water."[15] Slaves flooding into Luanda and Benguela became far more numerous after Lunda wars of expansion had erupted. From a base 600 miles inland on the Kasai River, the Lunda warriors moved eastward as far as Lake Tanganyika and westward to the Kwango River. In the mid-18th century, the Lunda capital, Mussumba, was the site of a massive slave fair. The supply line ran from Zambia to the coast at Loango.

By 1789, when Luanda derived 88 percent of its income from the trade in slaves, Brazil had been receiving Angolans by the million for more than two centuries.

The Bantu People

Who were the Central African people shipped to the seaports of Brazil? The Bantu languages spoken by people across most of Africa south of the equator are closely related and probably dispersed for approximately two centuries before the Atlantic Diaspora began.

Populations who lived in the western part of Sudan adapted successful crop cultivation in the moist woodlands, expanding to the edges of the Guinea forest. This happened during the third and second millennia BC.

Polished stone tools enabled them to move farther into the forests, where yams were a good source of food, along with fish from the rivers and coast. Bantu speakers migrated from Mount Cameroon along the Kongo forest and deep into the forest itself. This was phase one of the "Bantu dispersion" or "Bantu migration."[16]

There are numerous theories about the Bantu migration, some saying it never occurred. Linguistic and archaeological evidence shows migrations dispersed from North-Central Africa in the last millennium BC at a time when sub-Saharan Africa was still divided into isolated pockets of hunter-gatherers.

There was a migration south into the rainforests around the Congo and east into the East African highlands. One body of migrants may have moved southward through East Africa and another through the center toward South Africa. "In Zambia, there is evidence of at least three routes of migration—from the great lakes, from the Congo forest and from Angola. There is evidence that the Bantu ancestors of the modern Swahili peoples mastered sailing technology and possessed canoes and boats so they could make their way along the Zambezi River."[17]

These dispersions heralded the Iron Age in sub-Saharan Africa. The Iron Age originated in Africa around the 6th century BC in

Ethiopia, the great lakes, Nigeria, and Tanzania. At the end of the
Stone Age, Bantu speakers were already living in the Congo forest, so iron tools, axes, and hoes made the southern Bantu expansion from the Congo forest possible. Iron weapons were vital for
hunting and war, although the total presence of Bantu language
speakers over sub-equatorial Africa suggests a gradual expansion
rather than abrupt military conquests.

Farmers using iron clustered along river banks, the shores of
lakes, and the coastline and mountain valleys. Bantu cultural expansion came when the hunter-gatherers still using Stone Age tools
and weapons, who inhabited the drier savannas, traded with ironworking farmers, and settled in the same places, creating linguistic
integration.

"There are some 450 known languages in the Bantu family from
Gikuyu in the north to Setswana in the south."[18] Over the centuries,
iron-using Bantu speakers moved through very fertile regions, cultivating crops like yam, banana, and plantain. They gradually inhabited areas that were suitable for farming and livestock raising.

The Bantu people of West-Central Africa in the era immediately prior to the arrival of the Portuguese lived in the following
regions: the lower Kasai, the Kwa, the lower Kwango, the periphery of the Kalahari, along the rivers south of the Zaire, the Loje, the
Dande, the Bengo, the Kuvo, the lower Kwanza, the Lukala, the
Nkisi valley, the lower Zaire's main tributary, the middle Kwango
plains, south of the Kwanza at the upper Kuvo, the Kunene, the
Kubango, the floodplains of the upper Zambezi, and from
Kabompo and Lungwebungo Rivers as far as Victoria Falls.

They were gathered in the places with the highest rainfall and
fresh water. The lowlands, the valleys, and expanses of the central
highlands were well inhabited. In sandy terrain, such as the Kala-

hari, people lived only where there was regular rainfall and wetter ground. The rivers were the main centers of population and the people communicated and traded using canoes. Many occupied the low plains of the middle Kwango and the central plateau, with the heavier rains higher up encouraging agriculture. Farming communities lived in the river valleys coming down from the plateau's crest. Where rainfall was seasonal, farmers combined herding with agriculture. Even wilderness regions on the edges of the desert or in the swamps of the lower Kubango toward Lake Ngami were places with Bantu-speaking populations. Floodplains like the upper Zambezi also attracted settlers, as they had excellent natural conditions for people to live.

In West-Central and East Africa, states formed based on shared political and religious thought. They were pre-Muslim and pre-Christian, possibly originating in the Nile valley. "The basic ideas of the system ran sharply counter to the tenets of both these [Muslim and Christian] religions, and therefore . . . if the Nile valley was the point of departure, they must have started to disperse outward from that region before either Christianity or Islam became firmly established there."[19]

Bantus who went east came into contact with Islam in the 9th century, as Islamic settlers had come from the Persian Gulf to Manda Island, which is near the border with Somalia in Kenya.

Here were the most northeasterly Bantu groups, who became mariners and coastal traders, the main movers of goods on the coast from Kenya and Tanzania to Mozambique (although these places didn't exist as nation-states in those days, of course). They occupied islands like Zanzibar and northern Madagascar. The Bantu Swahili farmers and fishermen were original settlers of centers where great mosques were built. The 12th-century Kizimkazi in

Zanzibar or the early 13th-century mosque at Husuni Kubwa on the island of Kilwa are examples of this development. The intercontinental Bantu traders sailed with ivory, dried fish, vegetables, mangrove poles, and other goods.

This development on the east coast from the 9th to the 15th century was an era of Muslim expansion and there was general prosperity in the region. The traders imported Thai stoneware and porcelain from both Sung- and Ming-era China. Africa's first sub-Saharan mint was built for copper and silver coins by Kilwa sultans. Their governors were based in the gold port of Sofala and oversaw all the duties of sea trade and traffic between Zimbabwe, Katanga, and any other that passed through. Mombassa was a source of iron ore, a popular export to India, while Mogadishu was an exporter of cotton and camel hair cloth to Egypt.

Places like Kilwa and Sofala would become key targets for Portuguese occupation as the latter sought to replace Arabs as dominant factors in Indian Ocean trade as far as the Persian Gulf.

Bantu people also settled south of Angola. Bantu immigrants founded the civilization of the Mwenumatapa at Great Zimbabwe, a stone-built royal capital lasting from the 11th to the 15th century. This dynasty invested in vast cattle herds and controlled Zimbabwean gold exports from the Zimbabwean central plateau. It should be noted that the Lemba people of southern Africa claim to have built Great Zimbabwe. These are African Jews who are thought to have traveled from "Sena" in Yemen and dispersed throughout South Africa. "By the middle of the sixteenth century we know from Antonio Caiado, who accompanied Dom Gonçalo da Silveira to the court of the Monomotapa, that Moorish ngangas were the principle wizards of the country."[20] These "Moorish ngangas" are convincingly argued to have been Lemba. This question is thoroughly investigated in Tudor Parfitt's book, *Journey to the Vanished City.*

The origins of Great Zimbabwe are a riddle, not least because poor soil wasn't suitable to support agriculture sufficient to supply food for a large population, making imports essential. This riddle has intensified, as archeologists argue that the plateau's gold deposits, previously believed to have been the basis of Great Zimbabwe's prosperity, were not mined until possibly a century after the city's founding. The question today has as much to do with why that particular location as with who did the building.

Despite the Lemba claims to have co-built Great Zimbabwe, the widest consensus among archeologists is that it was constructed between the 12th and 15th centuries by the Shona, one of Zimbabwe's Bantu-speaking groups (who live in the area today).

The first Europeans to see Great Zimbabwe were the Portuguese. One explorer, Viçente Pegado, captain of the Portuguese garrison of Sofala, wrote in 1531:

> Among the gold mines of the inland plains between the Limpopo and Zambezi rivers there is a fortress built of stones of marvelous size, and there appears to be no mortar joining them. . . . This edifice is almost surrounded by hills, upon which are others resembling it in the fashioning of stone and the absence of mortar, and one of them is a tower more than 12 fathoms [22 m] high. The natives of the country call these edifices Symbaoe, which according to their language signifies court.[21]

The ruins occupy approximately 1,800 acres. In the late fourteenth century, the population of Great Zimbabwe was perhaps 18,000. At its peak, in the 14th century, this medieval capital controlled a large proportion of interior southeast Africa.

The amazing ancient buildings of Great Zimbabwe are situated east of
the Kalahari desert between the Zambezi and Limpopo rivers. They were
built by the Bantu-speaking Shona people of southern Africa and, despite
a mortarless dry stone construction, they have survived more than seven
centuries. Zimbabwe is a Shona word meaning, roughly, "house of
stone." The Great Zimbawe was used as a religious site for the worship
of Mwari (the creator of all things). The castle and intricately built
interlocking wall have a circumference of 250 meters and are over 5
meters thick and 9 meters high in parts. The interior was probably
reserved for the king as a place for smelting gold. Great Zimbabwe has
long been a symbol of ideological conflict, since many white Rhodesians
and then other racists have resisted accepting that sub-Saharan African
people were capable of building such impressive structures. Most of the
treasures disappeared when waves of Europeans ransacked the site after
its "discovery" in the late 19th century. Some of the artifacts from Great
Zimbabwe are examples of the way animals have been widely used as
religious symbols in African belief systems.

In southern Africa, the ancestors of the Zulu were the Nguni. There were also Xhosa, Tembu, and Pondo, all Bantu people who had occupied regions where rainfall and the climate made agriculture possible. The Transkei, Pondoland, Natal, and southern Mozambique were all inhabited by Bantu, while in the drier regions and desert, pastoralists and hunter-gatherers who were not Bantu (for example, the San, originators of the berimbau) tended to settle.

Another of the largest Bantu states, which we have already discussed, was the kingdom of the Bakongo. The capital of this kingdom was Mbanzakongo, situated at São Salvador in modern-day northern Angola.

Agogô

This kingdom was founded by people from the state of Bungu on the north bank of the lower Congo River. They were initially a small state but skilled ironworkers, giving them supremacy in the region. The Kongo language became widely spoken, supplanting Mbundu as the people were absorbed and subjected by the Bakongo conquerors. The position of metalsmith was held as an honorable role in the Kongo kingdom, and its practitioners were awarded privileges normally associated with chiefs. Iron products signified power and prestige associated with chiefdom. The *agogô* was an iron product with this symbolic and ritual importance.

Traveling in Angola and on the Congo River in 1875, Monteiro wrote:

> From Bembe we could descry . . . the "Quibucas" or caravans . . . of 200 and 300 natives, bringing as many as 100 large tusks of ivory. . . .

As soon as they came within hearing distance they beat their "Engongui" [agogô] as the signal bells are called, one of which accompanies every "Quibuca" and is beaten to denote their approach, the towns answering them in the same manner, and intimating whether they can pass or not, if there is war on the road, and so on. These "Engongui" are two flat bells of malleable iron joined together by a bent handle, and are held in the left hand whilst being beaten with a short stick. There is a regular code of signals, and as each bell has a different note, a great number of variations can be produced by striking each alternately, or two or three beats on one to the same, the lesser number on the other. . . . Only one "Engongui" can be allowed in each town, and belongs to the king, who cannot part with it on any account, as it is considered a great "fetish" and is handed down from king to king. To obtain the one in my possession, I had to send Pae Tomas to the "Mujolo" country, where they are principally made. . . . I believe he must have got it nearer Bembe.[22]

Bantus' traditional skills in iron and metal smelting, herding, and agriculture made them particularly popular among pombeiros representing the sugar industries of Brazil, where all these skills were needed. Monteiro wrote that "the "Mujolos" . . . are greatly prized as slaves by the Portuguese, as they are very strong and intelligent, and work at any trade much better than any other race in Angola." Monteiro was writing from Bembe, a Kongo province en route from the ndembu slave market, where captives traveled to the lower Zaire River and on to Cabinda.[23]

The kingdom of Kongo stretched from the Atlantic Ocean, bounded by the Congo, Kwango, and Dande rivers, and was estimated in the 17th century to have a population of 2.5 million people. On its periphery were smaller states, paying tribute to the ManiKongo, who formed part of the same political system. North of the Congo estuary were the Bantu kingdoms of Ngoyo, Kakongo, and Loango, all Bungu Kongo speakers like those who'd established the main kingdom. South and east were the regions of Okango, Matamba, and Ndongo. In Ndongo the most important of the local rulers were the hereditary monarchy, the Ngola (from which, we remember, Angola derived its name after Portuguese conquest).

In 1660, the kingdom of Kongo went to war with the Portuguese.

> The Manikongos were left too weak to maintain the internal unity of their kingdom . . . so that by the end of the eighteenth century . . . the former kingdom had shrivelled to a few villages around São Salvador. . . . Angola remained the supply-base for the Brazil slave trade, and during the seventeenth and eighteenth centuries was converted into a howling wilderness. . . . The Kongo kingdom . . . was near enough to the storm to be torn apart by it.[24]

Colonialism eventually overtook the slave trade and made Congo and Angola countries of European primitive extraction. During the later slave trade, as de Lima wrote in the 1830s, "Angola [became] far more a colony of Brazil than of Portugal." This began to change around the 1850s, when Portuguese imperialism regained its flagging energy and the Portuguese made efforts to conquer the Angolan interior. The governor of Luanda replied to any suggestion that free labor would replace slave by asking, "For what reason may the African Negro, who exercises no useful profession, not be subjected to forced labour?"[25] This view continued during the era of Portuguese extraction from Angola, which continued until the 1970s. By then, Angola and Congo were embroiled in the U.S.-South Africa and Russian conflicts of the Cold War, ensuring that military aggression in the Congo and Angola were maintained, virtually uninterrupted, for 500 years.

Chapter Seven

ISLAMIC REVOLUTION
IN WEST AFRICA

At the time when the Portuguese were colonizing Brazil, the Mande people, the Mandinga, were the most important state-builders on the upper Guinea coast of Africa. The Mandinga were centerd in Gambia (called Guabuu).

Farims ruled provinces at a distance of around every seventy miles. Mandinga territory was split into two principle provinces, Braço and Cabo. The Farim at the upper Cacheu in Gambia was the Farim Braço. The Farim Cabo was the Mandinga ruler at the capital of Cantor, south of the Gambia.

Politically similar to the kingdom of Kongo, the provinces of the Mandinga were subdivided under the rule of local chiefs giving allegiance to the Farim. There was a complex hierarchy and tribute was paid by subjects living in the Farim's sphere of influence.

Ultimate power lay with the emperor of Mali, to whom chiefs and Farim technically owed tribute. The Portuguese were very impressed by the way Mandinga always uncovered their heads in reverence whenever the emperor's name was mentioned, although Walter Rodney observed, "This was in most cases likely to have been the full extent of their homage to the ruler of Mali, given the system of delegated authority, which left most individuals on the coast virtually under the sole authority of their own chief."[1]

The people of the 16th- and 17th-century Mande territories—the Balantas, the Banhuns, and Djolas—mixed agriculture and cattle ranching successfully. They supplied their own food and had a surplus for the Portuguese settlers and supplies for slave ships. Rice, yams, millet, goats, and other livestock were traded between different villages according to the yield and surplus they possessed.

Populations were divided into modestly sized villages of 200–300 people, with the family being the integrating unit. Tribute to the Farim was less readily handed over where the physical presence of the Mandinga was more scattered farther inland up the rivers. "The reverence which the peoples of the upper Guinea coast continued to give to the mandimansa (emperor) can only be taken as evidence of the fact that the past glory of the Mandinga emperors continued to live in their minds, and they considered themselves subjects of the mandimansa even when there was no longer a Mandinga at the head of the Sudanese empire."[2]

At the time of the slave trade, lançados, Mina's answer to pombeiros (initially Portuguese settlers), regularly chose a convenient African village situated on a river as a base for delivering captives to the coast. On the upper Cacheu, the Mandinga called the Portuguese village the *tubabodaga* (the white man's village).

In the 1480s, Portuguese had traveled up the Gambia to have an audience with the Mandimansa in the city of Mali. In the earliest period of the slave trade, up to the late 17th century, the Portuguese moved inland from the coast. After a while, though, the Portuguese ships and merchants became themselves a draw for trade-motivated migrations of African people (Susu and Fula) toward the coast.

During river explorations and attempts to reach western Sudan, the Portuguese made many contacts with the Mande people. Besides gold, the Mandinga provided hides, gum, dyes, ivory, civet, and slaves. Lançados were prepared to journey inland to Mande territory to collect such trade goods and captives.[3]

The main trading centers were ruled by Mandinga. Cantor, 250 miles up the river Gambia, was the last port of call for lançado settlement. More than 100 miles up the river Cacheu, there existed a slave market, and another seventy miles up the river Geba at Malampana.

As the slave trade intensified, Mandinga traders focused on the Atlantic coast. Portuguese lançados, usually as desperate as their counterparts, the pombeiros, in Angola, were prepared to travel any distance to funnel supplies and slaves to the ships waiting to sail to Brazil.

The pattern of European influence on the upper Guinea coast was familiar. Local wars erupted that were totally unrelated to gaining territory or political power. Lançados, with a few notable exceptions, didn't raid for slaves on their own account, but encouraged local animosities, offered incentives, and provided weapons and everything possible to convert local populations to the cause of selling captives into slavery.

> No tribe was free from involvement in these hostilities. Some did not take an aggressive stand, but were liable to attack from other tribes: the Nalus from the Beafadas, Papels and Bijagos; the Balantas from the Papels and Bijagos; and the Djolas from the Mandingas. . . . Sailing south of the estuary of the Gambia, the Mandingas fell upon the Djolas as they gathered seafood in large parties on the coast. At first, the Djolas were taken unawares, but obviously they soon began to prepare for these attacks, and many Mandingas were in turn made captive.[4]

Mercenary slave hunters called *gampisas* operated in bands. An infamous one was led by Salim, dubbed "the highwayman" by the Portuguese in the late 17th century, who had sixty slave hunters under his control.

Mandinga Magic

There were many ways to be captured by gampisas and sold into slavery down the Cacheu, Mansoa, or Geba rivers in the 16th and 17th centuries. One of the most famous portrayals of a random slave kidnap comes on the banks of the Gambia River in the television series of Alex Haley's novel, *Roots,* when Kunta Kinte is overpowered by African *slatees* on the orders of an American factor. As John Thornton pointed out, such kidnaps, though possible, were not the norm. "Most were enslaved in Africa as a result of wars between African armies, or by raiders and bandits that arose from these wars, or from the breakdown of social order that often accompanies war, especially civil war."[5] Random kidnaps of the unwary were far less likely than sale as a prisoner of war to a Muslim slave trader in the deep interior.

Wadström, in Senegambia, wrote:

> Unhappy captives, many of whom are people of distinction, such as princes, priests, and persons high in office, are conducted by the Mandingoes in drives of twenty, thirty, and forty, chained together either at Fort St. Joseph on the River Sénégal or . . . to places near the River Gambia. . . . These Mandingoes perform the whole journey, except at certain seasons of the year when they are met by the traders belonging to the coast, who receive the slaves from them, and give them the usual articles of merchandise in exchange. . . . I was curious enough to wish to see some of those that had just arrived, [and] I applied to the director of the Company who conducted me to the slave prisons.

I saw there the unfortunate captives, chained two and two together, by the foot. The mangled bodies of several of them, whose wounds were still bleeding, exhibited a most shocking spectacle.[6]

Another cause of enslavement was punishment for criminal offenses after Mande law became thoroughly corrupted by the slave trade. A regularly fabricated crime was adultery or the much misused charge against the "fatal fetish." Citizens were routinely accused whenever people got sick and died without clear physical evidence of murder. Such deaths were attributed to evil and magic and the guilty party was charged with "eating the spirit" of the deceased. Technically, it was the dead person who made the charge and gave the evidence against the accused witch. This unlikely feat was accomplished by means of necromantic rituals, which gave unlimited scope for deceit. "When anyone was successfully arraigned on a charge, his family and dependents often followed him into slavery. . . . This was always so in witchcraft cases, and sometimes an extended family could be wiped out in one sale."[7]

Accidental death was often blamed on witchcraft performed by the deceased themselves. The dead *feticeiros* obviously had no defense and so their extended family were then liable for transportation to the Atlantic ships in their stead. This corruption of the law was commonplace by the end of the 16th century and may be why Mandinga became associated with witchcraft and magic in Brazil.

The Mandinga were the main collaborators with the Portuguese in Upper Guinea throughout the slaving era. Farim Cabo was the prime slave raider in his locality. The Muslim Mandinga were particularly prone to trade in captured prisoners. The Djolas suffered attack for hundreds of years from Mandinga aggressors. Djola, sometimes written Dyula, was also the guild name for Islamic Mande traders. Small satellite states, subject to Mandinga Farims, such as the Cocolis of the river Nunez, also provided slaves in significant quantity. When Portuguese slavers needed to make up the numbers of their intended quota, they sailed up the Nunez River until they reached Kagandy and were provided with captives by Mandinga agents of the Farim Cocolis.

As in Angola, the captives hailed from the interior, particularly the hinterland plateau and regions of the Futa Djalon and from the Tenda land tract along the Gambia. In Brazil, people who were not truly Mande or Mandinga, but Tenda or others of the hinterland plateau, were also termed Mandinga because these areas had been intensely culturally influenced for some time past by the era of the Atlantic trade.

On the Guinea coast, Tendas, Coniagas, Djolas, Papels, Nalus, Bijagos, Badjarances, Bassaris, Manes, the Casangas, the Cocolis, Susus, and Fulas were all shipped at various times to Brazil, especially between the latter half of the 16th and the latter half of the 17th century.

The Guinea cycle of slave imports to Brazil coincided with the Angola cycle, which continued throughout the 17th century. There was increased trade on the Mina Coast during the gold boom due to the Brazilian preference for Mina slaves between 1700 and 1775. From 1770 to 1851 the Bight of Benin was more heavily used. The slave trade brought revolutionary changes to West Africa after the centers of wealth and political power shifted from Sudan toward the coasts, boosting the development of the states in the immediate coastal hinterland from El Mina to Wydah.

Gold Coast, Slave Coast, Fanti, and Ashanti

For about half a century up to 1730, the Akan state of Akwamu won territory in the hinterland, which ran parallel to the Gold Coast and the western Slave Coast. Yet no chief could gain long-term loyalty from the Ga or Ewe subjects. This left a power void that was soon filled by the Ashanti. The Dutch, British, and Danish occupied many forts along the coast. These bastions of European representation leased land from coastal Africans who were usually Fanti. The joint interests of the Europeans and the Fanti were threatened by the expanding states inland. By 1743, the Mina trade had been organized in favor of Brazilian merchants instead of Lisbon bankers. Thirty ships a year sailed from Brazil, twenty-four from Bahia and six from Pernumbuco. They ensured good prices on the Mina Coast for Brazilian goods. By the 1750s the profits gained from Mina slaves were running at 45 percent, and were mainly based around trade in tobacco.

> It . . . relied on Bahian risk capital. . . . Given the African smokers' partiality toward the Bahian leaf, it became a small gold mine in itself for American growers and merchants . . . since Bahians sold it to the Dutch on the Gold Coast for African gold, while providing slaves for the plantations of the sugar captaincy at virtually no cost at all in réis. This Mina trade left Bahia, secondarily Pernumbuco . . . less dependent on labor from Angola in the 18th century . . . and confirmed a century-long decline in the presence of Bahian slavers at Luanda.[8]

In Brazil, when Mina slaves were spoken of, it usually referred to Fanti or Ashanti, while in the Caribbean, those from the Mina Coast were routinely called Coromantees.

> Of these Ashanti slaves one West Indian planter, Dr. Collins (author of a . . . manual, *Practical Rules for the Management of Negro Slaves in the Sugar Colonies . . . 1803*) writes that "being habituated from infancy to war, the necessary movements of which give flexibility to the muscles, and energy to the mind," the Coromantees were by far the most hardy

and robust; yet bringing with them into slavery lofty ideas of independence, they are dangerous inmates on a West Indian plantation.[9]

Captain Snelgrave sailed in the Guinea slave trade for approximately thirty years. His account of his voyages was published in London in 1754. He wrote:

> It had been the custom, time out of mind, for negroes to make slaves of their captives taken in war, and when they had taken more than they could well employ on their plantations they were often obliged to kill many. It followed that they welcomed an opportunity to sell their surplus slaves to traders. . . . I have been several Voyages, where there has been no Attempt made by our Negroes to mutiny; which, I believe, was owing chiefly, to their being kindly used, and to my Officers Care in keeping a good Watch. But sometimes we meet with stout stubborn People amongst them, who are never to be made easy; and these are generally some of the Cormantines, a Nation of the Gold Coast.[10]

Indeed, the "Cormantines" were an Akan-speaking people of the Gold Coast and their presence is noted in a great many rebellions in America, the Spanish Americas, and Carribean. On St. Jan in the Danish West Indies, Ray Kea has demonstrated that leaders of a major revolt in 1733 had been commanders in Akwamu before that state was defeated by Akyem in 1730.

These Gold Coast wars were fought in Ghana. By the early 1800s there were three categories of Ashanti state: (1) true Ashanti, with strong kinship, linguistic, and cultural ties; (2) southern Akan states, bordering the true Ashanti and sharing close cultural links; and (3) the northern provinces like Gonja and the southern Mossi, which were subjects but shared neither language nor cultural bonds.

The Ashanti occupied primary roads where they collected taxes and tributes or moved trade caravans to areas they controlled. They watched these roads closely to stop guns and ammunition reaching farther into the interior beyond the Ashanti sphere of power.

At the time of the Mina Coast slave trade to Brazil, the Ashanti wanted to control the narrow strip of land that lay between their territory and the sea.[11] This strip was occupied by Fanti kingdoms. Britsh trader Henry Meredith wrote:

> In the Fante country, and as far as Accra, [government] is composed of a strange number of forms; in some places it is vested in particular persons, and in other places lodged in the hands of the community. In the Fante country they very often change their forms of government on certain occasions, and unite, for their general safety. . . . when the cause of this union is annulled, they recede into their accustomed form of government.[12]

The Ashanti had wanted to invade the Fanti territories since the 1760s, after they'd consolidated states like Bono, Banda, Gonja, and Dagomba to the north. To the east they saw the kingdom of Dahomey conquering such Aja states as Allada and Wydah. These conquests characterized a general push toward the coast activated by the Atlantic trade in slaves.

Wars between the Fanti and Ashanti raged through the first two decades of the 19th century. It was as prisoners taken in these wars that many of the Mina slaves arrived in Brazil. But "after the Portuguese became middlemen. . . . West Africa looked to Europe and forgot about each other."[13]

Intra-African trade, such as that between gold-producing Akan and the specialist bead and cloth craftsmen of Benin (Dahomey), had all but completely stopped. Before the Atlantic factors destroyed it, this healthy trade had been conducted via the small rivers and creeks inland of Dahomey and Togo. The Atlantic trade was more profitable for the Akan, Ashanti, and Dahomey rulers, so the slav-

CAPOEIRA

ing frontier moved eastward from Ashanti territory toward the littoral that became known as the Slave Coast.

Islamic Jihad

The Malê (Muslim) influence in northeast Brazil originated because of the instability in West Africa at that time. The Islamic reform movement was arguably "as central to West African history as is, for example, the French Revolution to Europe."[14]

What began as an elitist, intellectual movement became a popular mass movement and ended in sectarian warfare. West African Islam (pre-18th century) was a "private craft" of scholars who congregated in towns and operated as advisors or political lobbyists to kings and ruling-class enclaves.

They engaged in intellectual competition, paying marginal heed to the masses in the countryside that practiced traditional Yoruba sacrificial rites in areas of Oyo, Ondo, Ogun, Lagos, Kwara, and the Bendel states of Nigeria. Such traditional Yoruban religions were also worshipped in Dahomey, Benin, and Togo to the west of modern-day Nigeria.

Many African kings were Muslim by the late 18th century and sympathized with pro-jihad urban reform scholars. These in turn were vehemently criticized by rural scholars. The rural group preferred teaching old-school Islam and accused urban scholars of breaking Islamic law. Some rural scholars traveled great distances, preaching and challenging urban reform scholars with accusations of their ignorance of Islamic legal minutiae.

The most famous of these men was Umar b. Jibril, who attracted followers in Hausaland in the late 18th century. Hausaland was ripe terrain for Muslim scholars at the time and many came from

populations of pastoralists and cattle herders, from the desert borders of Mauritania to Ahir. Fulbe pastoralists from the interior of
the Slave Coast were living through difficult economic changes
and many journeyed from Borno and Katsin to Sokoto in the northwest of Nigeria, where the career of a teacher-scholar provided an
alternative livelihood during economic crises.

The slave trade was disrupting the savannah economies. Wealth
was with those able to send caravans of slaves to Wydah and the
Bight of Benin, ruining villages and communities along the route.
During this exodus of people, Islam, unattached to ancestral sites,
became particularly attractive as a religious solution to the rup-
ture of ritual ancestral links.

Unannounced and Unplanned

The entry [of Islam] was unannounced and unplanned . . . and might
have dated back to the 17th century because . . . the northern neighbors of the Yoruba who live, for example, in Kano and other parts of
Hausaland in Northern Nigeria had received Islam as early as the 14th
century, and the Nupe, the immediate northern neighbors of the
Yoruba, were Islamized in the 18th century. As many Yoruba were (and
still are) traders, they might have come in contact with these northern
Muslim brethren from about the 17th century or even earlier.[15]

If Islam's entry was unplanned, its diffusion certainly wasn't. Its
spread in West Africa, particularly in Nigeria, had precedent in the
jihad movements on the upper Guinea coast. The Futa Jalon reform
movement and jihad of the mid-18th century transformed the territory of the river Gambia and river Senegal from:

[a] decentralized Mande society into a centralized federation with
mosques, an education system and Islamic law. . . . Though these

wars failed to increase the numbers of believers, they certainly reduced the numbers of unbelievers. . . . The most important export soon came to be captives for sale into the Atlantic slave trade; indeed, the Islamic state of Futa Jalon became the largest supplier in the region. The propriety of Muslims selling people to Christians was not, it seems, questioned, as it was in later reform movements. Jihad, then, became in part a quest for slaves.[16]

The Sokoto Caliphate

It was in Futa Jalon that Umar Jibril's student, the scholar-teacher Usuman dan Fodio, cut his teeth as a fomentor of jihad. Usuman dan Fodio was born in northwest Hausaland in 1754. His career evolved from that of a popular itinerant preacher to a militant leader of jihad. He became the leader of the largest reformed Islamic state of the 19th century, the Sokoto Caliphate, which covered thousands of square miles with its headquarters in Sokoto.

After his death in 1817, his son, Muhammad Bello, took over leadership of the realm, leading forty-seven military campaigns to defend the Caliphate and spread new emirates. In the south, Sokoto expanded into Nupe in the second decade of the 19th century; in the 1830s an emirate of Sokoto was established there. On the other side of the Niger, there was Muslim expansion into territories previously part of the old Oyo kingdom, which had collapsed and split into various Yoruba chiefdoms.

Eventually even Yoruba generals, like the most powerful Edun of Gbogun, were crushed by Islamic forces coming from Ilorin under the control of Abd al-Salam. Communities of Hausa traders were established in the caliph's domains and linked the Sokoto Caliphate economically across Benin and Togo as far as Ashanti in Ghana to the west and northeast through Borno to the area occupied by modern-day Chad. Hausa became the language of trade and empire, which in turn led to certain misconceptions about West Africans in the diaspora to Brazil.

Lovejoy commented:

Gambari is a Yoruba term for Hausa, Nago is a subsection of Yoruba speakers but was sometimes used as a generic term for Yoruba; Tapa refers to Nupe. . . . In the Sokoto Caliphate, conversion to Islam often meant becoming a Hausa . . . hence the recognition of Hausa-speakers in [Bahia] does not necessarily establish that these "Hausa" have much in common with 20th century "Hausa" since many were probably non Hausa in origin. . . . being "Nago" in Bahia in the early 19th century was not the same as being "Yoruba" in West Africa, but uncovering the difference and what was meant by these labels at the time is a major task whose undertaking must inform any analysis of the slave conditions.[17]

Islam in Salvador, Bahia

The reforming jihads led to prisoners being taken on all sides, which also changed the population of Bahia in the early 19th century.

Between the years 1820 and 1835, Nagos, Jejes, Hausas and Tapas (Nupes) made up 57.3 percent of Bahia's African-born slave population. . . . Nagos brought with them either the Oyo militaristic tradition or their experience resisting that tradition. As the [Oyo] empire crumbled during the first two decades of the 19th century, local inhabitants entered a period characterized by small, independent, mutually hostile armed factions formed and led by all powerful warrior chiefs—ologuns or oloroguns. Many slaves coming to Bahia had been leaders in Africa. The 1835 [Bahia slave rebellion] rebels were stirred not solely by religious fervour but also by men with experience in intra- and interethnic warfare, that is, in civil and national wars. These men, besides having lived peacefully within their ethnic traditions,

The powerful influence of religion in Nigerian politics can be traced to
the Islamic legacy of the 19th-century Sokoto Caliphate. The Caliphate
was founded by the Fulani religious and political leader Usuman dan
Fodio in 1809. After his successful jihad against the king of Gobir in
1808, dan Fodio's followers, and subsequently those of his son, Muhammad Bello, conquered most of the Hausa states of northern Nigeria by
the 1820s. The repercussions of war in West Africa were felt strongly in
northeast Brazil, as a great many prisoners of war were shipped from
Nigeria and Benin as slaves to Brazil.

had put their ethnic and native identity on the line in the most extreme
case of political contention—war. Ethnic identity continued to be an
organizing and sociopolitical cornerstone of African life in Bahia.[18]

The military conflicts in West Africa weren't always "ethnic."
Even though Usuman dan Fodio counted the Fulbe pastoralists
among his staunchest supporters and wrote his Islamic verse in
Fulbe, not all Fulbe pastoralists were converts.

Even in pre-colonial Africa, multi-ethnic nations existed. The Benin

Empire comprised . . . Yorubas and [many other groups]. The influence of the Oyo Empire extended into modern day Ghana. The Sokoto
Caliphate was multi-ethnic, in fact most of the great African empires,
Mali, Songhai, Ashanti, Zulu, etc. were composed of more than one
ethnic group. . . . Even the indigenous pre-Islamic Hausa-Fulani culture was not much different from that of other Nigerians. The difference
came with the violent enthronement of Islam in the 1804 jihad. Prior
to that most Hausas were pagans (Maguzawa) who had little or no
interest in Islam even though they had been aware of it for over 800
years. Like other indigenous pre-colonial Africans, the pre-jihad Hausas
never fought, killed, persecuted or discriminated on the basis of religion. They intermarried freely . . . with neighboring African peoples.[19]

Britain's abolition of its slave trade in 1807 had little impact on
exports. West African rulers gained huge revenues from it. They
weren't excited by the prospect of abolition. The compensation
offered by Britain, for instance, £400 to King Gezo of Dahomey
against his £60,000 annual returns, was hardly an incentive to shut
down a business that was built into African economy by the likes
of Britain in the first place. "In 1817 the British Foreign Office estimated that slave exports were about 25 percent more than they
had been in 1807. Between 1821 and 1845 roughly 654,000 slaves
embarked from the major supply zones: Western Guinea, the Bight
of Benin and the Bight of Biafra."[20]

Beware and take care of the Bight of Benin,
Few come out, though many go in.[21]

The verse clearly wasn't referring to Africans, as eventually 2
million people were shipped from a stretch of coast between the
river Volta and Lagos. Between the mid-18th century and the end
of the Brazilian slaving era (in the 1850s), 1 million of those people
were aboard Portuguese or Brazilian ships.

Yoruba Culture In Bahia

During Bahia's Bight of Benin cycle (1770 to 1851), the early years belonged to the Oyo empire. It was:

> the principle supplier of slaves to [Lagos and Porto Novo] . . . using a large market, Abomey-Calavi, as its chief trading centre. . . . The Oyo not only ensured that the merchants there had prisoners of war to sell but also bought slaves from their Arab northern neighbours and resold them to their southern ones, including the Dahomeyans . . . The Oyo still dominated the region, directly or indirectly at the end of the eighteenth century. . . . Only in the 1790s did Oyo power begin to decline.[22]

In the late 18th and early19th century, the Yoruba people spoke the same language and shared a unified culture. Originally the word *Yoruba* (said to have been Hausa slang for the Oyo), was applied only to the Oyo. There were many other groups—Egba, Egbado, Ife, and so on—who weren't Yoruba by name, but were culturally related. After the first Yoruba dictionary was written in the late 1800s by a repatriated Oyo Anglican of Sierra Leone, it became a British custom to call the people of western Nigeria and Benin Yoruba and this custom took hold.

Ife was the royal city and home of the most ancient hereditary kingship in Yorubaland. The creation tradition asserted Ile-Ife to be both the cradle of the Yoruba people and the cradle of the human race. It was said that in Ile-Ife, Oduduwa came down from heaven onto primordial waters and brought into being material earth.

Another tradition held that the Yoruba migrated to Ile-Ife from somewhere else in the northeast, possibly Mecca or Egypt.

Aja-speaking Ewe such as the Fon had a different language, but shared some of the Yoruba's religious ideas. They both believed in a Creator and Supreme Being. In Yoruba the god-head is Olodumare. There were also divinities brought into being by Olodum, such as the Orisa-nla, the arch divinity Esu, a primordial divinity, and Ògun, a powerful warrior. The Yoruba deified ancestors such as Sango, an Alafin Yoruban supreme ruler of Oyo. Sango, initially a king, later became elevated to divine status.

> The Fon . . . shared several deieties with the Yoruba and at times they came together for religious festivals. . . . current research indicates that neither the Fon [nor the related Mahli] claim descent from Ife. However [some branches] of the Ewe, who are found far to the west of the Nigerian epicenter, center of Yoruba culture, claim descent from Ife. . . . The Yoruba word to describe deities which are subordinate to God is Orisha. The Fon [word] is Vodun, from which the word voodoo is derived.[23]

Alafins were rulers but their power never extended over the whole of Yorubaland. Many towns founded by the Yoruba grew and developed autonomously, outside of the sway of leaders such as the Alafin of Old Oyo. Yoruba towns were subject to the laws and controls of their own rulers, rather than those of the Alafin. This made the economic and political quality of life dependent on the strengths and weaknesses of these individual rulers.

The Oyo was split into two provinces east and west of the river Ogun, which runs down to the sea at Lagos. It became the most powerful of the states coexisting within the Yoruba monarchical-political-linguistic system. The Oyo were powerful but totally subject to the Alafin. They developed a very strong cavalry, which they used to expand Oyo power and keep in check competing obas (chiefs), ensuring the Alafin's wealth. "Political and military allegiance did not follow ethnic lines: there were many non-Yoruba peoples in the Oyo empire as there were several Yoruba peoples who owed allegiance to Benin. But in spite of the sub-cultural differences, the Yoruba emphasized the importance of speaking the same language, worshipping the same gods and sharing similar political institutions."[24]

The Oyo empire at its most powerful (the latter half of the 18th century) could send forces into any state of Yorubaland or make vassal states supply military forces to assist Yoruba subjects against enemies. Old Oyo provided stability for Yorubaland as a whole even where Yoruba weren't allied to the Alafin. Oyo's cavalry or the military forces of satellite towns were always available as enforcers if they were needed.

Having been attacked by the Oyo in the past and resenting the rule of the Alafin, not all of Oyo's subjects were happy with this situation. In the 17th and early 18th century, areas that were independent of the Oyo empire coexisted in uneasy peace as long as they agreed to Oyo's economic policies. These areas included parts of Nupe to the south of the Niger, and Dahomey, including Aja-speaking populations such as the Gun, the Fon, and the Ewe. The Fon were responsible for the rise of the kingdom of Dahomey on Yorubaland's west flank. The Aja claimed ancestry to Ife way back, but they'd migrated so that Yoruba and their languages were now so different as to be unintelligible when they spoke to each other.

Islam, the Fall of Old Oyo, and the Rise of Dahomey

Contributing factors leading to slaves being exported from the Bight of Benin to Brazil were the Islamic Sokoto Caliphate, the fall of the Old Oyo empire, and the rise of the kingdom of Dahomey. Tensions on the Oyo empires peripheries got worse at the beginning of the 18th century due to the rise of the kingdom of Dahomey. Allada was conquered in 1724 and Wydah fell to the kingdom in

1729. Those who lived on the Abomey plateau (Benin) became subjects of the Dahomey absolute monarchy.

Internal conflict in Oyo played as much a part in its crash as the influence of Europeans. Atlantic trade was largely controlled on the African side by Dahomey or the Muslims to the north. The Alafin had competition within the empire, mainly from political chiefs (*Basorun*) who maintained their own contingent of troops. While the Alafin enjoyed a kind of ritual power it was the Basorun cavalry who were the real muscle in Yorubaland.

The chiefs preferred careers as professional soldiers and dedicated their lives to the art of war. Traditional Oyo cavalry units were archers and swordsmen. Because of the tsetse fly, horses were imported from the north and tended by Hausa vets. The horses became important symbols of wealth and status.

In the mid-1700s the Basori and the Alafin's own slave captains began to drift away from his direct control and a three-way power struggle emerged. Alafin tried to purge his kingdom of the Basorun and family, but the Oyo kingdom and its monarchy collapsed and provincial war chiefs broke away, becoming independent kings. In 1797, Kakonfo Afonja led an Oyo army mutiny allied to Basorun leaders, causing Alafin Aole to commit ritual suicide. His successors were weakened beyond repair.

In the 19th century, particularly after the fall of Old Oyo, professional soldiers emerged in Yorubaland who had no interest in maintaining any lasting peace in the region. Internecine wars and a chaotic political situation created intense competition for control, both political and military, in territories once dominated by the Oyo empire. In this climate, a new breed of very well trained professional soldiers became a significant regional influence.

Oyo refugees, now without a home because of the Fulani (Muslim) invasion, joined the wars. There was widespread use of guns for the first time, while "hitherto the major war implements were arrows, bows, clubs and cutlasses."[25]

Muslim Fulani invaders successfully defeated Yoruba war chiefs in battle. They provided Muslim charms for Yoruba warriors, while Hausa Muslims who controlled the cavalry's horses were also influential. Muslim slaves rose up and joined a rebellion in a special force called the Jama. They were victorious at the Islamic town of Ilorin, which evolved from an unruly part of Oyo into a vanguard of the Fulani jihad.[26]

The jihad was changing. Hostility to the Islamic reformers in Yorubaland was intense. The original scholars and sufi had always emphasized true jihad, the jihad of the heart and defeat of the self. Now Muslim communities needed protection, which led to jihad of the sword. Many great scholars died and a new generation of reformers ignored many parts of Islamic law, focusing only on jihad of the sword. Whole towns and villages of nonbelievers were carried off into slavery or killed along the way.

> As a result of the collapse of Old Oyo and the Fulani pressure the Yoruba people became increasingly pressed into the forest area. The Oyo abandoned the open savannah, except around Ilorin, and poured into the forest zone. . . . The forest belt became more thickly populated . . . and the coastal areas attracted more settlements than ever before. Through this enforced colonization, Oyo cultural influences on the rest of Yorubaland became more intense . . . such as drums slung from the shoulder as opposed to standing drums, and the royal cult of Sango, all spread more rapidly in the days of Oyo decline than in the days of Oyo hegemony.[27]

As the 19th century progressed, guns, professional soldiers, and standing armies increased. Warlords grew in power. This bore similarities to Angola, although the warlords' armies here were better trained and larger. Many of the big names in Yorubaland were young men who were bored by the prospect of life on a farm. Ibadan, the "city of warriors," provided such men with opportunities.

The city, home to the densest population of renowned warlords, was about 40 miles west of Ife and 70 miles northeast of Lagos. Ibadan had evolved from a military barracks into a city-state and those who wanted to gain military training or become a soldier in a private army made their way to Ibadan. There were many in this position after the collapse of Oyo towns. Another attraction of Ibadan was a difference in the laws of the town, so that regulations concerning career, apprenticeship, and norms of family alliance were overlooked, giving young men considerably more freedom to fulfill the highly prized ambition of becoming a professional soldier in the army of an Ibadan warlord.

This had obvious regional ramifications. For example, Egba-land, which lay between Ibadan and the coast at Lagos, was over-run and a large number of Egba's inhabitants were made homeless and either sold into slavery or became assimilated with the forces in Ibadan. After 1829, Oyo warriors who had settled in Ibadan occupied much of the Egba territory.

The Egba had access to the coast and wanted to remain in this advantageous position as middlemen between Europeans at the coast and the Yoruba of the hinterland. Many in Ibadan were hungry for access to the coast themselves, mainly to obtain guns. In the latter half of the 19th century, it was Ibadan's invasions of Egba territory that sparked off major wars involving the whole of Yorubaland.

Jeje and Nago

The West African economy was in a state of flux. Farms and plantations were dependent on slave labor. The motive of the jihad had much to do with the procurement of slaves. Prisoners were diverted to the port of Wydah, bound for Brazil. The Dahomey kingdom was particularly dependent on the Atlantic trade and Dahomey was largely responsible for the many Fon and Ewe people who entered Bahia, Saint Domingue, Cuba, and North America in the 18th and 19th centuries.

Since the 1730s, Dahomey's King Agaja had resented his enforced suzerainty to Oyo. The Dahomeans planned a revolt. King Agaja began dealing with the Europeans at the coast and Dahomean raids gradually depopulated the interior, even north of the capital city of Abomey where the king had his palace.

The Europeans made no headway in Dahomey. They were not allowed any farther inland than Wydah. Control of slave caravan routes from the interior was overseen by the king's army, paid from the royal treasury. The king used profits from the trade to acquire guns, which the army used to expand the kingdom further. The king allowed no other males of royal descent (or secret societies) to gain independent power. Chiefs were hand-picked and were not chosen by lineage. Only female family members gained autonomous political sway in the kingdom.

Royal festivals have become infamous in the history books because of the mass sacrifice of hundreds of slaves and captives that took place. By the 1770s, with the kingdom suffering from diminishing returns on its raids against its own subjects, King Kpengla decided the time had come to throw off the Oyo yoke. Dahomey (including Ewe and Fon Aja speakers) attacked the Yoruba kingdom of Ketu. These wars are said to have been the cause of animosities between Jejes (Fon) and Nagos (Yoruba) in Bahia during this period. "Jejes and Nagos . . . made up nearly 45 percent of urban African slaves and almost 47 percent of manumitted Africans. Nagos and Jejes divided the so called Sudanese Africans (i.e., West Africans) living in Bahia in 1835."[28]

In 1818, King Gezo seized power in Dahomey and strove to reverse the kingdom's flagging fortunes by securing new sources of slaves. By 1822, Dahomey extricated itself from Oyo power, which was already breaking up into chiefdoms. It was King Gezo who raided the Yoruba (Egba) stronghold of Abeokuta, and Dahomey became heavily involved in the early-19th-century Yoruba civil wars. By the 1830s, the Oyo empire had also been sacked by an invading army of Fulani and Hausa Muslim soldiers of the Sokoto Caliphate.

The summary in this chapter indicates why, during the Bight of Benin cycle, the ethnic makeup of African people in Bahia was recorded as shown in the following table.

Population from Manumission Lists and Probate Records

	Freed, 1819–36		Slaves, 1820–35	
	Number	%	Number	%
Nago (Yoruba)	275	11	424	19
Hausa	111	4.5	141	6.3
Jeje (Aja-Fon-Ewe)	288	11.6	240	10.8
Tapa (Nupe)	45	1.8	43	1.9[29]

Other African people listed according to their region, ethnicity, or port of departure were Bornu, Gurma, Calabar (Nigeria), Mina (Ghana), Bagba, Mundubi, Congo, Cabinda, Angola, Benguela, other Africans, and unknowns. Of the population in Bahia, nearly 60 percent were from the region of the Fulani-occupied Sokoto Caliphate, Yorubaland, or Dahomey. Many were Muslim by birth or were converted after being conquered by the Islamic reform jihad.

Chapter Eight

THE ST. DOMINGUE REVOLUTION

A series of upheavals in the colonies directly affected the enslaved of the Americas and Caribbean. These began in 1775 when the thirteen British colonies of North America went to war with Great Britain in the American war for independence. They formed the constitutional republic of the United States of America in 1787.

The American Revolution awakened the French peasantry and the newly powerful French bourgeoisie. They brought together the National Assembly in 1789 and the "Commons" pressed for reforms by the monarchy and King Louis. The National Assembly and its followers stormed the Bastille prison, which had become a hated symbol of monarchical power and repression in France. French revolutionaries organized a new government with the intention of abolishing feudal privilege in France. In 1791 King Louis tried to flee the country, but was arrested and guillotined two years later, closely followed by his wife, Queen Marie Antoinette.

As a result of the French Revolution, Napoleon Bonaparte was able to seize power in 1799. In an unprecedented surge of imperialist fury, Napoleon subdued most of Europe and pushed through political reforms that heralded the transition from feudalism to bourgeois capitalism throughout Europe.

The Rights of Man

On August 26, 1789, France had passed the Declaration of the Rights of Man. This document stated, "In the eyes of the law all citizens are equal," and in Article II, "The aim of all political associations is the preservation of the natural rights of liberty, property, security and resistance to oppression."

Across the Atlantic, thousands of miles from where these noble principles were being hammered out, the African workers slaving on France's sugar plantations were conspicuously not sharing these "natural rights."

At that time, the French Caribbean island colony of St. Domingue, previously part of Spanish Hispaniola, produced more sugar than Barbados, Jamaica, and all the other British sugar-producing islands combined.

The plantation system in St. Domingue was run in a very similar way to the sugar industry in northeast Brazil. Slaves on the island outnumbered planters by fifteen to one, and the deeply paranoid slaveholders treated the slaves of St. Domingue with a level of cruelty extraordinary even by the degraded standards of the time.

Many historians attribute the events that began on the night of August 22, 1791 exclusively to the influence of the French Revolution. Commenting on this bias, Lovejoy, particularly thinking of Eugene Genovese and C. L. R James, says:

> The French Revolution had such an obvious impact on the St. Domingue uprising that the African dimension is not relevant. As Thornton has demonstrated however, even the uprising in San

Domingo had its African antecedents, especially the legacy of the Congo civil war. . . . Moreover, influences from Africa remained a strong force in the struggle against slavery well after the 1790s, especially in Brazil and Cuba, where there was a continuous infusion of new slaves from Africa, from places where slaves had been coming for some time.[1]

Many uprisings and rebellions in the slaveholding colonies began with newly arrived African slaves. In St. Domingue, however, the Creole slaves born on the island shared the Creole language and the Dahomey version of Yoruba religion, Vodun (voodoo). They provided the grassroots base of an uprising that resulted in the overthrow of slavery in St. Domingue (later, Haiti). Early leaders of the revolution probably had no military training, but as these leaders attested, their strength was in the fighters who had served in African armies of Oyo and Kongo, and who did much of the fighting in the first weeks of the revolution. This explains "how the rebels, in a matter of two weeks, were able to coordinate large-scale operations, hold their own against soldiers sent against them, manage artillery, raise their own cavalry and acquit themselves well against colonial cavalry."[2]

Creole knowledge of the local situation and the newly arrived war veterans' combat skills enabled St. Domingue to bring the only slave revolution in history to a victorious conclusion. In the French Caribbean it was said:

The "new" slaves who escaped during the first days or weeks after they were bought from the slave traders were both the most numerous and least dangerous of all maroons, since they knew neither the countryside nor the Creole language. . . . Creole maroons were not as rare as one might think, but this was perhaps less because they were Creoles than because they lived in cities, where more slaves fled than on plantations . . . because they had almost unlimited freedom of movement as domestics, artisans' helpers or skilled laborers hired by the week or month.[3]

Quilombos, or *grand marronage*, had been a fact of life in St. Domingue since its inception as a colony. Settlers had engaged in battles with maroons for decades before the revolution. For example, in 1761, it was reported, "Protected by an epaulement [a kind of earthen parapet], the Negroes defied their adversaries by dancing. These latter became infuriated and rushed right into ditches, the bottom of which had been filled by pointed stakes of pine wood and then covered with lianas and creeping plants."[4] The maroon fortifications in St. Domingue were similar to those in Brazil's quilombos. Falola and Oguntomisin explain that by the 1800s, the majority of Yoruba states had a history of warfare and many towns had erected walls for defense and dug deep ditches for the protection of the residents within.[5] These Oyo fortifications carried over to the sugar colonies.

C. L. R James writes:

As early as October 1789, in Fort Dauphin, one of the future centers of the San Domingo insurrection, the slaves were stirring and holding mass meetings in the forests at night. In isolated plantations there were movements. All were bloodily repressed. Revolutionary literature was circulating among them. . . . In March 1791 . . . the French soldiers, on landing at Port-au-Prince, had given the fraternal embrace to all Mulattos and all Negroes, telling them that the Assembly in France had declared all men free and equal. At many places near Port-au-Prince the Negroes were seizing arms and rebelling.[6]

A week before the first attacks against the whites in St. Domingue, a voodoo priest named Boukman, an inhabitant of a maroon town, held a mass voodoo ceremony in Creole, in which the lead-

The Haitian revolution began in 1791 and, after thirteen years of fighting, ended with the establishment of the Republic of Haiti in 1804. This first independence from colonial rule in the New World was achieved with the military expertise of Kongolese, or Central African, infantry and West African Oyo soldiers enslaved on the sugar plantations of the French island colony of Saint Domingue. In 1814, merchants and citizens of Bahia wrote to the Portuguese prince regent, "Nobody with good sense can doubt that the fate of this captaincy will be the same as that of the island of Saint Domingue . . . gatherings of blacks can be seen at night in the streets . . . they know about and discuss the disastrous occurrences that took place in the Island of Saint Domingue, and one hears mutinous claims that by St. John's day there will not be one white or mulatto alive."(Source: Conrad, ed., *Children of God's Fire: A Documentary History of Black Slavery in Brazil*, p. 405.)

ers of the uprising pledged allegiance. "There Boukman gave the last instructions and, after Voodoo incantations and the sucking of the blood of a stuck pig, he stimulated his followers by a prayer spoken in Creole."[7]

Vodun was the religion of Africans in St. Domingue because many of the slaves there were Fon and Ewe from Dahomey, where Vodun is sill today the official religion of the country (Benin).

On the night of August 22, 1791, in the northern plain, fires were lit, plantations burned, and whites put to the sword. This marked the beginning of the twelve-year revolution.

Though France abolished slavery in 1794, Napoleon Bonaparte, the "people's champion," sought to reinstate it in the French Caribbean in 1802. Toussaint Louverture, a former Creole slave, emerged as the military and political brains behind the St. Domingue revolution. He took on Napoleon's troops and defeated them. Napoleon later described his invasion of St. Domingue as the greatest folly of his life. His troops found devastation everywhere: plantations and sugar mills burned to the ground, livestock slaughtered, mutilated white corpses decaying under the tropical sun.

The rebel commander, Dessalines, said, "The whites from France cannot hold out against us in St. Domingue. They will fight well at first, but soon they will fall sick and die like flies. . . . We will harass them and beat them, we will burn the harvests and then take to the hills."[8]

The French army was decimated by yellow fever and protracted guerrilla hit-and-run tactics. Even after the arrival of 20,000 French reinforcements, the writing was on the wall and Napoleon's army surrendered to the former slaves of St. Domingue.

Fear Spreads to the USA and Brazil

The St. Domingue rebellion inspired uprisings all over the Americas.

> Reports of the fury vented by the Haitian slaves on their white oppressors reached the United States, transmitted by refugees fleeing St.

Domingue. One eyewitness reported seeing "young children trans-
fixed upon the points of bayonets." Others described slaves dragging
white planters from their homes and tearing off their limbs one by
one or strapping them to wooden racks and sawing them in half. . . .
Slave uprisings in the United States greatly increased. . . . In the case
of one major slave revolt . . . in 1802, to burn Charleston, South Carolina, for example, evidence established that Vesey [the leader] had
communicated with Haitian blacks and even expected a Haitian invasion to support his rebellion in South Carolina.[9]

Napoleon and St. Domingue created wide repercussions in Brazil
at the turn of the19th century. First, the world's sugar markets had
been deprived of their biggest producer, so Bahia and Pernambuco
experienced increased demand for their sugar. A consequence of
this was increased transport of Africans from the Bight of Benin
to Bahia.

France was aiming to complete a total blockade against Britain.
To achieve this, Napoleon needed to seize power in Portugal.
French soldiers crossed the border from Spain in 1807. Prince Dom
João VI of Portugal, along with his entire court and 15,000 others,
fled to Brazil, escorted by British ships. Britain, enjoying an industrial revolution that had been significantly financed by Brazilian
gold, was becoming a world power and Portugal's main ally against
Napoleon. Dom João VI had little room to manuever. If Britain
said jump, the prince jumped. He ensured that Britain's export
advantages to Brazil were even better than Portugal's.

Abolition

The power brokers in Brazilian society, often referred to as the
elite, were gravely worried about Britain's domestic policies. In

January 1807, a bill was passed in the British Parliament to abolish Britain's own 200-year-old slave trade. Using their stranglehold on Brazil, the British forced Portugal to sign treaties restricting slave trade to its colonies and making vague promises to restrict internal slave trade in the future.

Brazilian planters were horrified by these developments, which only added to their other expressed or inner terrors. A climate approaching hysteria had been created by news of the killings on the sugar plantations in St. Domingue. The rumors slowly infiltrated Brazil's plantations. Up to now, the main African solution to bondage had been the quilombo, manumission, paramilitary service, insubordination, or attempting to achieve less punishing workloads. After St. Domingue, either by inspiration or because of the huge influx of trained African soldiers to Brazil, the solution to slavery increasingly veered toward armed revolt.

The following petition was sent to the Prince Regent by "merchants and citizens of Bahia" in 1814:

> Nobody with good sense can doubt that the fate of this captaincy will be the same as that of the island of Saint Domingue, and for two reasons. First because of the enormous advantage they have in numbers, and this in a people accustomed to hardship, and so barbarous that when they attack they don't fear death. . . . And the second reason for reaching this conclusion is the relaxation of customs and lack of civility which are commonly observed in this city because of the many liberties that have been granted to them. . . . What is most amazing in this lamentable and disastrous situation is the government's indifference. . . . it even permits and recommends in its first and only order of the day . . . that the blacks be allowed to entertain themselves with their dances in the two plazas named Barbalho and Graça, places as dangerous for a gathering as any that exist, without

considering what they might do there, and when in fact, in the present circumstances, not even three should be allowed to walk together . . . it is even suggested in this first order that interference with the batuques which might be performed elsewhere should be carried out with great moderation. Perhaps we should ask them on our knees not to dance the batuque and not to convert this country into a new Mina Coast, as they have been doing up to this time.[10]

The nervous representative of the Bahian citizens group continued:

Failure to establish firm principles spoils these people; fear and rigorous punishment are the only way to make them behave correctly. Since their batuques have been allowed (they are in fact banned by statutes) and since they have been permitted to dress themselves with pageantry and public ceremony, and paying homage to one another, gathering together to play a kind of single stringed instrument resembling a guzla—it is since all this has been allowed that we have witnessed most of the acts of violence and disobedience. . . . gatherings of blacks can be seen at night in the streets as before, conversing in their language and saying whatever they like, and with constant whistling and other signals. They are so impertinent that even in our language they blurt out their reasons for putting off the day of the planned revolt. They know about and discuss the disastrous occurrences that took place on the Island of Saint Domingue, and one hears mutinous claims that by St. John's day there will not be one white or mulatto alive.[11]

The writers of that petition were abolitionists. The Bahian merchants were forever making demographic calculations and finding the math stacked against them. The whistling and hand signals the petitioner complained about were soon dealt with. "Slaves were also forbidden [by ordinance in 1825], and not only slaves but any Negro or colored person, to stand on the street corners without good reason and even to whistle or give any other signal."[12]

Every time the elite noticed Africans behaving in ways that threatened them, they decreed an ordinance. Musical gatherings and batuques were main targets, and capoeira would have been included as a batuque when it wasn't mentioned specifically by name. The measures were in vain. Peace or harmony was impossible under slavery. A representative of the planter class saw it clearly and wrote after the 1814 rebellion in Salvador:

> It can be calculated that there are twenty-four to twenty-seven blacks for every white or mulatto, and here we include only those in the city. Outside the situation creates a sense of horror. We need only to recognize that there are 408 plantations, including those growing sugar, tobacco and subsistence crops, and that, estimating one hundred head to a plantation, this comes to 40,800 blacks, whereas there are not more than six whites or mulattoes per plantation, if in fact that many. It is sometimes argued that they are of different nations and so unable to unite their forces. Well, the opposite has happened in the present revolt, in which, aside from Hausas [from Nigeria and Sudan], those of the Nagó, Calabar [mainly from eastern Nigeria], and other nations are involved. And so it must be, because the desire to free themselves is common to all.[13]

Revolts flared periodically. The so-called Revolt of the Tailors in 1798 heralded a proliferation of slave revolts. Also called the Inconfidência Baiana, the revolt actually involved a mix of intellectuals, soldiers, artisans, *mestiços*, and slaves. The leaders were tailors from Salvador who modeled their activities on the French Revolution. They placed handwritten bills on walls in Salvador, calling for the abolition of slavery and end to racial discrimination, free trade overseas, and the seizing of church property. Slave revolts in Brazil mainly involved *boçal* slaves—those born in Africa. They occurred more frequently after 1807, culminating in a famous conspiracy among *nagôs* in Bahia in 1835. The leaders were often individuals with revolutionary experience in Africa and knowledge of revolutionary ideas in Europe. Many of the Portuguese colonists were barely literate in Portuguese, let alone Arabic, and had no means to read Arabic bills posted in churches and other meeting places.

The authorities got wind of the tailors' revolt, and the famous Inconfidência Mineira in Minas Gerais. The leaders were arrested and executed before anything larger could come of them. Yet police and government agents weren't omnipotent. In 1810 groups of African rebels attempted to kill all the whites living in a cluster of plantations in Bahia. Starting at a warehouse about a league outside Salvador, they joined other slaves from plantations and farms in the area, shouting, "Freedom. Long live the blacks and their King and death to whites and mulattoes."[14]

In Brazil, as in St. Domingue, there was animosity between African slaves and mulattos, the latter having secured a degree of relative privilege and being likely to side with the whites when push came to shove. The battle lines were drawn along racial lines connected to skin color. Whether a slave was born in Africa or Brazil also had an effect. Unlike St. Domingue, where creoles played a crucial role in the revolution, Reis reported that "Native born blacks [from Brazil] and mestiços did not take part in any of the more than twenty Bahian slave revolts prior to 1835."[15]

Engenho Santana

Between 1800 and 1835, jejes and nagôs exerted a powerful cultural influence in the city of Salvador. Candomblé houses multiplied and Yoruban languages were spoken. Around 185,000 slaves from the

Bight of Benin (old Dahomey and Yorubaland) entered Bahia between 1801 and 1830.

At the end of the Napoleonic wars in 1815, at the Congress of Vienna, the Portuguese agreed to cease trading slaves anywhere north of the equator. Britain gained the right to board and seize ships suspected of slaving. The treaty, aimed at reducing slavery, had no such effect and in fact coincided with the most intensive period of Brazilian slaving since 1500.

Uprisings and rebellions continued constantly in the city and on the engenhos. Engenho Santana in Ilhéus provides a case history. It had originally been worked by Amerindian labor under the control of Jesuits. By the 1780s, an African workforce had become organized and unwilling to accept the conditions of their bondage.

Santana had 300 slaves. In 1789, the majority escaped into the surrounding countryside, led by a *crioulo cabra* (very dark-skinned mulatto) named Gregorio Luis (thus disproving Reis's contention that no creole slave had ever led an uprising prior to 1835). They dismantled and took the equipment, closing the sugar mill for two years. A Royal Magistrate's letter of 1806 explained: "The majority of the slaves . . . divided into errant and vagabond bands throughout the territory of the engenho, so absolute and fearless that the consternation and fright of their master increased in consideration that he might one day fall victim to some disaster. . . . Matters being in this situation, the rebels sent emissaries to their master [having already killed the sugar master and overseer]." Gregorio Luis was caught and imprisoned for life, while the rest were sold to the captaincy of Maranhão.

A document written by Gregorio Luis provides one of the few historical records of a Brazilian slave's voice. He made very specific demands:

Treaty Proposed To Manoel Da Silva Ferreira By His Slaves During The Time That They Remained In Revolt. . . .

My Lord, we want peace and we do not want war; if My Lord also wants our peace it must be in this manner, if he wishes to agree to that which we want. In each week you must give us the days of Friday and Saturday to work for ourselves not subtracting any of these because they are Saint's days. To enable us to live you must give us casting nets and canoes. You are not to oblige us to fish in the tidal pools nor to gather shellfish, and when you wish to gather shellfish send your Mina blacks.

Make a large boat so that when it goes to Bahia we can place our cargoes aboard and not pay freightage. In the planting of manioc we wish the men to have a daily quota of two and one half hands and the women, two hands. The daily quota of manioc flour must be five level alqueiras, placing enough harvesters so that these can serve to hang up the coverings. The daily quota of sugar cane must be of five hands rather than six and of ten canes in each bundle. On the boat you must put four poles, and one for the rudder, and the one at the rudder works hard for us. The wood that is sawed with a handsaw must have three men below and one above. The measures of firewood must be as practiced here, for each measure a woodcutter and a woman as the wood carrier.

The present overseers we do not want, choose others with our approval.

At the milling rollers there must be four women to feed in the cane, two pulleys, and a carcanha [a woman who swept the engenho and did other chores]. At each cauldron there must be one who tends the fire and in each series of kettles the same, and on Saturday there must be without fail work stoppage at the mill. The sailors who go in the launch beside the baize shirt that they are given must also have a jacket of baize and all the necessary clothing.

We will go to work the cane field of Jabirú this time and then it must remain as pasture for we cannot cut cane in a swamp. We shall be able to plant our rice wherever we wish, and in any marsh, without asking permission for this, and each person can cut jacaranda or any other wood without having to account for this.

Accepting all the above articles and allowing us to remain always in possession of the hardware, we are ready to serve you as before because we do not wish to continue the bad customs of the other engenhos. We shall be able to play, relax, and sing any time we wish without your hindrance nor will permission be needed.[16]

"We shall be able to play, relax, and sing any time we wish"

Notable is the demand that the slaves be allowed to "play, relax, and sing" without the master's permission or interference. On plantations and in the cities, the work was piecework, controlled by quotas. The day ended when laborers had completed their quota. It was usual for slaves to "multitask" slave work with private enterprises such as basketweaving, food selling, or music and play. The quota system enabled plantation managers to force work at the maximum pace from their slaves, who naturally wanted to finish as quickly as possible. The daily quota might take eighteen to twenty hours to complete. How was it possible in these circumstances for slaves to have a recreational social life involving music and play? Observers often wondered how slaves could toil for hours every day and then spend the night drumming and dancing.

Cultural life and activities not related to work were tolerated insofar as they provided the minimum morale needed for slaves to continue working day to day. Drumming, singing, dancing, playing the berimbau, even playing capoeira, were adapted to the conditions of slavery in different places in the town and country. Some music came in the form of work songs. Capoeira evolved with regional characteristics in Brazil. Forms, instruments, and activities that had one function in Africa changed function in Brazil.

Work Songs

In his *Viagem Pitorêsca e Histórica ao Brasil*, Jean-Baptiste Debret included a painting of an elderly blind slave begging in the streets of Rio de Janeiro. Begging was often the occupation of slaves who had been awarded manumission due to handicaps that stopped them from working. The blind man is shown playing a berimbau, accompanied by a young boy who carries a sugar cane, "destined to his nourishment."

Debret, who was in Brazil between 1816 and 1831, wrote:

> Initially amazed by the huge crowd of slaves spread through the streets of Rio de Janeiro, the calmer observer immediately recognizes the particular character of the singing and dancing, each of the black nations that are mingled there.

> It is mainly in the plazas, around the public fountain, usual places of meetings of slaves, that many times, one inspired by missing his homeland, remembers a song. Listening to the voice of his compatriot, the others suddenly enraptured, gather around the singer and follow each verse with a national chorus, or simply a specific cry, a kind of odd refrain articulated in two or three sounds, susceptible however to a character

> Almost always this chant that electrifies them is accompanied by an improvised pantomime, or varied successively by the spectators that want to figurate in the middle of the circle formed around the musicians.

Those African troubadors whose eloquence is fertile of love stories, usually end their naive stanzas with some lascivious words, followed by analogous gestures, an infallible way to make the black audiences cry with joy, and to mix applause with whistles, treble screams, contortions and jumps. Fortunately, this explosion is momentous once they run away in all directions in order to avoid the repression of the police soldiers that chase them with clubs.[17]

Two European visitors to Salvador in the early 19th century detailed how work and other activities were combined:

Immense numbers of tall, athletic negroes are seen moving in pairs or gangs of four, six or eight, with their loads suspended between them on heavy poles. Many more of their fellows are seen sitting upon their poles, braiding straw, or lying about the alleys and corners of the streets, asleep. . . . The sleepers generally have some sentinel ready to call them when they are wanted for services . . . they often sing and shout as they go, but their gait is necessarily slow and measured, resembling a death march.[18]

An English merchant described the singing of African slaves at work in Bahia:

During the time of carrying heavy burdens through the streets they sing a kind of chorus, a very useful manner of warning persons to get out of the way. This chorus generally consists of one of the blacks chanting a remark on anything he sees, and the other comes in with a chorus. . . . I have noticed, too, that when the work is heavy, or the burden is being carried uphill, that they become much more vigorous in their shouts, aiding their labour and varying their song . . . and they are extremely independent, they would rather lose the chance of gaining a wage than carry more than what they thought proper.[19]

In the countryside, a 19th-century American traveler wrote about a plantation in Paraíba:

For those who did the work of the fazenda—the slaves, men, women and children, many of them recent arrivals from Mozambique, Angola, the Congo, and Benguela—Saturdays and saints' days were eagerly awaited. . . . Two or three slaves played the drums placed near the fire, where they could be heated when necessary. The slaves—men in white pants and striped shirts, women in blouses and wide, gathered skirts, kerchiefs on their heads—danced separately near the drummers, moving in a counter-clockwise circle. A master singer sang the first line of a riddle [jongo], and the assembled slaves repeated the refrain. If no person could sing the answer to the riddle, a new one was sung. In the mixture of African tongue and Portuguese, the Negro slaves mocked their masters and themselves. There were other dances mentioned by contemporary observers, the lundú and the batuque. Often the dances continued far into the night with little thought of the early hour at which [the] fazenda routine was resumed.[20]

This dance, the *lundu*, along with the *modinha*, was a forerunner of samba, and was already popular by the late 1700s. From Pernambuco to Minas Gerais there were dances on feast days, often celebrating the coronation of African kings, sometimes called Kings of Congo. In the early 19th century, in Pernambuco, Henry Coster wrote:

The election of a King of Congo by the individuals who come from that part of Africa, seems indeed as if it would give them a bias towards the customs of their native soil; but the Brazilian Kings of Congo worship Our Lady of the Rosary, and are dressed in the dress of white men; they and their subjects dance, it is true, after the manner of their country; but to these festivals are admitted African negroes of other nations, creole blacks, and mulattos, all of whom dance after the same manner; and these dances are now as much the national dances of Brazil as they are of Africa.[21]

A German, Von Martius, in Minas Gerais in 1818, wrote of a local King of Congo and Queen Xinga, whose titles referred back to the famous Angolan Queen Nzinga of Matamba. A few years later, also in Minas Gerais, Count Francis de la Porte de Castelneau wrote:

> The king had a black mask. . . . The court, whose costumes mixed all colours with extravagant decorations, was seated on either side of the king and queen; then came an infinity of other characters, the most considerable of which were without doubt great captains, famous warriors or ambassadors of distant authorities, all dressed up in the style of the Brazilian Indians, with great headdresses of feathers, cavalry sabres at their sides, and shields on their arms. In this tumult, they mixed national dances, of dialogues between people, between these people and the king, or between the king and the queen, simulated battles and all types of somersaults.[22]

The judiciary and their cavalry made a full-time occupation of breaking up African gatherings, particularly those accompanied by music and dance. Brazilian politicians weighed the relative advantages and dangers of batuques and African drum sessions. Their usual conclusion was that any group of Africans massing for activities other than work was threatening. As far back as 1559 a Portuguese decree stated:

> The King, our Lord, orders that in the city of Lisbon, and one league around it, there might be no assembly of slaves or dances or playing of musical instruments performed in their [the African] manner, either at night or during the day, on feast days or during the week, under penalty of being arrested, and each one of those who play instruments or dance is to pay a thousand reaes to whoever captures him, and those who do not dance and are arrested for being present are to pay five hundred reas. And that the same prohibition be understood for free blacks.[23]

These laws extended to Brazil and continued to be updated throughout the captaincies. The labyrinth of rules made it seemingly illegal for African people to live at all. There were laws against religious worship, gambling, traveling outside their master's plantation, congregating in groups of more than three outside the plantation, begging, carrying weapons, wearing gold, wearing silk, wearing shoes, and wearing good quality cotton, fine wool, and Dutch linen. Any breach of this mid-18th-century dress code was punished by a fine. "Or not having the money to satisfy the fine, they will be whipped in the most public place in the town, in whose district they may reside; and for the second offence . . . they will be imprisoned in the public jail until they may be exiled to the island of São Tomé for the rest of their lives."[24]

Batuques Are Forbidden

Any slaves carrying knives or other weapons were punished with "one hundred lashes, administered on the pillory [*pelourino*], and repeated for ten alternating days."[25] But laws were just as prevalent to restrict music, dancing, and religious worship as they were for weapons. Many ordinances decreed against music, drumming, and dance gatherings. For example:

City of Desterro, Santa Catarina, Law of May 10, 1845. . . . Article 38. From this time on assemblies of slaves or freed persons intended to form batuques are forbidden, as well as those which have as their purpose the supposed African royal ceremonies.26

City of Diamantia, Minas Gerais, Law of March 26, 1846. . . . Article 41. Negro dances with hubbub and shouting [*batuques com algasarra*] which disturb the neighbourhood are forbidden.27

Town of Itajubá, Minas Gerais, Law of 1853. . . . Article 129. It is forbidden to dance batuque in the houses of the villages accompanied by loud noise either during the daytime or at night, in such a way that it disturbs the neighbourhood. . . . Article 130. Negro dances . . . which the slaves are accustomed to celebrate on certain days of the year are permitted, with the condition that they not be held at night.[28]

City of Recife, 1833. . . . Paragraph 3. From this time on the games which the blacks and vagrants are accustomed to play on the streets, plazas, beaches, and stairways are forbidden; under penalty of suffering, those who are free, from two to six days in jail . . . and slaves from 12 to 36 bolos [a crack on the hand with a wooden paddle] administered in the same jail.[29]

Town of Itamaracá, 1836. . . . Article 6. Screaming in the streets and in the churches . . . batuques of the blacks at any hour, and boisterous diversions are forbidden: violators will pay a fine of 4$000 reis or will suffer 8 days in jail, and being a slave will receive 36 palmatoadas [the same as bolas], and twice the number in case of recurrence.[30]

Town of Cabo, 1836. Tranquility and Public Morality Article 1. Every shopowner who allows slaves to remain in his shop longer than the time needed to do their buying or selling, or who there allows meetings, dances, and drumbeating will be fined 4$000 reis.[31]

Town of Brejo, 1836. . . . Article 20. Shouting after hours is forbidden in the streets of this town, as well as batuques of any kind . . . being a slave he will suffer 25 lashes, his master having the option of a fine.[32]

Legislação do Rio de Janeiro . . . 1836. Ordinance 6. Every person who in his house or residence, or in some other adjacent house, allows gatherings for dances, or Candomblé, in which outside slaves take part will be punished. . . . The slaves who are arrested at such gatherings will be punished with from fifty to a hundred lashes.[33]

Batuques had taken place in Salvador's town center for well over a hundred years. In 1802, a professor in Salvador made bitter complaints about "barbarous batuques through the city streets . . . to the beat of . . . horrible atabaques, indecently dancing to pagan songs [and] speaking various languages."[34] The Bahia assembly of merchants complained in 1814 of *batuques*, pinpointing blacks gathering together to play berimbaus.[35] The fact that so many laws were passed to contain Africans has led some historians to conclude that there would have been no sense disguising capoeira as a dance, as dance and batuques were banned by statute. And yet it was exactly in capoeira's most formative period in Salvador, when the Central and West African cultures began to merge in the city, that there would have been good reason to disguise the practice of capoeira as a harmless dance or batuque.

The Count dos Arcos was governor of Bahia from 1810 to 1818. During that time *batuques do Negros* were outlawed and there was a punishment of 150 lashes for groups of more than four slaves gathering together or being in town at night without their owner's permission. But the Count dos Arcos strongly believed enforcing this ban would only unite Africans from different nations to rebel, so he disobeyed Lisbon's orders and let certain kinds of batuque go ahead in Barbalha and Graça plazas. He was criticized for having weak policies and showing excessive friendliness toward blacks. Salvador citizens petitioned the king, but still the batuques, accompanied by berimbaus, continued. Nor was Salvador isolated in this situation; local governors often made allowances for batuques as long as they were peaceful and didn't create a disturbance. In Goiânia in 1796, for example, the military called for an end to batuques in the town. The government refused, "Since it is the main pleasure they can have throughout their days of bondage" (although they warned of severe punishments for disturbances).[36]

The disguise wasn't fooling everyone, of course, which is why people like the Count dos Arcos were criticized. Yet there was a significant period when it was definitely not only possible, but potentially life saving to disguise capoeira as a dance, because in the late 18th and early 19th century certain influential members of the elite argued for harmless dances to go ahead but for any sign of violence or disturbance to be crushed.

Witchcraft and Feitiçaria

Candomblé was attacked for drumming and dance, and for its supposed use of *feitiçaria*. These were illegal under Portuguese Catholic decrees against witchcraft.

> Between 1591 and 1786, at least 119 cases of witchcraft were prosecuted by visiting inquisitors in Brazil or were sent by Brazilian bishops to the Lisbon Inquisition. Witch-hunts elsewhere in Europe peaked in the seventeenth century, but Portuguese witchcraft trials peaked in the early eighteenth century. . . . the Portuguese Philippine Code, which governed Brazilian criminal law from 1603 through 1830 . . . defined witchcraft in three tiers: a death penalty for witchcraft involving Eucharistic objects stolen from churches, invocation of demons, or use of potions; whipping and banishment for divination and love-magic; whipping and a light fine for "rustic superstitions" . . . and particularly . . . healing practices.[37]

Candomble and other "creolized" African religions (voodoo, Macumba, Calundu, and Xangô) were practiced for healing ailments, psychological problems, and social and emotional calamities. The Portuguese Inquisition was abolished in 1821. Newly independent Brazil declared a constitution in 1824 that allowed the secret, private practice of non-Catholic religions. Brazil's 1830 criminal code covered Candomblé and capoeira automatically by banning assembly, by imposing curfews, and forbidding drumming, shouting, and dancing.

The Rio de Janeiro ordinances against Candomblé houses were enacted in 1836, and many other laws against dance gatherings were newly enforced that year as a reaction to slave rebellions, particularly one in Salvador, Bahia in 1835, in which religion played a part. Candomblé houses and mosques for Islamic slaves were used as planning centers for the conspiracy. Magistrates in Salvador had been concerned about the situation for a long time.

In 1829, a Brotas magistrate and his men raided a local Candomblé house, and wrote of seeing Africans (Jejes) worshipping

The so-called Voodum God. . . . On top of an elaborately prepared table [was] a heap decorated all over with ribbons and seashells, and a big African gourd full of seashells, and some copper coins mixed up with the alms. Male blacks were playing barrel drums and gourds decorated with seashells. Some black women were dancing, others were off in a room sleeping, or pretending to sleep. . . . It is true that the sacred Political Constitution offered by His Majesty the Emperor says in Article 5 that "the Holy Roman Catholic Church will continue to be the Religion of the Empire. All other Religions will be permitted, but their practice will be kept indoors and private [and] the buildings designated for worship [kept] with no external sign of a Temple." This is understood to apply to Europeans, never to black Africans, who, coming as they do from their country to ours, are brought up in our religious fold. How could we dare allow them to apostatize and feign catholicism only to turn the other cheek and worship their Gods in public?[38]

Sedan Chair Porters

Salvador's streets were filled with African people doing a huge variety of jobs. "They worked in the open air as artisans, washerwomen, tailors, street vendors, water bearers, barbers, musicians, artists, masons, carpenters, stevedores and sedan chair porters."[39]

Capoeira was played by these workers in the city where religion, work, music, and rebellion were all intrinsic to everyday life. Briefly consider the job of sedan chair porter as a keyhole to glimpse, however incompletely, that life.

Salvador's streets were uneven and very steep. The taxis of the day were not horse and carriage, the ubiquitous hansom cabs found in European cities or colonies like Australia and New Zealand. In Brazil, the usual mode of transport in the city was sedan chairs (*cadeirinhas*). In the 1820s, Maria Graham wrote, "They consist of a cane armchair, with the footboard and a canopy covered with leather; curtains, generally of moreen, with gilt bordering and lined with cotton or linen, are contrived to draw round, or open at pleasure; and the whole is slung by the top to a single pole, by which two negroes carry it at a quick pace upon their shoulders, changing occasionally from right to left."[40]

An English woman, Mrs. Nathaniel Kindersley, arrived in Salvador in 1764 and wrote, "The chair is carried by two negro slaves on their shoulders; at every step the foremost gives a groan, which the other answers: this helps to make them keep an equal pace; but is a melancholy disagreeable noise, and when we first came on shore, hearing the slaves, who were in parties, carrying any thing from one place to another, utter these kind of moans, we thought they were oppressed with burdens beyond their strength."[41]

As we have seen, slave workers took on additional jobs to make extra money. Many domestic servants doubled as sedan chair porters on the side, and sedan chair porters worked as tailors, barbers, meat cutters, or peddlers, so that one way or another, a high proportion of Salvador's slave population took a turn carrying these chairs. They were usually *ganhadores* (earners) who paid their masters pre-arranged amounts, keeping the rest for their own expenses and saving to try and buy themselves out of slavery.

In the city, slaves lived in residences called *loges*, the urban equivalent of senzalas and equally humble. The masters and their families occupied the upper floors while the slaves lived on the ground floor or basement. The *armazém* (storerooms) were home to the masses sleeping on mats on the floor, usually without any furniture except a wooden box for some belongings. They were locked in at night for the curfew.

These loges were overcrowded, so many slaves rented small rooms in the huts of freed Africans, where they could go during the day. Even the homes of the most financially secure blacks, who'd won their manumission and created successful small businesses, were run-down.

> The great majority can be described as "thatched hut dwellings," improvised [*de bofetão*] mud huts, or made of stone and whitewash. They were generally one-story, with a door and a window, almost always on rental lots belonging to convents, churches, or important urban land-owners. Some only own half of the dwelling they live in. The other half belongs to someone else with whom their relations do not go beyond that of co-tenants.[42]

Once someone had achieved manumission, it was usual to continue working in the profession followed as a slave. Two freed slaves, Domingos and João Borges, worked in Salvador as sedan chair porters in the 1830s. They were Hausas from West Africa and gained their manumission from the same master. As freemen they continued carrying the sedan chairs. It was very tough work, but the more journeys they made the more money they counted at the end of the day.

In the mid-19th century a journey of one mile cost the passenger the equivalent of ten pence. An Alexader Majoribanks wrote at the time:

> There are supposed to be a thousand of these cadeiras in Bahia, some of the higher classes keeping private ones of their own, so that you frequently meet cadeiras carried by two slaves dressed in livery. The cost of a cadeira is about £ 20.00 sterling. The owners of them generally let them out to their slaves at a certain sum per day, allowing them to pocket as much more as they can, and this makes them very active, and occasionally somewhat importunate, as when they see a decent person walking they are apt to ask if he wants a cadeira.[43]

Eventually João Borges broke his leg and soon Domingos, 78 years old, couldn't work either because of a hernia. They gained manumission, yet even as freemen they didn't enjoy a good standard of living in Salvador. It was disenfranchised, abandoned, and cheated men such as these who provided the impetus to rebellions in the city.

Dozens of white businessmen and town council members signed a petition arguing that of all the Africans in Bahia, it was the freed slaves who were the greatest threat to the status quo. The petition begged for their complete expulsion from the city. "They are the . . . surest support for slave conspiracies, since once they shared their lot. Being freedmen, they can judge the hardship of slavery better than anyone, and for this reason they can describe the pleasures of freedom to those still enslaved."[44]

Bad Night in Bahia: The 1835 Uprising

On the 19th of January, 1835, one particular sedan chair porter in Salvador, whose name was Aprígo, lost his temper with a belligerent and arrogant drunkard, refusing to carry him. A bailiff, backed up by a soldier, ordered him to carry the drunken passenger. The porter responded impatiently, "Just you wait. Before you know it, you'll look for a black man in this place and you wont find one—then it'll be you who has to heft these chairs."[45]

What was this porter talking about? Salvador's chief of police wrote a letter to the provincial president, painting a vivid picture of an uprising that the sedan chair porter must have been privy to that night. The letter is reproduced here, virtually in its entirety.

> When Your Excellency received the extraordinary fortunate warnings on the night of the 24th that the Africans, particularly the Nagos, would revolt at dawn, setting fires at various points in the city and attacking the guardhouses, the justices of the peace went into the streets and called upon the citizens to join the police. Soldiers and guards immediately took up their weapons, and the regular units sent to various places men who were capable of suppressing any initial uprising on the part of the blacks.

> Having received Your Excellency's message at about eleven o'clock at night, I inspected several places, gave some orders, and then went to the Ladeira da Praça where, according to the reports, many of the insurgents were to have been assembled in some houses. There I found the justices of the peace of the two cathedral districts with some citizens and municipal police who were searching some of those places.

> In compliance with your orders, and recognizing that there was no danger in the centre of the city where the police barracks and guardhouses are located, and with everything in a state of readiness. . . . I

headed straight for the cavalry barracks, which I found on the alert. Ordering a cavalry guard to follow me later to the Largo do Bomfim, I hurried immediately to that place while the soldiers were mounting up, fearing that any delay could be disastrous for so many unarmed families who were near the sugar mills and separated from the forces of the city and so in the worst possible location for such an attack. I had hardly given some orders tending to reduce the danger when a cavalry patrol arrived at full gallop to inform me that some Africans had attacked at various points in the city.

With this news, I ordered a municipal police detachment of eighteen men who were in Bomfim that, in the event of danger, they should make the families go into the church and lock themselves in, defending themselves from any attack until I could come to their aid. Returning to the cavalry barracks at three in the morning, I found it prepared, with one force mounted and the other on foot, along with some men of the National Guard. The latter withdrew into the building to defend the entrance and to fire on the Africans from the windows, while the cavalrymen waited for the attack in the plaza below.

Within a few minutes some fifty or sixty of them appeared on the scene armed with swords, lances, and even pistols and other firearms. Encountering pistol and rifle fire from the barracks windows, they advanced furiously, causing the cavalry to break up in pursuit of them to prevent their escape by way of the Noviciado road. At this moment the cavalry commander, Captain Carvalhao, who awaited them dismounted, was wounded and forced to withdraw.

As I and some horsemen again charged the Africans at the barracks door, the latter began to disperse, with the two groups of cavalry in pursuit of them. Meanwhile, more Africans appeared and with the rest of the cavalry absent, I entered the barracks, from which the firing continued for another quarter of an hour, until they were all overcome. This was accomplished mainly by mounted cavalry who bravely charged them, forcing them to leap into the sea or to hide in the nearby hills which are covered with underbrush. They left seventeen dead behind, others wounded and captured, aside from many who were drowned or, having been wounded, lost their lives among the waves. I have been informed that several of these have been found in various places.

With the danger reduced, knowing that the rest of the city was free from attack, and fearing an assault on the village of Bonfim, I went their with the cavalry. . . . There I remained until I was certain that there was no movement at all at the nearby sugar plantations. Returning to the cavalry barracks as dawn was approaching, I found forty men there from the frigate, whom Your Excellency had sent me. I ordered sixteen of these to embark for Itapagipe, and there they stayed until calm had been re-established.

Later I learned from reports that while the justice of the peace, following up a private tip, was attempting to search a house near Guadalupe on the Ladeira da Praça, a mulatto woman showed reluctance to open the door to him, claiming there was nobody there. Since he was prepared to break his way in, she opened the door, but just then another door inside was seen closing. With growing suspicion, the Commander of the Regulars, Lieutenant Lazaro Viera do Amaral, entered the hallway in the direction of the closed door, when suddenly, at a signal given allegedly by the mulatto woman, the door opened, a shot was fired from a blunderbuss from within, and a group of about sixty blacks came forth armed with various weapons, mainly swords, scattering the small, unsuspecting force and gravely wounding Lieutenant Lazaro and others who stood in their way.

This group then headed toward Nossa Senhora d'Ajuda in the Largo do Teatro, where it was met by a volley fired off by eight Regular

Guards commanded by the adjutant of the same unit. These soldiers were dispersed by the Africans after five of them had been wounded. From this place the blacks ran with a great deal of shouting to the Rua de Baixo killing and wounding people on the way, allegedly including two mulattoes. From there they went straight to the artillery barracks, perhaps with the intention of joining the group from Victoria, as was later verified. Near the barracks they killed a National Guard sergeant named Tito from the 2nd Battalion, who was escorting a justice of the peace seeking help from the fortress, but had stayed a bit behind to take a shot at them.

Afraid to attack the artillery barracks, they returned by the same road, and soon they made contact with the group coming from the Victoria area. These had crossed the new fortress road, despite some shots that were fired from there. Now united, they went to attack the Regular Army barracks where there were only twenty two soldiers, the rest having been sent to several other places. After an exchange of fire there in which two soldiers were killed and others wounded, the barracks gate being closed, they headed toward Barroquiha, arriving a second time at Nossa Senhora d'Ajuda. From there they went toward the school, attacking the retreating guardsmen. Some shots were fired there by a group of Regular Army reinforcements who happened to be at that place. There they also killed an Artillery soldier who had come to take away an image of the Saint. Before falling wounded, he defended himself courageously, killing one with a single shot and wounding many others. While descending the Baixa dos Sapateiros, they killed a mulatto and, I am told, a second one as well, continuing toward Coqueiros, as I have already informed Your Excellency. After the damage that was done to them in this last place, they never reassembled, and this was the only time that they were not on the offensive. . . .

I should also inform Your Excellency that the mulatto woman of the house where the blacks were found and her husband are under arrest.

There are reasons to suspect that they are co-conspirators or sympathizers.

From the cavalry barracks to the fortress of São Pedro many dead and wounded Africans have been found, but few were captured during the attacks. I calculate the number of dead found in all the places, including those found along the shore, at fifty. However, in addition to these, there were the wounded ones, who will certainly not escape death, considering the seriousness of their wounds and the length of time which elapsed before they were treated. These are in the hospitals where I ordered them sent, and the dead are in the Sea Fortress. In the morning some were found in the nearby forests with bullet or sword wounds, and some of these tried to escape using disguises.

At six or seven in the morning six blacks belonging to João Fransisco Ratis suddenly came out of his house armed with swords, pistols and daggers and dressed in battle apparel, in their fashion, and after setting fire to their master's house they ran toward Agua de Meninos and were quickly killed on the way. It can be assumed that these blacks were also in on the conspiracy but were unaware of the early morning events, since the sixty in the house near Guadalupe were forced to begin their attack prematurely.

I have given the necessary orders for the search of every house where Africans are living, without any exceptions, and the result will be sent to Your Excellency at the proper time. Your Excellency may already be assured, however, that the revolt was planned long ago with an unbreakable secrecy, and with design superior to that which we might expect from their brutishness and ignorance. Generally speaking, almost all of them can read and write in unknown characters which are similar to the Arabic used among the Ussás [Hausas?], who now evidently have made an alliance with the Nagós. Teachers exist among them who give lessons and have tried to organise the insurrection, in which many free Africans, even rich ones, were also involved. Many books have been found, some of which, it is said, must be religious precepts derived from the mingling of sects, mainly the Koran.

What is certain is that religion played a role in the rebellion, and the leaders managed to persuade the miserable people that certain papers could save them from death. For this reason many of these have been found on the dead bodies and in the rich and exquisite vestments which were found during some of the searches and probably belonged to some of the leaders. It was also observed that many of the rebels were the slaves of Englishmen and were better armed. These facts should probably be attributed to the lesser amount of constraint in which they are held by these foreigners, who are accustomed to living with free people.

According to information I have received, in addition to the deaths of the National Guard sergeant, the artilleryman, four mulattoes, and two regular Army soldiers, many others were wounded, and some gravely.

There is no doubt, Sir, that if we had not been prepared by the warnings, the end result would have been the same, although the destruction would have been much greater. Therefore, to increase our security, it will be useful to reward the black women who gave us the warnings, granting them their freedom, if they do not already possess it, or a reasonable compensation.

Precautionary steps are still being carried out enthusiastically, and in all the districts procedures are being followed to discover any guilty persons who may still exist, in order to make effective examples of them to other Africans. To best achieve this, I have tried to establish procedures everywhere in a uniform and regular manner.

After such events, it is quite natural that there should be abuses, and these have taken place to such an extent that they completely justify

the well-founded complaints. Soldiers are arresting, beating, wounding and even killing slaves who, under their master's orders, are going
into the streets . . . otherwise peace has returned, and we will now
have time to establish measures, by legislative means, so that it will
not be necessary to fight such people a second, especially free Africans.
Almost all the latter, while enjoying their freedom, bear the stigma
of slavery, and their presence is in no way profitable to this country.
Bahia, January 29, 1835. To the Most Illustrious and Most Excellent
President of the Province. (Signed) Fransisco Gonçalves Martins,
Chief of Police.[43]

The 1830s were a turbulent decade at all levels of Brazilian society up to and including the monarchy. It was also the decade that
marked a clear development in the fight against slavery, when
capoeiristas, slaves, and free Africans increasingly chose to fight
back in the city itself rather than flee to quilombos in the countryside.

Chapter Nine
AN AWFUL LOT OF COFFEE
(AND CAPOEIRA) IN BRAZIL

After British abolition, in 1810 the king of Dahomey sent a special ambassador to reassure the viceroyalty that Britain's actions would not interrupt the flow of captives leaving Wydah for Brazil.

By now Dom João was resident in Rio de Janeiro and he'd signed a treaty with Britain for the gradual abolition of the slave trade. The British Foreign Office conveniently overlooked that the Portuguese king would have no legal reason to honor this treaty and they decided to ignore that the British goods flooding into Brazil would certainly be flooding straight out to Luanda and Benguela for purchasing slaves.

Dom João's presence in Rio had enriched the city. Rio was still a boom town for the merchant class. There were "shops of every kind. . . . By 1799 the city had over 1,300 registered commercial establishments, including *boticas* (pharmacies), *casas de cafe* (coffee shops), *casas de pasto* (eating houses), and tobacco shops. Taverns were found along the Rua São José. Wholesalers were concentrated on the Rua dos Pescadores and the Rua Direita."[1]

Between 1790 and 1808, 200,000 people from Kongo and Angola arrived in Rio de Janeiro, where they built public promenades, statues, and fountains. The city's main slave market had been moved by the Marquês de Lavradio to Valongo in a less central area out beyond Conceição Hill. In the captaincy of Rio de Janeiro, half the 200,000 population were slaves. Among the urban population of 60,000, at least 40,000 were slaves or freed mulattos and blacks.

Vadiagem

Long before the court arrived in the city, Viceroy Conde de Resende named *vadiagem* (vagrancy) as the main evil of society. "Innumerable individuals who come here without occupation . . . poor people and mostly Mulattos and Blacks . . . abuse their liberty indulging in every sort of vice and passing their lives in complete inaction, either because they do not have any means to earn their living or because they are not subjected to anyone who looks after their conduct."[2]

The official understanding was that the black population was a serious internal threat to Brazilian security. It was no unusual sight to see the heads of decapitated slaves captured in quilombos placed on stakes in public places and along roadsides. Rio's Viceroy Conde de Resende led the war against vadiagem. Resende had made a name for himself when he arrested and oversaw the torture and hanging of the conspirator Tiradentes. Active fifteen years before the Portuguese court arrived in Brazil, Resende had led an offensive campaign of prosecution against leading Rio intellectuals and others he suspected of harboring revolutionary ideas.

Unfortnately for Resende, the same black military regiments established to control quilombos were soon perceived to be part of the problem. "Just one year after Haitian independence, in 1805, the image of the Haitian General Jean Jacques Dessalines appeared on the medallions of several members of Rio's black militia. It was 'notable,' wrote a horrified local magistrate in an order to have the portraits 'ripped from their chests,' that such an image should be worn by cabras and freedmen who were skilled at handling artillery."[3]

The city's population continued growing rapidly in the early 19th century, soon reaching 80,000. Badly built houses clung to the mountains surrounding the city with no adequate drainage, resulting in disease and social chaos for impoverished residents.

As Rio de Janeiro was the home of the imperial court, Brazilian politicians were intent on improving its image. They particularly wanted to heighten security for merchants, vassals, and European citizens. They feared that the filthy, crime-ridden city undermined the authority of the monarch living at its center. It was vital to keep up appearances.

"United Kingdom of Portugal, Brazil and the Algarves"

In December 1815, Dom João declared, "By the grace of God, Prince Regent of Portugal and the Algarves, in Africa and Guinea, and of the conquest, navigation, and commerce of Ethiopia, Arabia, Persia, and India, etc., make known . . . my kingdom . . . shall form from henceforth one only and united kingdom under the title of the United Kingdom of Portugal, Brazil and the Algarves."[4]

The newly revamped Rio de Janeiro created the first state police force in Brazil. This force joined together many branches of previously separate constabulary. Led by a magistrate, the city's parishes, Santa Rita, São José, Candelária, and Se, had to register every resident and business within their borders.

It was during Dom João's era in Rio that the state police first took over duties that had previously been in private hands. That was domestic policy, though foreign policy remained unchanged. James Prior of the British navy wrote in 1813 that everything faded "into insignificance in comparison with the slave trade; Portugal and Spain, England and France, Wellington, Bonaparte, the Prince Regent can all vanish into the land of the shades; what does it matter provided that their dear traffic, the subject of their dreams, day and night, can be maintained? This attachment, no power of reason can shake, only the argument of force can have any effect."[5]

Now the problem for the elite was the physical danger of living in close proximity to a volatile majority of oppressed people. Their solutions were never subtle and they invariably focused on crushing insurrection by force.

The police force was commanded by an intendent who cooperated with the Royal Guard. The guard was founded by Paulo Fernandez Viana, a very well connected politician who knew his way around Rio and also knew that security needed tightening up if, as he put it, the "decorum and perfection of the Court"[6] were to thrive there. The most visible obstacles to that decorum and perfection were gangs of capoeiristas and other vagrants who challenged the "personal security and tranquility of loyal vassals."[7]

Capoeiristas, Spies, and Conspiracies

What Viana and the prince regent feared were capoeira gangs, foreign spies, and court conspiracies.[8] These were atop the law-and-order hit list in Brazil's capital city.

The intendent and the guard patroled the streets by night; they broke up batuques and gatherings of Africans wherever they found them. They closed down taverns and gambling dens, and arrested anyone suspected of vadiagem. Vadiagem became synonymous with capoeira.

The strategy of the guard was to lie low, "in inconspicuous places, and in silence, so that they might hear whatever row, or racket, and then suddenly appear at the location of the disturbance."[9] They were chronically understaffed, however. In 1818, there were 218 reserved places in the force, but only 75 were occupied.

Viana ordered taverns and rowdy food stalls closed anywhere in the vicinity of the palace. As a kind of mayor, he was also responsible for theatrical street entertainments. He had a problem on his hands as the popular public spectacles that drew crowds also drew capoeiristas and what he called "the licentious liberty that the people had taken to clapping and whistling . . . without decency and without any attention to the good order that they should maintain."[10]

Fear and Loathing in Rio de Janeiro

Thirty thousand whites arrived in Rio de Janeiro with the prince regent; the number of slaves who were to serve them also increased, by 200 percent. Political economists of the day suggested immigrating poor whites instead of Africans. The court adviser, Manuel Viera da Silva, urged that it would be "in the Prince Regent's interest to increase the number of whites, be they Brazilian, or European, rather than propagate [the population] of blacks."[11]

The vast majority arrested by Brazil's earliest police force were slaves. Despite vadiagem among the white poor, it wasn't beyond the means of most of them to acquire one or two slaves of their own. As Viera da Silva conceded, such loafers lived "only from the

Coffee exports from southeast Brazil grew rapidly in the late 19th century. Importation of slaves from Angola enabled Brazil's plantation owners to expand their output without raising wages in the Brazilian economy. The financial advantages of the slave trade to the coffee sector caused the Brazilian state to resist British abolitionist interventionism for fifty years. During this period of time, capoeira was practiced widely by slaves and free blacks in Rio de Janeiro, Bahia, and Recife.

work of these miserable men."[12] He suggested making slaves much more expensive. Viana said bluntly that Brazil's "population is black [with] . . . ten times as many slaves as whites, and because of this . . . more propensity to be led astray, and [the population therefore] requires more police."[13]

Ninety-nine percent of those arrested by the intendency's guard and sent to prison were black or mixed race. Of those imprisoned, 80 percent were from Angola or Congo. In 1817, the magistrate, António Felipe Soares de Andrada de Brederode, wrote, "As the crimes perpetrated by individuals of this city, some freed and others enslaved, known as capoeiras, are frequent, the vigilant police has sought to capture them, and judges have sought to try them, and the casa de suplicação has sought to sentence them with exemplary zeal."[14]

The guard was a vicious force. Even Viana, who was not known for his tender heart, struggled to keep them under control. In 1811 he reminded them that their role wasn't to create trouble but to contain it. They attacked black women who worked as street vendors. It's clear from Viana's reports that many of the street-fights between the guard and Rio's blacks were started by the guard and weren't reported by their commander.

In early-19th-century Rio there was also widespread use of capoeira by African people in fights and as part of gang activity in the city. The capoeira gangs, called *maltas*, were important organizations for young males, parallelling black churches, trade organizations, and brotherhoods. Capoeira was a common and necessary tool of self-defense in an environment where violence against Africans was casual and sadistic.

Thomas Holloway cites the case of an English visitor, who traveled to Brazil in 1819. A parked carriage stood in the street, attended by a driver and footman, who were idly awaiting their passenger's return. A slave walking down the street tried to get by the carriage and its two attendants. The Englishman wrote that "so good an opportunity of mortifying the half naked negro was too good to let slip, and the coachman gave him a very severe cut with his whip over the bare shoulders. . . ." This created a visible welt. The driver whipped the slave again, obviously causing him great pain. The footman then took the whip and started beating him. The English visitor described it as "gratuitous and unprovoked brutality" and was amazed that he put up with it. But he wrote, "Blacky had, however, his reasons for thus appearing passive; he was watching his moment, and having found it, a flash of lightning is not more prompt than were his movements." He bent low and head-butted the driver back against a wall, knocking him unconscious. He rapidly spun upon the footman and, as the Englishman said, "gave him with the sole of his foot a kick in the stomach with such force and dexterity that he stretched him lifeless. Leaving both his victims, he then took to his heels with the swiftness of a deer."[15]

It is interesting that this incident took place in 1819, in the decade before the Austrian artist Rugendas painted his famous "Jogo de Capoeira," accompanied by a description of the game that only described head-butts and *esquivas* (escape movements). The slave in the passage above was able to render both of his attackers unconscious with a single *cabeçada* (head-butt) and one *chapa de frente no peito* or *bênção* (a front kick with the sole of the foot).

It has been argued at length (see Nestor Capoeira's *Capoeira: Roots of the Dance-Fight-Game,* pages 295–296) that capoeira in Rugendas's time did not possess kicks. Yet there is evidence from various observers of kicks being used by African slaves in Brazil and other South American and Caribbean colonies. Two examples are John Stedman in Suriname in the 1780s, who described a (sometimes fatal) kicking game played by slaves from Loango. Africans entering Brazil from the Loango coast, which was situated north of the Zaire River mouth and north of Cabinda, were generally termed "Angolan" once they reached their destination (many of the slaves leaving from the Bay of Loango were from the area north of the Zaire River and Kongo and from the forest to the northeast of the Loango Coast). The cross-kicking game resembled capoeira and was played for points, as was capoeira sometimes in Bahia up until the 1930s. James Wetherell, the British vice-consul in Salvador from 1822 until the 1850s, wrote of slaves playing capoeira with kicks and open hands. The above quoted 1819 description from the anonymous English traveler is another example of the efficacy of kicks in pre-1830s Brazil.

By 1810, arrests for capoeira accounted for approximately 10 percent of total arrests in Rio. The only crime that caused more arrests was slave escape attempts. The punishment for capoeira was whipping and jail time.

Viana was opposed to public flogging. He said he'd "always been afraid to punish [blacks and common people] outside [the jail] . . . because whipping them in the streets and in the places of their infractions provokes uprisings."[16]

Judges generally agreed. Whites were whipped publically in the pelourinho or the *praça do rocio*, because this wasn't a cause of mutiny. Slaves received their punishment in jail or behind the closed gates of police barracks. Where capoeiristas were concerned, even cautious judges sometimes recommended public lashing to "make a terrifying example of . . . slave capoeira practitioners," as one judge said in 1817.[17]

The police state took over from private foremen on the plantations. In Rio's jail (*calabouço*), prisoners were punished by officers rather than by the feitor of the fazendas. Prison chain gangs worked on road building and public monuments. After Dom João arrived, massive building projects were undertaken, with chain gangs from the calabouço as the main source of manpower. Slave owners paid the intendency 160 reis per 100 lashes inflicted on capoeiristas inside the calabouço.

Holloway writes that in November 1821, there was a vicious fight involving capoeiristas in which six people were killed and many others were injured. After this, an official order complained about the massive expansion in the number of capoeiristas, and the same order recommended that whipping was "the only punishment that intimidates and instills fear." The document further ordered the court's royal guard, which was the forerunner of the military police force, to give out corporal punishment "as soon as blacks are arrested for disorder, or with a knife or suspicious instrument."[18]

Soon after this, the intendent gave an order that those arrested on a charge of capoeira would suffer 100 lashes and be held at the calabouço.

Coffee and Capoeira

To describe the capoeiristas of Rio de Janeiro under Dom João's reign, or that of his son, Dom Pedro I (who personally called for Rio's police to extinguish capoeira), it is necessary to look to Africa.

The southern Brazilian merchants in Rio de Janeiro "multiplied their actvity at Benguela many times over in the eighteenth century . . . developing a considerable fleet that carried people originating from deeper and deeper in the southern highlands of Central Africa. They also replaced Pernambucans as the major buyers in the government's slaving port at Luanda."[19]

Joseph Miller writes, "These years of Rio traders' dominance at Luanda and Benguela—when they carried as many as 15,000–20,000 captives to South-Central Brazil in some years—consolidated Central Africans as the dominant groups among the slaves in and around the city of Rio de Janeiro."[20]

Portuguese and Brazilian traders from Rio used the European wars of the 1790s to their advantage. Replacing French and British shippers, they delivered Cabindas, from Kongo through Cabinda. Benguela and Luanda were favored ports of call and many from Mozambique entered Southern Brazil via Rio de Janeiro between 1811 and 1830.

Central Africans had been living in large numbers in Rio since the second half of the seventeenth century.

> The increasingly commercial nature of primary slaving within the new communities of eighteenth-century central Africa preyed on isolated individuals, particularly children, many of them of slave origins themselves. . . . The recent experiences of their enslavement, the immediacy of slavery in Brazil, and the Afro-Brazilan cultures they found in the streets and on the plantations there would have provided more resonant bases for forming communities of their own, amidst nostalgic personal awareness of many different roots in Africa. Increasing characterizations of the slave cultures of southern Brazil as generically "Bantu," largely in contrast to the Western African tone of those in the Brazilan Northeast, thus reflected the depth to which slaving had penetrated all of Western central Africa by the late eighteenth century.[21]

After 1770 coffee production was centered in Rio de Janeiro, São Paulo, Espirito Santo, and Minas Gerais. The climate in these places was well suited to growing coffee, just as the climate in the Northeast had suited sugar cane. In the 1800s, exports from Rio de Janeiro multiplied.

Although coffee houses had been very popular in cities like London and Paris since the 17th century, coffee hadn't made much of a stir in Brazil or Portugal until now. By the 1790s, there were about forty coffee houses in Rio de Janeiro. "In spite of its reputation for tasting bitter because of improper drying procedures, Brazilian coffee was to be found in markets all the way from Moscow to Venice, in Hamburg, Copenhagen, Amsterdam, Paris, Lisbon, and parts of the Barbary Coast."[22]

An agrarian revival had picked up speed just as the gold cycle was declining in Brazil. The main cause of this agrarian boom was coffee. "The need for African labor to work Brazilian agriculture . . . completed the portrait of a Brazilian economy more in need of new Angolan slave labor from the tropical north to the far south than it ever had before."[23]

Paradoxically, the most intense slave trade from Africa began after it had been made illegal in Brazil. Masses from Angola and Kongo were transported directly to the Paraíba Valley during the coffee boom.

"Neither man nor his land rested"

The quoted phrase in the heading above "is the way the restless cycle of transient coffee agriculture was described, the cycle of tearing from the virgin soil as much as possible in the shortest possible time to move on to new clearings."[24]

From 1800 to 1850, a million slaves entered Brazil, and 700,000 after 1831. Children could more easily harvest coffee than sugar and the average age of slaves was decreasing. Slavers in the past had been reluctant to take children onboard if they could help it, but by the 1780s, West Central African captives were often male children of female Angolan farmers. Most of the children were adolescents and the figures generally point to a ratio of two males to each female. These figures were similar to those for St. Domingue and 19th-century Cuba.

Coffee plantations had sixty to hundreds of field slaves working in gangs. Coffee bushes generally produced beans for 25–45 years, which was much greater than the life expectancy of the slaves employed to harvest them. Stein writes, "The period of maximum productivity in the life of a slave was relatively short, from eighteen to thirty years of age, and fazendeiros had never enjoyed what they considered an adequate labor force even during the busiest days of the slave trade. . . . the constant complaint of the fazendeiros concentrating more and more on coffee became the lack of hands for fieldwork."[25]

The coffee estates spread around a big house, or casa grande. "From his shaded veranda or a window of the house, the fazendeiro watched his slaves clean the terreiro of sprouting weeds or, at harvest time, revolve the drying coffee beans with wooden hoes. . . . The senzala itself had changed little . . . a tile roof, perhaps a cooling outside corridor surrounded by wooden bars, never any flooring. The narrow, windowless cubicles of the mated slaves— the single men and women lived in separate, undivided senzalas— contained the few possessions a slave could have."[26]

Freyre described the masters' life, which "tended to become a life which was lived in a hammock: a stationary hammock, with the master taking his ease, sleeping, dozing. Or a hammock on the move with the master on a journey . . . or a squeaking hammock, with the master copulating in it. The master did not have to leave his hammock to give orders to his negroes."[27]

Stanley J. Stein reports:

A few fazendas had been established on poor locations, near bottom-lands or on badly drained terrain that left stagnant water near the living quarters. To the fazendeiros who would not recognize the evils of such conditions, one observer wrote that because of such negligence, many fazendeiros "suffer immense damage not only to their slaves, but also to their cattle." On other fazendas, owners had allowed tile roofs to deteriorate, and under heavy rainfall, unprotected mud-and-wattle walls rapidly disintegrate.[28]

Rio Coffee Carriers

Coffee carriers had one of the most crippling jobs in Brazil and many employed at Rio's docks and plantations were given this task. The coffee carriers were porters who carried the bags of coffee from the plantations to the shipping place, or from different warehouses in the town to the ships. A Royal Navy surgeon, speaking at a House of Lords Select Committee, said:

> If we take coffee-carriers, who are the hardest worked of any of the Brazilian slaves, the average of their life is said to be about eight years after they are imported into the Brazils. They gain from 1 shilling four pence to 2 shillings a day carrying coffee, and they have to support themselves, taking 300 working days per annum, you have a very enormous sum realized at the end of eight years. . . . The master gets the whole of it. The system with the coffee-carriers is to send them out, and they have to bring home to the master a certain amount of money, and of course, to make a little over and above the sum for themselves they work remarkably hard, and drink to a fearful amount; they drink very hard; about eight years is said to be the average of the life of the coffee and sugar carriers, who are the hardest worked."[29]

A North American living in Rio in the 19th century wrote:

> Every gang of coffee-carriers has a leader, who commonly shakes a rattle, to the music of which his associates behind him chant. The load,

weighing 160 lbs., rests on the head and shoulders, the body is inclined forward, and the pace is a trot or half run. Most are stout and athletic, but a few are so small and slightly-made that one wonders how they manage to keep up with the rest. The average life of a coffee-carrier does not exceed ten years. In that time the work ruptures and kills them. . . . On returning, some kept up their previous chant, and ran as if enjoying the toil; others went more leisurely, and among them some noble-looking fellows stepped with much natural grace. . . . No wonder that slaves shockingly crippled in their lower limbs are so numerous. There waddled before me, in a manner distressing to behold, a man whose thighs and legs curved so far outward that his trunk was not over fifteen inches from the ground. I observed another whose knees crossed each other, and his feet prematurely apart, as if superincumbent loads had pushed his knees in instead of out. . . . the heads of Africans are hard, their necks strong, and both, being perpendicular to the loads they are called to support, are seldom injured. It is the lower parts of the moving columns, where the weights are alternately thrown on and off the jointed thighs and legs, that are the weakest. These necessarily are the first to give way under excessive burdens, and here are examples of their having yielded and broken down in every direction.[30]

Visitors commonly wrote about the songs and chanting of the Rio coffee carriers, who also marked time with a rattle. Many of these porters must have been capoeiristas. This is true because the majority of men arrested for capoeira were slaves and a massive amount of slaves were stevedores at the docks and warehouses.

Capoeira became a generic term for any type of violent activity perpetrated by groups the police labeled capoeiristas. If a gang set about a rival in the street, or robbed someone at knife point, that was capoeira. Most of our information about capoeira in Rio comes through police records, though as the police weren't interested in the details of African culture, if capoeira was accompanied by music the police didn't mention it.

There was a great deal of ignorance about capoeira in Brasil. As late as the 1930s, capoeira was still defined as "a pastime in which the participant, armed with a razor or a knife, with rapid and characteristic gestures goes through the motions of criminal acts . . . one who takes part in this pastime."[31]

Even while there isn't solid documented evidence of musical accompaniment to capoeira in 19th-century Rio, the scale of musical activity that accompanied work, religious gatherings, and social life makes the argument for a martial art practiced to music rather compelling. Acting on royal authority, the judiciary distinguished between different types of dance and entertainment. Many slave owners wanted all social gatherings of slaves prohibited. A *Cópia do Ordem do Dia* of 1814 banned some African dance and drum batuques but allowed others. A royal order explained, "In all the policed cities of the world public entertainment is permitted to even the most inferior classes of the nation."[32]

One interpretation of the legal distinction between one type of musical gathering and another could be the presence or absence of capoeira. In 1869, for example, four military police in civilian clothes were arrested for associating with capoeiristas near the imperial palace. Their commander ordered the further arrest of soldiers "found in the company of musicians, or in groups of civilians on the streets of the city."[34] His focus on groups of musicians is significant when considering how closely capoeira was linked to the Bantu, Congo, and Angola slave population of 19th-century Rio de Janeiro.

Chapter Ten
O BERIMBAU

It is highly likely that capoeira in 19th-century Bahia was played to one or more berimbaus, accompanied by the caxixi, the atabaque, the pandeiro, agogô, and reco-reco. Mestre Pastinha was born in 1889 and began learning capoeira from an African named Mestre Benedito at the age of ten. He described Mestre Benedito as a "great capoeirista" who in 1900 was already in his seventies. Mestre Pastinha also emphasized that "the one we call Capoeira Angola, the one I learnt, I didn't let change here in the academy. This one is at least 78 years old."[1]

He said, "The connection between percussion and berimbau is not a modern arrangement—it's something from the origins. A good capoeirista, besides playing, must know how to play the berimbau and sing. . . . You can't forget the berimbau. The berimbau is the primitive mestre. It teaches through the sound. It gives vibration and swing to our bodies."[2]

Mestre Benedito was an old man when he taught Mestre Pastinha, and Mestre Pastinha didn't change what he was taught, suggesting the berimbau was already the principle musical instrument of capoeira by the mid-19th century. That this tradition must have been long established is affirmed by the fact that many other Bahian capoeira masters of the early 20th century, including Mestre Bimba, all used the berimbau as the main intrument of capoeira.

As we have seen, in 1814, Dom João, the prince regent, received a petition complaining that "a group of blacks of the sort who normally hire out their services at the customhouse dock [cut] the ropes that bound [a] prisoner, they released him, threatening the two [guerreiros, or warriors or professional bearers of arms] with knives. . . . Since their batuques have been allowed (they are in fact banned by statute) . . . [the petitioner identified Hausas, those of the Nagô, Calabar and other nations] gathering together to play a single stringed instrument . . . and agitating the city. . . . it is since all this has been permitted that we have witnessed most of the acts of violence and disobedience."[3] By 1814, the Rio police were already tackling capoeira, and, although this Bahian petitioner calls these berimbau gatherings batuques, the imaginative leap needed to place capoeira in Bahia is not that great.

In Pastinha's ghost-written book, *Capoeira Angola* (with an introduction by Jorge Amado), the ensemble was said to include berimbau, pandeiro, reco-reco, agogô, atabaque, and *chocalho* (a generic term in Brazil for any type of shaker and often for the long, tube rattle).

"O berimbau é o instrumento principal e indispensável"

The translation of Mestre Pastinha's tribute to the berimbau,[4] in the heading above, is "the berimbau is the principle and indispensable instrument." With the exception of the pandeiro, the instruments of capoeira are traceable to the people who came from the Central African Kongo-Angola area and the people who came from West Africa, Nigeria, and Benin.

The musical ensemble in Bahia was a fusion of instruments and rhythms from both these regions of Africa. Two of the instruments, the atabaque and the agogô, were used in both capoeira and Candomblé.

The agogô was found in Yorubaland and in Central Africa. It was called the *gã* in Fon. It's a clapperless double bell that could be struck with a metal or wooden stick. In the music of Candomblé and its antecedent in Yorubaland, the agogô "generally sets the fundamental pulse at the start of each song and seldom changes in the course of a song."[5]

In Central Africa too, the double bells of the flange-welded type with a bow grip were played in a two-tone pattern with a wooden beater, and their sound could be varied by holding the opening of the agogô closer or farther from the chest or the floor.

Similarly to Candomblé, the agogô of capoeira is played as a pulse beater before the drum/atabaque starts to play. It reinforces the beat laid down by the berimbaus. This pulse is sometimes described as a timeline. Timelines are mainly one-pitch asymmetric rhythmic patterns that guide music and dance. They can be played on iron bells, bottles, or drums.[6]

Timelines were the basis of musical traditions dispersed throughout the New World in the Diaspora from Africa and differed depending upon where in Africa they originated. Each timeline variation is extremely stable and leaves no margin for change. Accentuation, tempo, and the relationship to dance steps might change from place to place, but the timeline patterns remained the same over the centuries.

Hundreds of Years of Tradition

"The most important drum rhythms [the Fon and Yoruba] used for summoning the gods, have been passed down unchanged in Brazil, from generation to generation for some 450 years."[7]

According to Gerhard Kubik, "Though West African music has changed considerably during the past three centuries and has produced in the last hundred years high-life, juju music, and many other new types, the timeline patterns are still there. . . . they were not 'invented' in some recent historical period. They were present in West Africa in the 16th century and much, much earlier."[8]

Kubik continues: "Where the twelve-pulse standard pattern occurs, especially in its seven-stroke version and when it is played on a bell or bottle, we have an almost certain clue that we have a West African Coastal tradition before us, Yoruba, Fõ, Akan or the like." And: "In Brazilian Candomblé the slow left-right alternating steps of the ceremonially dressed women clearly go in the Yoruba way to the bell."[9]

On the other hand, in most samba, in capoeira, *maculêlê*, and the rarer Angola Candomblé, there is a sixteen-pulse timeline pattern. This, according to Kubik, "is always an indication of an Angolan or Congo/Zaïre connection. Its nine-stroke variety points . . . to the vast hinterland of the port of Benguela (the country of the Ngangela group of peoples) as far as Lunda and even Katanga. The seven-stroke version points to southwestern Angola."[10]

The significance of the agogô and other instruments of Candomblé and capoeira goes deeper than their potential for making music. This was true in Africa, in a social, religious, and political sense, long before the days of Atlantic slavery.

There isn't a consensus on the origin and diffusion of the clapperless double bells in Africa. It is thought that they spread from eastern Nigeria and central Cameroon along the same lines as Late Iron Age technology. Double bells were an emblem of chieftain-ship, though they have a broken distribution that is bridged along the Ubangi and Congo valleys.[11]

The spread of Iron Age technology, as it is represented by the presence or absence of "Guinea-type" double bells followed the same routes as the great Bantu migrations, although probably at a later period. Archaeological findings have confirmed that dou-ble bells were played west of the Niger, in Ghana and the Côte d'Ìvoire, as well as in ancient Ife during the Classical Period, approx-imately dated from the tenth to fourteenth centuries.[12]

Double bells had a political function in Africa as an emblem of chieftainship. They were used to send signals and in religious cer-emonies. The double bell was one of the ritual emblems taken by the mythical kinguri on his route west from the lands of Lunda in Angola.

Atabaques

The main instrument in Candomblé is the drum, skinned with cord-and-peg tension. Like agogôs, these drums implied cultural cohesion among the musicians who used them. Whatever politi-cal or military rivalries existed regionally, common cultural traits could be traced by following the certain musical instrument along specific routes. Not surprisingly, considering the similarity of their functions, cord-and-peg tension atabaques had a distribution area roughly corresponding to the Guinea-type double bell.[13]

With atabaques, the distribution area was the Guinea Coast from the Niger River and west to Dahomey (Benin), Togo, and Ghana. Beyond West Africa, the only other place where cord-and-peg tension drums appeared was the New World, where, in Bahia, Suriname, in St. Domingue, Cuba, and the southern states of America, these drums signaled the presence of the Ewe people, the Fon, the Akan, and the Yoruba, who preserved the technological know-how wherever they went.[14]

The atabaque is constructed from a hollowed log, or more frequently today, barrel staves. Pegs are driven into the wood and follow a circle around its body. The single skin membrane of the drum is held in place by a ring attached to rope. This binds the drum and creates the tension of the skin. The pegs are hammered tighter to stretch the cord or rope, which is wound in a complex criss-cross pattern around the drum's body. The design is so specific, it's believed unlikely to have been used or invented in more than one place.

These are "talking drums," varying in size from place to place; in Ghana and the Ivory Coast, they were long and slim, beaten with crooked L-shaped sticks. Shorter talking drums called *atumpan* were used by the Ashanti of Ghana. The Ewe used barrel-shaped cord-and-peg drums. The Fon reserved very tall, single-headed cord-and-peg drums for Vodun ceremonies. For instance, the *oynvie* ("child drum"), *kpezi,* and *jikp* make up a three-drum setup in which all three drums are beaten with a curved stick.

Atabaques were depicted on Nigerian ceremonial pottery dating from the Classical period of Ife art during the 10th to 14th century. Between 1280 and 1295, Benin metal workers began to make bronze ceremonial plaques. One such plaque, made in Benin in the mid-1500s, shows cord-and-peg drums.

In Nagô and Gêge setups, the drumheads were held secure with the pegs inserted into the body of the drum, and the heads were struck with sticks called *oguidavis,* from the Yoruba *ò igi dá wiwo.*

In Kongo-Angola rhythms and some Candomblé, the drums were struck with the hands. The drumheads were held in place with cords, which were fixed halfway down the drum to a hoop or another cord, held fast and tuned by peg wedges.

It was in Yoruba and then Candomblé ceremonial music that the three conical drums were used. They varied in size. Traditionally the largest, called the *rum* (Fon *hun*, Yoruba *ìlù*) was 1.1–1.4 meters high with a deer- or calfskin head of 35–40 cm diameter.

The middle-size drum is called the *rumpi* (Fon *hunpevi*), and the smallest atabaque is called the *lé*. Often the rumpi and lé had goatskin heads. There was some variation in the way the drums were played and this remains true today. Some played all the atabaques with sticks, some with combinations of stick and hand, and others hit the atabaques only with their hands.

Custom of the Black People

The term *Candomblé* is a combination of two words from the Central African Kikongo language: *Ka* and *ndonbé*, together meaning "custom of the black people."[15] The drums play an essential and dominant role in Candomblé ceremonies. The master drummer plays the *rum*, which improvises intricate variations. The rumpi and lé play relatively unchanging patterns as they repeat one steady rhythm. The master drummer or *alabê* (Yoruba *alá agbè*) always has overall control of the ceremony, so it is important that drummers never go into a trance.

In Candomblé the initiates gain their knowledge from a male *babalorixá* or *pai de santo* or a female *ialorixá* or *mãe de santo*, as leader of their *terreiro*. The leaders are trained in the liturgy and musical and dance sequences. They also have knowledge of a massive body of ritual and esoteric information concerning the ceremonies. This knowledge has no doubt undergone some change in Brazil. Even in the 1930s, Ruth Landes wrote of Bahia's senior *babalaô*, Eliseo Martinio do Bomfim: "He denounced indifference to the ancestral languages of the Yoruba and Ewe . . . passionately he condemned ignorance of African morals and traditions. He found it terrible that the new generation did not care much about cult practices, and that present day standards for these practices were being lowered and cheapened."[16]

"Nobody trusts you if you keep visiting around"

The traditional values that Bahia's Martinio held are still to be found among some capoeira mestres today. Referring to Candomblé houses (although it could also apply to capoeira mestres), he said (of his son): "No, no use . . . he just can't learn. He won't apply his head . . . he moves around from one temple to another, and that doesn't go among the African people. Nobody trusts you if you keep visiting around. They think you're snooping on secrets, and evading responsibility to one temple. You're supposed to be loyal to one temple."[17]

A typical period of apprenticeship to the first level of initiation in Candomblé was seven years. Initiates serve a tough and lengthy period of education to learn ritual behavior, dance, music, and ritual language, which will be used for serving their personal deity.

Orixá

An *orixá* is a deity, a god or goddess of Candomblé. The Yoruba believe that a Supreme Godhead created heaven and earth and all the people and lesser divinities within. The divinities and spirits are usually called Órìsà or Imolè and Ebora. They serve in God's spiritual world. The Órìsà are naturally complicated. Some of them were with the Godhead before this Being created the earth and its population. These are "Primordial Divinities."[18] Others are important figures from history: monarchs, legendary Yoruba cultural heros and heroines, famous warriors, and so on who have been promoted to the level of god or goddess. Others are the divine personification of forces and landscape in nature: mountains, earth, air, lightning and thunder, trees, sea and river, and so on. The actual number of the divinities is not possible to calculate. Yorubaland possesses many of these divinities and it's hard to say exactly how many exist. Some are popularly worshipped and others are only significant regionally.

In Brazil, the religion is subject to some variation from terreiro to terreiro. The term *terreiro* comes from the Portuguese for "large, flat, clear piece of land." Religion in Brazil is often described as "syncretic" because the African deities correspond to Catholic saints. This is disputed by some who argue that religions related to Candomblé, like Umbanda, Macumba, Caboclo, and Quimbanda are syncretic, but Candomblé is totally African, using saints only as disguise in the face of repression. Odé Kayode-Mãe Stella de Oxossi's assertion that "Iansã is not Saint Barbara" draws attention to one often-stated syncretic correspondence between Catholicism and Candomblé, albeit to profoundly disagree with it. This connection will be familiar to capoeira players through the capoeira *corrido* "O Santa Bárbara que relampuê, O Santa Bárbara que relampuá," which translates to "Saint Barbara will bring lightning."

This wouldn't make any sense unless the singer knew that Saint

The contrast between an
African ngonge and a
Brazilian agogô

A Brazilian agogô

Cord-and-peg atabaque
from Brazil

The iron double bell was a symbol of power and
kingship all over Central Africa and in Nigeria. In
Brazil, the ngonge, sometimes spelled engongui,
became known as the agogô and is used widely in
the percussive music of capoeira and Candomblé.
Modern African names include: Bantu (Congo)—
n'gogo; West Africa (Nigeria)—n'gongo; and
Mandinka—nèkè.

In Africa, cord-and-peg tension atabaques had a distribution area roughly
congruent with the iron double bell. This included the Guinea Coast from
the Niger River and west to Benin, Togo, and Ghana. Beyond West Africa,

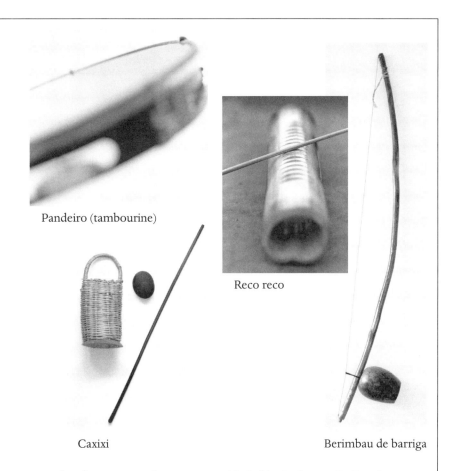

Pandeiro (tambourine)

Reco reco

Caxixi

Berimbau de barriga

cord-and-peg tension drums appeared in Bahia, Suriname, St. Domingue, Cuba, and the southern states of America. These drums traveled with the Ewe, Fon, Akan, and Yoruba people during the New World diaspora.

The berimbau developed from the San musical hunting bow some five to seven thousand years ago. The change from using the mouth to a gourd (cabaça) resonated instrument is thought to have occurred in Angola and South Africa among Bantu people.

Moquoque, also called *ngonge* or *gange,* was a military instrument of the black people. Queen Ginga (Nzinga) was said to have taken up the moquoque when she became an Imbangala. (Source: Cavazzi da Montecuccolo, Istorica Descrizione de tre regni Congo, Matamba ed Angola.)

Barbara is associated with Iansá, a goddess of storms, wind, and lightning in Candomblé. Whether one agrees or disagrees with Mãe Stella de Oxossi, the syncretic correspondences are made, just as they are between other types of non-Christian religions, archetypes, and Catholicism, whether Celtic, Qabalistic, Greek, or Roman. Saint Barbara, for example, also corresponds to the planet Mars, the angel Michael and the Egyptian archetype Sekmet.[19]

Ruth Landes spent a year with the priestesses of Candomblé at the terreiro of Menininha do Gantois (described in the glossary). At the time when Menininha was *mãe* at Gantois, in the 1930s, she had appointed a priestess named Maria José, nicknamed Zézé. This woman's husband was very jealous of the time devoted to her religious duties at Gantois, so sometimes she neglected to do them. Her goddess was Iansá, or, as she was known even in the 1930s, "St. Barbara of the lightning." Maria José even referred to herself as Zézé of Iansá and was quite clear that she belonged to her goddess rather than her husband. Landes reported that Zézé told her when she didn`t do her work at Gantois, Iansá would beat her up; one time the goddess battered her so that her eyes were blackened for many weeks, and on another occasion twisted her arm so that she couldn`t use it for months.

Indeed, possession by a god or goddess of Candomblé could get very rough and it was essential that there were experienced mães or assistant mães (called *ekedis*) there to dispatch the gods after the ceremony, which could take up to twelve hours.

When soldiers and a Brotas magistrate raided a Candomblé house in Bahia in 1829, he wrote in his report, "Some black women were dancing, others were off in a room sleeping, or pretending to sleep."[20] They didn`t know that this room was a specially reserved place called a *roncô*, where elaborate rituals were performed to send the orixás away. But even once dispatched, in their place came misbehaving imps known as *êre,* said to be the children of Xangô and Iansá. During this second phase of lighter trance, the women were allowed to eat and drink and they would begin to run around and act in sometimes bizarre ways, during which time those who were not entranced would move things out of the êre's way to avoid accidents, and the mãe might lock doors and windows to stop them running out of the terreiro, causing havoc to themselves or others.

It was the mãe who would decide when it was time for the êres to sleep, and when they did they might sleep straight through for a full twenty-four hours before once again being taken into the roncô for some final ablutions. In another, earlier, stage some of the priestesses might have been nodding off or appearing to sleep as they were attended to by their ekidi.

The 1829 Brotas magistrate will have caused more harm than he imagined when disrupting the ceremony. If the religious protocol were not followed in the correct order, or if the worshippers were rushed and interrupted during, for instance, a ceremony when orixás were being sent away from laywomen or men who had become possessed, the possessed worshippers might be sent back into the normal world still in a state of confusion and vulnerability, still in thrall to the "Saint" and often very unhappy.

Capoeiristas were drawn from among the same milieu as the Candomblé worshippers and the influences of one on the other are often marked. Many capoeira players will be familiar with the habit of touching the floor at the entrance to a capoeira roda, or touching the forehead to the floor before a game. These things were the custom of Candomblé and Yoruban religious practitioners centuries ago. Mestre Pastinha told a Finnish researcher in 1964:

"Capoeira is religious. It comes from the same religion as Candomblé, as the Batuque and the Samba. Candomblé has the same amount of religious meaning but now with the modification it is a little bit different. The manifestation is a little bit different but the amount is the same. The religion is the same."

When the research anthropologist asked if there was a rivalry between Candomblé and capoeira, Mestre Pastinha said, "It doesn't have rivalry; it is together. The capoeirista is the same as a Candomblé priest. Now he has abandoned one part for another. We follow the Candomblé priest. We practice the Candomblé. If it wasn't like that we wouldn't go in the Candomblé house. We are from the same base. But now, one runs to capoeirismo, the other to Candomblé."

Compared to Yoruba and Vodun religions, Candomblé trimmed down the number of orixás to a core group. These include:

- *Iansã* (Yoruba = ìya = mother + sán = thunder), associated with St. Barbara, in the dominion of wind, storms, thunder, lightning, and vengeance.

- *Ibêji* (Yoruba = ìbi = birth + èji = two), associated with the Saints Cosmus and Damian, the twins, in the dominian of fertility and duality.

- *Iemanjá* (Yoruba = yè yè = mother + omon = animals + eja = fish), associated with Our Lady of the Conception, of the Rosary, the Virgin Mary, in the dominion of water, under the sea, families, and mothers.

- *Nanã* (Yoruba = na nón = oneself), associated with St. Anne, who is the mother of orixás, in the dominion of the sea, of ruins, and the "guardian of the Portal of Death"; also known as *Mãe-d'água* (mother of the water).

- *Ogum or Ogún*, associated with both St. George and St. Antony, in the dominion of war.

- *Omulu* (Yoruba = *omu* = sharp + *oolu* = hole-maker), associated with St. Benedict, in the dominion of sickness and illness, cemeteries, infectious diseases like small pox and yellow fever.

- *Oxalá*, associated with Jesus Christ and Christ of the Bonfim and known as the father of orixás and in Yoruba as the Great Orixá, in the dominion of procreation, creation in nature, and peace and death.

- *Oxóssi*, associated with St. Sebastion and the God of the Caboclos, in the dominion of the hunt and the forest.

- *Oxum*, associated with Our Lady of the Rosary and St. Catherine, named after an African river, in the dominion of the sea, femininity, and the womb, and symbolizing charity.

- *Oxumarê* (Yoruba = *osumàarè* = rainbow), no regularly used associative saint, in the dominion of the rainbow and the sky.

- *Xangô,* associated with many, including St. Gerome, St. Michael, St. Peter, and St. John, in the dominion of law, tempests. Xangô is also a ritual in itself practiced by Gegê and Nagô people in northeast Brazil.

The atabaques used in Candomblé to call the orixás are treated with reverence. The drums are dressed with a cloth adorned with beads and shells, called an *ojá* in Yoruban, which is also used to decorate alters, or sometimes as a sash used to carry babies in Bahia. After being built the drums are baptized; they have a godfather and godmother. The drums are refreshed each year at ceremonies with holy water, chicken blood, honey, and oil.

Certain drum rhythms are associated with particular orixás. These include:

- *Adarúm* to quicken the orixá's descent
- *Aderé* for Oxum and Iemanjá
- *Agueré* for Oxóssi and Iansã
- *Aluj* for Xangô
- *Barravento* for many orixás
- *Bravun* for Oxalá
- *Egô* for Iansã
- *Ibi* for Oxalá
- *Opanijé* for Omulu
- *Saté* for Oxumarê

Set dance steps correspond to the rhythms associated with specific orixás. Drummers are vital in calling these deities. In Nigeria, "the dances take definite forms, depending upon the divinities to which the offerings are made. These ritual dances are not mere emotional responses to the rhythm of the music. They are symbolic; often re-enactments of something sacred. . . . the devotees do not dance anyhow but are constrained to conform in their dance to certain forms and patterns."[21]

In the Yoruba religion of Nigeria, "there are many songs sung in connection with the worship of the different divinities in Yorubaland . . . many of which are sung on festival occasions. In some cases, a fixed number of songs has to be sung and in a particular order. Although the songs are not recorded, the officiating priests never forget the order in which they should be sung."[22]

In Candomblé, "the extensive repertoires of song originate from the association of specific songs with each deity. . . . The ritual power of musical sounds, combined with the liturgical significance of lyrics as components of myths, explains the length and complexity of Candomblé ritual songs."[23]

There is a reciprocal relationship, a kind of conversation between the dancers, singers, and drummers. "The master drummer is the 'mainspring of the ritual, its focal point.' Cutting across the established beat with the rhythm of a particular orixá, he is able to trigger . . . the dancers' brain. . . . From that moment on, the dancer is the orixá, and behaves accordingly. He or she first salutes the drums, and is then dressed in the appropriate costume and handed the appropriate . . . emblems, arms, or ritual tools."[24]

Even though the song is more important in the liturgy, the three drums command the music. They are accompanied by call-and-response singing. Candomblé songs are still sung in Yoruba language in Brazil. The same drum patterns used to summon Ogún in pre-Sokoto Caliphate Yorubaland are used to summon Ogún in a Candomblé ceremony in Bahia in the 21st century.

"Berimbau bateu, angoleiro me chamou"

The atabaques of Candomblé have influenced the use of the berimbau in capoeira. Before exploring how, a glossary and some backgound history. (The following is formatted like the larger glossary at the end of this volume; see that glossary for additional terms.)

benta: Described in *Stedman's Surinam:* "a branch bent like a bow, by means of a slip of dry reed, or warimbo, which when held to the teeth, the string is beaten with a short stick, and being shifted back and forward sounds not unlike a jew's harp."

berimbau de bacia: Played vertically using a hand basin as resonator, and a sliding bottle to change pitch while striking with a stick.

berimbau de barriga: A gourd-resonated bow (literally, belly bow).

berimbau de boca: A mouth bow or jew's harp, "used by old Angolans and played with a cord of limbo, a kind of vine—the cord is made to vibrate by striking it with a knife."[25]

bilimbano: Mandinga word for the berimbau.

brimbale: French word for berimbau de barriga.

bucumbumba: Another Brazilian term for berimbau de barriga.

burumbumba: Cuban name for berimbau de barriga.

chipendani: Zimbabwean name for a bow identical to the berimbau de barriga.

gubo: A similar unbraced gourd bow recorded in 19th-century Mozambique.

guimbarde: Portuguese word for jew's harp or mouth harp, sometimes claimed to be the root of the word berimbau, as guimbarde de barriga was a distinction for the belly bow as opposed to the guimbarde de boca (mouth bow),which turned into the word berimbau de barriga over time.

humbo: 19th-century name for the berimbau de barriga in Luanda.

hungi, hungu: Variations on the 19th-century name for the berimbau de barriga in Luanda.

lungungu: Regional Congolese name for the berimbau (Mbala and Sonde).

lukungo: Regional Congolese name for the berimbau (Luluwa, Mwanza, and Bapende).

madimba lungungu: Early 19th-century name for berimbau de barriga in Rio de Janeiro.

mbulumbaniba: Southwestern Angolan name for the berimbau.

mbulumbumba: Bantu term for the gourd-resonated bow used by the Ngumbi and Handa in southwestern Angola.

mbirimbau: Angolan Kimbundu word for musical bow.

mbilimbano: Name for the berimbau on the Island of Guam.

nkungu: Another reported 19th-century name for the gourd-resonated musical bow in Angola.

oburububa: A berimbau played by Africans in Benguela, as described in 1881.

ombumbumba: Berimbau de barriga used by the Ovimbundu of central Angola in the early 20th century.

onkhonji: The hunting bow and the mouth-resonated musical bow in the Luhanda language spoken in Huíla, southwestern Angola by the Bantu peoples of that region, including the Nkhumbi, the Handa, and the Cipungu.

oricongo: Debret's name for the berimbau in his celebrated drawing in *Voyage pittoresque et historique au Brésil*. This is one other name for the instrument in early 19th-century Brazil.

rucumbo: 19th-century name for the berimbau on the Angola-Congo border.

sambi, pandiguaro, gorokikano: Three Cuban terms for the berimbau.

urucungo: Another Brazilian term for the berimbau.

urucongo: A berimbau reported in 1858 as accompanying the batuque in Brazil.

violâm: Reputed 19th-century Portuguese name for the berimbau,
but coined by the Lundu people.

warimbo: A term for a bent bow, mouth-resonated and beaten with
a stick, used by Stedman in the 18th century.

The San Hunting Bow

Berimbaus originated when San hunter-gatherers used hunting
bows to create musical sounds with the vowel and click consonants
in the San language. A resonator was formed when the end of the
bow was put into the mouth.[26]

"Khoisan" is a compound word taken from the African names of
two peoples, Khoikhoi and San, who were hunter-gatherers on the
open savannah between modern-day Somalia and central Angola
at least seven or eight thousand years ago. San people penetrated
south and Khoisan languages are still today, according to Professor J. H. Greenberg, the primary languages of Southwest Africa.[27]
In Western terms, the Khoikhoi were called Hottentots and San
called Bushmen. They were the indigenous nomads of this region
before the arrival of the Bantu people.

Discovery of a harmonic counterpoint could have occurred at
any time up to seven thousand years ago. San and Bantu contact

began in Southern Africa in approximately the fourth century after
Bantu migrated over the Zambian and Zimbabwean plateaus. The
Bantu learned of San harmonics, which hadn't been developed
anywhere else in Africa. Bantu migrants incorporated San musical forms into their own music. This included the harmonic series,
because the San were able to play on the stretched string of the
hunting bow.

Up to 1300 A.D, San speakers still lived in Angola and Zambia
and had a significant influence on Bantu musical tradition. The
change from using the mouth as a resonator to using a gourd probably occurred in Angola and Southern Africa among the Bantu.
The gourd-resonated mbulumbumba in southwestern Angola was
a San-Bantu musical collaboration.

Today:

> In Angola's southwestern province of Wila (Huíla) . . . the !Kung
> [San] hunter-gatherers remain a population segment, however small;
> and they have long lived in intensive economic cooperation with their
> Bantu neighbors. In Luanda, one of the languages of this group of
> peoples, onkhonji, is the name for both the hunting bow and the
> mouth resonated musical bow. The villagers themselves acknowl-
> edge it as a San heritage . . . the idea of using a hunting bow as a
> mouth bow with alternate performative techniques—(a) inserting
> one end of the bow stick into the mouth, and (b) passing the center
> of the back of the bow stick past the lips—came from the !Kung,
> many generations back.[28]

Studies of late-19th-century !Kung/San music in southwestern
Angola recorded the indigenous use of only two types of musical
instrument: musical bows, and stamping tubes. Stamping tubes
were also used in the Christian ring shouts already alluded to in

connection with North American circle dancing: "The ring shout was most often a ritual in which bondsmen would form a circle and dance counterclockwise. The dance was accompanied by the clapping of hands and the beating of poles against the ground in African polyrhythmic patterns."[29]

Calabash gourd-resonated instruments traveled to the American South and Caribbean islands. As we have noted, the berimbau is present in Cuba, and a variety of the instrument was described by Jonathan Boucher, "recalling his Chesapeake days in the 1760s and 1770s, . . . well remember[ed], that in Virginia and Maryland the favorite and almost only instrument in use amongst the slaves . . . was a bandore; or, as they pronounced the word, banjer. Its body was a large hollow gourd, with a long handle attached to it, strung with catgut and played on with the fingers."[30] This type of berimbau probably originated in Senegambia and often had a skin stretched over the mouth of the gourd and strings stretched outside the skin. It could either be plucked or hit with sticks and was the prototype for the modern banjo.

When Angola's Kwanza River became the largest slave route in history, the area north and east of Lubango was heavily exploited via the slave trade. The mbulumbumba, as it was called there, traveled to Brazil too. In capoeira, the berimbaus and the circle (*roda*) reflected a variety of the same elements as the roda de Candomblé. This is something that may have started in Salvador in the 19th century when Candomblé and Yoruba culture began to cross-fertilize with the Bantu *jogo de angola* that had already become established.

Gerhard Kubik writes:

> The Nigerian socio-linguist Valentine Ojo told me . . . that the large
> Yoruba lamellophone called agidigbo . . . was used long ago as an

instrument to accompany a wrestling game called gidigbo. . . . I am not suggesting that the Yoruba wrestling game was exported [to Brazil] and merged with the older capoeira. Culture is not necessarily exported in its visually and auditively perceptible dimension only. There was a readiness in Yoruba culture to use melodic instruments for the accompaniment of such games.[31]

Caxixi

The rattle, caxixi, which was used by the Rio porters, fills a gap noted by Gerhard Kubik, who acknowledges that the musical bow from southwest Angola, the mbulumbumba, is identical:

> in the construction and the playing technique, as well as in the tuning and in a number of basic patterns played [to the berimbau]. The mode of attachment of the calabash . . . and most significantly, how the player holds it with his left hand are all identical. . . . More important is the finger set. I have not seen it anywhere else so far besides in Angola. There was only one minor difference: the Angolans stopped the string with the nail of the thumb in a kind of pincer movement of thumb and index finger, while the Brazilians had adopted a coin instead.[32]

Kubik writes of the caxixi: "In some way its presence is a riddle. In Angola I did not see musical bow players holding a rattle at the same time. Historical illustrations of the gourd-bow in Brazil of the 19th century also show no trace of a caxixi."[33]

In the few tantalizing pictures of 19th-century berimbau players, the caxixi is missing, but it was very evidently in use by the work gangs in the city of Rio de Janeiro. Sometimes it was made of tin. A Reverend Charles Samuel Stewart wrote:

The jingling and drumming of the tin rattles or gourds borne by the leaders of the gangs, transporting on their heads all manner of articles . . . the dull recitative, followed by the loud chorus, with which they move along; the laborious cry of others. . . . The first sight which arrests the eyes of the stranger on landing in Rio is the number, varied employments, and garb of the negroes. The first and chief human sounds that reach his ears are also from his class. Their cries through the streets vary with the pursuits they follow. That of the vegetable and fruit vendors is monotonous and singular; but so varied, that each kind of vegetable and fruit seems to have its own song. The coffee-carriers, moving in gangs, have a tune of their own to which they keep time, in an Indian-like lope, with a bag of one hundred and sixty pounds weight, poised on their heads. The bearers of furniture form a regular choir. One or two, with rattles of tin in their hands, resembling the nose [sic] of a watering pot, perforated with holes and filled with shot, lead the way in a style truly African. To this is allied, with full strength of lungs, a kind of travelling chant, in which at times all join in chorus. It is full and sonorous.[34]

The British artist Robert Ewes wrote: "The best and strongest negroes not brought up as servants or to any trade are employed in carrying coffee from the stores to the custom-house, where it is shipped. They work in gangs of ten or twelve, each carrying a bag of coffee on his shoulders. They . . . work cheerfully, one singing a song and often carrying a rattle, whilst the others join in the chorus, and always go at a jog trot."[35]

The rattles that the workers shook were cone-shaped like the caxixi, and were called *ganzás* or *canzas*. These words derived from the Angolan Kimbundu word for gourd, *nganza*.[36] Ganzas differ from the caxixi in that they are held by a handle and they are metallic rather than woven from wicker. Call-and-response chanting, emblematic of capoeira, was indispensable to slaves in Rio de Janeiro (who made up the body of the capoeiristas in the city during the same period).

Rio de Janeiro magistrates tried unsuccessfully to ban such singing in the early 19th century. Two American clergymen described how this was received by the African workers, who, they said:

usually go in troops, numbering ten or twenty individuals, of whom one takes the lead, and is called the captain. These are usually the largest and strongest men that can be found. . . . Each one takes a bag of coffee upon his head, weighing one hundred and sixty pounds, and when all are ready they start off upon a measured trot, which soon increases to a rapid run.

As one hand is sufficient to steady the load, several of them frequently carry musical instruments in the other, resembling children's rattle boxes: these they shake to the double-quick time of some wild Ethiopian ditty, which they all join in singing as they run. Music has a powerful effect in exhilarating the spirits of the Negro; and certainly no one should deny him the privilege of softening his hard lot by producing the harmony of sounds, which are sweet to him, however uncouth to other ears. It is said, however, that an attempt was at one time made to secure greater quietness in the streets by forbidding the Negroes to sing. As a consequence they performed little or no work, so the restriction was in a short time taken off. Certain it is that they now avail themselves of their vocal privileges at pleasure . . . in singing and shouting to each other as they run. . . . The impression made upon the stranger by the mingled sound of their hundred voices falling upon his ear at once is not soon forgotten.[37]

There are many other descriptions of gourd rattles and caxixis accompanying the rhythm of the work and the singing. Thomas Ewbank coined the phrase "Angola warble" to describe it. His journal from Rio de Janeiro recalled: "Chanting only at intervals, they passed the lower part of the Cattete in silence, and then struck up the Angola warble that surprised me. There they go, jog trotting on! The foremost . . . in his hand a gourd-rattle . . . beats time and leads the way." This gourd rattle was possibly a Yoruban *agé* or *sèkèrè*, in Brazil an *aguê* or *xequerê,* which was covered with netting and cowrie shells.[38]

A French painter, François Baird, described the cone shape of the rattle: "being like the nose of a watering can and . . . having little pebbles inside." An American naturalist, H. Smith, wrote of the porters moving "in time to the leader's rattle, and to a plaintive chant."[39]

Observers reported that though the lead singers' verse varied, the chorus was rendered as a steady response to the call. The British vice-consul in Salvador wrote in 1851: "This chorus generally consists of one of the blacks chanting a remark on anything he sees, and the others come in with a chorus . . . which is seldom varied, however much the recitative solo part may."[40]

"Negroes fighting with their open hands"

British vice-consul James Wetherall wrote a derogatory description of capoeira in Rio in 1856: "Negroes fighting with their open hands is a frequent scene in the lower city. They seldom come to blows, or at least sufficient to cause any serious damage. A kick on the shins is about the most painful knock they give each other.

They are full of action, capering and throwing their legs about like monkeys during their quarrels."[41]

Porters who had free hands would also clap. The U.S. attaché to Spain, J. E. Warren, in Pará in 1840, "met with a party of some thirty or forty blacks, each one of them bearing a large basket of tapioca on his head. . . . They marched on at a slow and measured pace, chanting at the same time a singularly monotonous air, to which they beat time with their hands. . . . they were free blacks, and called themselves Ganhadores. Their business was that of loading and unloading vessels."[42]

Elements of capoeira music were inherent to the everyday working life of slaves in Brazil. Kubik suggests how the caxixi rattle may have been included in capoeira music: "More than one musical bow is needed in capoeira to control the game. And there must be something to mark the beat of the music. In many African traditions rattles are the most important beat-carrying instruments. So it is apparent why the caxixi could have been integrated into the playing techniques of the bow."[43]

The shakers described were percussive instruments shipped or inspired from Africa. The ganzá (canzá or xeque-xeque) was an Angolan intrument made from a tin-plated tube filled with small beads or pebbles; the aguê was a whole gourd covered with netting and shells.

Kubik found not much evidence of bell-shaped, bow-gripped caxixis in Angola. In Nigeria and Cameroon he found them made in the same way as a berimbau's caxixi, the bottom sealed off by a calabash disc. Large plaited rattles similar to the caxixi have also been used in Benin. In northern Angola and southwestern Zaire, musicians use a large fibre-plaited caxixi.

Berimbau in Capoeira

There are no written records of the berimbau accompanying capoeira prior to the 20th century, although in Rio de Janeiro glimpses exist. We've already referred to the order during the reign of Dom Pedro II that officers should arrest any soldiers "found in the company of musicians, or in groups of civilians on the streets of the city."[44]

Also during the Paraguayan War, in Dom Pedro's time, Frenchman Émile Allain was alarmed by capoeira gangs in Rio: "They are present at all large gatherings. One sees them especially in the front of parades at popular festivities, engaged in a gymnastic performance or special dance . . . called capoeira."[45]

Charles Dent, who was at the Rio carnival in the 1880s, described "every kind of horse-play [being] exercised. Numerous mulattos, called Capoeiros [sic], dance about and run amok with open razors strapped to their hands, with which they rip people up in a playful manner. The police are always on the look-out for these gentlemen, and rush out on them with drawn swords."[46]

In Recife, capoeira was played at the front of carnival parades more than a hundred years ago. Carnival clubs were formed by urban laborers. Feared capoeristas like Nascimento Grande led these parades, which were accompanied by military marching music. This gave birth to *frevo da rua*, noisy syncopated rhythms from clarinets, saxophones, trumpets, trombones, tubas, snare drums, and tambourines, played in a fast duple meter.

Recife was a center of political protectionism (*capangagem*). There were violent clashes between capoeira gangs who led the carnival parades. Recife's elite didn't like frevo da rua, because of its association with capoeira. Frevo was characterized by elaborate drum rolloffs with brass and woodwind countermelodies and per-cussion. This created non-stop musical accompaniment to march-ing dances. Frevo da rua was banned in the same time as capoeira. In its place came *frevo de bloco*, a softer version, featuring flutes, bandolins (similar to mandolins), violins, a female voice chorus— and slower tempo. This became the accepted and legal form in Recife by the early 20th century.

Did the music accompanying capoeira in the 19th century include berimbau? The berimbau had been played in Brazil at least since the 1700s. Maria Graham, governess to Pedro I's daughter, lived in the imperial palace on the quayside in Rio. She said it was completely open to "the noise and dirt of the city."[47] She wrote of "uncouth airs, played on rude African instruments . . . the most inartificial things that ever gave out musical sounds . . . yet they have not an unpleasing effect. . . . [a musical bow] simply com-posed of a crooked stick, a small hollow gourd, and a single string of brass wire. The mouth of the gourd must be placed on the naked skin of the side, so that the ribs of the player form the sounding-board, and the string is struck with a short stick."[48]

Regarding the question of the caxixi's use with the berimbau, researcher Peter Fryer found that in the Kongo-Angola area the caxixi is used as an instrument by itself. "The Baluba people of Lunda call it cassaca, the Libolos [call it a] quissaca." Yet the berim-bau was being used with the caxixi in Brazil by the mid-19th cen-tury. James Wetherall wrote in 1856: "Between the finger and thumb of the right hand is held a small stick with which the wire is struck, producing a tinkling sound; on the other fingers is hung a kind of rattle made of basket-work, confined in which are some small stones which are made to rattle as the hand moves to strike the string. A very monotonous sound is produced, but, as usual, seems to be much appreciated by the Negroes."[49] (This was the same James Wetherall who wrote about the open-handed fighting games in Rio, although he didn't say whether they were accompanied by the berimbau.)

Also in 1856, Ladislaus Magyar was traveling in South Africa. He painted a bow of the same description, gourd-amplified, called a burumbumba. This is the name given to the Angola bow in Cuba today. A few years later, in *Ethnographía e historia tradicional dos povos da Lunda,* Henrique Augusto Dias de Carvalho wrote:

> This instrument is well known in our province of Angola. They take a stick of a particular pliable wood and bend it into a bow, joining the ends with a thick string which is made beforehand from cotton fibre and stays very taut. On the lower part of the bow is fixed a small gourd with an opening of a size calculated to secure good vibrations. This opening is turned outwards and the string goes above it. . . . The Loandas [Lunda] call it violâm. They play it when they walk around and also when they are lying in their huts. It is very handy and portable.[50]

The Lunda had been procuring slaves from the Kwango Valley and inland from Luanda Bay and south of Kongo since the early 1600s, and berimbaus were probably in Brazil even then.

Rugendas's famous painting of 1824 shows the dance-fight of capoeira performed to the drum, not the berimbau:

> The negroes have another, much fiercer, war game, the Jogar capoeira: two champions run at each other, each trying to strike with his head the chest of the opponent he is aiming to knock down. The attack is thwarted by leaping sideways or by equally skillful parrying; but in springing at each other . . . they now and again butt each

other's heads very roughly; so one often sees jesting give place to anger, with the result that the sport is made bloody with blows and even knives.[51]

No definitive analyses of early-19th-century capoeira can be achieved solely based on Rugendas's description of the game he saw. Even if he was the perfect observer, we can still wonder whether berimbaus were played in other rodas where Rugendas wasn't present with his sketch book in hand.

Signs, Crosses, Circles, Rodas

In the early 1700s, a Capuchin missionary, Father Lorenzo, stationed in the Kongo kingdom, wrote of *nsanga,* the armed war dance: "Some of them commenced to 'sangare,' that is, to make contortions to demonstrate their force and dexterity."[52]

T. J. Desch Obi describes how collective nsanga (*sangamento*):

involved dancing out large scale encounters during ritual contexts such as Imbangala initiation ceremonies, the feast day of Saint James— patron saint of the Kongo kingdom, or prior to war . . . participation was a demonstration of group loyalty to the officiating ruler [and] . . . individuals also exhibited their dexterity in their own nsanga solos against imaginary foes in attempts to outshine their rivals for the praise of the ruler.[53]

Recall Count Castelneau's 1850s account from a crowning of the king and queen of Kongo in Minas Gerais: "With great headdresses of feathers, cavalry sabers at their sides, and shields on their arms . . . [the African participants] . . . mixed national dances . . . and . . . simulated battles and all types of somersault."[54]

Desch Obi argues that nsanga and the ngolo dance were practiced inland from the Loango coast at the Zaire (Congo) River, down through the Kwango Valley and to the highlands. "As a combat system, the art of ngolo and its cognates utilized kicks and powerful head-butts for attack and acrobatic evasions for defence."[55]

From observations made on field trips in Angola, Congo, and Zaire, Desch Obi describes "a circle of singers who were at the same time potential combatants. Individual singers/fighters took turns leading call and response songs in which all those present answered back with the chorus."[56] He doesn't mention drums, berimbaus, or any other instrument being played, and he explains the circle functioning "to bring the practitioner into the spiritual world through circling or physically enacting the counter-clockwise cosmograms to draw on spiritual power."[57]

Miller also describes Mbundu war preparations: "For days and weeks before a battle, the Mbundu conducted rituals which, they believed, could determine which army would prevail, arming themselves with the best magical charms available, waiting for omens to indicate the most propitious moment to attack, and cementing their good relations with spiritual forces which could turn the actual battle in their favour."[58]

"A canoa virou marinheiro, e no fundo do mar tem dinheiro"

Translating the heading: "The ship turned over, in the depths of the sea there is treasure."

This traditional folkloric capoeira song is an apt metaphorical lyric to represent Kongolese religious ideas that have been described by T. J.Desch Obi. He explains that the counter-clockwise roda, or *elola,* was essential to central African cosmology, which "linked human combat to the interplay of spiritual forces from across the kalunga, or the threshold between the lands of the living and the dead."[59]

Kalunga in Central Africa, in N'Bunda language, meant the sea. The word also means rivers and the kingdom of the ancestors. In Kongolese cosmology, the counter-clockwise circle represents a solar cycle. If a cross were drawn within the circle, the horizontal east-to-west line is the kalunga. The kalunga divides the material world from the spirit world or afterlife. East represented birth, north was the peak of strength, west was death at the intersection with the kalunga line, and regeneration came at the southern extreme of the cross.[60]

This African cosmic cross is also found in the Western mystery tradition. William Gray writes:

> We may suppose we can think in straight lines, but in fact we do not. We just cannot see curvature of consciousness through Time anymore than we feel the curvature through Space of our planet spinning on its axis, or completing its annual cycle round the Sun. Nevertheless, if we do not learn how to live in harmony with the natural laws behind our beings, we can scarcely be very healthy or happy creatures of the Cosmos.[61]

The ngolo dance is sometimes argued to be "linked to the cosmological paradigm of the crossing of the kalunga."[62] Many movements in capoeira reflect this. The cartwheel into the circle inverts the player to the kalunga line, as the otherworld is inverted. Some *chamadas,* the "calls" of capoeira, and *volto do mundo* also follow the circular pattern.

The roda, or circle dance, is found everywhere Bantu people were spread by the Diaspora. For example, in *ladya* in Martinique, Thompson observed, "The first thing players of ladya do is to run in a mystic circle to 'close' their bodies off from emanations of jealousy and envy."[63] *Corpo fechado,* "closing the body" to attack, was traditionally achieved by the greatest capoeira masters. Besouro Mangangá (nganga) was said to possess corpo fechado, which protected him from knives and bullets.

The Caribbean and the U.S. southern delta had a high population of Bantu people. The Louisiana State Penitentiary is still today called "Angola" after the cotton and sugar plantation that once stood there. There were many regional variations to Central African cosmology.

As Christianity had spread to Kongo by the 1500s, many of the slaves transported to America were already Christian or became Christian soon after arrival. But on their own terms: "Musical ministry of black Christians [was transformed] into a deeply coded liturgy of rebellion and transcendence. Traditional hymns, with their devout tales of trials, earthly betrayal, and ultimate deliverance formed only an allegorical text to which black Christians added a wealth of painful personal experience."[64]

"Look out sister, how you walk on the cross / Your foot might slip and your soul get lost"

The verses in the heading come from what is called a ring shout.[65] In North America, Christian ring shouts involved counter-clockwise dancing and handclapping. "The use of the circle for religious purposes in slavery was so consistent and profound that one could argue that it was what gave form and meaning to black religion and art."[66] The circles of the ring shout affected "knocking and kicking." Some praise houses hired watchmen to expel worshippers who cross-stepped during a shout (to stop them doing leg sweeps).

This chapter has briefly reviewed the African contribution to fighting and musical instruments in Brazil by the 19th century. Call-and-response singing, the berimbau, caxixi, agogô, atabaque drum, pandeiros, rodas, kicks, head-butts, and other elements associated with capoeira were all in place in Brazil by 1850.

Chapter 11
THE EMPIRE OF BRAZIL

The Brazilian elite and their henchmen became deeply suspicious of foreigners. In 1816, Rio Intendent Viana was jailing anyone, white or black, who arrived in Rio de Janeiro from the Caribbean. Since the uprising in St. Domingue, the Brazilian ruling class suffered from a morbid collective paranoia.

In 1816, Carlos Romão, "a black man . . . of the French nation," was thrown into Rio's jail and interrogated to see if he was "from the Island of São Domingos, or from there had come [with] others, or mulattos, if he had been in Bahia, or if he knew of anyone who was there [in Bahia] and had come from São Domingos, and their names and the marks by which they could be identified."[1]

The elite were aware of the revolutionary atmosphere in Bahia and didn't want it spreading to Rio de Janeiro. Viana thought that by holding interrogations in private, he could stop the spread of "contagious" ideas to his own back yard. He detained "Blacks from Martinique. . . . with these men I have always sought to avoid entering into judicial enquiries or investigations involving witnesses which always give body to formless things, and raise ideas unknown to the great body of the people."[2]

Rio's ruling class was afraid of many things, not least that the new prince regent, Dom Pedro, would go back to Lisbon, leaving Rio just one of many colonial capitals in Portugal's kingdom. But instead of leaving Brazil, in September 1822, he declared independence from Portugal with the battle cry "Independence or Death!"

The empire had no education or transportation system, no national administration, a free press that was only a year old. One-third of the population were slaves, half of them born in Africa. The majority of the population were illiterate and Brazil's wealth was in the hands of a very limited group of landowners and politicians. This oligarchy controlled Brazil through town councils and the various branches of the armed forces.

It took Dom Pedro a year to oust the Portuguese troops from the country. By declaring himself emperor, Dom Pedro I had obviously antagonized his father, Dom João IV, the king of Portugal. European monarchs despised Brazil's new emperor so much that when he was searching for a wife in Europe, no royal house would supply one of their daughters.

His single friend in Europe was Great Britain, which gained extraordinary financial benefits from Brazil and wanted to resolve the new empire's problems as quickly as possible. Britain suggested that if Brazil would guarantee abolition of Atlantic slave trade, Britain would recognize the empire. The Brazilians were becoming attracted to the idea of replacing slaves with European laborers because they feared a permanent and increasingly radical and restless black majority.

Portugal didn't like the idea of an independent Brazil; neither did Dom João IV relish his eldest son taking a title even more high and mighty than his own.

To please Britain, Brazil agreed to end the Atlantic slave trade within four years and Britain put heavy diplomatic pressure on Portugal to recognize the Brazilian empire, which it did in 1825. For their diplomatic help, Britain won privileged commercial treaties with Brazil.

Dom Pedro I was very unpopular in Brazil. He was generally considered an ignoramus and certainly wasn't an astute leader. One of his first acts of leadership was to order troops from the Rio garrison to dissolve the empire's brand new Constituent Assembly by violent force. This was such an error of judgment he never really recovered from it.

It was the death of Dom João IV, in 1826, that hurried along Brazil's treaty to end slave trade with Africa. Pedro I automatically became king of Portugal, but as he was already the self-styled emperor of Brazil, he abdicated and crowned his eldest daughter, D. Maria, queen of Portugal instead. The Portuguese weren't overjoyed at being ruled by a seven-year-old girl who lived in Rio de Janeiro. Once again Britain stepped in and Dom Pedro I was so deeply indebted he ended up signing anything the British envoy handed him.

As Lord Canning had already told the Cabinet in London, "The great mart of the legal slave trade is Brazil."[3] And as Jean Suret-Canale points out, "The 'economic imperatives' of expanding liberal capitalism had finally got the better of those of the slave plantation. . . . Thus English industrialists, who in the first half of the 19th century reduced their own workers to unimaginable misery, exhaustion and degradation, condemned slavery as an abomination in the name of humanity."[4]

Dom Pedro I's new laws were a great shock to the many Brazilians whose money was tied up everywhere in the purchase of Africans. The illegal slave trade eventually eased their misgivings, but for now they simply increased imports ahead of abolition. By 1829, 60,000 Angolans a year were arriving in Rio de Janeiro.

Traveling from Rio to Minas Gerais that year, the Reverend Robert Walsh wrote of slave caravans:

> winding through the woods, the slave merchant, distinguished by his large felt hat and poncho, bringing up the rear on a mule, with a long lash in the hand. It was another subject of pity to see groups of these poor creatures cowering together at night in the open ranches drenched with cold rain, in a climate much more frigid than their own . . . [and] . . . such a glut of human flesh in the markets of Rio that it has become an unprofitable drug.[5]

Major Nunes Vidigal

The police chiefs themselves, even though they were the scourge of the capoeiristas in Rio de Janeiro, were sometimes said to be adepts of the art too. Major Nunes Vidigal is a famous example—a capoeirista who was also the first commander of the *Guarda Real do Palácio*. As the main character in the novel *Memórias de um Sargento de Milícias*, Vidigal was, according to Almeida, "an expert of person-to-person combat and his remarkable skill with weapons, such as the club and straight-razor, gave him the reputation of being invincible in their use. He instituted a special kind of torture called cêia de camarões (shrimp supper) which was a nightmare of violence for his brothers in capoeira."[6]

Gilberto Freyre elaborates:

> Elysio de Araujo tells how, in Rio de Janeiro at the beginning of the nineteenth century, the talk of the town was the so-called "shrimp dinners": the severe cudgeling by the grenadiers of the Royal Police Guard of "vagabonds" or "idlers" who were rounded up in the "dances

which were at the time frequent in the outskirts of the city." . . . After their severe trouncing by the grenadiers of the notorious Major Vidigal, who, with his gentle air and sweet voice, was often the evil spirit of the Royal Police Guard, and their imprisonment for some time in the guardhouse, the "able-bodied" on their release "joined the army."[7]

The shrimp supper torture sometimes involved cutting the hamstring of the prisoner. Its creator, Major Vidigal, was reportedly present in June 1828, when 2,000 German and Irish mercenary troops were billeted in Rio de Janeiro. Pedro I had hired these men to fight in the Crisplatine Province of Rio de la Plata in a war with Argentina that led to the formation of Uruguay.

Various accounts about the development of the fighting in Rio differ in detail. According to Bira Almeida, "Once in a while, capoeiristas were considered heroes, as . . . when they helped to suffocate a rebellion of foreign soldiers in 1828. . . . The incident ended when the soldiers were confronted by a group of capoeiristas. Although armed with rifles, the soldiers could not defend themselves against the clubs, razor blades, sticks, stones and cunning of the capoeiras."[8]

Thomas Holloway says, "In Rio the idle foreign troops irritated the native population with their arrogance and drunken sprees. When their officers attempted to impose more rigorous discipline and ordered corporal punishment for some of the more egregious offenders, the mercenaries broke out of the barracks in revolt."[9]

Essentially, one German and two Irish battalions were in conflict with their commanders. It was said that the Germans quartered at São Cristovão began the trouble. They burned their barracks and were soon joined by other German soldiers from Praia Vermelha. They killed Major Benedito Teola, looted vast quantities of liquor, and carried on with their spree. Forty-eight hours passed.

It was said that the Germans tried to encourage the Irish mercenaries quartered in Campo de Santana to break out of their barracks and join in. Brazilian militia cut off the Irish before they could reach the streets. When Irish soldiers given the job of guarding public buildings went to join their countrymen, the police of the Corte were unable to contain the mutineers.

Vidigal, of the infamous shrimp dinner, led a large contingent of capoeiristas who confronted the soldiers, some of whom were armed with muskets. Gangs of capoeiristas carried on running battles with English, Irish, and German northerners, taking revenge for the previous week's agitation and violence. It took five days before the mercenaries were eventually put down.

Holloway points out that it was unlikely the police force actively requested the slave capoeiristas' assistance when they were "the day before and the week after . . . subject to 100 lashes and a term in the Calabouço [for capoeira]." Holloway suggested, "An interpretation is . . . that gangs took advantage of the generally anarchic situation . . . to strike out at a group of white strangers who nobody wanted to protect anyway."[10]

It was the capoeiristas who eventually beat the mercenaries: "By stones, clubs, and bodily skill . . . they fell in the streets and squares, many of them wounded and a considerable number dead."[11]

Robert Walsh, a clergyman from Finglas in County Dublin, had recently been appointed as chaplain to the British Embassy in Rio de Janeiro. Walsh traveled in the interior of Rio de Janeiro and to Minas Gerais on the same route that Rugendas had taken five years before. In 1828 he was a witness to the events of the Irish insurrection in Rio and his account gives a different perspective.

Foreigners were not popular in Rio in 1828. Since the Portuguese had been expelled, there was extreme prejudice against all foreigners, shared by both white Brazilians and African slaves. Pedro I had assigned a Colonel Cotter of the imperial service in Rio, an Irish officer, to hire a large contingent of mostly very poor Irish agricultural workers and some mechanics from Cork, who were told they'd receive one shilling, a pound of beef, and a pound of bread, and be employed in four hours of military training each day. They would act as soldiers, and would reside in Rio unless there was an invasion or war in which they were needed elsewhere in Brazil. These Irish "soldiers" were told that after five years of military service they would each be assigned fifty acres of agricultural land.

Walsh reported, "Two thousand four hundred persons were collected, some of them, as was to be expected, of indifferent characters and dissolute manners; but the majority decent, respectable people, who brought out with them their wives and families."[12]

What the newly arrived immigrants from Cork didn't know was that their dream of beginning a new life as Brazilian farmers had led them into a nightmare of alcoholism, jail, violence, and degradation. Everything went wrong, from the day of their arrival at Rio de Janeiro. Nothing was ready for them; their accommodations and barracks were squalid. There was no food, no training, and most of the time they were tricked out of whatever wages were supposed to be given to them. They slept on the floor, often without a mattress, and lived in dirty clothes, hungry and virtually forgotten. There was no regularity or routine, no discipline, and the mainstay of their existence was the many rum houses, filled with cheap *cachaça,* where a youngster could spend his days in reverie, drowning sorrows and, as Walsh put it, drunk with both rum and fever, Many Irish, he reported, were seen "crawling about the streets of Rio" daily.

At the same time, Walsh observed:

The miserable slaves of Rio, employed only as beasts of burden in the streets, are, of all classes of the human race, by far the most abandoned and degraded. Used merely as inferior animals, without the smallest reference to their being endowed with the faculty of reason, they are driven all day, and turned loose in the evening; and by a strange inconsistency, allowed the most licentious and un-restrained habits. They go along in the streets frequently drunk, shouting, hallooing, and fighting; and when one considers that there are fifty or sixty thousand of this class, in a large and licentious city, and the great majority of its population, it is fearful to contemplate the consequences which may arise, some time or other, from their ferocious passions.[13]

Rio de Janeiro's African population and the newly arrived soldiers from Cork didn`t make friends with each other. The Irishmen were dubbed *escravos brancos* ("white slaves") and, according to Walsh, reminded of this fact every time they encountered African slaves outside the barracks. There were constant fights in the streets, and it seemed to Walsh that African slaves and capoeiristas (whom he does not call by the name capoeira, referring instead to "moleques") were being used to deliberately attack and harrass the soldiers by the white Brazilian citizens of the city, who looked on with satisfaction when these fights took place. The Irish were punished for fighting by being sentenced to life as galley slaves and, according to Walsh, being chained along with African galley slaves, and imprisoned in the same way.

Walsh continued:

In this state of things, a body of the Irish, quartered in the barracks of Praia Vermelha, were marched to the Campo d'Acclamacão, and in their way it was necessary to pass the Carioca, a fountain where a large collection of blacks continually attend to draw water. The moment they appeared, an immediate insurrection of the blacks took place, and an attack was made on these unarmed men, quietly passing through the streets; they repelled it with sticks and fists, and the blacks fled, but from that time no recruit could appear in any part of the town, without being assaulted. Even the officers failed to preserve that respect for their rank, which would be secured to any others; they were the indiscriminate object of attack by any slaves they met, as if the general system was to degrade and exasperate the whole corps without distinction. In the Rua dos Barbonios is a barrack, near a fountain attended by blacks, and here the parties came into constant collision. The blacks, who seemed, as it were, trained to insult the Irish, constantly attacked the sentries, and even climbed up the windows, and assaulted, with stones and other missiles, those who were inside quietly sleeping in their quarters.[14]

Walsh said the condition of the German troops was much the same. They too had been left to rot. Their pay was cheated out of them and pocketed, not least by their officers; one in particular, Major Teola, had a reputation for this. The situation had become explosive by June 1828. On the 9th of that month, a low commissioned officer passed a German soldier who neglected to take off his hat out of respect to the officer's superior rank. The officer ordered the soldier to be jailed and he was sentenced to fifty lashes for insubordination. The punishment was to take place in the barracks square at São Christovão. The soldier asserted his right to be tried by a court-martial, and would not take off his jacket. After he'd been tied up, the jacket was cut off his back and the fifty lashes were raised to 250—effectively, a death sentence. After 210 lashes, the other German soldiers could see he was close to death and they demanded that the punishment stop. When the officer continued whipping the prisoner, the whole corps began a spontaneous mutiny and released their fellow soldier. Dom Pedro I refused their demands to see him. Meanwhile the Irish at the Campo d'Accla-macão heard what had happened and headed for the palace barracks at São Christovão. They wanted to join the Germans and continue the attack. The ammunition magazine was forced open and the mutiny got fully underway.

Major Teola was, according to Walsh, an Italian who had been a waiter at the Hotel du Nord in the Rue Direita. It was rumored that the reason he had received his commission to major in the German regiment was that he was married to an extremely attractive woman whose charms had somehow accelerated his career prospects way beyond his natural abilities. He was hated by the soldiers in his charge; they quickly used the opportunity of the insurrection to capture him and stab him to death with bayonets.

As the insurrection spread throughout the city, Brazilian troops were ordered to take up arms. The war minister also ordered the commandant, the Conde de Rio Pardo, "to destroy every man, to give no quarter, but to exterminate the whole of the strangers."[15]

It was at this point that the authorities also decided to call in Major Vidigal and a large number of capoeiristas armed with clubs, knives, *facas,* daggers, and swords.

> A large crowd of them was soon collected in the Campo d'Accla-macão, and a tumult immediately commenced with the Irish. These latter had now become infuriate like the Germans—had attacked the police barracks in the neighborhood, and having seized the arms, began to fire in all directions. They then broke open the vendas [rum houses], and many of them having drank caxas [cachaça] to excess, burst into private houses and committed great excesses. A regular warfare soon ensued between them and the armed Moleques, joined by a number of Brazilians of the lowest description,

and the Campo and the streets adjoining were filled with dead and wounded bodies.[16]

The Brazilian government then called on the assistance of a large force of French and English marines from warships anchored in the harbor. The German and Irish only had fifty to sixty muskets they had stolen from the police and armory, which were useless as they were by now out of ammunition.

The fighting so far had left approximately a hundred people dead. Having sobered up, many mutineers had returned to their barracks. The Germans surrendered on the 12th of June after some three days of anarchy.

Walsh said that the moleques, the term by which he described members of malta gangs and capoeiristas, were by no means finished with the fighting, even if the German and Irish had lost their taste for it.

[The maltas] rushed on every foreigner they met in the neighborhood, with their knives, and butchered them. Several of the Irish, who were artisans, industriously exercised their trades, and were doing well at Rio. One of them, a tailor, was returning to his barracks, with a bundle of clothes under his arm, entirely ignorant of the insurrection that had taken place.

He was met by two Moleques in a street leading to the Campo, who rushed at him with their facas, and having stabbed him in several places, ripped up his belly, and left him, with his bowels hanging out, weltering on the pavement. One fellow, a corpulent mulatto of a very ferocious aspect, was pointed out to me afterwards at [a] butchery . . . where he has now some appropriate employment. He was seen, after tranquility was restored, brandishing a bloody sabre over his head, and boasting it was stained with the blood of five foreigners, whom he had killed. Many of the insurgents lay down in the streets and fell asleep, overcome by fatigue and intoxication; and in that state of insensibility were stabbed by the Moleques. As this disposition for blood continued after the cause was past, and the excitement over, it was found necessary to issue, on the 13th of June, a second [decree], prohibiting any person from carrying arms, but especially slaves . . . under severe punishment. They had been most imprudently called on to take them up para salvar a patria, and it was found imperatively necessary to compel them to lay them down, for the same reason.[17]

Of the 2,400 Irish who arrived in Brazil, only some 200 were involved in the mutiny, but it was decided to send the majority of Irish back to Cork. The problem now was finding them, as many were incarcerated, in some of the most notorious jails for which Rio de Janeiro was famed in the early 19th century.

Numbers of inferior rank remained behind, till they were altogether forgotten. Such was the case of these poor men. When they emerged from these catacombs, they were in the most miserable state of destitution and disease, their bodies ulcerated with sores and covered with vermin, and their skins so raw and tender from putrescency and mortification that when it was necessary to clothe them for the sake of decency, to enable them again to appear, they could not bear the painful touch of any covering.

They had been called on to take the military oath [which would have contracted them to permanent military service under Dom Pedro I], but they refused. They affirmed they had come out as settlers. . . . they had no objection to be enrolled as militia, learn military duty, and be ready to turn out to defend their own or any other part of the country invaded, but they persisted in refusing to take the oath tendered to them as mere soldiers, for unlimited service.[18]

Unlimited military service would have made the soldiers effectively slaves of the emperor in everything but name. In fact, he frequently attended church services for the Irish at the Praya Vermelha and knelt down among the common soldiers. Every one of them suspected a plot, as a rumor had been circulated, that if this ceremony took place three times, they were legally obligated to him, as soldiers, for unlimited service. Therefore, on the third Sunday, only the officers were in church. The regular troops stayed away to avoid entrapment.

Walsh said that for the offense of refusing to take the military oath, "They were represented as mutineers, and thrown at once into these dismal dungeons, where they had remained totally neglected, and must in a short time have perished in a state of putridity, had they not been relieved. . . . in all 1,400 persons [were carried] back to their native land."[19]

As an epitaph to those Irish who returned, it should be said that the majority were injured, particularly lame, and remained destitute in Ireland for the rest of their lives, which were soon to be overtaken by the Irish potato famine of the 1840s.

Walsh pointed out that the policy of bringing the Europeans to Brazil in the first place had been a deliberate strategy of the government, aimed at increasing the population of whites. (This policy would be very strongly increased during the reign of Dom Pedro II). He mentioned the St. Domingue revolution and surmised that the planters in Brazil entertained "serious apprehensions . . . that some time or other, in the present diffusion of revolutionary doctrines on this continent, they [the slaves] will discover their own strength, assert independence for themselves, and Brazil become a second St. Domingo." He continued:

This is particularly the case at Bahia and Pernambuco, where almost all the negroes are brought from the same part of the coast of Africa; and there is a general union and understanding among them, as speaking the same language, and feeling an identity of interests; and here several conspiracies have been formed, and risings attempted. . . . But at Rio the case is different. The negro population consists of eight or nine different castes, having no common language, and actuated by no sympathetic tie; insomuch . . . they frequently engage in feuds and combats, where one, or even two hundreds of a nation on each side are engaged. This animosity the whites cherish, and endeavor to keep alive, as intimately connected with their own safety.[20]

Nationalistic feeling, which a century later would find common cause with the political ideas of National Socialist Germany and Fascist Italy, was already emerging strongly in Brazil. Walsh said that many nationalistic newspapers, particularly the *Aurora* and the *Astraea,* wrote of "delivering themselves from the German and Irish invasion," though they failed to mention that the "invaders" were mostly blind drunk and the Brazilian soldiers had been assisted by armed capoeira gangs and a number of French and English marines.

And so the insurrection was over. The slaves were forced to put down their arms once again. Only shortly before, in 1825, the chief of police of the court, Fransisco Alberto Teixeira do Aragão, decreed that slaves would be flogged and searched, day or night, to prohibit "not only the use of any weapon of defense, but to carry clubs."[21] As knives and clubs were one of the main weapons used against the mercenaries, Major Vidigal had guaranteed an amnesty, though this held only for the duration of the crisis.

After this mutiny, the emperor agreed to the dissolution of every foreign army unit. That strategy caused Pedro I eventual difficulties as they were the very soldiers who were defending the imperial palace. In 1830 there was a total breakdown of trust between the emperor and the Chamber of Deputies, who had no faith in his commitment to constitutional rule, and were suspicious of him anyway as a Portuguese-born monarch. Full-scale riots broke out on the streets of Rio. Rival gangs marched and fought pitched battles with one another. Dom Pedro I believed the best thing to do was replace all his ministers, sack the commander of the Rio garrison, and dissolve the Chamber of Deputies, just as he had done with such misjudgment in 1823.

By April 1831, central Rio had become a war zone. Masses of armed cariocas occupied the Campo de Santa Ana. The sacked ministers had armed supporters, including gangs of capoeiristas called maltas. The name *malta* is thought to come from old Lisbon slang, where itinerant road builders, laborers, and street gangs often came from the island of Malta. In Rio, capoeira gangs called maltas were allied to political parties as henchmen and mercenary fighters. The malta for Santa Ana was called Cadeira da Senhora (the Lady's Chair) after St. Anne, who is usually depicted in paintings sitting down. The crowds of people in the street were joined by garrison troops who were encouraged by their officers to leave their barracks and demand that Dom Pedro reinstate the sacked ministers.

"There remains in the imperial palace but one silver spoon"

Dom Pedro and his family were at São Cristovão palace a few miles outside of Rio de Janeiro city center. Not a single sentinel patroled the avenues leading to the palace, as even the imperial bodyguard had abandoned the family and were marching into Rio to join the throng. Messages came from Rio that if the emperor didn't restore the sacked ministers, they'd form a government without him—

and there was a strong chance of that being a republican government. Dom Pedro I had his back to the wall and, perfectly in character, he rushed into his study and scribbled a letter of abdication.

Upstairs a five-year-old child slept, unaware that his father and stepmother were about to step out of his life forever and that when he awoke it would be as Dom Pedro II, Emperor of Brazil. Dom Pedro I, his wife, and eldest daughter took refuge on a British warship anchored in Rio harbor without waking up their son to kiss him goodbye. They did, however, find time to arrange for the removal of every gold and silver object or item of expensive furniture from the palace.[22]

Cops and Capoeiristas

Despite the 1830 criminal code and a complex police system, the readiness of Rio's population to take to the streets (with troops running wild in fraternity with armed civilians) shows just how close to the surface the revolutionary potential lay. Republicanism and anarchy loomed to a degree that had the British envoy distinctly worried: "Large bodies of the populace, armed, continue to parade the streets . . . and a renewal of the past scenes of tumult may, upon the slightest cause, take place."[23]

The enthronement of the child emperor was reported by the Austrian envoy, Baron Daiser:

> We were at the palace [in Rio city] a little after mid day. . . . the coach having reached the front of the church, a man of the people, since there were present neither courtiers, nor guards, nor servants, picked up the emperor, put him on his shoulder and in this fashion carried him into the church. The people cheered him to the echo, smothered him with caresses, and kissed his hands and even his face. . . . [After-

wards] . . . a review of the troops took place, their ranks interspersed with armed common folk, and then came some 500 to 600 of the same, also armed but by themselves, without any soldiers. . . . On leaving the palace we were with difficulty able to traverse the crowd composed of all classes and all colours. It was not until 5 o'clock that we returned from this sad and unpleasant ceremony.[24]

It took until the end of the month before the troops returned to their barracks. Swords of honor were handed out in Campo de Santa Ana and the armed crowds there were eventually persuaded to hand over their weapons and disperse from the public squares.

In 1832, to curb the power of the emperor, a Code of Criminal Procedures gave more judicial and legislative power to the state. A revamped police system soon turned the police into a far more organized branch of the judiciary, led by a powerful chief of police.

The chief had two delegates, bailiffs, clerks, and sub-delegates who were assigned to Rio's eight parishes. The sub-delegates had six deputies each to assist them. There were also block inspectors who were dispersed among 195 *quateirões,* each block housing at least twenty-five residences. The block inspector could arrest as he wanted, call for backup from police, and look out for illegal activities in his own block. More than 100 armed patrolmen were spread throughout the city, on stand-by day or night to help delegates or block inspectors. There were also approximately 400 military police on night patrols. They were well trained and each was armed with two guns and a sabre. More than a hundred of them were cavalry officers by 1850. Military police collaborated with the regular police or broke up into small units to walk the beat at night. The delegates, block inspectors, and police on patrols ensured a powerful surveillance network in Rio de Janeiro.

It was in this environment that the capoeiristas existed. Paradoxically, capoeira was never formally made a crime until after the abolition of slavery, yet it was always near the top of the activities the police wanted to punish and control. In November 1832, the intendent explained to the military police commander that "the black capoeiras and individuals of a similar bent customarily carry daggers and other weapons of that nature hidden in marimbas [gourd-resonated xylophones], pieces of sugar cane and in the handles of small black whips made in this country [so practice] the utmost vigilance and carefully search such individuals, arresting those found with these instruments so that they can be punished under the law."[25]

In the early part of the century the majority of those arrested for capoeira were slaves. This began to change after 1850, with a greater percentage of free blacks and even whites arrested specifically for capoeira.

Punishment was a short term of imprisonment or 100–300 lashes in the calabouço. The police favored this as it was immediate and bypassed court sessions and decisions of judges. The police resented legislative attempts to protect slaves "convicted" of capoeira, even though it wasn't a crime.

A Britisher in Brazil in 1821, James Henderson, described what would have amounted to a typical punishment for capoeira in Rio:

> The negroes . . . in the interior . . . are treated much better than at Rio de Janeiro. . . . For a trifling offence, they are sometimes committed to the charge of two or three soldiers, who pinion them with cords, and beat them in the most unfeeling manner along the streets, to the Calabouço, a prison for the blacks. . . . Their owners procure an order from the intendent-general of the police, for one, two or three hundred lashes . . . which punishment is administered to those poor wretches by one of their own countrymen, a stout, savage-looking,

degraded Negro. . . . The black degredado set to work very mechanically, and at every stroke, which appeared to cut part of the flesh away, he gave a singular whistle. The stripes were repeated always upon the same part, and the negro bore the one hundred lashes he received at this time with the most determined resolution. On receiving the first and second strokes he called out "Jesu," but afterwards laid his head against the side of the post, not uttering a syllable, or asking for mercy; but what he suffered was strongly visible in the tremulous agitation of his whole frame. . . . he received the other one hundred lashes on the third day following, after which, a heavy iron chain to his leg, and an iron rivetted round his neck.[26]

Chief Eusébio de Queiroz became famous eventually as the man who ended illegal slave traffic to Brazil after 1850. He began his political career as Rio police chief from 1833 to 1834. In this capacity he wrote to the minister of justice: "The capoeiras, who always required the utmost vigilance by the police, today infest the streets of the city in a most scandalous way. It will not be easy to avoid the dire consequences of this situation as long as the police, with respect to slaves, are not authorized as formerly to punish, with no further legal formality, those caught in the act."[27]

Queiroz instigated a harsh and relentless campaign against the capoeiristas. He ordered police patrols to "search all blacks on the street and dissolve their gatherings, whether in the streets or in the taverns, and to take action against tavern keepers who permit such meetings [and] . . . from time to time operations should be carried out against . . . capoeiras, as soon as word arrives that they have gathered."[28]

African-born slaves received the worst beatings for capoeira. Slave owners were ambivalent about whipping and hard labor in prison because it meant slaves were no longer productive and the slave owner lost money. A mid-century prison inspector and criminal court judge complained, "Presently when a slave is arrested for capoeira, with no further formality whatever he is sent to the House of Corrections, where he immediately suffers 150 lashes."[29]

The inspector knew this punishment was far too harsh, but the system was embedded in an ancient colonial mindset and was too popular with the police to allow for effective regulation. Angolan slaves accounted for the majority of those held in the calabouço. In 1850, three slaves from Mina, nine from Congo, six from East Africa, and twenty-two from Angola were arrested and sent to jail for capoeira in Rio.

The ubiquitous nature of capoeira among the young Central African slaves in Rio is something that baffled the authorities of the day. Membership in maltas often ran into the hundreds, and there were many maltas spread throughout the parishes, often fighting over territorial claims.

Paraguay

One effective method of controlling the maltas and sweeping the streets of capoeiristas was military impressments. Never was this more evident than when Brazil embarked on the Paraguayan War. Clashes between the Uruguayan government and local Brazilian land barons escalated into violent battles. Rio politicians with economic links to Rio Grande do Sul saw this as an opportunity to expand into Rio de la Plata. In September 1864, Brazilian army units marched over the frontier toward the Uruguayan capital, Montevideo. The navy blocked key ports on the Uruguay River. Argentina, Brazil's traditional enemy, was strangely silent about this, though Paraguay's president, Francisco López, was not. He was disputing territorial claims in the Brazilian province of Mato Grosso, which could only be reached via the Paraguay River. He was convinced that Brazil wanted to absorb both Uruguay and Paraguay into its own territory.

Pedro II didn't give a damn about Paraguay, as he demonstrated by killing more than 500,000 Paraguayans (half the population) over the course of the next few years. He wrote, "They boast of having thousands of soldiers . . . but most without military training and with the slight or non existent energies of the Guaraní race."[30]

In 1864, Paraguay invaded Mato Grosso and Brazil declared war. Capoeiristas played a significant role as fighters in the Brazilian army, called the *Voluntários da Pátria* (volunteers of the fatherland).

Paraná ê, Paraná ê, Paraná

The only way to attack Paraguayan positions was over Argentine territory up the Paraná River. Argentina and Brazil were unlikely bedfellows, but President López also declared war against Argentina, making Brazil, Uruguay, and Argentina the "Triple Alliance" in 1865. Pedro II pledged that the alliance would make no peace until President López was driven from Paraguayan soil. He took this pledge literally and dragged his countrymen through hardship, financial ruin, and starvation to achieve it.

After some shuffling, the leader of the Brazilian conservative party, the Marquis of Caxias, became commander in chief. After he resigned, Pedro II's son-in-law, Count d'Eu, took over. Commander in chief of the Triple Alliance was an incredibly horrible job that nearly crushed the spirit of both men. They needed to be begged and bullied into doing it. Pedro II only came close to the action once, in September 1865. Wearing the uniform of the Vol-

The Paraná River is approximately 2,000 miles (3,200 kilometers) long and is formed by the junction of the Paranaíba and the Rio Grande in Brazil. It forms the border between Paraguay and Argentina, flowing to the Uruguay River at the head of the Río de la Plata. The only effective way to get into Paraguay during the War of the Triple Alliance was through Argentine territory up the Paraná River. To finally gain positions in Paraguay, the Brazilian forces had to cross the Paraná River. This they achieved in April 1866. The Paraná River was the site of hard-fought and cruel battles during the Paraguayan war, in which many capoeiristas fought and died in the service of Brazil. The war left Paraguay ruined, with its population reduced by more than half, to only 221,000; of these, only 28,000 were men. (Source: Kraay and Whigham, eds., *I Die with My Country: Perspectives on the Paraguayan War 1864–1870.* See especially Chapter 4, "Patriotic Mobilization in Brazil: The Zuavos and other Black Companies.")

untários da Pátria, at Caçapava, he wrote, "The stay here has bored me rigid. . . . The enemy was unworthy even of being beaten. What a rabble." He also noted that Uruguay's leader was "an old and very ugly caboclo, but cunning."[31]

Pedro II also recorded, "The war is going well and I hope that it will last only a short time. Internally there is much that needs to be done; but that will be worked on."[32]

In fact, only Pedro II held the opinion that the war was going well. The Triple Alliance armies battled a network of dense fortifications on the Paraguay River. In 1866, with the war in its third year, they launched a major assault against the Paraguayan fort of Curupaití, but were badly defeated with many deaths.

"Club and Rope" Impressment

The internal problem Pedro II referred to was the abolition of slavery. The Paraguayan War hindered abolition and crippled Brazil's economy. With its economy propped up by British finance, the pressure to abolish slavery and end the war successfully was growing. Patriotic fervor in Brazil had long since died away and a rising majority of the Brazilian elite, politicians, and common people wanted the war to end.

But Pedro II was determined to go down in history as the final nemesis of Paraguay's uppity leader. He needed at least another 10,000 men for the next stage of the assault and wrote, "Efforts are being made to send more troops and everyone feels that the war should be concluded as honour demands, cost what it costs."[33]

This war was much bigger than anything the Brazilians had undertaken before. It mobilized four times as many soldiers as any previous campaign, including the war with the Dutch. One hundred thousand died on the Brazilian side—mostly soldiers who had been press-ganged into military service. They were called "club and rope" recruits. The British envoy wrote, "Few persons would have believed at the beginning of the war, that Brazil could have furnished so large a force."[34]

The pace of "manumission" of slaves increased as it never had been before. A senior government officer observed in 1867, "For some time now titles and honours have been given in exchange for slaves who are freed and enlisted in the army. In these measures have been detected the Emperor's intention to take advantage of the war to begin the abolition of slavery. What confirms this viewpoint is that for some days now, there has been talk of a decree which will order the expropriation of 10,000 slaves."[35]

The elites in Rio de Janeiro were under great pressure from

Pedro II to donate slaves. As slaves weren't permitted to enlist in the armed forces, however, manumission was necessary. The government purchased slaves by the thousand and freed them straight to the front line. Added to ex-slaves were the hundreds and thousands of poor, mainly black or mixed-race, men captured by the police, or by army and navy press gangs for transport to the front.

Those eligible for capture were men who weren't in the National Guard, who had no skilled trade, who weren't legally married, who couldn't buy an exemption, and who were homeless or unemployed. Vagrants, capoeiristas, street children, and freed slaves were all collected in massive sweeps by squads of well-armed police and military. Convicts in the calabouço were also enlisted. Press gangs roamed Rio and other cities' districts taking captive anyone who didn't move fast enough.

National guardsmen were mobilized for front-line duty for the first time, but if they had money they could buy a substitute, a slave who was then "free" to serve in their place. One in eight fighters in the war came from Rio de Janeiro. Added to the ranks of the press-ganged were the so-called "volunteers of the fatherland." The government promised volunteers a list of incentives to enjoy once the war was over. Pensions and land grants were offered, although in the end only a negligible number of veterans ever saw those grants, which were protected behind a solid wall of mystifying beaurocracy or turned out to be in distant provinces unfit for habitation. The war veterans' home for invalids was built right beside Rio's rat-infested rubbish heap on Bom Jesus island in Guanabara Bay.

To maintain the war effort, Dom Pedro rigged elections without shame. The elections of the late 1860s were mere charades of liberal democracy, where parties used any and all means, "from force to fraud to win the legislative elections."[36]

Capangagem

Capoeiristas who were useful as cannon fodder on the Paraguayan front were also useful in other ways. "In the 1870s and 80s . . . factions in Rio employed gangs of toughs who used capoeira techniques to protect polling places for favorites, disrupt the rallies of rival candidates, and intimidate opposition voters."[37]

Moraes Filho wrote in the 1880s, "Until recently many of those in government rose by the flash of the razor, and the senate and the Chamber [of Deputies] supported themselves on the swarthy shoulder of the capoeira."[38]

Capangagem was described in Manuel Antônio de Almeida's 1855 novel *Memórias de um sargento de milícias.* Kirsten Schultz summarized Almeida's fictional vision "of early 19th century Rio de Janeiro [where] . . . the city's residents [are] revealed as agents of political and social allegiance, repression, and resistance, and where courtiers, officials, petty functionaries, soldiers, merchants, and artisans emerge in a web of relationships that suggest links between the elite and popular experiences of constructing the New World empire and New World court."[39]

Holloway noted that "members of the police, national guard, and army soldiers were involved in capoeira . . . at the level of the street, the social division between the forces of order and the forces of disruption was more like a permeable membrane than a solid barrier."[40]

The capoeirista aligned himself to a political patron, often on a temporary basis at election time. This practical *malicia* gained capoeiristas some favors in Brazil's generally dangerous cities. Capoeiristas were also in all branches of the armed forces, which caused grumbling among the commanders of the police and army.

The chief of police complained that men who were arrested for capoeira couldn't be punished under the usual vadiagem laws. They were "national guardsmen, soldiers on pass, retired members of the armed forces, [Paraguayan War veterans], or artisans in the army and navy arsenals, and were thus looked after by their respective commanders."[41]

In the introduction to the post-Paraguayan War novel, *Os Capoeiras,* Placido Abreu wrote, "The solution for an ex-slave remained in the area of 'the favour,' which opened to him opportunities inside the group of capoeiras."[42]

Freyre writes:

Many free Negroes in Imperial times became professional body-guards, a group which in the cities formed "a real power, contracted by political figures for personal protection, whose services were especially useful during elections." In 1873, Police Chief Ludgero Gonçalves da Silva declared these capoeiras "a disgrace to the capital of the Empire"; they were "inordinately bold," they "promoted disorder," and often "committed assault and murder in cold blood, sometimes merely for amusement."[43]

Yet politicians regularly employed capoeiristas for electoral purposes. The politician's strategy was described by Luiz Sergio Dias as "the exercise of one law in a manner that doesn't succeed in breaking another one, often carried out in an underhand way, 'aiding and abetting,' showing a versatility to arrange things without giving even a hint of the presence of corruption,"[44] In *Os Capoeiras,* the more deadly the capoeirista's skill, the further his fortunes advanced. This web of relationships between capoeiristas and the political elite created the "permeable membrane" of legal illegality described by Holloway above.

In the mid-1850s, a Rio newspaper article said, "The night before last, after eight o'clock, an individual named Maurício was attacked by a band of capoeiras, who fell on him with clubs, striking him upon the forehead, and gashing his thigh. . . . [Capoeiras are] . . . a secret society among the negroes, in which the highest rank is assigned to the man who has taken the most lives. . . . During a festa they will rush out at night and rip up any other black they chance to meet. They rarely attack the whites, knowing perhaps, that it would cost them too dearly."[45]

In fact, the capoeiristas did target whites, particularly the immigrant Portuguese. The police and press argued that capoeiristas drew blood for the simple pleasure of it. In fact, the maltas were characterized by extreme loyalty among members and the police or journalists were rarely privy to the cause of any particular attack. Capoeiristas operated in a world where violence was the means to achieve a desired end. Rio de Janeiro rested on a foundation of violence or its threat. From the slave driver's whip to the punishment in the jails, the torture, the chain gangs at work in the streets, to the guns and swords of the military and police, the culture of force to make things work was evident everywhere. The maltas' hierarchical structure, the loyalty within the group, their readiness to fight the police and other gangs to defend their own territory, and willingness to hire out their services to political benefactors were exactly the adaptations needed to win space and relative power in Brazil's urban capital.

Razor attacks were very common. The police were at pains to say that the motive for these attacks wasn't theft. Most of the rackets that have existed in cities since time immemorial were present in Brazil. Extortion of businesses and taverns took place, and strict laws against blacks gathering in taverns were a cause of conflict and violence. The antagonism felt by black cariocas for immigrant whites from Portugal who set up in business right next door to established slums was often intense.

The maltas' rank and file were male slaves and free blacks. Maltas had their own meeting points and training grounds in different parishes, *freguesias.* Children and adolescent boys were apprentices called *carrapetas* or *caxinguelês,* who had to prove themselves on missions into rival parishes. Almeida wrote, "Young capoeiristas . . . paraded before the adults during street parties, religious festivities, political meetings, or at any event that gave them the chance to play the brincadeira de angola."[46]

Nagôa and Guayamu

The maltas tended toward allegiance with two main camps, the Nagôa and the Guayamu. (See Appendix B.) Each of these had a degree of backing and protection from different political parties and enjoyed membership from the ranks of policemen, national guardsmen, and firemen. The maltas had their own way of dressing, gang signs, nicknames, and slang. In the *Relatório do Chefe de Policia da Corte* of 1872 and then again of 1878, the police chief reported:

> They form a sort of association, divided by neighbourhood, with specific leaders. They not only do battle among themselves, but also injure and murder innocent passers-by. . . . there are still trouble makers who, armed with knives and razors, occasionally fight among themselves, with tragic consequences. [Capoeira is] . . . one of the strongest moral diseases of this great and civilised city [like] . . . the bloody sect of those who worship Siva, or the homicidal Druses . . . a regularly organized association, subdivided into gangs with their own special signs and slang terms . . . [and during public festivals] . . . that is the time that some, the most cruel, disperse themselves among the people, razor in hand, wounding at random those whom they encounter, sometimes committing murder.[47]

"A capoeirista . . . with his odd gait"

References to capoeiristas turn up all over 19th-century Rio de Janeiro, Recife, and Bahia. For example, this 1820s description of Rua do Ouvidor, the center of Rio's elite nightlife:

In the midst of that parade of elegance . . . it was not rare to see a pitch-black Negro burst in, drunk, to stagger, shoving and driving away the passers by, [or] on the sidewalk, a cabrocha, exposing a shiny, jelly-like breast outside of a ragged blouse, or a capoeira from Saúde or Saco de Alferes with his odd gait, a soft hat drooping down the back of his head, a cigarette behind his ear, and a club in his hand, smelling of cheap rum, shouting like a madman.[48]

Or Freyre's account:

At times there was a Negro who had been slashed by a razor, some black boy with his intestines hanging out who was carried off in a white hammock (the red ones were for the wounded; the white for the dead). For these processions with bands of music were the meeting place of the capoeiras, a curious type of urban Negro or mulatto, whose counterpart was the capangas and cabras, the hired gunmen of the plantations. The speciality of the capoeira was his razor or sharp-pointed knife; his trademark, the kinky hair combed in the shape of a turban, the light sandals on his feet, which were almost those of a dancer, and his loose-jointed gait. His art included . . . a variety of difficult steps and movements of incredible agility, in which the street vagabonds were initiated almost as in a Masonic rite. . . .

Forbidden the use of firearms, swords, walking sticks with concealed rapiers, the arms of the gentry and the masters, the slaves—principally those hired out as porters, who together with blacksmiths, metalworkers, machinists, seem to have comprised, in Rio de Janeiro as in Recife, the fighting aristocracy of the slave population—became experts, like the ruffians and street loafers, in the use of daggers and knives, but above all, in head-butting, tripping, kicking the feet out from under an adversary. . . . (others made use of spells, witchcraft, mysterious poisons, which crippled and killed whites). . . . The art of capoeiragem enabled them to compensate for the lack of firearms with their agility, with movements of the body which were almost those of the dance. The "dancers" of capoeiragem, with their small, swift, delicate feet, almost those of a girl, and shod, like the women of Bahia, in slippers with oriental trimming, could confront armed soldiers, powerful northerners, English sailors, Portuguese "he-men" and wreak havoc on them and to a certain degree, demoralize them. Challenging their technical superiority as soldiers or men armed with pistols, swords, daggers and their social superiority as whites, gentlemen. Perhaps these clashes account for the antipathy of the Portuguese for Brazilian mestizos, with their small, agile feet, to whom the former gave the name "goat-feet"; and that of the mestizos for the Portuguese, who as a rule had big feet, often broad and clumsy, known in our folklore as "lead feet."[49]

Gilberto Freyre was given to picturesque portrayals of Brazil's past. In *Order and Progress,* he notes that the Frenchman Émile Allain "saw no lack of safety in Imperial Rio de Janeiro; on the contrary, he claimed there were few cities where both the center and suburbs were equally tranquil both day and night."[50]

Yet elsewhere Émile Allain is said to have complained that capoeiristas were "a stain on the civilization of a great city. . . . Almost all people of color, they are organized in 'maltas' and divide themselves into two or more rival groups. The weapon of the capoeiras is the knife, and often the razor, which they use in fights among themselves, against their enemies, or against those at whom they direct their revenge."[51]

Malta Slang Names

Some of the maltas' parish nicknames were Cadeira da Senhora (lady's chair) in Santa Ana, Três Cachos (three bunches) and Flor da Uva (flower of the grape) in Santa Rita, Franciscanos in São Fransisco de Paula, Flor da Gente (flower of the people) in Glória, Espada (sword) in Lapa, Lança (lance) in São Jorge, Luzianos in Santa Luzia, Ossos (bones) in Bom Jesus do Calvário, Santo Inácio in the Castelo, and Guaiamu in Cidade Nova.

Some nicknames of capoeiristas in the mid- to late-19th century included Quebra-Coco (skull buster), Clave de Sol (treble clef), Chico Africano (Frankie the African), Zé Maluco (Crazy Joe), Desdentado (toothless), Trinca-Espinha (spine splitter), Carrepeta (ironwood), Boca-Negra (black mouth), Manduca (chomper), Corta-Orelha (ear cutter), Grego das Ostras (oyster Greek), Camisa Rôxa (pink shirt), Quarto (the fourth), and Espanha (Spain).[52]

Camisa was also the nickname given to men who scrubbed the decks and supervised slaves getting exercise aboard some mid-19th-century slave ships. This was because the camisas wore special sack-cloth shirts.

Espanha and Quarto gained their names from military bands. The maltas' informal attachment to the military enabled politicians and members of the elite to make contact with them and it wasn't rare for capoeiristas to be in the forces. The wide use of capoeira among Africans and mixed-race people in Rio made it inevitable that the National Guard would be full of capoeiristas.

The National Guard had been a somewhat exclusive force in the rural areas since its establishment in 1831. Only free citizens were eligible for membership and only those with money and property could get promoted to officer. But the National Guard in Rio was not such a privileged enclave. Its members were working class and, as the Paraguayan War proved, were not exempt from active service. More than 10 percent of Rio's "free" population were members by 1849 and most of those were of low rank. During police and military dragnets to catch capoeiristas in Rio during the last forty years of the slave era, firemen, police, soldiers, and national guardsmen were caught with unerring regularity.

"A special crime and punished with new penalties"

The police wanted to make capoeiristas front-line soldiers in Paraguay or at least barracked far from Rio. This was the same strategy as exiling quilombolas to distant plantations after recapture. The Rio police chief in 1881 declared, "The capoeiragem must be delineated as a special crime and punished with new penalties. . . . it should be punished with exile in military colonies, where under rigorous discipline, delinquents would acquire habits of order and work in obedience to the law and authorities."[53]

Police didn't want capoeiristas to become members of the National Guard because this membership would protect them from military exile. In 1849 the chief of police argued that the National Guard, "where so many honest and upstanding citizens serve, should not also be a refuge for vagrants and malefactors."[54]

A decade later, a national guardsman by name of Felisberto do Amaral was recommended for dismissal and military exile by the chief of police, who said, "He is very dangerous, and known to be the head of the capoeiras who gather in Santa Rita parish. He is the one who, during the pursuit of a capoeira gang there, threw a brick at a patrolman . . . wounding him on the head."[55]

Big religious festivals like the feast of Saint Sebastian brought the maltas out onto the streets in force. Rio's police chief often told military commanders to restrict all off-duty soldiers to barracks during the festivities. "The capoeiras are accustomed to taking advantage of the celebration to engage in their forays, committing crimes and alarming peaceful citizens, and it is undeniable that among them are a large number of soldiers in civilian dress."[56]

During the Paraguayan War, Brazil's justice minister made a special recommendation to conscript to the army four national guardsmen who, "although members [of the Guard] were arrested as members of the capoeira gang which . . . created a disturbance in Lapa Square."[57]

It seems that during the empire, politicians were reluctant to commit themselves to formal laws, preferring an ad hoc system of justice because they sought to protect certain capoeiristas and prosecute others. The government opposed a formal policy of conscription to the army for national guardsmen arrested for capoeira, recommending in 1870 that "other means be found to repress them."[58] The police, even at a high level, numbered among the ranks of Rio's capoeiristas. A late empire military police lieutenant was arrested for being in the "well known and incorrigible gang of capoeiras that caused the disorders in Constitution Square [and had also] . . . beat up an individual and roamed through the bars and taverns in the company of capoeiras and troublemakers. . . . the most deplorable example of indiscipline . . . keeping company with individuals of the lowest class, with whom he equaled himself in committing indecorous acts."[59]

In 1855, a capoeirista created an incident in Velha Street and was "said to be a fireman of the Carioca station [and] . . . threw a sharpened round file into the tavern at number 23, where it stuck in the front of the counter. The cashier of the tavern narrowly escaped injury."[60]

Rio de Janeiro Quilombos

In the same period, 1824, the Rio police chief, Estavão Ribeiro de Rezende, sent a letter to the Brazilian minister of justice, outlining his suggestions for destroying quilombos on the outskirts of Rio:

> Most illustrious and excellent sir: day after day in this city and its neighbourhood there is an increase in the number of runaway slaves who join the many others in the various quilombos which exist in the sierra and forests of Tijuca or the surrounding region. . . . I have ordered assaults against some of these quilombos with a police squad and another force whose assistance I asked for, along with soldiers of the militia, but all has been in vain. Such attacks are never undertaken without a great deal of alarm and confusion, and when the assault begins the blacks (and the deserters who live among them) have already been informed and have abandoned the place. . . . As long as expeditions are launched with military fanfare, they will always be given this kind of warning. The reason for this is that, both day and night, the fugitives carry on a regular trade with tavern keepers and other black men and women of this city, who transport and sell stolen goods which the fugitives acquire from country houses and from highway robbery. Moreover, as long as they are carried out by ordinary soldiers, these attacks can never accomplish anything . . . because it is not practical for booted, uniformed, and armed men to penetrate into those steep, lofty mountain jungles, caves, and grottoes where the blacks hide out and move about with total freedom.

> The so called bush captains, which the town council appoints, are worthless. . . . The evil is growing and must be stopped. I have been informed that there are quilombos with a considerable number of slaves, and even freedmen and deserters. . . .

> In Minas Gerais . . . there are foot soldiers and bush captains . . . peo-

ple who can penetrate mountainous jungles because of their use of leather clothing which protects them from briers and thorns. . . . It would be advantageous if a dozen of these men were allowed to come here, released by the government of Minas Gerais . . . bringing along their weapons and clothing. . . . Thus, picked and able men could come here to be employed each day in entering the forests and destroying quilombos, and even capturing runaway black slaves in the city and its suburbs. . . . I am convinced that in a few months we would be able to eliminate the quilombos, establish public security and protect the private interests of proprietors and slaveholders.[61]

The government granted the funds to pay for the special squadron of slave hunters, although they never totally defeated the quilombos, which were also the retreat of military deserters and free blacks who often preferred to live there than the city. Fifty years later, the Rio de Janeiro police were still venturing into the mangrove swamps of Guanabara Bay, attacking the old and well-fortified Quilombo Grande (also known as Bomba) and Quilombo do Gabriel at Iguassu.

These quilombos bordered Benedictine plantations and lay in a swamp that stretched to the ocean, giving easy access to boats and communication with Rio de Janeiro. The boat owners transported firewood provided by the fugitives back into the city, and "always warned them when there was reason to suspect that the authorities were trying to capture them."[62]

There was evidently much interface between black residents in the city and the escaped slaves in the Iguassu swamp by way of mutual trade. The quilombolas of Bomba and Gabriel supplied firewood to Rio de Janeiro for many years, often in exchange for food and rum. It goes without saying that many of Rio's capoeiristas must have been living in the quilombos during this period.

During the Paraguayan War, when the club-and-rope recruitment officers scoured the city, blacks and mulattos escaped to the hills en masse. Rio's businesses and workforce were adversely affected, making the war universally unpopular. The quilombos, including Bomba and Gabriel, received many new inhabitants fleeing not only slavery, but also conscription to the Paraguayan front. Newspapers lampooned the government and satirical cartoons mocked the recruitment policy by showing cities full of wild animals because all the men had fled to escape the press gangs.

The Beginning of the End of Empire

In 1869 the political violence in the streets assured the conservatives a win so complete that the chamber didn't admit a single opposition member. The liberals were disgusted by the conservatives' fraud and intimidation campaigns, in which the maltas played a significant part.

Pedro II didn't believe the liberals could assure him the total victory in Paraguay that he demanded. He badly undermined his own authority and the monarchy's supposed impartiality by coming out so obviously in favor of the conservatives. The empire looked more unstable than it had since Dom Pedro I had abdicated.

Despite the liberals' complaints, they and the conservatives spoke for much the same constituency, so the conflict wasn't exactly ideological. It was more a case of family and kinship ties. Political factions were dominated by Brazil's prestigious families and their strategies for gaining votes were imaginative.

> Cabinets . . . created parishes where they had friends, and abolished them where they had enemies. They harassed rank-and-file opposition voters, threatening them with conscription, rewarded

those who supported the cabinet with jobs, promotions and sinecures; mobilized the National Guard to intimidate the opposition by forcing its voters to stay home on election day [and] they resorted to violence. Opposition voters were often expelled from the churches where they were supposed to vote. Ballot boxes were stolen and reappeared filled with more votes than there were voters or with ballots replaced by others.[63]

Many tricks were enacted by paid henchmen in the maltas, or as Melo Morais Filho described them, "profissionais do crime . . . the capoeiras who filled the church towers, bell ringers who mounted the head of their bells and followed the sway of the ringing, blessing from above the heads of the people congregating in the squares and streets below, who watched them with admiration."[64]

Brazil had won the major battles in Paraguay. The commander in chief, Luis Alves de Lima, marquis and duke of Caxias, was sick of the war. As far as he was concerned, the war was won though Paraguay's president was still at large. As Pedro II's son-in-law, Count d'Eu, said, Caxias still had "the abominable task of chasing López God knows where"[65], and the only man still remotely concerned with catching López was Pedro II. In January 1869, Caxias not only handed over his command, but issued a final order of the day, which declared the war over.

Furious with Caxias, Pedro II managed to persuade the Count d'Eu to take over the command in Paraguay and keep the war going. López used this lull in the hostilities to reform an army out of the few troops remaining to him. They dug in among the hills to the east of the capital. This last vestige of the Paraguayan army was slaughtered at Piribebuy and cut down further in retreat, but d'Eu failed to capture López once again. He had but a few hundred men left, and conventional warfare was out of the question.

The Brazilian army were men conscripted against their will, hastily trained and poorly equipped. A special squadron of capoeiristas attacked enemy positions without even being equipped with guns. The Zuavos, as they were known, were armed with knives, swords, and other weapons particular to the capoeiristas.

The soldiers regularly outran their supply lines so that Brazilians starved to death as they hunted down López in the Paraguayan wilderness. Count d'Eu had to reorganize his forces for guerrilla war. He needed flying columns and intelligence networks to supply accurate information about Paraguayan movements. But d'Eu was losing his grip. One of his staff wrote, "It was at Caacupé that there appeared this tendency of the prince to be irritable . . . which soon after transmuted into melancholy and attacks of complete apathy which his physician . . . combated as far as he could."[66] d'Eu had the same desperate desire to leave Paraguay that had hit Caxias. He insisted to Pedro II and anyone else who'd listen that the war should be declared over.

López was finally caught and killed on March 1, 1870, after more than five years of war in which nearly half of Brazil's 200,000 soldiers had died. Count d'Eu recovered quickly from his melancholia. "It was a really beautiful day. You cannot have an idea of the excitement which existed throughout the entire city of Rio. During four consecutive evenings, there was not a single house which was not illuminated."[67] However, according to the *Anglo-Brazilian Times,* even though more than 8,000 invitations were sent out to elite and very important persons for the "victory parade," none of them showed up and the spectator stands remained "utterly quiet" when the emperor arrived for the review. Instead, the stands were dotted with the poor relatives of the working-class veterans who marched past.

The absence of applause at the Paraguay War victory parade was the least of Pedro II's worries, for now the army itself was becoming a problem. After the "victory," soldiers were promoted because of their military ability rather than their monarchic connections. These officers were disillusioned and ambitious, and were beginning to form a class of their own, rather than being an appendage of the elite.

Pedro II made no effort to befriend or reward these new officers. After showing he could recruit 10,000 soldiers at the swivel of his fountain pen in the late 1860s, he soon allowed the army to dwindle to only 12,000 total. This arrogant oversight was being scrutinized closely by soldiers like Manuel Deodoro da Fonseca, a man of humble origin who'd risen through the ranks due to his bravery during the Paraguayan War.

Abolition and the Brazilian Republic

Some 80,000 veterans returned from the war, many of them ex-slaves granted their freedom for military service. The term "free" can be misleading. Agostinho Marques Perdigão Malheiro worked as a *curador* (guardian) of free blacks in Rio de Janeiro and he painted a very different picture of "freedom":

> The lot of these miserable people, both those working in towns and in rural areas, was in fact equal, or even worse, than that of slaves. Belonging to the black race like the others, they were placed on the same level because of their colour; but, not being slaves, they were not treated as well as the latter, or at best, the same. Service and labour day and night; punishments; a lack even of necessities, or a scarcity of food and clothing, they slept on the ground in unsuitable places, exposed to disease; education was a dead letter. The children were

cast into foundling homes in order to hire out their mothers as wet nurses. . . . In the cities the blacks were sent out to work or were employed in other profitable ways by private persons, not as the personal servants of those highest bidders, as they ought to have been according to the instructions. . . . To sum up, the free African was dealt with exactly like a slave. The abuse and scandal reached the extreme of substituting dead slaves having the same name for free Africans, in this way reducing the latter to slavery! And the children of free African women were baptized as slaves.[68]

The Law of the Free Womb

By now a republican manifesto was circulating the city. To undermine the republicans' main grievances, the police force was reformed, the National Guard was demobilized, and military impressment was made illegal. The conservative, Visconde do Rio-Branco, enacted the Law of the Free Womb in 1871. This stated:

The children of women slaves that may be born in the Empire from the date of this law shall be considered to be free. The said minors shall remain with and be under the domination of the owners of the mother, who shall be obliged to rear and take care of them until such children shall have completed the age of eight years.

When the child of the slave attains this age, the owner of its mother shall have the option either of receiving from the State the indemnification of 600 dollars, or of making use of the services of the minor until he shall have completed the age of twenty-one years.[69]

As Joaquim Nabuco observed, "A black girl born on the eve of the proclamation of the law might give birth to a child in 1911 who would remain in provisional slavery until 1932."[70]

The Law of the Free Womb quieted the abolition debate and initially it seemed that the battle against the *escravocrats* (slavocrats) had been won. The law was supposed to phase out slavery gradually. In reality, nothing had changed and by the end of the 1870s, it was obvious that children born of slave mothers were still slaves. The government's emancipation fund had failed and slaves were being shipped from the Northeast to work for the coffee industry in São Paulo. By the 1870s a broad-based popular front for abolition was active.

An abolitionist confederation was formed. The *Cidade do Rio,* the *Emancipationist,* the *Gazeta da Tarde,* the *Gazeta de Notícias,* and *Radical Paulistano* were all Black-owned media outlets. The black lawyer Luíz Gonzaga de Pinto Gama, an ex-slave, said, "Every slave who kills his master, no matter what the circumstances may be, kills in self-defense."[71]

He succeeded in freeing slaves in at least 500 cases. There were white abolitionists as well, whose intentions were often fueled by concern about Brazil's economy and the safety of the whites. Joaquim Nabuco was well aware that Brazil hadn't kept pace with the USA or Argentina since those republics had abolished slavery.

Because slaves had no money, slavery thwarted internal economic development and deprived Brazil of a consumer market. Joaquim Nabuco wrote the influential *O Abolicionismo.* His father, Tomás Nabuco de Araújo, had been responsible for compiling reports of slave uprisings and rebellions. Attacks against sugar estates, armed slaves, poisoned-tipped arrows, quilombos—all these would have been part of the Nabuco household's table talk when Joaquim was growing up.[72] Uprisings, quilombos, and capoeira were grist for the "official" abolitionist's mill.

The slave calabouço in Rio was in some years virtually a jail for capoeiristas. In 1857–58, the greatest number of slaves in prison for any reason was for capoeira. Most of them were arrested on a Sunday, a traditional rest day for slaves. This adds weight to the contention that capoeristas practiced playing the game of capoeira on Sundays, and the police knew that on a Sunday they'd make many more arrests.

By the 1870s, the percentage of free Africans arrested for capoeira had risen to 50 percent in Rio de Janeiro. Records from 1889–1890 show a huge increase in the number of whites and mulattos arrested for capoeira. Almeida also draws attention to the increasing diversity of the ethnic or social status among capoeiristas at the end of the 19th century: "The great majority of capoeiristas . . . were Brazilian mulattos from the lower classes [yet] capoeira was also practiced by blacks, whites, some rich citizens from renowned families, and occasionally by citizens of other nations who were living in Brazil."[73]

Freyre relates:

> Horácio Pires Galvão states that he and other members of the élite learned aspects of the capoeira from Negro soldiers during the [Paraguayan] war. This Afro-Brazilian art became highly prized by some upper-class whites, not only for self-defense but also as an expression of physical elegance. . . . Coelho Neto recalls associating with coloured laborers—shortly after the Paraguayan War—in order to "learn the secrets of capoeiragem, so useful for those in politics, in teaching, or in the Army and Navy."[74]

A certain level of social mobility was possible in Brazil. Some intellectuals mixed openly with capoeiristas and sambistas. Machado de Assiz, for example, wrote widely about capoeiristas and was quite familiar with the underworld. He was a mulatto himself, and became an elder statesman of Brazil's "belle époque." Coelho Neto said of people like Machado de Assiz:

They went out to the theaters, for conversation at Garnier's [book-store] or at the Deroche [café], or remained [at home] talking about the future, making literary plans—a great work of art that would shatter the indifference of a lazy public, a strong work, made with love and talent, the form well-studied, the analysis minute; a book magisterial in style that would cross the ocean and make the foreigner talk of the fatherland and its artists.[75]

La Belle Époque

Already by the second half of the 19th century there was nostalgia for cultural purity and "authenticity" in Brazil. An 1878 advertise-ment for a samba show in Rio offered "true and reputable samba, that great Bahian dance, executed by four graceful women of Bahia."[76] The artistic and intellectual elite in Brazil had ample oppor-tunity to observe African art and music. The poorest of the poor lived side by side with the elite in the cities. In the famous 1835 Sal-vador uprising, many of the captured Nagôs lived in Sé parish, where slums and grand government buildings were next door to each other. Rua da Oração, the cathedral, the Salvador jail, Ladeira da Praça, the Palace Square, and City Hall were all in Sé parish.

In Rio too, the Cidade Velha, the old city, was a warren of nar-row overcrowded streets near the port, occupied by rich and poor alike. They were separated by their social and economic circum-stances and by occupying the ground or upper floors of the build-ings they lived in. In the Cidade Velha, on the Rua do Ouvidor, it wasn't unusual to see capoeiristas rubbing shoulders with mem-bers of the elite during the belle époque. In this same area were the Chamber of Deputies, the Paço de Cidade, and the Imperial Palace, just a stone's throw from the charity hospital, the Santa Casa de Misericórdia, behind which stood the cemetery reserved for black and poor people. Capoeiristas who died in the calabouço after excessive punishment were usually dumped in this cemetery.

> Nothing more wretched and nasty can be imagined than this ceme-
> tery, which in fact looks more like a trash deposit than a cemetery.
> Here no cypress tree mourns over expensive cenotaphs, in this place
> of horror and death we do not find the usual loving messages with
> which gratitude and dedication ornament the tombs of absent rela-
> tives. Putrefaction and decomposition have here installed their throne
> composed of skulls and human limbs, with empty eyes visible over
> the entire length of their silent and deserted realm. The surface is of
> eighty square meters, and in such a small space thousands of people
> are buried every year.[77]

The Brazilian elite followed the British and other foreigners out to Flamengo, Botafogo, and the Jardim Botânico, escaping the Cidade Velha and epidemics of yellow fever that swept the city. They built villas in these hilly valleys away from the overcrowded tenements of inner Rio.

"Scientific" Racism

The Brazilian ruling class both worshipped and despised the African contribution to Brazilian culture, often simultaneously. Racist theories had already become popular among Europeans by the late 19th century. These theories were mechanical and simple, based on the idea that the white race was at the top of a hypothetical evolutionary tree and the black race at the bottom. Followers of this idea were pessimistic about "race mixing," believing it to have a weakening effect on the constitution. Culture, according to this theory, whether art, literature, music, nation building, or any other, was an extension of race. The Brazilian racists saw European (particularly French) culture as the pinnacle of human achievement. African culture was believed primitive and detrimental to the country's development.

As the majority of people in Brazil were African or mestizo, racists had various ways of dealing with their dissapointment. The first was economic and involved "whitening" Brazilian society by encouraging a surge of immigration by Europeans. This economic necessity was glorified as a racial development strategy. Immigration from Europe rose to around 194,000 in the 1870s and 450,000 in the 1880s.[78] In 1891 alone, 215,000 immigrants entered Brazil, mainly to feed the labor needs of coffee plantations. Significantly, none of these people were African.

The racial origin of the immigrants was a matter of supreme importance to the policy makers. A plan to replace slave workers with Chinese was met with strong opposition from those who declared the Chinese a "decadent" racial stock that wouldn't mix with the European. In 1879, representatives of the coffee industry fought to gain Chinese labor. In Parliament, opponents spoke of "mongolizing" the country, and that the Chinese "were drug addicts, naturally corrupt, weak and indolent."[79] The major coffee interests were split on the issue, which was founded only on racial grounds. The Chinese envoy left Brazil in November 1883, unable to secure a deal to deliver workers from Hong Kong and Macao. The consensus among the elite favored southwestern Europeans and debates about the desirability of different races went regularly to the National Assembly. After 400 years of African slavery, laws were eventually enforced *against* free Africans entering Brazil.

Pedro II worshipped the French. His good friend, Joseph Arthur de Gobineau, a French philosopher, was influential among the Brazilian elite, who devoured racist literature and tinkered endlessly with theories that might fit Brazil's African and mixed-race profile.

Gobineau is recognized as the father of modern racism. As a virulent reactionary, he devoted his whole life to pseudo-scientific racist gobbeldygook and his *"Essai sur l'inégalité des races humaines"* (1853–55) was his most influential work, taken to heart by European philosophers, the Brazilian elite, and a later generation of German Nazis alike. In this essay, Gobineau asserted that "Aryans" (Germanic peoples) were the summit of human civilization. In his view, Aryan civilization might only prosper when it was unmixed with "black and yellow strains." It was the French quasi-scientific racist ideas of Gobineau and his followers that began to stir the shift from religious anti-Semitism in Europe and Germany (which had existed for centuries) to the specifically racial anti-Semitism that developed toward the end of the 19th century.[80]

Gobineau held an explicitly sexual theory of race, in which whites were "male" and blacks were "female." He wrote, "The black element [is] . . . indispensable for developing artistic genius in a race, for we have seen what outbursts of . . . vivacity and spontaneity are intrinsic to its soul and how much the imagination, that mirror of sensuality, and all cravings for material things, prepare it."[81]

Gobineau advocated that race mixing sowed the seeds of the destruction of civilization. In Brazil, a country founded on race mixing, the elites' folklorists molded Gobineau's ideas to their own vision. Sílvio Romero championed the cause of the Romantics and the romanticization of the Indian. He argued that the true Brazilian was a product of race mixing: "There can be but one source of nationality in Brazilian poetry . . . the genius, the true spirit of the people that emerges from the complex of our ethnic origins."[82]

Romero expressed a wish to see the gradual and complete

whitening of Brazil through miscegenation over three or four centuries. When German immigrants moved to southern Brazil in the late 19th century, Romero criticized them because they wouldn't mix with black Brazilians sexually. He believed that their role in Brazil was to whiten the population and Brazilianize themselves.

Contemporaries of Romero, like Joaquim Nabuco, advocated race mixing to move steadily in the direction of whiteness. It wasn't until the emergence on the scene of Gilberto Freyre that racial mixture was advocated as a thing of value in itself and not simply a means to a desired end of eventual whiteness.

Freyre's usefulness in paving the way for the "nationalization" of African arts can be gleaned from the following passage cited by Hermano Vianna and written by the novelist Jorge Amado: "It was an explosion, a new fact of life, something like we never had before, and right away there was a feeling that we had grown and become more capable. Nobody who didn't live through those times can know how beautiful it was. . . . Gilberto's book [*The Masters and the Slaves*] dazzled the country, people talked about it the way they had never talked about other books."[83]

Freyre today is widely disparaged, yet he was far in advance of those who preceded him. At the turn of the century, the elite wanted to destroy African cultural symbols such as capoeira and Carnaval and rebuild the colonial city of Rio de Janeiro in the image of Paris or Lisbon.

"In the pulverization of the earth, there was a long groan"

Work began on the Avenida Central. The neighborhood of Cidade Velha was pulled down and the writer Olavo Bilac cried:

A few days ago, the picks, intoning a jubilant hymn, began the work

of the Avenida Central's construction, knocking down the first condemned houses . . . we begin to stride toward our rehabilitation. In
the collapse of the walls, in the crumbling of the stones, in the pulverization of the earth, there was a long groan. It was the sad and lament-
ing groan of the Past, of Backwardness, of Shame. The colonial city,
filthy, backward, obstinate in its old traditions, was weeping with the
sobs of those rotten materials falling apart. But the clear hymn of the
picks smothered the impotent protest. With what happiness they
sang, the regenerating picks! And how the souls of those who were
there understood well what the picks were saying, in their unceas-
ing, rhythmic clamour, celebrating the victory of hygiene, of good
taste, and of art.[84]

The Empire Strikes Back

In 1884 the Liberal Party announced that the Law of the Free
Womb wasn't good enough. "The government needs to intervene
with the greatest seriousness so that this problem can be resolved
in a progressive form," said their leader.[85] They introduced a bill
granting freedom to all slaves over the age of sixty and abolishing
slave trade between Brazilian provinces. By now, very strong emancipation movements in Ceará and Amazonas had almost completely
ended slavery in those provinces; abolitionists in Rio Grande do
Sul had done the same.

The Liberal Party was defeated and Pedro II invited the baron of
Cotegipe's Conservative Party to form a cabinet. This cabinet constantly harassed abolitionists and denied their right to hold meetings or gain access to the press. Cotegipe also amended the liberals'
bill so that sixty-year-old freed slaves were still obligated to serve
for a further five years until they were sixty-five years of age.

Around this time an incident happened that was usual in Brazil, yet served as a catalyst for accelerated mass movements against slavery. A sentence of 300 lashes was handed down to four slaves by a jury in a small coffee town in Rio de Janeiro province. Severe punishments like this usually killed the victims. In this case, doctors had attended them during the six days of punishment and they were given fifty lashes a day. On the way back to the plantation, bound by the wrists and beaten all the way, two of the slaves (Alfredo and Benedicto) died, supposedly of pulmonary apoplexy. Joaquim Nabuco wrote many articles decrying these killings and as a result of the outrage among the people, in 1886 the General Assembly passed a law against whipping in the calabouço or other public buildings.

Santos

By now there were approximately 1.25 million slaves in Brazil, three-quarters of whom were centered in Rio de Janeiro and São Paulo. In Santos, São Paulo province, a radical abolitionist movement reacting to the Cotegipe government's attempt to silence them, encouraged slaves to flee their fazendas and workplaces. Santos was the main port for the export of coffee from São Paulo to the rest of the world. In November 1886, the Santos chief of police tried to arrest and return four slaves to their owners, but his officers were attacked at the Santos railroad station. The first major sanctuary for escaped slaves was established in Santos, protecting fugitives from professional capitaos de mato and government troops. Santos became the center of a popular anti-slavery movement, and a massive haven for runaway slaves from all over São Paulo. This movement had been encouraged by the new law banning corporal punishment in jails.

Pedro II questioned Cotegipe and was assured that he would "repress these activities with prudence but with energy."[86]

The military, liberals, republicans, and abolitionists were all completely dissatisfied with Pedro II. Impressment may have been outlawed after Paraguay, but like so many of Brazil's laws, this one was usually disregarded by the authorities when it suited them. Ninety percent of regular soldiers were impressed on six-year contracts and the main targets were unemployed free blacks and mulattos who would never be promoted to the rank of non-commissioned officer.

The army was overloaded with Paraguayan War veterans at the level of captain and major, who languished in resentment for years in poorly paid positions. In peacetime they were hardly more than glorified capitaos do mata—bush captains and slave hunters. But younger officers who hadn't fought in Paraguay tended to be better educated and more overtly political than their elders. They felt no sense of loyalty to the monarchical system.

Deodoro da Fonseca

By 1886 Deodoro da Fonseca had risen through the ranks from brigadier general and field marshal to quartermaster general in command of all the military forces in the province of Rio Grande do Sul. The Conservative Party wanted Deodoro da Fonseca on their team, but Cotegipe looked on with gritted teeth as the hero aligned himself to the opposition. Deodoro was relieved of his command, but was shown instant "kindness and understanding" by the republicans. He chaired a meeting of 200 army officers, most of whom were republicans involved in the abolitionist movement. He was sacked as quartermaster general and immediately established the Clube Militar (military club) with himself as its popular leader.

Through the early part of 1887, Dom Pedro II was suffering from headaches, fevers, a swollen liver, gallstones, biliary colic, pancreatitis, cramps, vomiting, nausea, and worsening diabetes. His speech was slow and he became forgetful. He may have suffered a minor stroke. Still worrying over the trouble caused by the killing of the slaves in Rio province the previous year, he wrote to the countess of Barral, "I have opposed public prisons being used to incarcerate slaves and I have said that it is for the owners to take measures so that they don't run away and to inflict on them the punishments that the law allows."[87]

As Pedro's health deteriorated, Cotegipe stood in for him. There were too many mass escapes for individual slaveholders to deal with privately. Cotegipe ordered the military to round up and return escaped slaves to their masters. Black soldiers, impressed into service in the first place, were in no mood to hunt down thousands of slaves and drag them back to farms in the countryside, and neither were officers happy ordering them to do it.

In June 1887, Cotegipe and the Council of Ministers called Princess D. Isabel home to Rio de Janeiro from a trip she was taking with her husband and children in Europe. Pedro II was so sick that the doctor had ordered a period of complete rest in Europe. As he set sail, the *Jornal do Comércio* wrote, "Depart in peace our sovereign. God protect him and return him to us. All Brazilians unite their voices to that of the Church in a fervent prayer: 'Lord save the emperor.'"[88]

But peace was the last thing on Brazil's agenda in June 1887. Cotegipe's conservative cabinet was defending the interests of the powerful pro-slavery Rio de Janeiro planters, while the São Paulo planters faced a mass of radical black abolitionists and the fugitive slave town of Santos. Princess D. Isabel, now the acting regent in Brazil, wrote to her father in December 1887, "It would be good if everything copied the example of São Paulo planters. . . . Rio de Janeiro is currently very resistant, but sooner or later it will be forced to do the same as the rest."[89]

Cotegipe was more extreme in defense of Rio planters than they were for themselves. Even after they followed the lead of those in São Paulo and Minas Gerais, Cotegipe refused to budge on slavery and used every weapon in his political arsenal to maintain it in Brazil for as long as possible.

Urged on by the liberal Joaquim Nabuco, Marshal Deodoro da Fonseca asked Princess D. Isabel to relieve the army of having to hunt for escaped slaves, while the São Paulo assembly asked Parliament to decree immediate abolition of slavery in Brazil.

At the same time, another important army leader, Floriano Peixoto, wrote to a fellow officer, "Our poor country is in an advanced state of moral corruption, and needs a military dictatorship to cleanse it. As a liberal, I cannot wish for my country a dictatorship by the sword, yet everyone knows—and examples abound—that only this type of government knows how to purify the blood of a social organism, such as ours, which is in such a corrupt state."[90]

In March 1888, the hostilities that had been building between the baron of Cotegipe and Princess Isabel came to a head when she insisted on the dismissal of Rio de Janeiro's chief of police. Rather than obey, the conservative leader Cotegipe handed her the whole cabinet's resignation, which she happily accepted. She wrote, "I confess that a blind irritation took command of me, and in conscience I could not continue with a ministry when I personally felt and was convinced that it did not meet the country's aspirations in the present circumstances."[91]

"Slavery is declared abolished in Brazil"

In May, D. Isabel issued the following decree:

> The Princess Imperial Regent, in the name of His Majesty the Emperor Dom Pedro II, makes known to all subjects of the Empire that the General Assembly has decreed, and she has approved, the following law:
>
> Art: 1. From the date of this law, slavery is declared abolished in Brazil.
>
> Art: 2. All contrary provisions are revoked. . . . Given in the Palace of Rio de Janeiro, May 13, 1888, the sixty-seventh year of independence and of the Empire.[92]

At the ceremony where D. Isabel signed the law, she said, "Today would be one of the most beautiful in my life . . . if I did not know my father to be sick."[93] But Pedro II's health had improved in the French Alps and he returned to Brazil on a French steamship called Congo. His son-in-law, Count d'Eu, remarked, "The avidity and the enthusiasm of the public for the Emperor have been very great . . . but it is a totally personal homage. . . . the republican creed has made since his departure last year enormous advances . . . never, for the past 40 years, has the situation of the Brazilian monarchy appeared more shaky than today."[94]

By May 13, 1888, there were approximately 650,000 slaves in Brazil. The new policy of employing foreign immigrants meant many of these slaves were soon unemployed and moved to the cities in search of work.

Dom Pedro II had dominated the political process for decades, but he wasn't the man he'd been before his illness. Gone were the days he could bully a nation into fighting a war to satisfy his own vanity. He was now doddering and shaky, spending much of his time writing poetry that wasn't destined for critical acclaim. He went to the Petropolis train station every morning and evening to meet the Rio train. A British diplomat wrote, "It was a novelty to see the head of a State in full evening dress and high hat at half-past six in the morning, listening to an extremely indifferent brass band braying in the waiting room of a shabby railway station."[95]

With Pedro II home, D. Isabel wasn't acting regent anymore. She turned her back on politics to concentrate on religion. Her "Golden Law" assured her a level of popularity among African Brazilians, but she was loathed by members of the Chamber of Deputies, and seen as a traitor by slavocrats and traditionalist planters in Rio province and southern Minas Gerais.

They said the monarchy had betrayed them without the promise of indemnification. The republicans promised indemnification for lost slaves, so every malcontent in the country began to join their cause. In August 1889, the liberal leader, Ouro Preto, instigated the reformation of the National Guard. All this did was encourage the military to take immediate action against the government.

Deodoro da Fonseca returned to Rio de Janeiro without the government's permission and Floriano Peixoto joined him in a military coup. The pretext they gave for the mutiny was that they feared the 1st and 9th Regiments of Cavalry and the 2nd Battalion of Artillery were about to be attacked by the Guarda Negra. In the final days of the empire, the republicans and the uniformed forces of the Guarda Negra had been involved in many fights. The Guarda Negra were monarchists and former slaves, armed to defend D.

Isabel after she declared the Golden Law, when "the streets of Rio de Janeiro were the stage of actual battles."[96]

The cavalry and the army said they were going to avenge Deodoro da Fonseca against the Guarda Negra, and that they'd destroy them as if they were "killing dogs." Republican forces presaged the policy the republican government would adopt toward capoeiristas in all their dealings with African Brazilians loyal to the monarchy:

> In Rio de Janeiro, [African Brazilian monarchists] were shot down by republican youths armed like the soldiers with rifles against a so-called "Black Guard" carrying simple razors or clubs bearing the legend "Petrópolis." . . . the bravos of the Republican Club . . . set out to repel what seemed to be "aggression" on the part of the negroes of a Black Guard armed only [according to Medeiros e Albuquerque, a republican agitator] . . . with clubs and razors. It is not surprising that the volleys of the Club produced many victims among the heroic blacks whose bodies, according to Medeiros, "were hidden by the police." "The Travessa da Barreira was literally jammed with a bloody and panicky multitude," that is, of a mass of Negroes from the Black Guard, all of whom had relied only on their skill in capoeira or upon the said clubs and razors. . . . "We loaded our revolvers and, opening the windows a crack, extended one arm outward, discharging the five bullets in the chamber. Then we reloaded and repeated the process."[97]

After hearing the claims about the Guarda Negra, the minister of war and the rest of the cabinet, including Ouro Preto, trooped over to army headquarters in the city center. Going inside, protected by a large armed force, they watched the arrival of Deodoro da Fonseca and his 600 rebels, who were backed up by Floriano Peixoto and 2,000 of his troops. Ouro Preto wanted the men inside the barracks to attack Deodoro's rebels with the same valor they'd shown in the Paraguayan War, but a general reminded him that in Paraguay they'd faced armed enemies and not fellow Brazilians.

The rebels marched into the barracks. Deodoro paraded with Benjamin Constant and Quintino Bocaiúva through Rio de Janeiro. His troops surrounded the royal palace and took over the naval arsenal and the telegraph office. Later that afternoon at City Hall, some accounts say Deodoro was absent, others that he was the one who announced that "the people, the army and the navy, in perfect harmony of sentiment with our fellow citizens resident in the provinces, have just decreed the dethronement of the imperial dynasty, and consequently the extinction of the representative monarchical system of government."[98]

The following day, Pedro II and Princess Isabel were informed that the Bragança family had just twenty-four hours to pack their bags and leave Brazil. This came as a surprise to Pedro II, who'd grown rather out of touch, but Count d'Eu observed that "all the troops were massed in front of the ministry of war with Deodoro and Bocaiúva at their head. In that case, I could not stop myself saying, 'the monarchy is finished.'"[99]

It was the end of an era. d'Eu noted, "The boat began to move during the night of the 17th to the 18th and when about 5 A.M., I opened my window, we were in front of . . . the Sugar Loaf with the entry into the bay spread before us in all the splendour of the morning. Some time after midday, we passed cabo frio; and shortly after that we lost sight of land."[100]

Chapter Twelve
THE REPUBLIC

The Republic wasn't the golden dawn of a new and better era for African Brazilians or the poor in Brazil, nor was it going to be a holiday for capoeiristas. On the contrary, Deodoro da Fonseca used his newly gained power to persecute capoeira through law and police action in the most aggressive manner.

Republicanism was all about changing political representation among the ruling class. The main concerns were issues like senatorial representation for São Paulo, Minas Gerais, and Bahia. Planters' and landowners' interests were paramount in this process. Addressing unemployment, lack of public health, educational weakness, and the grinding poverty of the majority were way down at the bottom of Deodoro da Fonseca's things-to-do list. Republican reforms and laws swept the poor and black to the margins, both geographically and socially.

Deodoro was the chief of the provisional government, Benjamin Constant was war minister, Bocaiúva was minister of foreign relations, Ruy Barbosa of Bahia was minister of finance, and Campos Salles held down the justice ministry.

Ruy Barbosa's office was in the Cidade Velha, but his home in Botafogo had the best-stocked library in Brazil. He was a bibliophile who spent his life collecting books and documents. But on December 15, 1890, he ordered that all papers in the ministry of the treasury relating to slavery or the slave trade were to be burned. Hugh Thomas said, "It remains a matter of controversy what was, and was not, thereafter consigned to the flames."[1]

The avowed intention of Barbosa's resolution was to cleanse from history, by their "complete destruction," those papers that recalled "the lamentable institution which paralyzed for many years the development of society."[2]

Burning treasury papers did nothing to cleanse from history the shame of Brazilian slavery, though it did cleanse from the ministry of the treasury much of the documentation former slave owners might have used to bring indemnification claims for lost property against the provisional government, especially after the hasty promises about indemnification made by republicans during the dying days of empire.

The Republic brought mass immigration to Brazil. Particularly represented were the Italians, Germans, Spanish, Portuguese, Arabs, and Japanese. Their arrival ensured the unemployment of many of the emancipated, who were migrating between provinces after abolition.

Vadiagem and Bens do Evento

It had always been an uphill struggle for free blacks to remain free in Brazil. Since the early 18th century there had been the so-called laws concerning *Bens do Evento*, or "those properties which without an owner, go wandering from place to place, or move as the wind moves, from whence comes the name."[3] The Bens do Evento laws were a means of disposing of those "stray blacks, beasts, and cattle" that had no brand. This weird Portuguese and Brazilian legal concept made it virtually impossible for any individuals arrested to claim freedom effectively, and they were sold at auction in the same way as cattle. The concept of human bens do evento was in effect right up to 1872.

After abolition, new laws registered unemployed people, to stop their moving between states. Local authorities could expel those they officially labeled beggars and anyone registered as unemployed could also be expelled. Many states banned begging unless an individual was born in the state. Minas Gerais, for example, had such a law; the only reason people would migrate to Minas Gerais, if they had no family there, would be to keep from starving. But the law forbade begging and there were no longer any jobs. Slaves had been freed and that was the end of the government's resposibility toward them, except in creating imaginative laws that covered all aspects of life. The legislators in Minas Gerais banned unemployed people from singing, for example.

No funds were provided toward the welfare of emancipated ex-slaves. The Minas Gerais laws, and those of many other states, defined vagrancy as a crime: "If he [the vagrant] is found capable of working, he will be dealt with accordingly."[4] Dennis Newsome of San Diego has written of the parallels between Brazil and the USA after emancipation. He points out that the Confederate states all passed "Black Codes" to re-establish slavery in plantation prisons, chain gangs, farms, and factory prisons. The Black Codes provided the means for a free man to be re-enslaved: "Africans caught without 'visible means of support' could be made 'indentured servants.'"[5] Black orphans could be turned over to white masters until coming of age, excessive fines for minor crimes were paid off by local landowners in return for free labor, and so on.

Brazilian republicans admired the federalist government of the USA and learned some judicial tricks from them. The Black Codes in the USA made free use of vagrancy laws to imprison black men migrating between states. It was, according to Newsome, during the time of Black Codes that fight styles like "knocking and kicking" developed in U.S. prisons. These had regional names: "Jail House Rock, Closing Gates, 52, 42, Strato, PK, Mount Meg, Comstock, Gorilla, Barnyard."[6] The regional derivatives came from Bantu fights in prisons like Louisiana's Angola penitentiary. Newsome says his speciality, "52," was "named after a card game in which you throw up a deck of cards and where they land they land."[7] The fights were adapted for enclosed spaces such as corridors or stairs and, like capoeira, they are all based on deceptive and unexpected attacks. Newsom says that, "Jail House Rock is very rhythmic, pretty, and dance-like in execution."[8]

Other similarities existed between the American South and Brazil—for example, the popularity among planters of watching "boxing" matches between the slaves of different plantations. Dog- and cock-fighting were also common. Freyre noted that in Brazil, the plantation owner had a taste for "having capoeiras, cocks, and male canaries fight in his presence."[9]

In 1898, Araujo wrote of "idlers, thugs, ruffians . . . in taverns in the lowest quarters of the city [who practiced] feats of bodily skill and dexterity, to the vast delight of sailors and seamen, who, between puffs of smoke and reeking of alcohol, applauded this entertainment."[10] Famous capoeira master Pastinha told *Black Belt* magazine, "Even the plantation foremen would applaud the 'performances' as the 'players' would jump, weave, gambol, trip, and kick their opponents, then avoid retaliation by slithering on the ground like serpants."[11]

It was during this time that capoeira became so identified with vagrancy in Brazil that it was known as *vadia,* or idleness.

"The exercise of agility and corporal dexterity known by the term capoeiragem"

After abolition, many black people migrated from Bahia to downtown (north) Rio de Janeiro. Candomblé and new rhythms came with new residents, changing the music in the streets. Before reform policies totally annihilated the old downtown, there was contact between poor, black musicians and writers and members of the upper class who were predominantly white. Some capoeiristas also had contacts in the elite. This occasioned some political scandals at a very high level in the early years of the Republic.

One scandal came to be known as "The Capoeiristas Deportation and the General Quintino Bocaiúva."[12] The Republic's first chief of police in Rio was João Batista Sampaio Ferraz. He'd been ordered by Deodoro da Fonseca (the provisional president) to annihalate capoeira in the city by whatever means necessary.

To put this into practice, capoeira was finally outlawed on October 11, 1890, in the same penal code that forbade witchcraft and Candomblé. The penal code was designed to replace the 1830 criminal code, and it was tailor made for complete repression of rodas de capoeira, as well as afoxes and terreiros de Candomblé.

The code prohibited "practicing, in the streets and public squares, the exercise of agility and corporal dexterity known by the term capoeiragem."[13] Articles 157 and 158 also made it illegal "to practice spiritism, or magic and its conjurations, or use talismans and cartomancy, in order to arouse sentiments of hate or love, to insinuate the cure of a curable or incurable disease . . . to administer . . . a substance from any of the kingdoms of nature, thus performing or exercising the profession of folk healer [curandeiro]."[14]

Freyre suggests:

> The Republic is generally praised for having succeeded, through its energetic police chief Sampaio Ferraz, in crushing the capoeira in Rio de Janeiro. The truth is that the republican police seem to have acted against this group—all of whom were Negroes or mulattos—with a rigor which seemed to stem less from impulses of police order than of republican revenge against the group who had supported the Empire through activity in the Black Guard.[15]

In the 1870s, the windswept and lonely South Atlantic island of Fernando de Noronha, was chosen as the new high-security penal colony for Brazil's unwanted criminals. Given extraordinary powers, the new police chief, Sampaio Ferraz, sent his forces into areas where the capoeira maltas were most active and arrested capoeiristas for deportation to the island.

The police chief and his forces were inflexible and thorough in rounding up all the known capoeiristas in regular dragnets through Rio's streets. On one expedition, they caught a famous capoeirista from the upper class, Jose Elisio dos Reis, brother of the Count of Matosinho. The count was also the owner of the newspaper *O Pais*. General Quintino Bocaiúva was one of the newspaper's directors and a top minister in the new republican government. Like most of the capoeiristas arrested in Rio during the first years of the Republic, the count's brother was deported to Fernando de Noronha. Outraged, and working on the count's behalf, Bocaiúva publicly stated that he'd resign from the government if the capoeirista wasn't released from prison. The row was covered at every stage by the press, and was a huge public scandal.

Deodoro de Fonseca wasn't prone to back down when it came to capoeiristas, so Reis wasn't released from prison immediately. The Count of Matosinho was so disgusted that he sold his paper and left for Portugal.

Here was a breach in the *do favor* system of old. That system had assured favors and privileges to a limited number of capoeiristas for services rendered to influential politicians. During the empire period of Dom Pedros I and II, politicians were very familiar with capoeiristas, and they used African fighters for any number of duties from bodyguard service to intimidation of political opponents and others. We may recall the way in which "moleques" (a Brazilian Portuguese slang term for African capoeiristas, meaning, simply, "boys") were encouraged by Brazilian slave owners to attack the Irish and German soldiers in Rio in the 1820s, even before the soldiers had mutinied. Many of the seemingly illogical attacks by knife- and razor-wielding capoeristas of the malta gangs on businessmen, foreigners, and European immigrants during the Empire period could have been explained by this capangagem (bodyguard service). It also extended to attacks against republican rallies by capangas who became semi-officially known as the Guarda Negra. But times had changed.

The intransigent republican police were determined to destroy the ground on which capoeira grew. Bocaiúva was very influential in Rio de Janeiro. That the government didn't acquiesce to his demands demonstrated a determination to deal with capoeiristas in the harshest way. Decree no. 847 of the penal code against vagrants and capoeiristas was a declaration of war against capoeira.

Playing favorites wasn't completely obsolete, of course, and politi-

In the era of the Industrial Revolution, railroads were a symbol of modernity. Brazil's first railroad legislation happened in 1835, but actual railway building came later. The earliest railway, built in 1854, extended only 15 kilometers. As late as 1890, the country only had 9,973 kilometers of railroad track—this in a country with a total expanse of some 8.1 million square kilometers. An increase in railway construction toward the interior began in the 1890s. The largest increase in railroad track happened only in the twenty years before 1914, by which time the country had 26,060 kilometers of track—a figure the United States had already surpassed in the 1850s. This demonstrates that by the coming of the Republic, Brazil was already underdeveloped in relation to two of its main trading partners, Britain and the United States.

cians still intervened successfully in individual cases when they felt like it. Hermano Vianna tells the story of a favored musician:

> João da Bahiana played the tambourine, and once, in 1908, when he was playing it at the Penha street fair that many sambistas attended, the police confiscated it. "Samba was prohibited, tambourines were prohibited," explained João in an interview half a century later. Yet shortly after the police took João's instrument, senator Machado Pinheiro asked him to play at his house, and hearing of the lost tambourine, he bought a new one and had it inscribed: "For João da Bahiana, with admiration, senator Machado Pinheiro."[16]

Men like Pinheiro were the politicians behind the very public attacks on African Brazilian culture. He was a leading member of the government that criminalized João da Bahiana's music (and also the food hawking that João da Bahiana's mother, Aunt Prisciliana de Santo Amaro, had undertaken in the city). Yet Pinheiro was still a welcome guest at Aunt Prisciliana's parties, and João da Bahiana likewise performed at Pinheiro's home. Ruy Barbosa wept openly when the famous Rio stevedor and modinha master, Catulo da Paixão Cearense, sang at his Botafogo home.

This type of paradoxically sympathetic relationship between the elite and those they were legislating to repress was surprisingly common in Rio de Janeiro.

Old Portuguese Bantu-Land

Most of the old city was razed to the ground. In destroying the Cidade Velha and the Carnaval, the politicians were hoping to expunge African culture. This was an openly expressed policy. Olavo Bilac, the writer who so poetically rejoiced to the sound of pick axes pulverizing the old buildings, wrote about his desire to see the extinction of Carnaval. "The abominable cordões . . . that ancient custom of bacchic processions. . . . I believe, that of all civilized cities, Rio de Janeiro is the only one that tolerates this shameful exhibition. . . . it is revolting that these orgies spill out onto the street in erotic processions."[17]

The man-about-town and belle époque journalist, João do Rio, wrote that the street processions of Carnaval:

Come from the festival of Our Lady of the Rosary, back in colonial times. I don't know why the blacks like Our Lady of the Rosary. . . . In that period they already liked her and went out in the street, dressed like kings, animals. pagans, and policemen, playing African instruments, and they would stop in front of the Viceroy's house to dance and sing. . . . the origin of the cordões is the African Afoché, the day in which religion is mocked. . . . Carnaval would have disappeared . . . if it were not for the enthusiasm of the groups from Gambôa, Saco, . . . Saúde, S. Diogo, cidade nova, that burning enthusiasm . . . which captures and leads astray the entire city.[18]

João do Rio's fellow journalist, Luis Edmundo, wrote:

The country, until the time of the African slave trade's end, was still a land that seemed more like a corner of Africa than a nation of the New World. And it was more or less the same until the dawn of this century. Bilac, quite accurately, called Rio de Janeiro of his time, Old Portuguese Bantuland. . . . Rio is becoming civilized, the papers report. And the barbarous noise is invited to disappear from a city that is beginning to worship civilization.[19]

The Carnaval's strongholds were all working class, poor neighborhoods. Alternative accommodation wasn't provided for residents fleeing flattened homes in Cidade Velha. Favelas had been developing and spreading to the hillsides of the northern dock area. The marshes northwest of the city were drained and the Cidade Nova was filled with favelas where many of the Bahians who had immigrated lived.

In the wake of the police crackdown after the 1890 penal code, the maltas were broken up and capoeira no longer featured in police reports as public enemy number one. Capoeira in Rio de Janeiro experienced the banishment of a whole generation of its practitioners to penal colonies. Once "the strongest moral infirmity" of the city, capoeira was no longer even a police problem. And yet within only thirty years, the "barbaric" and "criminal"

African pastimes of samba and capoeira were destined to become valuable national assets.

Bahia and the End of the Beginning

The birth of the Republic, so destructive to capoeira, coincided with the birth of many great capoeiristas and Brazilian outlaws. Manoel Henrique Pereira is said to have been born in 1895 in Santo Amaro da Purifiçao in Bahia. He would later become known as Besouro Mangangá. Vincent Ferreira Pastinha was born in Bahia on April 5, 1889. Manoel dos Reis Machado (Mestre Bimba) was born on November 23, 1899 in Salvador, Bahia. Virgulino Ferreira da Silva was born in the Passagem das Pedras region of Pernambuco on July 7, 1897. Virgulino da Silva would later gain the nickname Lampião, king of the *cangaceiros* (bandits) "because he could fire a lever-action rifle so fast that it created a continuous light in the darkness."[20]

Recalling the first decades of 20th-century capoeira, Mestre Pastinha said, "Legendary names appeared—invincible fighters, men with flesh impenetrable by knife or bullet, men under contract to the devil; men with charms against the most powerful of enemies; men who could liberate themselves from any kind of trap."[21]

Besouro Mangangá always carried amulets, *patua*, for his own protection. His birthplace, Santo Amaro, was at the heart of the sugar Recôncavo. As far back as 1745, the region of Santo Amaro had gained a reputation as a place where traveling the highways was hazardous and many carried firearms because of the region's highwaymen. Landowners employed capitães-do-mata in large numbers to hunt fugitives from the sugar mills, who lived by banditry on the outskirts of the Recôncavo in a network of quilombos.

The Recôncavo was aflame. A "king" of the blacks in Cachoeira led an insurrection in August 1826. In December, a pitched battle was fought against a quilombo at cabula, on the outskirts of Salvador. The quilombo had served as a Candomblé for the Yoruba religious activities. . . . Arrests revealed that the quilombos depredations were intended to draw troops away from the city to set the stage for a general uprising. . . . The fires continued to smolder and ignite . . . at engenhos in Santo Amaro.[22]

By 1900 there'd been Yoruba and Hausa people in Bahia and Santo Amaro for centuries. Hausas did a lot of trading in the Recôncavo, such as buying tobacco to sell in Salvador. Hausas and Nagôs also practiced Candomblé and Hausas additionally sold Muslim charms for protection. In Congo and Angola, charms were also popular for protection in battle, for success in hunting, or other purposes. Angolan charms, called *nkisi,* were sometimes very heavy (up to 5 kg). Like the Hausa and Yoruba charms, they could be personally fashioned by priests for clients and put to specific purposes. Charms were often worn in pouches strung around the neck or waist. Besouro Mangangá was said never to go anywhere without his patua, hence the name Mangangá, a practitioner or disciple of magic. Mangangá derives from the Kimbundo term for doctor, nganga. Mangangá was also a "term applied in north-eastern Brazil to a species of large wood-gnawing beetles."[23]

Yoruba Magic

Muslim, or as it is sometimes expressed, "Islamicized," Africans in Brazil were known by the collective Yoruba name *malê.* Hausas from northen Nigeria were a significant group among those classed as malê in Bahia. In using these terms, however, it is important to remember Paul E. Lovejoy's warning that labels like "Hausa," "malê," and "Yoruba" in Brazil had possibly quite different meanings in Africa, and the context has also changed between today and the early 19th century. He maintained that today's ethnic labels can't be used backwards through time, nor are religious practices static. European categorization of African populations were not in many cases the names used by African slaves themselves. It is with these reservations that the terms Hausa, Yoruba, and malê are used here.

After the 1835 uprising, the authorities scrutinized the occupations of the 500 malês who were sentenced either to death, the pelourinho prison, or deportation. A glimpse of the life of the times is achieved through the eyes of the judiciary. One Jeje called José was a butcher, but according to one witness worked also as a curador de feitiço (witchdoctor). A small minority in Bahia were able to live off the proceeds of their healing or *feitiço* work. At his trial, José testified that he'd been raised in Nagôland, where he practiced Yoruba religion and magic. One slave woman, Marcelina, was arrested in the house of a curandeiro on the night of the uprising. She'd been sent there by her mistress to get her foot treated. The curandeiro was a healer of the Yoruba religion. Because of illegal smuggling of slaves into Brazil after 1850, there were still many Yoruba Africans in Bahia in the late 19th century; in fact, there were still Yoruba speakers in Recife up until the 1950s.

Muslims sold amulets and charms to heal physical or psychic sickness and to protect against physical danger. One Hausa arrested after the uprising made four *patacas* every day selling prayers to protect his customers. Ganhadores in Salvador had to pay about one pataca (320 reis) to the slave owner each day they worked. Yet this Hausa was clearing a thousand reis a day from his charms, which put him among the top earners of the African population of the time.

Religion and magic were so closely connected in Yorubaland (Nagôland) that the boundary between one and the other wasn't clear. The Yoruba had and still have a strong belief in the reality of a supernatural kingdom. Yoruba people have used magic to harness supernatural forces by a wide variety of means. Incantations, all kinds of amulets and charms, miniature cabaças (gourds), padlocks, animal horns, rings, alligator pepper, and many other objects and substances have been applied to supernatural work that might have a good or sometimes an evil intention, depending on the will of the practitioner. Magical recipes have been commonly used for psychic self-defense against witches, enemies, poison, or a gamut of potentially harmful evil spirits. Such concoctions or enchanted amulets have also been widely used to achieve invulnerability to knife, gun, and machete attacks.

Corpo fechado was a possibility in the Yoruba religion. The correct words in the correct order had to be spoken and ritual actions performed. If a combatant wanted to cut his adversary, he might prepare a knife in a bowl of water and call the spirit of the enemy into the bowl, using the weapon to attack the spirit in the water.

Practitioners of magic followed a series of taboos if they wished to be effective. At certain times they might not eat particular foods or they refrained from sex so that their charms and spells became more potent.

> In consequence of belief in magical power, many . . . are found wearing all kinds of charms—copper rings (órùkao bàbà), amulets (ifúnpá), preparations sewn up in a leather girdle/belt (onde) . . . some babies wear coils round their necks and waists; men and women have some

black powder injected into their bodies through incisions (*gbéré*). . . . Some of these preparations are protective measures, others are intended to bring good health, fortune or prosperity. But some others are employed for nefarious deeds and they make people live in constant fear.[24]

In the Candomblé of Salvador there were different traditions. These were Nagô or Ketu, Ijexá, Egba, Efan, Gêge, and Kongo-Angola, called Angola in Rio de Janeiro and Salvador. A Kongo language was still spoken in the 1940s in Angola Candomblé ceremonies.

Charms were prevalent in Central African religions. In Kongo-Angola they were hung on the body, in the home, or buried in the ground, depending on the purpose.

> The proper creation of the charms depended on the knowledge and skill of a religious expert to assemble the suitable ingredients, speak the appropriate words of invocation, and follow . . . the correct behavior and dietary prohibitions. Practitioners such as the nganga-ngudi-a-nambua and mpombolo also earned renown for their ability to enchant animals and draw them to hunters for the kill.[25]

Besouro Mangangá

Manoel Henrique Pereira was born to João Grosso and Maria Haifa in 1895 or 1897. Much of what is known about him was described in *Capoeira Angola Ensaio Sócio-Etnográfico* by Waldeloir Rego, and was originally passed on by Rafael Alves França, Mestre Cobrinha Verde. Accounts say that he learned capoeira fighting from an elderly slave, Mestre Tio Alipio, at the Rua do Trapiche de Baixo in Santo Amaro da Purificação.

Manoel Henrique gained his nicknames because of his fighting prowess and ability to escape death and capture in the tightest of situations. He had a reputation for possessing supernatural powers, not only because he had a closed body that was invulnerable to bullets and blades, but also employed shape-shifting magic that enabled him to transsubstantiate into a black beetle. In northeastern Brazil mangangá was a variety of beetle, as well as being associated with nganga, the Bantu term for doctor. His other nicknames were Besouro Preto and Besouro Cordão de Ouro.

He lived during the era of police chief Pedro de Azevedo Gordilho, who controlled the Salvador police 1920–1926. Gordilho's name became synonymous with the persecution of capoeiristas. He ordered his cavalry squadron to attack capoeira rodas wherever they were discovered.

Police and arrest records mention Manoel Henrique Pereira in Salvador. For instance, on September 8, 1918 he was arrested and given a short stay in jail for an altercation with police officers, including Cláudio de Souza, who had a confiscated berimbau at the police station in São Caetano. Besouro Mangangá fought with three officers who refused to return it to him. There are numerous records of fights in Salvador, and records in the jurisdiction of Salvador indicate he worked as a stevedore at the quay in Cachoeira.

Besouro Mangangá never held a fixed profession, but was an itinerant laborer in factories, mills, and farms in the area. He was known to attack police who arrested his friends, and then steal police weapons and return them to the police station later. He disliked the police and went to lengths to humiliate them whenever he could.

Among the stories that circulated from Mestre Cobrinha Verde is the occasion when Besouro was employed for a period at the Colônia mill (which in the 1960s was called Santa Elisa). The foreman there acted much as he would have during the days of slavery. When it was time to distribute wages he would call out the

workers' names and if they didn't answer for their money immediately, he wouldn't pay them. He'd say the money had "broken
São Caetano." Besouro knew the foreman's trick and when it
came his turn for wages he deliberately remained quiet. Sure
enough, the foreman called out again, and when Besouro asked
for his money, he was told to go away. At the Colônia mill, if
workers argued about this they were strapped to a tree and
whipped.

This didn't happen to Besouro; instead, he rushed into the foreman's house and easily overpowered the man, shouting "Are you
going to pay Besouro or not!" The foreman, in a trembling voice,
ordered for Besouro to get his money.

Another time, Besouro took a soldier hostage, forcing him to
drink cachaça until he was drunk in a tavern at Largo da Cruz.
When the soldier went back to his barracks and told his commander, José Costa, where Besouro was drinking, Costa organized
ten armed soldiers to take him, "dead or alive."[26] Besouro knew
when they arrived and went out toward Largo da Cruz, shouting
that he wouldn't give himself up, so they shot him on the spot. He
fell, but when they went to confirm that he was dead, Besouro got
up, kicked his way free, and made his escape. These stories circulated widely and give an indication of the qualities that were valued
among capoeiristas. Physical, even supernatural, prowess, cunning,
bravery, loyalty to the underdog against the police and soldiers—all
these were looked upon with admiration by a wide enough peer
group for the legends about Besouro to continue growing and
spreading in Santo Amaro.

He usually traveled by night and remained on the move. He
could leap great heights and move so fast it appeared he'd vanished
into thin air. His body was impervious to bullets, or at least he sur-

vived so many battles with police armed with guns, it might as well have been.

Jean-Jacques Dessalines, the leader of the Haitian revolution, was believed to have the same power. Jean-Baptiste Cinéas described his powers:

> Before each battle the spirits enabled him to make himself invisible so that he could inspect the enemy's camp. The most striking example of this protection was at Crête-à-Pierrot where eighteen thousand French soldiers surrounded his fort with its fifteen hundred men. The French sent a spy to give Dessalines poison, but he threw up the poison. Each night he left the fort, slipping through the French army without being seen and conferred with Haitian officers outside the fortress.[27]

"Besouro quando morreu / Abriu a bôca e falô / Adeus Maracangalha / Qui é terra de matadô"

Besouro has also been called "Danado," meaning that he was damned. He traveled regularly between Santo Amaro and Maracangalha. His final demise came after gaining employment as a cattle herder on the ranch of a Dr. Zeca. Besouro had a furious argument with Zeca's son, Memeu, who swore to Besouro that he would see him dead. Zeca had a friend called Baltazar who was the administrator at Maracangalha. Zeca told Besouro, who couldn't read or write, to take a letter to Baltazar. Unknown to Besouro, the letter said, "Kill the messenger who brings this note." Baltazar read the letter in a leisurely way and asked Besouro to return the next morning so he could give him a reply for Dr. Zeca.

Plans were already afoot to assassinate Besouro. It was well known that he had the power to resist gunshot, so a special wooden knife of the tropical palm tree *tucum* was prepared to counteract Besouro's own magic. The fact that he delivered the letter ordering his own death was probably part of this magic ritual, as there were many other means to have Baltazar informed and ready for the ensuing ambush.

Besouro spent the night in the arms of a local prostitute and returned the next morning for Baltazar's reply. As he walked through the gate into the enclosure, forty armed men took aim and fired straight at him without hitting him. One man, said to be named Eusébio de Quibaca, approached Besouro very slowly and, in a treacherous way, plunged the tucum knife into Besouro's chest. Besouro Mangangá died in 1924; he was only 27.

As well as Mestre Cobrinha Verde, Besouro's capoeira disciples included Mestre Siri de Mangue and there is also a possibility that Mestre Olivio Bispo dos Santos (Mestre Bispo de Santo Amaro) of Grupo Bahia do Berimbau was a disciple of the late Besouro Mangangá.

Lampião

Another figure who loomed large in capoeira folklore was a contemporary of Besouro Manganaga. This was the famous cangaçeiro, Lampião.

> Ê sim, sim, sim
> Ôi não, não, não
> Oia a pisada de Lampião
> Ê sim sim,sim
> Ôi não, não, não
> Oi a pisada de Lampião
> Oi a pisada de Lampião.[28]

Two particular cangaçeiro leaders, Antonio Silvino and Lampião, have achieved national folkloric fame in Brazil. The media for that notoriety were ballads, and the poetry that resulted when ballads were transcribed into chapbooks. Also important for creating the legend were newspaper reports. Fame kept alive through ballads and song is a marked feature of northeastern Brazil's cultural life. It is certain that, if not for the songs of capoeira, the fame of Besouro Manganga would never have spread beyond Santo Amaro.

Both Lampião and Antonio Silvino were heroes of what is known as *cordel* literature. This working-class literature originated from forms of Iberian ballad that have been influenced by African oral traditions in northeast Brazil. The ballads were printed in self-published chapbooks (*folhetos*). The folhetos had their parallel in the old *folhas volantes* and *folhas soltas* of 17th-century Portugal (Spain and France also had equivalents). The chapbooks, typically made from paper folded over, had as few as four or as many as thirty pages. Their covers were originally designed using stencils made from blocks of wood. The authors made just a couple of hundred copies per printing on very basic equipment. *Cordel* means string and comes from the fact that the small books were sold suspended from a string in a market stall; thus, cordel literature is, literally, "string books." The marketplaces of the Northeast multiplied after Brazil gained indepedence from Portugal. Before that, the captaincies of Brazil were divided into *sesmarias*, vast land tracts ruled by *coronéis*. It was these coronéis who decided the laws, as this capoeira song sung by Mestre Beija Flor shows:

Coronel, Coronel, Coronel,
Dona Sinha mandou lhe chamar
Coronel, Coronel, Coronel,

Que a preta Iaia desobedeceu
Qual o castigo que vamos lhe dá pele avoar
Amarra essa preta no pelô
Pra que ela sinta muita dor
Assim ela não vai desobedecer

[Translated]
Colonel, Colonel, Colonel,
the Mistress has asked me to call you
Colonel, Colonel, Colonel,
The black girl disobeyed
What punishment shall we give her
We can tan the hide off her,
Tie that black girl to the pillory post,
Let her feel the pain
So she wont do it again.[29]

After 1822, the sesmarias were broken up into smaller ranches and farms, worked by poor subsistence farmers and sharecroppers who traveled to the marketplaces to sell their produce. Illiteracy was the norm, so storytellers were popular at the markets and served the function of providing entertainment and passing on news.

After the technological innovation of the printing press finally arrived in northeastern Brazil, literacy increased and ballad singers and poets began to reproduce their work in ink. So in the first half of the 20th century cordel literature became popular. It is still sold today, although its heyday has passed. Due to its readership, firmly rooted among the poor of northeastern Brazil, the literature was characterized by a set of values in which the people are perpetually in a struggle to resist exploitation by the ruling class and landowners who were the descendents of the hated coronéis.

Obvious heroes and archetypes of the Northeast's "backland"

resistance were cangaçeiros and messianic itinerant preachers who meant more to the local people than the distant pontiff residing in Rome. There are countless cordels about two of the most famous cangaçeiros, Lampião and Antonio Silvino (with titles like "The Debate Between Lampião and St. Peter" or "The Fight Between Lampião and Antonio Silvino in Hell"). Silvino lived from 1875 to 1944 and was known as the "the "terror" [or] "king of the backlands" from around 1896 until 1914, in which year he was captured and Lampião took over his crown as the bandit king.

Cordel literature and its heroes had a vital impact on the development of Brazilian literature in the 20th century. For example, Euclides da Cunha's classic book *Os Sertões* (or *Rebellion in the Backlands*) described the resistance of backland people and their leader, a religious mystic by name of Antonio Conselheiro, at Canudos. They defied the federal goverment and the Brazilian army for a year during 1896–1897.

Padre Cícero was another priest from Juazeiro, near Canudos, in the Northeast. He, like Conselheiro, became a backland messiah and hero as he traveled the sertão. As a figure of hope to geographically isolated and extremely poor people, Cícero was a popular character in Cordel poetry, and he was a personal hero of the bandit Lampião.

Lampião, Virgulino Ferreira da Silva, was born just two months before the event that inspired Euclides da Cunha to write his masterpiece, *Os Sertões* (Rebellion in the Backlands). Da Cunha wrote:

> Around twenty or twenty-five miles from Xique-Xique is the bandit capital, the settlement of Santo Ignacio, built among the mountains and to this day inaccessible to the police . . . lending sanction to the unpunished reign of gangsterism. . . . It is accordingly not surprising if these crimes have increased in number, with the bandits extending

their sway over the entire valley of the São Francisco and overflowing to the north. . . . For the cangaçeiro of Paraíba and Pernambuco is an identical product under a different name. He is distinguished from the jagunço by perhaps the slightest variation in weapons, the *parnahyba* of the long and rigid blade taking the place of the famous and traditional bell-mouth blunderbuss.[30]

Lampião was the second of nine children. His mother and father had a small farm and were known to be very hardworking and honest. Virgulino was reputedly pulled into *cangaço* by escalating rows over stolen cattle with his family's neighbors, the Saturninos. There was a rigid code of revenge in the backlands; "feud [was] the almost invariable starting point of a Brazilian cangaceiro's career."[31]

He bought a rifle and dagger
In the town of São Fransisco.[32]

After an initial shooting incident where nobody got hurt, Saturnino and fifteen men rode to the Ferreiras' ranch, where Virgulino (Lampião) and his uncle were waiting. They were well armed and ready for the attack. They blasted the Saturnino men and critically injured one of them before the Saturninos retreated.

It had become a serious blood feud and the Ferreiras were surrounded by enemies. They admired the cangaceiro Sebastião Pereira, and decided to adopt his image. They never went out without their guns, and they wore classic bandit attire, "hats with the brims turned up, colorful kerchiefs around their necks and cartridge belts crossed over their chests."[33] The situation went from bad to worse in Nazaré, where Lampião and his brothers had built a reputation as ruthless cangaceiros. After a shootout with the town's leading citizens, they realized they'd have to escape for their own safety even though it would cost them land and cattle.

Lampião's reputation grew. His large gang was loyal to him but the family had to stay on the move. They traveled in two groups to Engenho. Lampião's mother became very sick on the journey; she died on reaching Engenho. A force of policemen snuck up on the house and opened fire with everything they had, hitting Lampião's father where he sat, killing him instantly.

The double death of his mother and father hardened Lampião's heart against the police. He demanded complete loyalty from his friends—if somebody crossed him he showed no mercy. He tore out the eyeballs of a comrade who betrayed him and rammed the barrel of his gun into the gaping sockets, blowing his brains out while the man's wife and six children watched.

> He killed for play
> Out of pure perversity
> And gave food to the hungry
> With love and charity.[34]

In 1922 he gained a measure of revenge against the politicians and police he held responsible for his parents' death. Fifty men invaded the home of the baroness of Agua Branca, stealing money, gold, silver, and all her valuable possessions. She was an extremely wealthy widow and the haul was huge, so Lampião's name was in every newspaper. In 1925 he met his hero, Padre Cícero. Backlanders (*sertanejos*) thought Cícero a saintly figure and he was extremely popular. "The sertão of north-eastern Brazil, which was the classic home of the cangaçeiros, was also that of the santos, the rural messianic leaders."[35] In the ballad about Lampião, he:

> Swore to be avenged on all
> Saying in this world I'll respect
> Father Cícero and no one else.[36]

The so-called "Prestes column" of guerilla rebels had just arrived in the Northeast. They were spreading the message of Luis Carlos Prestes, the future head of the Brazilian Communist Party. The government's plan was to enlist one armed rebel, Lampião, to destroy another one, and Padre Cícero acted as the middle man who fixed up this arrangement for the government.

The 1926 configuration of Lampiao the bandit, Cícero the saint, and Prestes the Communist revolutionary was a dynamic one. Lampião was carrying around "The Prayer of the Crystal Rock," enamored by his new relationship with Cícero. He was soon informed by a friendly colonel that even if he succeeded in defeating the Prestes column, instead of the promised medals and salvation promised via Cícero, he'd actually be receiving jail time or, more likely, a death sentence. Lampião understandably lost interest in pursuing Prestes through the backlands.

By now Lampião's fame had spread far and wide. He was operating as a gangster in the same era as John Dillinger, Bonnie and Clyde, Bugsy Siegel, Lucky Luciano, Meyer Lanskey, and Al Capone. It was the "Golden Age" of gangsterism but even in the United States Lampião was famous enough to fascinate the American press. He was filmed live in the act of banditry. The *New York Times* published a feature article about him in 1931.

He and his gang "would . . . use tree branches to clear footprints, put sheepskins on the bottom of shoes, walk backwards over their tracks or bury food skins so vultures wouldn't circle."[37] Lampião was very good to the poor people in the areas where he held power, which won him sympathy and popularity, although he was singularly cruel to his enemies. It was said "He massacred laborers, tortured an old woman who cursed him . . . by making her dance naked with a cactus bush until she died. . . . [He] killed one of his men who had offended him by making him eat a liter of salt."[38]

In the end the police went undercover and discovered his movements from an informer within his inner clan, the *coiteiros*. At the Fazenda da Angicos, Pôrto da Fôlha em Sergipe, on July 28, 1938, the police ambushed and killed him. Ruth Landes, in Bahia during 1938–39, wrote:

> The Bahia police had lately captured in the Highlands a notorious young caboclo bandit named Lampeão and also his young sweetheart Maria Bonita. Having pursued his bandit group for so many years that the chase had given rise to exciting ballads indicating the sympathy of the people, the federal soldiers decapitated Lampeão and Bonita when they finally captured them. They sent the heads to the office of the médico-legista where they were put in a preservative brine. The heads, each in a separate jar, Dr. Eustacio showed me enthusiastically. . . . "She must have been pretty for a caboclo," he observed, intent on the girl's face, "she was so fair. You can't see Lampeã very well; he doesn't show up because he's already turning black." I know many Bahians would have envied my privilege.[39]

As in the case of Zumbi (who was beheaded), Tiradentes (who was hanged, drawn, and quartered), and Besouro Mangangá (executed with a wooden blade), Lampião's legend long outlived his mortal body, and his name is still sung in capoeira rodas all over the world.

"The art form was slowly extinguished in Rio and Recife, leaving capoeira only in Bahia"

"Capoeira was all but extinct in Rio de Janeiro and Recife by the first decades of the twentieth century," writes J. Lowell Lewis.[40]

Mestre Nestor also writes, "The art form was slowly extinguished in Rio and Recife, leaving capoeira only in Bahia."[41]

Mestre Pastinha said of Bahia in the times of Besouro and Lampião:

> The capoeira is as aggressive as it is dangerous. He who doesn't know how to fight is always caught unawares. Crooks and misguided people transformed these moves into a means of assault, to avenge their enemies and confront the police. It was a sad time for capoeira. I knew, I saw it. Around the docks . . . it's a violent fight, nobody can restrain it. . . . Once I saw a capoeirista driving away a whole patrol. Another thing; a dark place, a woman, a man arrives wanting something, and the man wanting a woman is always taken by surprise. Then suddenly he receives a punch. Just one and falls hurt, unconscious or dead. Yes man, there were double dealing capoeiristas who dressed as women to steal from Don Juans. . . . I know that this is a dirty blemish on the history of capoeira, but is a gun guilty of the crimes it practices? And the knife? And the cannons? And the bombs? What I always like to remember is that the capoeira appeared in Brazil as a fight against slavery. . . .
>
> Everything I think about capoeira I wrote one day on that picture that is on the front of the Academy. At the top, only these three words: "Angola, capoeira, mother." And at the bottom, the idea: "Mandinga of a slave longing for freedom." Its beginning doesn't have a method; its end is inconceivable to the wisest capoeirista.[42]

Street capoeira in Rio de Janeiro went underground and followed its practitioners into the *favelas* after the destruction of the Cidade Velha. It's improbable that a movement so ubiquitous was totally extinguished or that every capoerista was deported to Fernando de Noronha island.

"National representative symbol"

In 1906, the Rio-based magazine, *Kosmos,* published, "Two great capoeiras, equally distinguished, equally agile, with precise, perfect and complete knowledge of the game, will never injure each other, maybe just insignificantly and not seriously, which indicates the defensive value of this popular strategy that places it, therefore, above any national representative symbol."[43]

The capoeiristas of old had often been armed, as Rio's newspapers had complained daily. The long stick made of *lei* wood, nicknamed a petropolis, was a favored weapon, along with the so-called "Santo Christo" straight razor. Both these weapons were likely to be so named because they were used by the capoeiristas of the Black Guard of Princess Isabel, who had resided in Petropolis at São Cristóvão Palace.

In calling capoeira a game and a *"popular strategy,"* the *Kosmos* article was clearly not describing an art form breathing its last gasp in Rio de Janeiro, although its presentation had changed. The phrase "national representative symbol" foreshadowed a perspective that became common thirty years later. Nor were these ideas new, even in 1906. In the 1880s, Melo Morais Filho wrote, "The capoeiragem as an art, as an instrument of defense, is Brazil's own fight . . . with its muscular force, the fluid articulation and rapidity of its movements."[44]

Many decades later, Gilberto Freyre recalled whimsically how useful this trend in education might have been if only the republicans had immediately adopted it:

> Another error might have been the failure of the police to employ
> the capoeira, then in its fullest flowering, as a weapon in their own
> arsenal for the preservation of order. The Armed Forces also could
> have used the technique, both in suppressing disorders and as an exer-

cise in physical conditioning, an adjunct to the imitations of Swedish and Japanese exercises already employed at the time. . . . The Brazilian Army, composed mainly of mestiços and plebeians, could have developed the same virtues as the Japanese by adopting the capoeira and would at the same time have developed a technique that was ecologically nationalistic.[45]

In 1906, Lieutenant Santos Porto wrote a preface to a book by jujitsu specialist H. Irving Hancock on Japanese physical education (*Educação Fisica Japonêsa*). He inferred that the criminal practice of capoeira was a thing of the past and recommended mixing jujitsu with capoeira for an effective self-defense system.

There began a new trend to clean up capoeira's image in Brazil. It was becoming organized as a sport. Bouts took place in Rio de Janeiro between Japanese jujitsu fighters and capoeiristas. On May 1, 1909 at the Concerto Avenida I, Ciríaco Francisco da Silva (Macaco Velho) knocked out jujitsu champ Sado Miako with a single, lightning-fast *rabo-de-arraia*.

In 1916, Captain Ataliba Nogueira, Lieutenant Lapa, and Lieutenant Leite of the Rio military police published *Manual de Capoeira,* for use by military personnel. In 1922, in a widely read magazine, *Eu Sei Tudo*, Professor Mário Aleixo put forward a self-defense system combining capoeira with other martial arts. He explained that in capoeira classes he had observed deficiencies in its effectiveness, and he suggested a cross-section of supplementary techniques from a whole stew of styles, including jujitsu, boxing, wrestling, and *jogo de pau*.

Capoeira wasn't dying, but it was changing. Mestre Sinhozinho was born in Santos in 1891 and learned capoeira on the docks. He continued his practice in Rio and opened a school to teach fighting techniques of capoeira without music to middle-class white students, much in the way encouraged by Santos Porto. In 1928, Professor Aníbal Burlamáqui published *Ginástica Nacional (Capoeiragem) Metodizada e Regrada.* In this manual, the author added blows from other styles to those from capoeira. He devised bouts of three minutes with two-minute breaks. Capoeiristas in this system wore trunks and boots. Bouts were played on a special pitch. Burlamáqui argued that as football, boxing, and Greco-Roman wrestling had pitches and courts, so should capoeiragem. Burlamáqui's influential manual shaped Rio de Janeiro's capoeira in the '20s and '30s, when it began to be taught in academies. A poet named Felix Peligrini, author of *Liria de Crisemo,* established a thriving "scientific" school of capoeira in Cidade Nova in the 1920s.

The trend of teaching capoeira in Rio to whites, the military, and police—a capoeira divested of its African content—continued up to the Second World War and beyond. In 1945, for example, the Ministerio de Educaçao e Saude sponsored Penna Marinho to produce the *Subsídios para o Estudo da Metodologia do Treinamento da Capoeiragem,* modeled on the ideas of Aleixo and Burlamáqui. The systematized, martial arts-oriented capoeira in early-20th-century Rio had none of the ritual and musical components of the jogo de angola. To see how the jogo, the roda, and the music that we know today came into being, we have to look elsewhere.

"Bahia de todos os santos, Bahia dos orixás, Bahia de Menininha, Menininha do Gantois"[46]

The historical point at which this volume ends was the time of Menininha do Gantois. Capoeira, Brazil, and indeed the world were at a crossroad and the future of all three would be permanently changed by the events that occurred.

When a Jewish-American anthropologist from Columbia University took a German boat from Rio de Janeiro to Bahia in 1938, the army of the Third Reich had recently annexed Austria. German families who had been established in Santa Catharina in southern Brazil were leaving the country to return to the Fatherland.

As she stared, depressed, at the many pictures of Hitler adorning the walls of her cabin, her mind started to wander. She knew that five years earlier her own university professor's books had been among those burned on the huge bonfires lit by "students" of Germany's oldest university at Heidelberg. She didn't dare share her thoughts with anybody because she had noted that everyone on the boat saluted each other with "Heil Hitler." She wisely kept her mouth shut when her fellow passengers loudly discussed the vital importance of banishing Jews from Greater Germany and theorized that they could go to Brazil instead.

The previous year, Getúlio Vargas had declared the Estado Novo (New State) in Brazil. He was surrounded by ministers who were active supporters and admirers of Adolf Hitler and the Italian dictator Benito Mussolini. It would be far too simplistic to make direct parallels between the Estado Novo and the totalitarian states of Europe. However, the 1937 constitution was by no means the product of a constituent assembly; the constitution was the brainchild of a Minas Gerais lawyer named Francisco Campos. A promised plebiscite for its approval never happened, so Campos's 1937 constitution was effectively forced onto Brazil.

In an open letter to Getúlio Vargas, the Rio de Janeiro Communist party eventually warned, "The Fifth Column in Brazil is so well organized that . . . Francisco Campos was able to say, to friends, that whenever he wants to, Hitler can take Brazil by picking up the telephone."[47]

A famous chronicler of Bahian life, and admirer of Stalin, Jorge Amado had been arrested in 1936, due to the 1935 *Intentona*, a failed coup led in Brazil by Luís Carlos Prestes, the leader of the Brazilian Communist Party. But by 1940, after Russia and Germany had signed their non-aggression pact, Amado was the cultural editor of *Meio Dia,* a pro-Nazi newspaper. At a Communist Party meeting, writer Oswald de Andrade accused Amado of being a "cheap spy of Nazism."

Oswald de Andrade later said:

> In a writers' committee meeting, in front of 15 people from the Party . . . I accused him of being a cheap spy for the Nazis, as former eminent editor of *Meio Dia.* I told them—and Amado didn't dare to defend himself since everything is absolutely accurate—that in 1940 Jorge invited me in Rio to have lunch at Brahma with a high-ranking German man at the Embassy . . . so that this German could offer me to write a book defending Germany. Jorge informed me later that this book would pay me $30 *contos.* I refused and Jorge was surprised because he had accepted various orders from this very same German.[48]

This story is told to illustrate the way in which world events, Brazilian politics, and local culture intertwined and could destroy relations between comrades.

At the same time that Ms. Landes (the Jewish-American anthropologist) was in Brazil, another American academic was there, visiting from the City College of New York. He noted that the Ministry of Education was busy revising texts and removing volumes of "liberal" literature from the college libraries. Among other characteristics of the Estado Novo was the absence of freedom of the press and the banning of opposition parties.

The New York academic, Bailey W. Diffie, one of the leading Luso-Brazilian scholars in the world in 1938, warned colleagues that the official Brazilian propoganda line was that liberalism was the "greatest evil of the age, the source of all trouble, a Jewish plot for the disruption of society" and that Jews generally were communists and their liberal idea was simply the disguise behind which communism was hiding. He also noted that previous education minister (by then the justice minister) Fancisco Campos was dangerously powerful and a strong supporter of the European dictators.

Francisco Campos wasn't the president though. Vargas was, and he was a Brazilian nationalist through and through. Vargas was not in the business of handing over power to the Italians of São Paulo or the Germans of Santa Catharina. Vargas saw European totalitarianism on the one side and British shareholding and ever expanding U.S. imperialism on the other. Between these powerful forces was poised Brazilian nationalism, with its own paradoxical relationship to African-Brazilian culture.

In 1937 and 1938, some Nazi sympathizers had an influence within the Estado Novo government (such as the joint chief of staff, Pedro Góes Monteiro, and the federal district chief of police, Filinto Müler), but there were others, like Vargas himself, and second successor to Campos at the ministry of education, Gustavo Capanema, who were far more interested in cultural management within a Brazilian nationalist context.

Francisco Campos had been minister of education from 1930 to 1932. A politician named Washington Ferreira Pires held the post from 1932 to 1934, when Gustavo Capanema took over, holding the post until 1945. In 1935, Capanema had expressed his core belief in a memorandum: "The Ministry of Education, and the government as a whole, can be summed up in one word: culture. Or perhaps better stated, national culture."[49]

Ruth Landes set out to study Candomblé temples in 1938 and met many new friends in Bahia. Among them was Doctor Eustacio da Lima, an ogan of the Candomblé terreiro at Gantois. Dr. Eustacio was even ogan to Mãe Menininha's own goddess, Oxum. When Vargas seized power, many of the Estado Novo's political opponents had to go into immediate hiding for their own protection. A number of these people were influential ogans to various Candomblé temples, and the temples proved very effective for hiding those in danger of arrest.

One of those who was interrogated and jailed more than once for his opposition to Vargas was the journalist and ethnologist Edison Carneiro. To be jailed in the first years of the Estado Novo was not an unusual occurrence. "Red hunting" had become something of a national pastime for various branches of the judiciary and police, and universities were being purged. Carneiro, who became a firm friend of the American anthropologist, told her in 1938 that he had helped to organize a capoeira club in Bahia that would perform exhibitions each Sunday.

Brazil's new guardians of culture had not failed to notice capoeira, samba, frevo, and Candomblé on their travels. Gustavo Capanema wanted to "improve" Brazilian culture. He tried to convince Vargas that the word "culture" should be incorporated into the official name of his ministry: which at the time was Ministério da Educação e Saúde (ministry of education and health). Vargas resisted, although he collected many previously diverse areas of Brazilian cultural life into the Ministério da Educação e Saúde. Capanema became what Daryle Williams termed the de facto culture minister in Brazil, controlling radio, film, and historical and artistic patrimony, including art schools, museums, libraries, publishing, theatre, music, singing, and national symbols.

It was the Ministério da Educação e Saúde that sponsored Penna Marinho to publish the *Subsídios para o Estudo da Metodologia do Treinemento da Capoeiragem,* modeled on the ideas of Aleixo and Burlamáqui. In this Marinho said:

> [The] irremediable mistake, and one for which we can't find excuses, was to have persecuted and finally abandoned to itself the destiny of our capoeiragem, this style of fighting which is so typically Brazilian, which could easily be enlisted among the most prestigious world wide systems of attack and defence, considering the important moral qualities that its apprenticeship and practice can develop.[50]

Penna Marinho's words seemed to echo the constant refrain of a generation of cultural managers during the first Vargas regime. A 1938 editorial in the Estado Novo public service periodical *Revista do Serviço Público* said:

> Those nations that do not demonstrate active consciousness of their unique characteristics will find it difficult to survive in this tempestuous era in which we live. No aspect of national life can be left at the margins of state action, as the State is the sole entity capable of imprinting upon each citizen a truly nationalist mark. . . . Cultural development merits the highest level of attention from those in power, as it is the linchpin to real and lasting national progress.[51]

The purveyors of cultural criticism were unified in believing that greater central organization of diverse folkloric arts would solve social ills. At the Departamento da Imprensa e Propaganda (department of press and propoganda), Álvaro Salgado argued: "Although we find it intolerable that there exist street children prone to all types of mischief, we do not eliminate them from society; we ask for schools for them. What the samba, marchinha, maxixe, embolada, and frevo need are schools."[52]

Times were changing and allegiances were switching with the tides of history. It was a period of suspicion and watchfulness, when friends could turn out to be enemies or spies, and sometimes people didn't know who to trust. Our anthropologist noticed real fear on the streets of Bahia, as she was followed relentlessly by secret police and was eventually ordered out of the country.

As nationalism and cultural management became defining political philosophies during the Vargas era, many people were used and manipulated or drawn involuntarily into the fray. It was only a decade since police chief Pedro de Azevedo Gordilho had set his cavalry squadrons against capoeira players, and his men had dragged them through the streets, harnessed to galloping horses. There were many capoeiristas in Bahia who remembered those days and had lived through them.

One very tough and charismatic capoeirista, who was by now in his late thirties, had been teaching a small group of students, mostly privately, throughout the 1920s. During 1936 he'd been issuing challenges to fight anybody who wanted to take him on. He was often featured in Salvador newspapers for his many swift and brutally decisive victories against a wide variety of good-quality opponents from other fight styles. Naturally, he had come to the attention of the government, and had even been (in 1936) the subject of a piece in *A Tarde* newspaper, which took the virtually unprecedented line of representing the capoeira player as the good guy and the police as the bullies in an altercation in Vila America in the Engenho Velho area of Salvador where he lived. The police had tried to stab the capoeira player with a bayonet, but failed, and the piece was titled "It's not easy to catch a capoeirista."

He was well versed in all aspects of the traditional capoeira of Salvador. He was also a fearless fighter. One of his most loyal students had begun with him at the age of 11 in 1929. This child's name was Altenísio dos Santos (later known as Mestre Atenilo); he recalled that when he was around twelve or thirteen, his mestre had called a meeting at his house in Bogum in Engenho Velho. He invited other capoeiristas, who played the traditional style that some called Angola, and who were active in the early 1930s, to discuss matters concerning the future of capoeira in the city. Mestre Vademar [da Paixão] was there, along with Mestre Aberrê, Mestre Pastinha, and Mestre Bimba, who had called the meeting. This is the same capoeira master who would soon come to the admiring attention of the Ministério da Educação e Saúde in Salvador.

Probably nobody could have guessed that the activity they had come to discuss that afternoon would be a source of speculation, inspiration, and great passion to people beyond Salvador and beyond Brazil, throughout the world, even into the 21st century. It is rare that those at the epicenter of making history ever live long enough to know it, especially when they don't have the benefit of funding for history-making ventures.

Capoeira had traveled a long way on one of history's hardest roads. It had been kept alive by generations of people sold into slavery and transported to Brazil for 400 years and by their descendents. After a schism born in Salvador in the 1930s, divergent paths were taken and loyalties were maintained. Capoeira went through an amazing evolution, transported to all corners of Brazil and exploding onto the international scene as a live, virtually spontaneously reproducing phenomenon that has regularly benefited and changed the lives of practitioners worldwide.

This will be the subject of the second volume of *Capoeira: The Jogo de Angola from Luanda to Cyberspace.*

Appendix A

MICRO-TIMELINE OF THE NGOLO "ZEBRA DANCE" THEORY

1965: Álbano Neves e Sousa, an artist from Angola, visits Brazil. He visits the Candomblé terreiro of Dona Alice Maria da Cruz (Mestre Bimba's wife). He also visits the Centro Esportiva de Capoeira Angola, run by Mestre Pastinha.

After the trip, Neves e Sousa carries out mutual correspondence with Luís da Câmara Cascudo, a Brazilian writer and academic scholar of folklore. Having been impressed by the similarity of the movements of Capoeira Angola that he had seen in Brazil, and a dance called the ngolo, practiced by the Mucope in Angola, Neves e Souza supplies Luís da Câmara Cascudo with considerable information about the rituals of the ngolo dance.

1967: Luís da Câmara Cascudo quotes Neves e Sousa's information about the ngolo in his book *Folclore do Brasil*. It is after this date that the ngolo is said by Mestre Pastinha and others in the Bahian capoeira community to be the original progenitor of the Capoeira Angola.

In *Capoeira: The History of an Afro-Brazilian Martial Art,* Matthias Röhrig Assunção has presented an occasionally scathing critique of later advocates of the ngolo theory of Capoeira Angola's origins, especially of the scholar T. J. Desch Obi. Having made his point, and apparently attempting to rub Desch Obi's nose in it for not finding it himself, Assunção has uncovered a gem provided by Rosa Cruz e Silva from the National Archives in Luanda. He accurately acknowledges this as a "precious reference" from a 1908 account of the Benguela district, written by Augusto Bastos: "The Quilengues have an exercise, which they call ómudinhu. It consists in prodigious jumps in which they throw the legs into the air and the head downwards. It is accompanied by strong hand clapping." (Augusto Bastos. "Traços gerais sobre e etnografia do distrito de Benguela," *Boletim da Sociedade Geográfica de Lisboa*, 26a Série, 198, 1908. Cited in: Assunção, *Capoeira: The History of an Afro-Brazilian Martial Art.*)

Further discussion of the contemporary academic roda de capoeira and some of its themes will be found in the second volume of this book.

Appendix B
FACTS ABOUT THE MALTAS: NAGÔAS AND GUAYAMUS IN THE 1870S

Nagôas

Mainly situated in Glória, Lapa, and the Santa Luzia beach area of Rio, the Nagôas were affiliated with the Conservative party, the party favored by Pedro II. The Nagôas trained male children in head-butts, kicks, and razor and knife fighting at Russell beach and Pinto hill. The capangas of the Nagôas malta had been effective in winning the Conservatives the 1869 election, and in 1872, powerful political patrons from the Conservative party openly associated with capoeira capangas from Glória parish who had just as openly and recently attacked Liberal voters with razor blades and knives.

The very close association between Rio politicians in the Chamber of Deputies and tough gang members from capoeira maltas was an extraordinary feature of the late Empire of Brazil, and one which the first republican government set out to destroy.

The centrality of capoeiristas to the political process in D. João II's day was notable considering that, as far back as the 1820s, the Prince Regent Dom Pedro had ordered that slave capoeiristas would not only receive 100 lashes but that "any soldier who caught a capoeira would receive four days of leave." (Cited in Shultz, *Tropical Versailles,* 145, from J.F. de Almeida Prado. *D. João e o início da classe dirigente do Brasil (depoimento de um pintor austríaco no Rio de Janeiro).* São Paulo: Companhia Editora Nacional, 1968.)

Guayamus

This malta was mainly situated in the Santa Rita and Sacramento parishes of Rio de Janeiro. The Guayamus were affiliated with the Liberal party. The Campo de Santana, scene of so many violent battles during the late Empire, was an area held securely by neither malta, and over which much blood was spilt.

Appendix C
EIGHTEENTH-CENTURY WRITTEN REFERENCES TO CAPOEIRA

In *Capoeira: A Brazilian Art Form*, Bira Almeida says that the written history of capoeira begins in the 18th century. He then cites Melo de Morais Filho (who was a late- 19th- century author) and Joaquim Manuel de Macedo, who wrote about a Portuguese lieutenant named João Moreira, a capoeirista and bodyguard to the viceroy, the Marquis de Lavradio. Almeida says this was around 1700. In the book *Ring of Liberation*, J Lowell Lewis picks up on this error in his notes, and states that the earliest reference to capoeira as a sport or fight dates from approximately 1770, and also attributes this to Joaquim Manuel de Macedo. In fact, Joaquim Manuel de Macedo was born in 1820 and wrote of the capoeira bodyguard to the viceroy, nicknamed Amotinado ("the unruly" or "the mutineer") in his 1878 book, *"Memorias da Rua do Ouvidor"*. (The book refers to Amotinado the historical character, who ha'd been bodyguard to the viceroy a hundred years earlier, in the 1770s.).

There is, however, a late- 18th- century reference to capoeira by name, which. It is an arrest report of a "mulatto" slave, taken for being a "capoeira", dating from 1789. This reference was uncovered by Nireu Cavalcanti and cited by A. Gonçalves in "Capoeiragem: rebeldia e habilidade negra no Rio" in *Jornal da Tarde*, as well as. Also by M. Röhrig Assunção in *Capoeira: The History of an Afro-Brazilian Martial Art.* In this way, Bira Almeida's initial assertion that the written history of capoeira begins in the 18th century is correct.

Appendix D
PRIMARY SOURCE CITATIONS

Abbreviations Key:

ABNRJ: Anais da Biblioteca Nacional do Rio de Janeiro

AG/PMERJ: Arquivo Geral da Polícia Militar do estado do Rio de Janeiro.

AGCRJ: Arquivo Geral da Cidade do Rio de Janeiro

AGP: Arquivo Grão Pará, Petrópolis.

AHMI: Arquivo Histórico do Museu Imperial, Petrópolis

ANRJ: Arquivo Nacional, Rio de Janeiro

BNRJ: Ms., Biblioteca Nacional, Rio de Janeiro, Seção de Manuscritos

POB: Coleção Pedro d´Orléans e Bragança

RIHGB: Revista do Instituto Histórico e Geográfico Brasileiro, Rio de Janeiro

Barman, Roderick. J. *Citizen Emperor Pedro II and the Making of Brazil, 1825–91.*

Page 31: Public Records Office, Foreign Office Archives, 13: 81. Arthur Ashton, chargé d'affaires, to Lord Palmerston, foreign secretary, no.28, Rio, April 9, 1831.

Page 32: BNRJ TM Arm.32 Env. 145-I Leopold von Daiser-Silbach, chargé d'affaires, to Prince von Metternich, no. 4b, Rio, April 7, 1831.

Page 214: João Batista Calógeras to Michael Calógeras, Rio de Janeiro, March 21, 1867, in A.G. de Carvalho, *Ministério*, 234.

Page 341: AGP XL-2 D. Isabel to Pedro II and D. Teresa Cristina, Sáo Cristóvão, Mar.14, 1887 (transcribed in Magalhães Jr., Deodoro, 2: 385-86).

Page 359: Letter from Count d'Eu to the Countess of Barral, Palácio Isabel, Rio, November 14, 1889 in AHMI POB Maço 207 Doc. 9,435 and transcribed in "A deposição," 227–40. The present quote from "A deposição," 227–28.

Page 363: "A deposição," 236.

Conrad, Robert Edgar. *Children of God's Fire: A Documentary History of Black Slavery in Brazil.*

Page 123: Thomas Ewbank, *Life in Brazil, or a Journal of a Visit to the Land of the Cocoa and the Palm* (New York: Harper & Bros., 1856), 92–95, 113–119, 277, 280–81, 436–437.

Page 125: *Second report from the Select Committee on the Slave Trade Together with the Minutes of Evidence and Appendix* (London, 1848), 119.

Page 129: Alexander Marjoribanks, *Travels in South and North America* (London: Simpkin, Marshall and Company, 1853), 94–95.

Page 135: J.B.A. Imbert, *Guia medica das mães de familia, ou a infancia considerada na sua hygiene, suas molestias e tratamentos* (Rio de Janeiro: Typ. Franceza, 1843), 51-53.

Page 249: *Colleção chronologica de leis extravagantes posteriores á nova compilação das ordenações do reino publicadas em 1603* (Coimbra, 1819), IV, 476–477.

APPENDIX D

Page 247: *Leis extravagantes colligidas e relatadas pelo Licenciado Duarte Nunez do Leão, per mandado do Muito Alto e Muito Poderoso rei Dom Sebastião Nosso Senhor* (Coimbra, 1796), 418–423; *Colleção chronologica de leis extravagantes posteriores á nova complcação das ordenações do reino publicadas em 1603* (Coimbra, 1819), I, 319.

Page 250: *Revista do Archivo Público Mineiro 7* (1902), 276–277.

Page 260: *Leis da provincia de Santa Catarina de 1841 a 1847*, 217–218, 224, 230, 241.

Page 261: *Livro da lei mineira. 1846. Parte 1a, Folha No. 5*, 41–43, 48–52.

Pages 262 & 263: *Colleção das leis da Assemblea Legislativa da Provincia de Minas Geraes de 1853*, 33, 38–39, 41, 46, 50.

Page 264: *Colleção de Posturas das Camaras Municipaes da provincia de Pernambuco, descretadas pela Assembléa Legislativa Provincial de Pernambuco dos annos de 1836 a 1845* (Recife, 1845), 5–7, 17–28, 32, 38, 41, 45, 54, 89–91.

Page 304: James Henderson, *A History of Brazil, Comprising Its Geography, Commerce, Colonization, Aboriginal Inhabitants* (London: Longman, Hurst, Rees, Orme, and Brown, 1821, 72–73.

Page 339: Agostinho Marques Perdigão Malheiro, *Escravidão no Brasil: Ensaio histórico-juridico-social,* 2nd ed. (São Paulo: Edições Cultura, 1944), II, 70–72.

Pages 369, 371, 373: Pedro Paulino da Fonseca, "Memoria dos feitos que se deram durante os primeiros annos da guerra com os negros quilombolas dos Palmares, seu destroço e paz aceita em Junho de 1678," *Revista do Instituto Histórico e Geográfico Brasileiro 39* (1876), Part 1, 293–321. Conrad says the original manuscript (Codex CXVI-2–13) was found in the Biblioteca Pública in Evora, Portugal.

Page 384–5: "relatorio apresentado ao Illm. e Exm. Sr. Conselheiro Fransisco Xavier Pinto Lima, Presidente da Provincia do Rio de Janeiro, pelo Chefe de Policia, Dr. Luiz de Hollanda Cavalcanti de Albuquerque," in *Relatorio do Rio de Janeiro apresentado no dia 22 de Outubro de 1876* (Rio de Janeiro, 1876).

Pages 391: *British and Foreign State Papers, Vol. XLIV (1835–1854), pp. 1241–1243; Class B. Correspondence with British Ministers and Agents in*

Foreign Countries and with Foreign Ministers in England, relating to the Slave Trade. From April 1, 1855, to March 31, 1856 (London, 1856), 234–235; ibid. *From April 1, 1855, to March 31, 1857* (London, 1857), 230.

Page 400: Stuart B. Schwartz, "Resistance and Accommodation in Eighteenth-Century Brazil: The Slaves' View of Slavery, " *Hispanic American Historical Review* 57 (1977), 69–81.

Pages 401, 402 & 404–5: Carlos B. Ott, *Formação e evalução étnica da cidade do Salvador,* (Bahia: Tipografia Manú, 1955, 1957), II, 103–108.

Page 406: Conrad cites the source as José Carlos Ferreira, "As insurreições africanas da Bahia," *Revista do Instituto Geográfico e Histórico da Bahia* 10 (1903), 107–115.

Fryer, Peter. *Rhythms of Resistance: African Musical Heritage in Brazil.*

Page 37: Reverend Robert Walsh, *Notices of Brazil in 1828 and 1829* (Frederick Westley & A.H Davis, 1830), II, 175–6.

Page 37: James Wetherall, *Brazil: Stray notes from Bahia, being extracts from letters, etc, during a residence of 15 years.* William Hadfield, ed. (Liverpool, Webb & Hunt, 1860) 106–7.

Page 40: Mrs. [Nathaniel Edward] Kindersley, *Letters from the island of Teneriffe, Brazil, the Cape of Good Hope, and the East Indies* (J. Nourse, 1777), 47.

Page 45: C.S. Stewart, *Brazil and La Plata: the personal record of a cruise* (New York: G.P.Putnam, 1856), 72, 271–2.

Page 45: R.Elwes, *A sketcher's tour round the world* (1854), 25.

Page 46: Reverend Daniel P. Kidder, *Sketches of residence and travel in Brazil* (Wiley & Putnam, 1845), I, 68–9.

Page 47: Thomas Ewbank, *Life in Brazil; or, A Journal of a Visit to the Land of Cocoa and the Palm* (New York, Harper & Brothers, 1856), 92–3.

Page 47: Herbert H. Smith, *Brazil: The Amazons and the Coast* (New York: Charles Scribner's Sons, 1879), 470.

Page 49: John Esaias Warren, *Para, or Scenes and Adventures on the Banks of the Amazon* (New York, G.P Putnam, 1851), 10–11.

Page 97: J.J. Monteiro, *Angola and the River Congo* (1875), II, 136–8.

Hemming, John. *Red Gold: The Conquest of the Brazilian Indians.*

Page 26: Fernão Cardim, *Do principio e origem dos Indios do Brasil e dos seus costumes, adoração e ceremonias,* RHGB 57 (1894) pt. 1, 196.

Page 92: André Thevet, "Histoire d'André Thevet Angoumoisin, Cosmographe du Roy, de deux voyages par lui faits aux Indes Australes, et Occidentales" (c.1585), in *Français en Amérique.* Suzanne Lussagnet, ed., 293–5.

Page 94: Pero de Magalhães Gandavo: *História da Provincia de Santa Cruz* (Lisbon, 1576) and *Tratado da terra do Brasil* (1576). Rodolfo Garcia and João Capistrano de Abreu, eds. (Rio de Janeiro, 1924). John B. Stetson, trans. (New York: The Cortés Society, 1922).

Page 94: Anthony Knivet, *The Admirable Adventures and Strange Fortunes of Master Anthony Knivet,*in Samuel Purchas, *Hakluytus Posthumus or Purchas His Pilgrimes,* 16–223.

Page 94: John Manuel Monteiro: *'Os Guarani e a história dos índios no Brasil* (São Paulo, 1992), 475–98.

Page 155: Vicente do Salvador, *História do Brasil* (1627), João Capistrano de Abreu, ed. ABNRJ (1885–6) 13:1–261. (Also São Paulo/Rio de Janeiro, 1931), 92.

Page 158: Letter from King Philip III to Governor Gaspar de Sousa, 19 January 1613, in an unpublished collection of "Cartas de El-Rei a Gaspar de Sousa," in Itamarati Library, Brasília.

Page 271: Diego de Boroa, Anua, 13 August 1637, Blanco, "Documentos para la Historia Argentina," Iglesia 20: 549.

Page 362: Letter from Domingos Jorge Velho to the Portuguese King, from Serra da Barriga, Palmares on July 15, 1694. In Ernesto Ennes, *As guerras nos Palmares,* Brasiliana 127 (São Paulo, 1938), 204–7, trans. in Richard M. Morse, *The Bandeirantes: the historical role of the Brazilian pathfinders,* 118.

Page 362: Letter by the Bishop or Pernambuco to Junta das Missões, 18 May 1697, quoted in Junta's Opinion of October 1697. Edison

Carneiro, *Guerras de los Palmares* (Mexico, 1946) 133–4. In Ennes, *As guerras nos Palmares,* 353, and Morse, *Bandeirantes,* 125.

Page 397: João Fernando de Almeida Prado, *História da formação da sociedade brasileira: Primeiros povadores do Brasil (1500–1530),* Brasiliana 37 (São Paulo, 1935), 20.

Page 398: Manuel Felix de Azara, *Viajes por la America Meridional* (Madrid, 1923), 66–7. Azara was the commander over the Spanish frontier in Paraguay from 1781 to 1801.

Page 411: Agostinho Lourenço, *Relação de uma viagem que fêz em 1752 de ordem do Capitão-general Dom António Rolim de Moura.* In Levenger, *Apontamentos cronológicas,* RIHGB 205 232, October–December 1949.

Heywood, Linda M., ed. *Central Africans and Cultural Transformations in the American Diaspora*

Page 172: Elizabeth W. Kiddy, "Who Is The King Of Congo?" In Henry Koster, *Travels in Brazil* (London: Longman, Hurst, Rees, Orme, and Brown, 1816), 411.

Page 359: T.J. Desch Obi, "Combat and the Crossing of the Kalunga." In *Lorenzo da Lucca, relations sur le Congo du père.* Laurent de Lucques (1700–1717). J. Cuvelier, ed. and trans. (Bruxelles: Institute Royal Colonial Belge, 1953), 47.

Page 367: Mechal Sobel, *Tabelin' On: The Slave Journey to the Afro-Baptist Faith* (Westport, CT: Greenwood Press, 1979), 142. Cited by Desch Obi regarding "cross-stepping" in the ring shout circle.

Hochschild, Adam. *King Leopold's Ghost.*

Page 8: Peter Forbath, *The River Congo: The Discovery, Exploration and Exploitation of the World's Most Dramatic River.* (New York: Harper and Row, 1977), 73.

Page 13: Affonso to João III, 6 July 1526. Affonso I. Correspondance de Dom Afonso, roi du Congo 1506–1543. Louis Jadin and Mireille Decorato, eds. (Brussels: Académie Royale des Sciences d'Outre-Mer, 1974), 156.

Page 14: Ibid., 175.

Holloway, Thomas. "A "Healthy Terror': Police Repression of Capoeira in Nineteenth-Century Rio de Janeiro."

Page 667: AG/PMERJ. Ordens do Dia No.11, Dec. 16, 1869.

Page 670: Émile Allain, *Rio de Janeiro, quelques données sur la capital et sur l'administration du Brésil* (Paris, 1886), 271–272.

Page 671: AG/PMERJ. Ordens do Dia, No. 188, August 5, 1887.

Page 670: Charles Dent Hastings, *A Year in Brazil* (London, 1886), 239.

Page 648: Moraes Filho, *Festas e tradições,* 459.

Page 651: AG/PMERJ. Correspondência recebida November 16, 1832.

Page 651: Eusébio de Queiroz, in a letter requesting instructions from the minister of justice, June 1833.

Page 652: Arquivo Geral da Cidade do Rio de Janeiro. 40: 3–78, June 18, 1836.

Page 652: AG/PMERJ. Correspondência recebida August 10, 1836.

Levine, Robert M and John J. Crocitti, eds. *The Brazil Reader: History, Culture, Politics.*

Page 22: John Hemming, *Red Gold: The Conquest of the Brazilian Indians.* (Cambridge, MA: Harvard University Press, 1978).

Pages 79, 82, 84 & 86: Stanley J. Stein, "Middle Paraíba Plantations, 1850–1860: Aspects of Growth and Decline." In *Four Papers Presented to the Institute for Brazilian Studies, Vanderbilt University.* (Nashville, TN: Vanderbilt University Press, 1951).

Pages 140, 141 &142: Thomas Ewbank, *Life in Brazil, or a Journal of a Visit to the Land of the Cocoa and the Palm* (New York: Harper & Bros., 1856).

Page 126: "Relação das Guerras Feitas aos Palmares de Pernambuco no Tempo do Governador D. redro de Almeida de 1675 a 1678," *Revista Trimensal do Instituto Historico, Geographico e Ethnographico do Brasil,* Tomo XXII, n. 2 (1859).

Page 129: Condições Ajustadas com o Governador dos Paulistas Domingos Jorge Velho em 14 de Agosto de 1693 para conquistar e destruir os negros de Palmares," *Revista Trimensal do Instituto Historico, Geographico e Ethnographico do Brasil,* Tomo XLVII, Parte I (1844).

Page 135: *African Repository and Colonial Journal* (September 1841).

Page 136: *Remarks on the Slavery and Slave Trade of the Brazils* by Thomas Nelson (London, 1846).

Page 137: *O Captiveiro* by João Dunshee de Abrantes (Rio de Janeiro, 1941). Cited in Robert E. Conrad, *World of Sorrow: the African Slave Trade to Brazil.* (Baton Rouge, LA: Louisiana State University Press, 1986).

Price, Richard, ed. *Maroon Societies: Rebel Slave Communities in the Americas.*

Page 7: Ernesto Ennes "The Palmares Republic of Pernambuco: Its Final Destruction, 1697." *The Americas* 5 (1948) 209.

Page 8: Captain J.G. Stedman, *Narrative of a Five-years' Expedition Against the Revolted Negroes of Surinam from the year 1772 to 1777.* (London: J. Johnson and J. Edwards, 1796), II: 89.

Page 174: René Ribeiro, "Relations of the Negro with Christianity in Portuguese America," *The Americas* (1958) 14: 458.

Page 180: Sebastião da Rocha Pitta, *História da América Portuguêza*, 1st ed. (1730). (Lisboa, Portugal: F.A. da Silva, 1880), VIII, 236.

Page 180: Johan Nieuhof, "Voyage and Travels into Brazil and the East Indies." In *Collection of Voyages and Travels,* A. and J. Churchill, eds. (London: 1704), II: 8.

Page 182: Mario Martins de Freitas, *Reino negro de Palmares.* (Rio de Janeiro: Biblioteca do Exército Editôra, 1954), I. 291.

Page 184: Edison Carneiro, *O quilombo dos Palmares, 1630–1695,* 2nd ed. (São Paulo: Editora Brasiliense Limitada, 1958).

Page 192: Barros Latif, M.M. de As Minas Gerais, 169. (As referenced in Roger Bastide, *Les Religions Africaines au Brésil* (Paris: Universitaires de France, 1961).

Page 219: R.K. Kent, "Palmares: An African State in Brazil." *Journal of African History* 6 (1965), 170.

Page 214: "Información q. hize por mandado de VMg. sobre unos capitulos q. Duarte Gomez de Silveira Vezino de Parahiba embió a la mesa da Consciencia." *Archivo General de Simancas, Secretarias Provinciales, Libro 1583*, fols. 382–89.

Page 217: "Documentos historicos do Arquivo Municipal," November 25, 1640. Atas da camara [of Bahia] (Salvador: 1949), 1:477–78.

Schultz, Kirsten. *Tropical Versailles: Empire, Monarchy, and the Portuguese Royal Court in Rio de Janeiro, 1808–1821.*

Page 46: António Luiz de Brito Aragão Vasconcellos, "Officio," 34. In "Memórias sobre o Estabelecimento do Império do Brazil, ou novo Imperio Lusitano." ANN 43–44 (1920–21): 1–48.

Page 123: Paulo Fernandes Viana [representação], November 24, 1816, ANRJ MNB Caixa 6J 83.

Page 123: António Felipe Soares de Andrada de Brederode, Corregedor da Corte e casa, February 27, 1817, ANRJ ASH Casa de Suplicação Caixa 1707 Antiga Caixa 774 Pacotilha 3.

Page 125: Paulo Fernandes Viana to Sua Alteza Real, August 10, 1818, ANRJ MNB Caixa 6J 91.

Page 129: "[Cópia do Ordem do Dia]," April 10, 1814, BNRJ Ms.II 34, 6, 57.

Page 130: Paulo Fernandes Viana, "Registro do Oficio expedido ao Juiz do crime do Bairro de Santa Rita," April 11, 1816, ANRJ Códice 329 v.3.

Page 130: "Registro do Oficio expedido ao Ministro de Estado dos Negócios de Guerra," July 8, 1808, ANRJ Códice 318, f38.

Schwartz, Stuart B. *Sugar Plantations in the Formation of Brazilian Society: Bahia, 1550–1835.*

Page 144: Padre Antônio Vieira, *Sermon to the Slaves of Engenho Sergipe* (1633), cited by Barros de Castro, *Escravos e senhores*, iii.

Page 139: Reverend Robert Walsh, *Notices of Brazil in 1828 and 1829* (Frederick Westley & A.H Davis, 1830), II, 18–19.

Thomas, Hugh. *The Slave Trade: The History of the Atlantic Slave Trade, 1440–1870.*

Page 54: Zurara (Azurara), *Chronicle of the Discovery of Guinea*, 121. C.R. Beazley and Edgar Prestage, trans. and eds., Hakluyt Society, 1st ser., vols. 95 and 100 (London, 1896 and 1899), 95: 81–3.

Page 55: Ibid., 59.

Page 134: R&P, Commons Select Committee report, 1790, vol.1, 211.

Page 381: C.B. Wadström, *Observations of the Slave Trade* (London, 1788), 16.

Page 408: Olaudah Equiano, *Equiano's Travels*. Paul Edwards, ed. (New York, 1967), I, 76.

Page 412: Equiano, I, 78.

Page 433: Qu. Robert Edgar Conrad, *World of Sorrows* (Baton Rouge, 1986), 49.

Page 609: Robert Walsh, *Notices of Brazil in 1828 and 1829,* 1st edition (London: Frederick Westley & A.H. Davis, 1830), I: 465.

Thornton, John K. *The Art of War in Angola.*

Page 364–365: Cavazzi, *Istorica Descrizione*, book 6, para. 31.

Also Cadornega, António de Oliveira de, 1624–1690. *História Geral das Guerras Angolanas,* 1680/ Por António de Oliveira de Cadornega. Tomos 1–3. (Lisboa : Agência-Geral do Ultramar, 1972).

Page 366: Filippo Pigafetta, *Relazione del Reame di Congo* (1591), modern edition. Giorgio Cardona, ed. (Milan, 1978), 20–21.

NOTES

Chapter One: In the Beginning

1 Segal, *Islam's Black Slaves*, p. 92.

2 Rodney, *How Europe Underdeveloped Africa*, p. 69.

3 Okpewho, Davies, and Mazrui, *The African Diaspora: African Origins and New World Identities*, p. 347.

4 Segal, op. cit., p. 94.

5 Thomas, *The Slave Trade*, p. 53.

6 Ibid., p. 51.

7 Ibid., p. 54.

8 Ibid., p. 55.

9 Ibid., p. 53.

10 Hochschild, *King Leopold's Ghost: A Story of Greed, Terror and Heroism in Colonial Africa*, p. 8.

11 Ibid.

12 Thomas, op. cit., p. 70.

13 Conrad, *Children of God's Fire. A Documentary History of Black Slavery in Brazil*, p. 247.

14 Price, ed., *Maroon Societies*, p. 174 (Kent, "Palmares: An African State in Brazil").

15 Rodney, op. cit., p. 92.

16 Ibid., p. 93.

17 Hochschild, op. cit., p. 13.

18 Ibid., p.14.

19 Levine and Crocitti, eds., *The Brazil Reader: History, Culture, Politics,* p. 39 (da Nóbrega, "Letter to Governor Tomé da Sousa").

20 Levine and Crocitti, eds., *The Brazil Reader: History, Culture, Politics,* p. 22 (Hemming, "Noble Savages").

21 Steinberg, *The Cooking of Japan,* p. 21.

22 Davidson, *In the Eye of the Storm,* p. 99.

23 Ibid.

24 Birmingham and Martin, eds., *History of Central Africa,* vol. I, p. 143 (Miller, "The Paradoxes of Impoverishment in the Atlantic Zone").

25 Thomas, op. cit., p. 110.

Chapter Two: Sugar Blues

1 Burke, "The Bee, The Reed, The Root: The History of Sugar."

2 Ibid.

3 Schwartz, *Sugar Plantations in the Formation of Brazilian Society,* p. 144.

4 Levine and Crocitti, eds., *The Brazil Reader,* p. 142 (Ewbank, "Cruelty to Slaves").

5 Thornton, *The Kongolese St. Anthony,* p. 91.

6 Thomas, *The Slave Trade,* p. 134.

7 Lewis, *Ring of Liberation.* p. 22.

8 Price, ed., *Maroon Societies,* p. 192 (Bastide, "The Other Quilombos").

9 Giblin, "Issues in African History."

10 Kapuscinski, *Another Day of Life,* p. 132.

11 Davidson, *In the Eye of the Storm,* p. 121.

12 Miller, *Way of Death,* p. 386.

13 Mannix, *The History of Torture,* p. 43.

14 Ibid., p. 51.

15 Ibid., p. 47.

16 Malcom X, *On Afro-American History,* p. 75.

17 Schwartz, op. cit., p. 139.

18 Ibid., p. 111.

19 Pope-Hennessy, *The Sins of the Fathers*, p. 81.

Chapter Three: The Rise of the Quilombo dos Palmares

1 Pope-Hennessy, *Sins of the Fathers*, p. 81.

2 Thomas, *The Slave Trade*, p. 170.

3 Levine and Crocitti, eds., *The Brazil Reader*, p. 126 (Anonymous, "The War Against Palmares").

4 Ibid.

5 Ibid.

6 Stedman, *Stedman's Surinam*, p. 204.

7 Ibid.

8 Miller, *Way of Death*, p. 28.

9 Ibid.

10 Thomas, op. cit., p. 373.

11 Ibid., p. 129.

12 Miller, op. cit., p. 157.

13 Anderson, "The Slave King."

14 Ibid.

15 Miller, *Kings and Kinsmen*, p. 135.

16 Ibid., p. 139.

17 Ibid., p. 159.

18 Ibid., p. 163.

19 Ibid, p. 167. Miller gives a detailed description of the etymology of the word *samba* in *Kings and Kinsmen*.

20 Anderson, op. cit.

21 Ibid.

22 Campbell, *In the Heart of Bantuland*, p. 81.

23 Capello and Ivens, *From Benguela to the Territory of Yacca*, Vol. I, p. 26.

24 Levine and Crocitti, eds., op. cit., p. 127.

25 Stedman, op. cit., p 216.

26 Levine and Crocitti, eds., op. cit.

27 Anderson, op. cit.

28 Da Cunha, *Rebellion in the Backlands*, p. 59.

29 Miller, op. cit., p. 178.

30 Stedman, op. cit., pp. 211–212.

31 Da Cunha, op. cit., p. 60.

32 Holloway, "A Healthy Terror," p. 664.

33 Anderson, op. cit.

34 Thornton, *Warfare in Atlantic Africa: 1500–1800*, p. 105.

35 Ibid., p. 22.

36 Levine and Crocitti, eds., op. cit.

37 Heywood, ed., *Central Africans and Cultural Transformations in the American Diaspora*, p. 159 (Kiddy, "Who Is the King of Congo?").

38 Ibid., p. 160.

39 Ibid., p. 175.

40 Ibid.

41 Miller, op. cit., p. 33.

42 Levine and Crocitti, eds., op. cit., p. 126.

43 Ibid., p. 127.

44 Pope-Hennessy, op. cit., p. 127.

45 Thomas, op. cit., p. 171.

46 Ibid., p. 183.

47 Ibid.

48 Miller, op. cit., pp. 208–209.

49 Thomas, op. cit., p. 173.

50 Wheeler and Pelissier, *Angola*, p. 42.

51 Anderson, op. cit.

52 Ibid. (Anderson refers to Decio Freitas, *Palmares, a guerra dos escravos*. Rio de Janeiro: Graal, 1982.)

53 Ibid.

54 Ibid.

55 Thornton, *The Art of War in Angola: 1575–1680*, p. 365.

56 Miller, *Kings and Kinsmen*, p. 233

57 Thornton, *The Art of War In Angola: 1575–1680*, p. 365.

58 Cavazzi, *Istorica Descrizione de tre regni Congo, Matamba ed Angola,* Chapter 4. Translation by John K. Thornton.

59 Ibid., p. 362.

60 Price, ed., *Maroon Societies*, p. 152 (Herbert Aptheker, "Maroons Within the Present Limits of the United States").

61 Rath, "Drums and Power," side 3.

62 Thornton, *The Kongolese St. Anthony*, p. 212.

63 Newsome, *Kalenda*.

64 Ibid., p. 212.

65 Ibid., p. 213.

66 Thornton, *Warfare in Atlantic Africa: 1500–1800*, p. 105.

67 Robinson, "Haiti—A Call for Global Action."

68 Thornton, *The Art of War in Angola: 1575–1680*, p. 369.

69 Stedman, op. cit., p. 217.

70 Price, ed., *Maroon Societies,* p. 177 (Kent, "Palmares: An African State in Brazil").

71 Conrad, *Children of God's Fire*, p. 370.

72 Price, ed., *Maroon Societies,* p. 183 (Kent, "Palmares: An African State in Brazil").

73 Ibid., p. 180.

74 Conrad, op. cit. p. 369.

75 Price, ed., *Maroon Societies,* p. 180 (Kent, "Palmares: An African State in Brazil"). Sebastião da Rocha Pitta published *Historia da America Portuguêza* in 1730; Johan Nieuhof published *Voyage and Travels into Brazil and the East Indies* in 1704.

76 Price, ed., *Maroon Societies*, p. 7 (Introduction).

77 Conrad, op. cit., p. 371.

78 Ibid., p. 373.

79 Price, ed., *Maroon Societies*, p. 184 (Kent, "Palmares: An African State in Brazil").

80 Conrad, op. cit., p. 375.

81 Anderson, op. cit.

82 Levine and Crocitti, eds., op. cit., p. 129.

83 Hemming, *Red Gold: The Conquest of the Brazilian Indians,* p. 362.

84 Price, ed., *Maroon Societies,* p. 177 (Kent, "Palmares: An African State in Brazil").

85 Ibid., p. 186.

86 Ibid.

87 Hemming, op. cit.

88 Ibid., p. 363.

89 Ibid., p. 365.

90 Ibid., p. 367.

91 Ibid., p. 368.

92 Levine and Crocitti, eds., op. cit., p. 130.

93 Almeida, *Capoeira: A Brazilian Art Form,* p. 181.

94 Howell, *Capoeira: Martial Art of Brazil,* p. 12.

95 Price, ed., *Maroon Societies,* p. 187 (Kent, "Palmares: An African State in Brazil").

96 Levine and Crocitti, eds., op. cit., p. 129.

97 Price, ed., *Maroon Societies,* p. 187 (Kent, "Palmares: An African State in Brazil").

Chapter Four: The Gold Rush

1 Library of Congress Country Studies: Brazil. "Gold Mining Displaces Cane Farming."

2 Thomas, *The Slave Trade,* p. 221.

3 Davies, *A History of Money from Ancient Times to the Present Day.*

4 Thomas, op cit., p. 808.

5 Rodney, *How Europe Underdeveloped Africa*, p. 107.

6 Ibid., p. 245.

7 Levine and Crocitti, eds., *The Brazil Reader,* p. 136 (Abrantes, "Scenes from the Slave Trade, Log Book Entries").

8 Dow, *Slave Ships and Slaving,* p. 148.

9 Miller, *Way of Death,* p. 136.

10 Dow, op. cit., p. 244.

11 Miller, op. cit., p. 136.

12 Dow, op. cit., p. 67.

13 Ibid., p. 304.

14 Thomas, op. cit., p. 309.

15 Dow, op. cit., p. 214.

16 Thomas, op. cit., p. 408.

17 Ibid., p. 412.

18 Ibid., p. 424.

19 Ibid.

20 Levine and Crocitti, eds., op. cit., p. 137.

Chapter Five: From Rio to the Gold Mines

1 Hemming, *Red Gold,* p. 155.

2 Thomas, *The Slave Trade,* p. 396.

3 Hemming, op. cit.

4 Dow, *Slave Ships and Slaving.* p. 223.

5 Miller, *The Way of Death*, p. 295.

6 Hemming, op. cit., p. 133.

7 Thomas, op. cit., p. 432.

8 Almeida, *Capoeira: A Brazilian Art Form*, p. 24.

9 Thomas, op. cit., p. 433.

10 Davidson, *In the Eye of the Storm*, p. 105.

11 Dow, op. cit., p. 225.

12 Ibid., pp. 225–226.

13 Ibid., p. 194.

14 Vandevort, *Wars of Imperial Conquest in Africa, 1830–1914*, p. 11.

15 Thornton, *Warfare in Atlantic Africa, 1500–1800*, p. 59.

16 Dow, op. cit., p. 198.

17 Ibid., p. 245.

18 Price, ed., *Maroon Societies*, p. 193 (Bastide, "The Other Quilombos").

19 Thornton, op. cit., p. 61.

20 Ibid., p. 71.

21 Ibid., p. 73.

22 Bethell, ed., *Colonial Brazil. The Gold Cycle.*

23 Salway, *Gold and Gold Hunters*, p. 55.

24 Almeida, op. cit., p. 23.

25 Ibid., p. 24.

26 Walsh, *Notices of Brazil in 1828 and 1829*, pp. 332–333.

27 Conrad, *Children of God's Fire*, p. 250.

28 Ibid., p. 249.

29 Kubik, "Angolan Traits in Black Music: Games and Dances of Brazil," p. 31.

30 Ibid., p. 28.

31 Falola and Oguntomisin, op. cit., p. 79.

32 Hemming, op. cit., p. 271.

33 Price, ed., op. cit., p. 196.

34 Price, ed., *Maroon Societies*, p. 217 (Schwartz, "The Mocambo: Slave Resistance in Colonial Bahia").

35 Hemming, op. cit., p. 411.

36 Schwartz, *Slaves, Peasants and Rebels: Reconsidering Brazilian Slavery*, p. 122.

37 Smith, *History of Brazil*, p. 12.

38 Price, ed., *Maroon Societies*, p. 214 (Schwartz, "The Mocambo: Slave Resistancc in Colonial Bahia").

39 Hemming, op. cit., p. 405.

40 Freyre, *The Masters and the Slaves*, p. 68.

41 Dow, op. cit., pp. 223–225.

42 Freyre, op. cit., p. 69.

43 Bethell, op. cit., p. 138.

44 Price, ed., *Maroon Societies*, p. 214 (Schwartz, "The Mocambo: Slave Resistance in Colonial Bahia").

45 Conrad, op. cit., p. 391.

46 Hemming, op. cit.

47 Ibid., p. 398.

48 Ibid., p. 397.

49 Ibid., p. 94.

50 Ibid., p. 26.

51 Ibid.

52 Ibid., p. 92.

53 Ibid., p. 166.

54 Price, ed., *Maroon Societies*, p. 12 (Introduction).

55 Ibid., p. 8.

56 Hemming, op. cit., p. 157.

57 Ibid., p. 215.

58 Ibid., p. 158.

59 Price, ed., *Maroon Societies*, p. 192 (Bastide, "The Other Quilombos").

60 Freyre, op. cit., p. 26.

61 Dow, op. cit., p. 247.

62 Levine and Crocitti, eds., *The Brazil Reader,* p. 140 (Ewbank, "Cruelty to Slaves").

63 Price, ed., *Maroon Societies*, p. 223 (Schwartz, "The Mocambo: Slave Resistance in Colonial Brazil")

64 Price, ed., *Maroon Societies*, p. 196 (Bastide, "The Other Quilombos").

65 Ibid.

66 Morwyn, *Magic from Brazil.*

67 Price, ed., *Maroon Societies*, p. 182 (Kent, "Palmares: An African State in Brazil").

68 Price, ed., *Maroon Societies*, p. 219 (Schwartz, "The Mocambo: Slave Resistance in Colonial Brazil").

69 Miller, op. cit., p. 272.

70 Conrad, op. cit., p. 130.

71 Bethell, op. cit., p. 141.

72 Conrad, op. cit., p. 135.

73 Reis, *Slave Rebellion in Brazil,* Chapter 9.

74 Landes, *The City of Women,* p. 36.

75 Ibid., p. 37.

76 Ibid., p. 147.

77 Ibid.

78 Ibid.

79 Ibid., p. 193.

80 Ibid., p. 147.

Chapter Six: "Brazilian Bantu Land"

1 Almeida, *Capoeira: A Brazilian Art Form*, p. 16.

2 Chomsky et al., eds., *The Cuba Reader*, p. 62 (Barnet, "Biography of a Runaway Slave").

3 Stedman, *Stedman's Surinam*, p. 276.

4 Ibid., p. 243.

5 Walsh, *Notices of Brazil in 1828 and 1829*, p. 337.

6 Ibid., pp. 338–339.

7 Miller, *The Way of Death*, p. 286.

8 Ibid., p. 285.

9 Thomas, *The Slave Trade*, p. 279.

10 Miller, op. cit., p. 469.

11 Ibid., p. 286.

12 Ibid., p. 88.

13 Ibid., p. 129.

14 Thomas, op. cit., p. 366.

15 Ibid.

16 Fage and Oliver, *A Short History of Africa*, pp. 18–19.

17 BBC World Service, *The Story of Africa: Early History*.

18 Ibid.

19 Fage and Oliver, op. cit., p. 36.

20 Tudor Parfitt, *Journey to the Vanished City*.

21 Information from Mcintosh,
    http://www.archaeology.org/9807/abstracts/africa.html.

22 Monteiro, *Angola and the River Congo*, volume 1, p. 204.

23 Ibid.

24 Fage and Oliver, op. cit., p. 109.

25 Davidson, *In the Eye of the Storm,* p. 105.

Chapter Seven: Islamic Revolution in West Africa

1 Rodney, *A History of the Upper Guinea Coast*, p. 26.

2 Ibid., p. 27.

3 Ibid., p. 81.

4 Ibid., p. 105.

5 Thornton, *Warfare in Atlantic Africa, 1500–1800*, p. 128.

6 Thomas, *The Slave Trade*, p. 381.

7 Rodney, op. cit., p. 107.

8 Miller, *Way of Death*, p. 462.

9 Pope-Hennessy, *Sins of the Fathers,* citing Collins, *Practical Rules for the Management of Negro Slaves in the Sugar Colonies,* London, 1803.

10 Dow, *Slave Ships and Slaving*, p. 121.

11 Ajayi and Crowder, eds., *History of West Africa*, p. 217.

12 Ibid., p. 218.

13 Rodney, *How Europe Underdeveloped Africa*, p. 120.

14 Ajayi and Crowder, eds., op. cit., p. 11.

15 Awolalu, *Yoruba Beliefs and Sacrificial Rites,* p. 183.

16 Ajayi and Crowder, eds., op. cit.

17 Lovejoy, "The African Diaspora: Revisionist Interpretations of Ethnicity, Culture and Religion under Slavery."

18 Reis, *Slave Rebellion in Brazil,* p. 141.

19 Bamaguje, *The "Mistake" of 1914.*

20 Ajayi and Crowder, eds., op. cit., p. 64.

21 Pope-Hennessy, op. cit., p. 27.

22 Thomas, op. cit., p. 357.

23 Reis, op. cit., p. 148.

24 Ajayi and Crowder, eds., op. cit., p. 177.

25 Ibid., p. 5.

26 Ajayi and Crowder, eds., op. cit., p. 190.

27 Ibid., p. 193.

28 Reis, op. cit., p. 148.

29 See Reis, op. cit., p. 140, for a fuller picture of defendants' nationality in the 1835 Salvador uprising.

Chapter Eight: The St. Domingue Revolution

1 Lovejoy, "The African Diaspora: Revisionist Interpretations of Ethnicity, Culture and Religion under Slavery."

2 Price, ed., *Maroon Societies*, p. 182 (Schwartz, "The Mocambo: Slave Resistance in Colonial Bahia").

3 Price, ed., *Maroon Societies*, p. 125 (Debien, "Marronage in the Maroon Societies").

4 Price, ed., *Maroon Societies*, p. 136 (Moreau de Saint-Méry, "The Border Maroons of Saint-Domingue: Le Maniel").

5 Falola and Oguntomisin, *Yoruba Warlords of the 19th Century,* p. 14.

6 James, *The Black Jacobins,* pp. 66–67.

7 Ibid., p. 70.

8 Thomson, "The Haitian Revolution and the Forging of America," paragraph 8, citing Carolyn Fick, *The Making of Haiti: The Saint Domingue Revolution from Below* (Knoxville: University of Tennessee Press, 1990), pp. 15–17, discussing the economic structure of St. Domingue and the caste society of the colony in the pre-Revolution days.

9 Ibid., paragraphs 16–17, citing Althia de Puech Parham, ed., *My Odyssey: Experiences of a Young Refugee from Two Revolutions by a Creole of Saint Domingue* (Baton Rouge: Louisiana State University Press, 1959).

10 Conrad, ed., *Children of God's Fire. A Documentary History of Black Slavery in Brazil*, pp. 404–405.

11 Ibid.

12 Freyre, *The Mansions and the Shanties,* p. 327.

13 Conrad, op. cit., p. 402.

14 Ibid.

15 Reis, *Slave Rebellion in Brazil*, p. 141.

16 Conrad, op. cit., p. 400.

17 Almeida, *Capoeira: A Brazilian Art Form*, p. 76. Almeida cites (with an English translation) Jean-Baptiste Debret. Debret was a painter of historical water colors and a writer for the French Artistic Mission, which stayed in Brazil for fifteen years between 1816 and 1831. Debret's visual and written works were published in Paris under the title *Voyage Pittoresque et Historique au Brésil* in 1834. Almeida translates into English from the Portuguese version: *Viagem Pitorêsca e Histórica ao Brasil*.

18 Reis, op. cit., p. 161.

19 Ibid.

20 Levine and Crocitti, eds., *The Brazil Reader: History, Culture, Politics*, p. 84 (Stein, "A Paraíba Plantation, 1850–1860").

21 Heywood, ed., *Central Africans and Cultural Transformations in the American Diaspora*, p. 172 (Kiddy, "Who is the King of Congo?").

22 Ibid., p. 177.

23 Conrad, op. cit., p. 247.

24 Ibid., p. 248.

25 Ibid., p. 249.

26 Ibid., p. 260.

27 Ibid., p. 261.

28 Ibid., p. 262.

29 Ibid., p. 263.

30 Ibid., p. 264.

31 Ibid.

32 Ibid., p. 265.

33 Ibid., p. 258.

34 Fryer, *Rhythms of Resistance: African Musical Heritage in Brazil*, p. 96.

35 Conrad, op. cit., p. 404.

36 Fryer, op. cit.

37 Salvatore, Aguirre, and Josephs, eds., *Crime and Punishment in Latin America*, p. 183.

38 Reis, op. cit., p. 152.

39 Ibid., p. 160.

40 Ibid., p. 162.

41 Fryer, op. cit., p. 40.

42 Reis, op. cit., p. 178.

43 Conrad, op. cit., p. 129.

44 Reis, op. cit., p. 173.

45 Ibid., p. 160.

46 Conrad, op. cit., pp. 406–411.

Chapter Nine: An Awful Lot of Coffee (and Capoeira) in Brazil

1 Schultz, *Tropical Versailles: Empire, Monarchy and the Portuguese Royal Court in Rio De Janeiro, 1808–1821,* p. 44.

2 Ibid., p. 46.

3 Ibid., p. 57.

4 Levine and Crocitti, eds., *The Brazil Reader: History, Culture, Politics,* p. 57 ("João VI, Decree Elevating Brazil to a Kingdom").

5 Thomas, *The Slave Trade,* p. 376.

6 Schultz, op. cit., p. 107.

7 Ibid.

8 De Oliveira, *Frevo, Passo e Capoeira,* p. 78.

9 Conrad, *Children of God's Fire,* pp. 404–405.

10 Price, ed., *Maroon Societies,* p. 176 (Kent, "Palmares: An African State in Brazil").

11 Schultz, op. cit., p. 122.

12 Ibid., p. 123.

13 Ibid.

14 Ibid.

15 Holloway, "A Healthy Terror: Police Repression of Capoeiras in 19th Century Rio de Janeiro," p. 646. Holloway cites: A.P.D.G., *Sketches of Portuguese Life, Manners, Costume, and Character,* pp. 304–306.

16 Schultz, op. cit., p. 125.

17 Ibid.

18 Holloway, op. cit., p. 674. Holloway is quoting from Goulart, José Alípio, *Da palmatória ao patíbulo: Castigos de escravos no Brasil,* p.195.

19 Heywood, ed., *Central Africans and Cultural Transformations in the Ameri-*

can Diaspora, p. 31 (Miller, "Central Africa During the Era of the Slave Trade, c. 1490s–1850s").

20 Ibid., p. 33.

21 Ibid.

22 Bethell, ed., *Colonial Brazil*, p. 329 (Alden, "Late Colonial Brazil, 1750–1808").

23 Miller, *The Way of Death*, p. 493.

24 Levine and Crocitti, eds., op. cit., p. 85 (Stein, "A Paraíba Plantation, 1850–1860").

25 Ibid., p. 86.

26 Ibid., p. 82.

27 Freyre, *The Masters and the Slaves*, p. 429.

28 Levine and Crocitti, eds., op. cit., p. 79 (Stein, "A Paraíba Plantation, 1850–1860").

29 Conrad, op. cit., p. 125.

30 Ibid., p. 123.

31 Freyre, op. cit., p. 482.

32 Schultz, op. cit., p. 129.

33 Holloway, op. cit., p. 667.

Chapter Ten: Music

1 Mestre Pastinha interview.

2 Ibid.

3 Conrad, *Children of God's Fire*, p. 403.

4 Pastinha, *Capoeira Angola*, p. 36.

5 Fryer, *Rhythms of Resistance: African Musical Heritage in Brazil,* p. 19.

6 See *The Garland Encyclopedia of World Music.* Volume 1 is on Africa.

7 Fryer, op. cit.

8 Kubik, "Angolan Traits in Black Music, Games and Dances of Brasil: A Study of African Cultural Extensions Overseas," p. 18.

9 Ibid., p. 19.

10 Ibid.

11 *The Garland Encyclopedia of World Music: Africa.*

12 Ibid.

13 Ibid.

14 Ibid.

15 Morwyn. *Magic from Brazil*, p. 13.

16 Landes, *The City of Women*, p. 23.

17 Ibid., p. 31.

18 Awolalu, *Yoruba Beliefs and Sacrificial Rites*, p. 20.

19 Mathews and Mathews. *The Western Way. A Practical Guide to the Western Mystery Tradition*, p. 148.

20 Reis, *Slave Rebellion in Brazil,* pp.151–152.

21 Awolalu, op. cit., p. 107.

22 Ibid.

23 *The Garland Encyclopedia of World Music: Afro-Brazilian Traditions*, p. 342.

24 Ibid.

25 Mestre Pastinha, "Brazilian Karate," Black Belt Magazine, March 1964.

26 *The Garland Encyclopedia of Music: Issues and Processes in African Music,* p. 305.

27 Fage and Oliver, *A Short History of Africa*, p. 17.

28 *The Garland Encyclopedia of Music: Issues and Processes in African Music,* p. 306.

29 Heywood, ed., *Central Africans and Cultural Transformations in the American Diaspora,* p. 366 (Desch Obi, "Combat and the Crossing of the Kalunga").

30 Morgan, *Slave Counterpoint: Black Culture in the Eighteenth-Century Chesapeake and Low Country,* p. 587.

31 Kubik, op. cit., p. 31.

32 Ibid., p. 34.

33 Ibid., p. 35.

34 Fryer, op. cit., p. 45.

35 Ibid.

36 Ibid., p. 46.

37 Ibid.

38 Ibid., p. 47.

39 Ibid.

40 Ibid.

41 Ibid., p. 29.

42 Ibid., p. 49.

43 Kubik, op. cit., p. 35.

44 Holloway, "A Healthy Terror: Police Repression of Capoeiras in 19th Century Rio de Janeiro," p. 667.

45 Ibid., p. 670.

46 Ibid.

47 Barman, *Citizen Emperor: Pedro II and the Making of Brazil, 1825–91*, p. 20.

48 Fryer, op. cit., p. 37.

49 Ibid.

50 Ibid.

51 Ibid., p. 28.

52 Heywood, ed., op. cit., p. 359.

53 Ibid.

54 Heywood, ed., op. cit., p. 177 (Kiddy, "Who Is the King of Congo?").

55 Heywood, ed., op. cit., p. 357 (Desch Obi, "Combat and the Crossing of the Kalunga").

56 Ibid., p. 358.

57 Ibid., p. 357.

58 Ibid., p. 356.

59 Ibid., p. 354.

60 Ibid., p. 356.

61 Gray, *Western Inner Workings*, p. 157.

62 Heywood, ed., op. cit., p. 357 (Desch Obi, "Combat and the Crossing of the Kalunga").

63 Ibid., p. 365.

64 Cooper, *The Gospel Box. Writing the Song of Songs: An Evolutionary History of Black Gospel Music*, p. 9.

65 Heywood, ed., op. cit., p. 367 (Desch Obi, "Combat and the Crossing of the Kalunga").

66 Stuckey, *Slave Culture: Nationalistic Theory and the Foundations of Black America*, p. 11.

Chapter Eleven: The Empire of Brazil

1 Schultz, *Tropical Versailles: Empire, Monarchy and the Portuguese Royal Court in Rio De Janeiro, 1808–1821*, p. 130.

2 Ibid.

3 Thomas, *The Slave Trade*, p. 608.

4 Suret-Canale, *Essays on African History*, p. 653.

5 Thomas, op. cit., p. 609.

6 Almeida, *Capoeira: A Brazilian Art Form,* p. 25.

7 Freyre, *The Mansions and the Shanties*, p. 287.

8 Almeida, op. cit., pp. 27–28.

9 Holloway, "A Healthy Terror: Police Repression of Capoeiras in 19th-Century Rio de Janeiro," p. 647.

10 Ibid., p. 648.

11 Freyre, op. cit., p. 287. Freyre quotes from Pereira da Silva's 1871 book, *Segundo Período do Reinado de Dom Pedro I no Brazil*, p. 289.

12 Walsh, *Notices of Brazil in 1828 and 1829*, p. 281.

13 Ibid., p.283.

14 Ibid., pp.285–286.

15 Ibid., p.291.

16 Ibid., p. 292.

17 Ibid., pp. 293–294.

18 Ibid., p.302.

19 Ibid.

20 Ibid.

21 Freyre, op. cit., p. 327.

22 Barman, *Citizen Emperor: Pedro II and the Making of Brazil, 1825–91*, p. 33.

23 Ibid., p. 31.

24 Ibid., p. 32.

25 Holloway, op. cit., p. 651.

26 Conrad, ed., *Children of God's Fire*, p. 304.

27 Holloway, op. cit.

28 Ibid., p. 652.

29 Ibid.

30 Barman, op. cit., pp. 203–205.

31 Ibid.

32 Ibid., p. 206.

33 Ibid., p. 211.

34 Ibid.

35 Ibid., p. 214.

36 Ibid., p. 224.

37 Holloway, op. cit., p. 648.

38 Ibid.

39 Schultz, op. cit., p. 152.

40 Holloway, op. cit., p. 671.

41 Ibid., p. 618.

42 Abreu, *Os Capoeiras*.

43 Freyre, *Order and Progress—Brazil from Monarchy to Republic*, p. 176.

44 Dias, *Quem Tem Medo Da Capoeira? Rio de Janeiro, 1890–1904*.

45 Holloway, op. cit., p. 662.

46 Almeida, op. cit., p. 27.

47 Holloway, op. cit., p. 670.

48 Needell, *A Tropical Belle Epoque*, p. 165.

49 Freyre, *The Mansions and the Shanties*, p. 324.

50 Freyre, *Order and Progress*, p. 12.

51 Holloway, op. cit.

52 Almeida, op. cit.

53 Holloway, op. cit.

54 Ibid., p. 635.

55 Ibid.

56 Ibid., p. 666.

57 Ibid.

58 Ibid.

59 Ibid., p. 670.

60 Ibid., p. 665.

61 Conrad, *Children of God's Fire: A Documentary History of Black Slavery in Brazil*, p. 384.

62 Ibid., p. 386.

63 Da Costa, *The Brazilian Empire. Myths and Histories*, p. 72.

64 Morais Filho, *Festas e Tradicões Populares do Brasil*.

65 Barman, op. cit., p. 225.

66 Ibid., p. 229.

67 Ibid., p. 230.

68 Conrad, op. cit., p. 339.

69 Burns, *A History of Brazil*, p. 260.

70 Ibid., p. 266.

71 Ibid.

72 Conrad, op. cit., p. 413.

73 Almeida, op. cit., p. 27.

74 Freyre, *Order and Progress*, pp. 11–12.

75 Needell, op. cit., p. 190.

76 Vianna, *The Mystery of Samba: Music and National Identity in Brazil*, p. 90.

77 Conrad, op. cit., p. 149

78 Schneider, *Order and Progress: A Political History of Brazil*, p. 66.

79 Da Costa, op. cit., p. 149.

80 Laquer, *A History of Zionism*, p. 30.

81 Bernal, *Black Athena: The Afroasiatic Roots of Classical Civilization*, p. 343.

72 Vianna, op. cit., p. 48.

83 Ibid., p. 53. Vianna cites Jorge Amado's "Casa grande e senzala e a revolução cultural," in *Gilberto Freyre: Sua ciência, sua filosofia, sua arte*, p. 31.

84 Needell, op. cit., p. 34.

85 Barman, op. cit., p. 325.

86 Ibid., p. 337.

87 Ibid., p. 327.

88 Ibid., p. 334.

89 Ibid., p. 339.

90 Da Costa, op. cit., p. 230.

91 Barman. op. cit., p. 341.

92 Levine and Crocitti, eds., *The Brazil Reader: History, Culture, Politics,* p. 145 (Princess Isabel and Rodrigo Augusto da Silva, "Abolition Decree 1888").

93 Barman, op. cit., p. 341.

94 Ibid., p. 343.

95 Ibid., p. 82.

96 Almeida, op. cit., p. 28.

97 Freyre, *Order and Progress,* p. 10.

98 Burns, op. cit., p. 285.

99 Barman, op. cit., p. 359.

100 Ibid., p. 363.

Chapter Twelve: The Republic

1 Thomas, *The Slave Trade,* p. 789.

2 Almeida, *Capoeira: A Brazilian Art Form,* p. 4.

3 Conrad, *Children of God's Fire: A Documentary History of Black Slavery in Brazil,* p. 323 (citing Viscount de Paraná).

4 Levine and Crocitti, eds., *The Brazil Reader: History, Culture, Politics,* p. 147 (Legislature of Minas Gerais, "Laws Regulation Beggars in Minas Gerais, 1900").

5 Newsome, *Planet Capoeira* interview.

6 Ibid., p. 5.

7 Ibid.

8 Ibid.

9 Freyre, *The Masters and the Slaves,* p. 76.

10 Ibid., p. 325.

11 Pastinha, "Capoeira: Brazilian Karate."

12 Almeida, *Capoeira: A Brazilian Art Form,* p. 28.

13 Holloway, "A Healthy Terror: Police Repression of Capoeiras in 19th Century Rio de Janeiro," p. 671.

14 Salvatore, Aguirre, and Josephs, eds., *Crime and Punishment in Latin America,* p. 181.

15 Freyre, *Order and Progress—Brazil from Monarchy to Republic,* p. 10.

16 Vianna, *The Mystery of Samba: Music and National Identity in Brazil,* p. 81.

17 Needell, *A Tropical Belle Epoque*, p. 34.

18 Ibid., p. 49.

19 Ibid.

20 Alexander, "Top Gun."

21 Pastinha, op. cit.

22 Schwartz, *Sugar Plantations in the Formation of Brazilian Society*, p. 486.

23 Freyre, *The Masters and the Slaves,* p. 490.

24 Awolalu, *Yoruba Beliefs and Sacrificial Rites*, p. 79.

25 Heywood, ed., *Central Africans and Cultural Transformations in the American Diaspora,* p. 310 (Brown, "Walk in the Feenda").

26 Rego, *Capoeira Angola Ensaio Socio-Etnografico*, p. 264.

27 Dayan, *Haiti, History and the Gods*, p. 23.

28 Rego, op. cit., p. 106.

29 Also see Xavier, "The Greatest Poet That God Creole." In addition toXavier's piece, I am also indebted for information from Kathleen Azevedo's "Tales on a String," available at www.brazzilmag.com 2002.

30 Da Cunha, *Rebellion in the Backlands,* pp. 263–264.

31 Hobsbawm, *Bandits*, p. 72.

32 Ibid., p. 65.

33 Alexander, op. cit.

34 Hobsbawm, op. cit., p. 64.

35 Ibid., p. 32.

36 Ibid.

37 Alexander, op. cit., p. 3.

38 Ibid., p. 67.

39 Landes, *The City of Women*, p. 73.

40 Lewis, *Ring of Liberation*, p. 50.

41 Capoeira, *The Little Capoeira Book*, p. 50.

42 From an article by Mestre Pastinha, source unknown.

43 "A Capoeira," *Kosmos*, Rio de Janeiro, March 1906, year 3, vol. 4. Quote cited in Sandler, *Capoeira, Rio Past and Present.*

44 Morais Filho, *Festos e Tradicões Populares do Brasil.*

45 Freyre, *Order and Progress—Brazil from Monarchy to Republic,* p. 177.

46 Lyrics from "Bahia de todos os santos" on the *Capoeira Angola* album by Mestres Boca Rica and Bigodinho. The CD was produced in July 2002 in association with Associaçao de Capoeira Angola Marron in Rio de Janeiro.

47 Levine and Crocitti, eds., *The Brazil Reader: History, Culture, Politics,* p. 181 ("Seized Correspondence from Communists, 1935–1945," Dossier 20, Police Archives).

48 de Andrade, Oswald, in Os Dentes do Dragão Magazine, cited by Janer Cristaldo in "Bahia's Dr. Faustas," www.brazzil.com, April 1998.

49 Williams, *Culture Wars in Brazil: The First Vargas Regime, 1930–1945*, p. 62.

50 Sandler, *Capoeira, Rio Past and Present,* citing Penna Marinho, Subsídios para o Estudo da Metodologia do Trainemento da Capoeiragem.

51 Williams, op. cit., p. 69, citing "Cultura e Serviço, Revista do Serviço Público, 1/3, no. 1 (July 1938), pp. 3–5.

52 Ibid., p. 86, citing Salgado, Radiofusão, fator social," *Cultura Politica,* vol. I, no. 6 (August 1941), pp. 79–93.

Glossary

1 Freyre, *The Masters and the Slaves,* p. 481.

2 Ibid., p. 482.

3 Ibid., p. 340.

4 Miller, *Kings and Kinsmen,* p. 301.

5 Capoeira, *Capoeira: Roots of the Fight-Dance-Game,* p. 58.

6 Miller, op. cit., p. 65.

7 For information about the Brazilian zuavos battalian, see Kraay and Whigham, *I Die with My Country: Perspectives on the Paraguayan War, 1864–1870,* especially Chapter 4.

GLOSSARY

abadá: Name for prayer shirt sometimes worn by malês in Brazil (from the Yoruban word agbada, for robe). A capoeira uniform. A capoeira group formed by Mestre Camisa.

academia: A school of capoeira.

acarajé: Beans fried in palm oil (dendê).

açoite de braço: A throw in Capoeira Regional.

adjá: Small bell made from metal played in xangô and Candomblé religious ceremonies.

afilhado (afilhada): Godson or goddaughter.

afoxé: Carnival marching groups, musical and sometimes religious.

africanos livres: African people enslaved illegally, manumitted after 1817 by British-Brazilian commissions, but often remaining de facto slaves.

agê (aguê): Gourd shaker covered with netting to which shells are attached.

agogô: Cow bell, double bell without clapper, sometimes iron or steel, or tin, used in capoeira ensemble and also in Candomblé.

agregado: Squatter or humble farmer on a fazenda.

agua: Water.

aguardente: Sugar cane rum, the same as cachaça.

aiê: Material world in Umbanda.

aimoré: Amerindian tribe of Espírito Santo and Ilhéus.

aldeia (aldea): An Amerindian village of the type developed by Jesuits and other religious orders in the colonial era.

alfândega: Customs house.

alforria: Manumission.

almude: 20-liter liquid measurement.

aluno/aluna: Capoeira student.

aluvanca: Backward leg sweep.

alqueire: Thirteen liters approximately of dry material, or an area of land ranging from 6 to 12 acres.

alta: High.

ama de leite: Slave wet nurse.

andar gingando: Walking with a swing.

Angola: A country in Africa; the style of capoeira which was initially distinguished from Regional style; a nation in the African Brazilian religion, Candomblé.

angolares: Quilombolas or slave fugitives on the island of São Tomé.

angoleiro: One who plays the Angola style of capoeira; a capoeirista.

angú: Flour made from corn or manioc or rice, and then boiled in water with salt.

anhanguera: A notably large bandeirante expedition.

anjinhos: A torture device; a thumbscrew used to punish slaves.

apanha: To be beaten

arame: Berimbau string; literally, wire.

Arawak: Amerindian tribe of the Amazon, Venezuela, Guiana, and the Caribbean islands.

areias: Soil with high sand content, where sugar cane doesn't thrive.

arqueação: The official slave carrying capacity of a slave ship.

armada: Capoeira turning kick; literally, armed strike.

armada pulada: Jumping armada.

armada real: Royal navy.

arraial: A mining camp or military barracks.

arrastão: Capoeira technique by which the player pulls both legs out from under the other.

arreador: Foreman of a mule train in Minas Gerais.

arriar: Antique capoeira slang meaning to change political allegiance.

arroba: 32-pound measurement.

Aruanda: As in "Caboclos de Aruanda," a reference to Luanda, "spiritland."

Ashanti: Gold Coast African ethnic group (of Ghana).

asiento: Contract granted (initially by the Spanish) to countries carrying slaves to Spanish colonies in the Americas.

atabáque: A varied size drum used in capoeira, Candomblé, and other activities. Can be beaten with the palm of the hand, fingers, or stick, depending on circumstances.

ataque: An attack in capoeira.

atual: A term for capoeira combining both Regional and Angola styles, invented by J. Lowell Lewis.

aú: A cartwheel.

aú batendo: Hitting aú.

aú coisa: Mule kick.

aú compass/aú siri: Closed aú.

aú chibata: Cartwheel with a one-legged "whip" kick.

aú duplo: Flying aú, in which both legs are thrown over with the feet together.

aú espinha: Cartwheel with a spinal twist.

aula: Class.

aviso: A rhythm on the berimbau, sometimes played to warn of approaching police.

axé: Cosmic force; life force; good energy; the power of the Orixás.

azenha: A water-powered sugar mill.

azul: Blue.

babalaô: Male diviner or seer.

bacalhau: Literally, codfish; a type of whip with leather thongs used for punishment.

bagaço: Stalks of the sugar cane after they've been pressed.

bagaceira: Place on a sugar plantation where cane waste was dumped.

baiana: From Bahia.

bairrista: One who is loyal to a bairro.

bairro: A neighborhood of a town or city.

baixa: Low.

balanço: Balance or quality of ginga and capoeira.

balcão: The platform where slaves dried and separated the sugar before it was crated.

bamba: A great capoeirista. An adept or expert.

banda: A band or a group of related rituals; a capoeira takedown technique.

banda amarrada: A takedown in pernada and batuque.

banda de costas: A takedown in pernada and batuque.

banda de frente: A takedown technique in the pernada or batuque game.

banda de lado: A takedown in pernada and batuque.

banda cruzada: A takedown in pernada and batuque.

banda dourada: A takedown in pernada and batuque.

banda jogada: A takedown in pernada and batuque.

bandeira: A large column of paulistas who explored the backlands in colonial days.

bandeirante: A member of a bandeira.

(de) bando: A ship with government authorization to load slaves as a freight carrier.

banguela: A berimbau rhythm.

banho de fumaça: Antique capoeira slang for rasteria (literally, smoke bath).

banqueiro: The sugar master's assistant.

Bantu: Kimbundu word for persons. An African people; tribes and language groups of 300 dialects that occupy two-thirds of sub-Saharan Africa. Bantu people live in both Congo and Angola.

banzo: A melancholy state born of a longing for the past or for Africa. A sad or depressed nostalgia. The blues. The "bundle" of goods equaling the price of a slave at Luanda.

baqueta: The wooden stick, about one foot long, used to strike the metal berimbau string.

barracão: A pen or shelter (barracoon) for slaves.

barravento: A berimbau rhythm, sometimes said to induce trance. A drum-beat of candomble that will serve any Orixá.

bater: To beat.

bateria: Set of percussion instruments of an orchestra.

batizado: Literally, baptism. A capoeira grading ceremony where belts are awarded.

batuque: A fight dance related to capoeira. A generic term for African dances performed to atabaques.

batuqueiro: One who participates in a batuque.

beira mar: Seacoast.

beixigas: Smallpox.

bênção: A direct front kick called chapa de frente in Capoeira Angola. Literally, blessing.

bênção pulada: "Jumping" blessing.

Benguela: A town on the Atlantic coast of Angola.

bens do evento: A stray animal, or "migrant" slaves who would be sold at auction.

benzedeira: Literally, she who blesses. A traditional healer.

berimbau: A bowed musical instrument amplified by a gourd, of central African/Angolan origin.

berra boi: Gunga cabaça.

bicho: A wild animal.

bico de papagaio: Another name for au quebrada.

bicuda: Thin pointed dagger.

biriba: The wood used for the verga, the main body of the berimbau.

boca: Opening or "mouth" of a cabaça.

boca de calça: A capoeira takedown, grabbing the ankles from the front.

boca de calça de costas: A capoeira takedown, grabbing the ankles from between the legs.

boca de siri: "Crab's mouth," a capoeira movement; also a slang name for straight razor.

boçal: An African newly arrived in Brazil, unacculturated. Uncouth.

bochecho: A block against cabeçada in Capoeira Regional.

bolo: A punishment inflicted by striking the hand with a wooden paddle.

bracear: Antique slang meaning to strike with the hands (literally, to swim)

bramar: Antique slang for shouting the name of a capoeira gang.

brincadeira: Playing, having fun in a childish way.

brincar: To play.

bumba meu boi: A northeastern Brazilian dance. A procession including some stock folkloric characters.

caapuera: Extinct forest. From the Tupi language.

cabaça: The amplifying and resonating gourd used on a berimbau.

cabeçada: A head-butt.

cabeleira: A mythical Pernambucan bandit of the sugar plantations, who was said to haunt Pernambucan engenhos in the 18th and 19th centuries.

cabocla/caboclo: Term (literally, copper-colored) to denote an Amerindian or mestizo. A mixed-race person of Amerindian and European heredity or a rural backwoods person.

caboré: Mixed-race person of African and Amerindian heredity.

cabra: Backlands assassin, "commonly a Negro."1 A young guy.

caçanje: Creole Portuguese spoken in Angola.

cachaça: Sugar-cane-based white rum made from first pressing of the cane.

cacubu: Handleless antique knife.

cadeirinha: Sedan chair carried by slaves, used for transporting passengers.

cafuso: Child of African Brazilian and Amerindian parents.

calabouço: Town jail.

calcanha: Female slave working in a sugar mill. Often swept up and tended lamps.

caldereiro: A worker in the sugar mill who tended the kettles. "Kettleman."

calhambola: Another name for a resident of a mocambo or quilombo.

calunga: An Orixá or divinity in Bantu religion. A small doll used for magical work by a nganga.

camara: Comrade. A stomach bug well known in colonial times.

câmara: Municipal council. Antique slang meaning to switch political allegiance.

Candomblé: Religion in Brazil deriving from West African Yoruban religion.

cangaceiro: A bandit.

cangaço: The burden or sack of weapons carried by the cangaceiro.

canhembora: A fugitive Amerindian.

canivete: Capoeira technique; literally, tin opener, can opener.

cantigas: Songs.

canto de entrada: The praising choruses following the ladainha.

capanga: Hired killer, "commonly a Negro of the backlands."2

capangagem: Use of hired muscle to achieve a desired end; for instance, the use of the maltas for political power.

capangueiro: Leader of a gang.

capitânia: Captaincy in colonial Brazil.

capataz: Overseer.

capitão do campo: Field captain, having the same purpose as capitão do mato.

capitão do mato: Bush captain used to capture fugitive slaves.

capitão-mor: A military rank given to commanders of local militias in colonial Brazil.

capoeira: Extinct forest (from Tupi language). Portuguese chicken coop. The African Brazilian martial art. (According to Waldeloir Rego, "capoeira" first appeared as a word in the *Vocabulario Português e Latino* in 1712.)

Capoeira Angola: A traditional style of capoeira that became defined as distinct from Capoeira Regional after Mestre Bimba began teaching in Salvador in the 1930s.

Capoeira Regional: So named after the style developed by Mestre Bimba at the Centro de Cultura Física Regional in 1937.

capoeirista: One who plays capoeira.

cariboca: Person of mixed European and Amerindian hereditary.

carimbo: Tool used to brand slaves; the brand mark itself.

carioca: Native of Rio de Janeiro.

carrapeta: Antique slang meaning small, brave, and quick.

carrasco: Undergrowth.

casa de santo: Shop selling religious supplies and artifacts for Candomblé and other sects.

casa do engenho: The building that housed the sugar mill.

casa grande: A big house where the rural aristocracy lived on plantations.

cavalaria: The cavalry. A berimbau rhythm used to warn of a police or cavalry raid.

caveira no espelho: Antique slang for a head-butt to the face of an enemy.

caxixí: The rattle that accompanies the berimbau.

cerrado: Forest.

chácara: Antique slang for a rural prison.

chamada: A passo a dois or "call" of capoeira used in Capoeira Angola.

chapa: A capoeira kick; literally, metal plate.

chapa com a perna de frente: "Sheet with the front leg."

chapa com a perna de trás: "Sheet with the back leg."

chapa de costas: Back kick (reverse kick).

chapa de frente: Front kick (the same as bencão).

chapa giratório: Turning sheet kick.

chapeu de couro: Literally, a leather hat; a swinging cross-kick delivered from the ground upward.

chibata: Small whip.

chicote: Whip.

chifrata: Antique slang for head-butt.

chula: A type of capoeira song that follows the ladainha.

chuta: To kick.

cinturra desprezada: The sequence of throws invented and taught by Mestre Bimba.

cocada: Coconut candy, or the name for a cabeçada technique delivered to the chin.

cocorinha: Literally, defecation; a variety of capoeira esquiva.

Código Filipino: Portuguese legal code used between 1603 and 1823, including slave laws and laws pertaining to the slave trade.

coffle: Gang or group of African slaves driven to a market.

coice: Mule kick delivered from a handstand with two feet.

como gérê: Roughly translated in Freyre as "I eat," relating to an African mythical creature called Quibungo who eats children. Singing "como gérê, como gérê."3

companha de emboscadas: Fighting patrol.

comprar o jôgo: Buying the game and replacing one of the players already in the roda.

confrarias: Black Catholic religious order.

contragolpe: Counterattack.

contramestre: An apprentice mestre, or foreman of an Academy.

contramestra: An apprentice mestra, or forewoman of an Academy.

conversos: New Christians or Jews who converted to Catholicism.

coqueiro: Coconut tree, coconut.

cordão: The colored belts awarded in capoeira batizados.

coronel: The political boss of a municipality.

corpo aberto: "Body open."

corpo fechado: Closed body. Invulnerability to knives, bullets, or psychic attack.

corridos: Short songs with verse and chorus sung during a roda.

corta capim: Grass cutter (foot sweep).

Côrtes: The Portuguese parliament.

cotovelhada: Elbow strike.

chique-chique: A Brazilian plant (*Opuntia brasiliensis*).

cria: A child. In old days it referred to a black child reared in the "big house."

crioulo: A black person born in Brazil.

cruz: Cross.

cruzado: Brazilian monetary unit. A Portuguese gold or silver coin with a cross marked on it, and used between the 15th and 20th centuries.

cruzeiro: A large cross built of stones in a public place like a square or a street.

curador: Public employee assigned as a guardian of orphans, slaves, or free blacks.

curandeiro: A practitioner of folk medicine.

cutelo: A "chopping" hand strike.

cutia: A forest-dwelling rodent of the family Caviidae (Dasyprocta aguti) found in the forests of Brazil. Featured in the capoeira song: "Eu vi a cutia com coco no dente, com coco no dente, com coco no dente."

cutilada de mão: A capoeira golpe (see Pastinha reference).

Dança do Rei, Reisado Guerreiro, or Congado: Brazilian dances that use wooden swords, according to information given by Mestre Bahia (António Rodrigues Clemente).

danado: Damned or cursed. Clever and cunning.

dá volta ao mundo: Literally, take a turn around the world; circle the roda.

dedeira: A strike to the eyes.

defesa: Defensive movement.

degredados: Exiled criminals, usually sent from Lisbon or Brazil to Angola.

dendê: "African palm" (*Elaeis guineensis*) imported and acclimatized to Brazil. Polyunsaturated orange palm oil widely used in Afro-Brazilian cooking. A term denoting spiritual power or energy.

desequilibrante: A technique that upsets an opponent's balance or equilibrium.

desgalhar: 19th-century malta slang meaning to flee from the police.

dgi: A sharp-edged tool made of diorite.

discípulo: Student of a capoeira master; literally, a disciple.

distorcer: 19th-century malta slang for disguise and concealment.

dobrando: Doubling on the berimbau.

dobrão: The coin used to play the berimbau.

donatário: Recipient of a hereditary captaincy in the 16th century.

é direito: 19th-century malta slang for being courageous.

Egbas: A Yoruba people.

elemento servil: "Servile element," a popular term for slave class at the end of the slave era.

emancipado: Free African

emboada: A pejorative term used by a native of an area to refer to an outsider.

emprenhar: The act of switching one ballot box for another in an election, for which capoeiristas were often responsible in the days of the maltas.

encruzilhada: Crossroads. A foot sweep.

engano: Phony and fraudulent.

engenho: Sugar mill or sugar plantation.

engenho real: Waterwheel-powered sugar mill.

entrada: A penetration by explorers from the coast into the sertão. Entrance.

eri ieiê ô: Salutation to Oxum.

escaupil: Padded or quilted armor, usually made of leather filled with cotton.

escolar: School; another name for academy.

esconder seu jogo: To hide or disguise the game.

escorpiao: A handstand with an extreme backbend.

escudo: Shield. Portuguese unit of currency.

espada: Literally, sword; a 19th-century malta gang of the Lapa district of Rio de Janeiro.

espelho: Mirror.

esquiva: Escape technique.

está pronto: 19th-century malta slang meaning to be hurt or wounded.

estância: Ranch or country estate, generally in southern Brazil.

estrangeiro: Foreigner or stranger.

fabrica: A mill, plant, or factory. Worker on a cattle ranch.

facão: Large knife, machete, or cutlass.

faiscador: Itinerant gold prospector.

falsidade: Falsity, treason, treachery, double dealing.

farofa: Toasted manioc meal (farinha de mandioca).

farinha: Flour.

favela: Slum, ghetto, or shantytown; often-used term in Rio de Janeiro.

fazenda: A large estate, ranch, farm, or plantation.

fazendas de canas: Cane fields.

fazendeiro: Fazenda owner.

fechar: Closed, effective defense.

fechar o corpo: Closed body. Spiritual and physical defense.

ferro: Iron knife.

feijão: Beans.

feijoada: Brazilian bean and meat stew. The "national" dish.

feira: An interior marketplace in Angola, designated by Portuguese for trade between African and European sectors.

feitor: Overseer or foreman on a plantation.

feitoras: Fortified Portuguese trading posts.

figa: Talisman of a fist with the thumb protruding between the first and second fingers.

fino: Highest quality sugar.

firma: 19th-century malta slang meaning "don't run."

floreios: Literally, flourishes; flashy movements in capoeira.

forasteiro: Scavenger for gold.

formado: A "formed" capoeira student. A graduate.

formatura: A "formed" capoeira student. A graduate. A grading.

foro military: Military privileges.

fortaleza: 19th-century malta slang for tavern; literally, fortress.

fouce: Short scythe or team of two slaves (man and woman) who cut and tied sugar cane.

freguesia: Parish.

frente: Front.

fretado: Freight carrier; a slave ship doing business in Luanda.

fubá: Corn or rice flour.

fuga: Flight and escape movements.

fundamentos: Basics and fundamentals of capoeira.

funidor: Backland slave hunter and buyer in Africa.

galo canto: Rooster song.

galopante: A strike to the ears with two cupped hands, sometimes called "telefone."

gameleira: A variety of tree of the *Moraceæ* family.

gan: Yoruba for bell (agogô).

Gantois: Gantois terreiro was the subject of written works by both Dr. Artur Ramos and Dr. Nina Rodrigues. Gantois was situated on a hill high above Bahia and stood in a clearing in the woods beyond the tram line which led from the Upper Town. It was reached by following a steep and circuitous footpath that had been hidden in the days of slavery to protect worshippers from arrest.

ganzá: Tubular metal shaker.

garapa: Another name for cachaça, a drink made from skimmings of heated sugar cane juice.

garimpeiro: Illicit miner and diamond hunter.

gargalheira: Iron collar worn by convicted runaway slaves.

gato: Back flip.

gaucho: Nomadic cattle herder or cowboy of southern Brazil.

gaunches: Indigenous people of Tenerife.

Gêges: Name in Brazil describing people of Dahomey, the Fon, who mainly worshipped the Vodun god.

gegê: Fon dialect of Ewe language.

gerebita: Brazilian sugar cane brandy of very high proof, which was important in the Brazilian slave trade.

ginga: To sway, the basic footwork and movement of capoeira.

godeme: A strike with the back of the hand.

golpe: Punch, blow, or hand strike. Attacking technique.

golpe de vista: The vision that instantly perceives a whole scenario from all angles.

grampear: 19th-century malta slang meaning to hold onto or hug an enemy.

gravata: Headlock.

gringo: Name given to Europeans by Brazilians and other South Americans.

grupo: Group (capoeira group).

guaiamus: 19th-century capoeira gang in Rio de Janeiro.

Guaraní: A sub-group of indigenous Amerindians of Brazil.

guardas: Defensive positions.

guerra: War or battle, fight.

gunga: Largest cabaça on the berimbau, giving the bass sound.

heré: A rattle made of copper used in Xangô ceremonies.

herva santa: Holy herb (tobacco).

hollandilha: Coarse linen tunic worn by prisoners taken by the Catholic Inquisition.

homens bons: "Good men," the upper-class men of colonial Brazil, who were permitted to vote for town council members.

iaiá/ioiô: Slang for senhora or senhor, or the daughters and sons of slave masters.

Iansã: The goddess of wind and storms, sometimes associated with Santa Barbara.

idalina: A berimbau rhythm.

Ilê: Spirit world in Umbanda.

Imbangala: Bands of mercenary, lineageless soldiers who first emerged in the south and east of Angola in the last decade of the 16th century.

inconfidência: A revolt.

ingênuo/ingênua: The freeborn son or daughter of a slave woman according to the Rio Branco Law of the "free womb" in 1871.

Ipueira: Lake that fills only in the rainy season. "Dead lake." Pueira, from the same Tupi root as poeira in capoeira, meaning "dead forest."

irmão: Brother.

irmandad: A religious brotherhood.

iuna: A berimbau rhythm customarily attributed to Mestre Bimba.

Iyá Kalá, Iyá Detá, Iyá Nassó: Three Xangô priestesses from Nigeria reputed to have established the first Candomblé terreiro in Salvador, Bahia.

jacaré: Literally, alligator; a broad-bladed, strong knife.

jagunço: Backwoods fighter or assassin. Or sertanejo, an inhabitor of the backlands.

jangada: Seagoing raft. Also 19th-century malta slang for a prison at the police station.

jeito: Skill.

jingola: The plural of ngola.

joelhada: A kick with the knee.

jogador: A capoeira player.

jogar: To play.

jogo: Game

jogo de baixo: Playing low.

jogo de braços: The arm and hand game.

jogo de búzios: Divination technique of throwing cowrie shells into a circle.

jogo de chão: The game on the ground.

jogo de corpo: Body play.

jogo de dentro: Playing in, or close to one's partner.

Keto: West African kingdom near the border of Nigeria and Benin, from whence came large numbers of people transported to Bahia. Their religion influences Candomblé today.

kibuka: The name given in Congo to a chain or coffle of slaves.

ladainha: Beginning prayer or "lament" of the capoeira roda, especially in the Angola roda.

ladja: A mock combat dance from Martinique with parallels to capoeira. Also danmyé.

lamparina: Literally, oil lamp. A straight razor, or 19th-century malta slang meaning to be hit on the face.

lançado: West African (Senegambian) word for an African-European trader.

lavrador: Tenant farmer, often of sugar cane.

leao de chácara: A bouncer.

Lei do Ventre Livre: Law of the Free Womb (also known as the Rio Branco Law).

lemba: A commercial "cult" used for trading in the hinterland of Loango. Sometimes said to be Elegba, a Vodun god of Dahomey/Benin. Jewish people of southern Africa who claim to have built Great Zimbabwe.

libambo: Iron chain used in Africa and Brazil to confine slaves, and the iron collar used to punish runaway Brazilian slaves.

liberto/liberta: A liberated slave.

ligeiro: Fast and agile, maybe cunning and dishonest.

limbabo: The same as kibuka, a chain or coffle of slaves in the area east of Luanda.

lingua geral: A "universal" language primarily of Tupi-Guaraní and Portuguese.

louvação: A tribute prayer.

luta: Fight.

macaco: Literally, monkey. The main village in Quilombo de Palmares; a back-flipping acrobatic capoeira technique.

Macumba: An African influenced Brazilian folk religion. Similar to Umbanda and Quimbanda, and centered primarily in Rio de Janerio.

macumbeiro: One who practices the Macumba religion.

machete: A banjo or small guitar.

macombeiro: An inhabitant of a mocambo.

maculêlê: A dance game using sticks, batons, or sabres, played to music, and reminiscent of African Brazilian folklore.

madrinha: Godmother.

mães de balção: Slave women who took sugar from pots and loaded it into crates.

mãe prêta: Black mother. Used in patriarchal families of colonial Brazil affectionately to describe black wet nurses and servants who cared for children.

malandragem: Street-wise actvities (often illegal) or street hooliganism; capoeira play.

malandro: Ragamuffin, street-smart trickster, bad guy or tough guy.

mal de Luanda: Scurvy.

malê: Africans of Hausa, Mandinga, or Fula origin, often muslims.

malícia: A way of being and thinking. Deception, speed, trickery, cunning.

maloca: An Amerindian village.

malta: 19th-century capoeira gang in Rio de Janeiro.

malunga: The plural term for lunga, an "ancient Mbundu authority symbol, associated with the Pende in particular; believed to come from the sea and have close connections with bodies of water."[4]

malungo: Comrade, an African term for one with a shared experience on a slave ship or in a quilombo.

mameluco: One born from European or Caucasian and Amerindian parents. This became a generic term for all mixed-race parentage.

mancebia: A form of slave marriage most commonly used, meaning "consensual union."

mandinga: Traders and people from Gambia. A cunning quality of playing capoeira. A kind of enchantment associated with pretos velhos.

mandingueiro: A capoeira player who possesses mandinga. A sorcerer or healer.

mandioca: Cassava and manioc.

manganga: Besouro's last name (Besouro Manganga). A healer who uses herbs or magic (from Angolan nganga, or doctor). A northeast Brazilian term for a large wood-gnawing beetle.

mangue: Swamp.

mani: Title of the kings of Congo.

maní: A mock combat dance from Cuba, with similarities to batuque.

mão-de-faca: Portuguese for knife hand.

maraca: A gourd filled with pebbles mounted on a short handle. Similar in use to ganzá.

marano: New Christian (or a Portuguese term for Sephardic Jews).

marcha: Literally, march; 19th-century malta slang meaning to go out in search of enemies.

maré: Tide.

marinheiro: Sailor. Also a name given to the Portuguese by Brazilians in colonial Brazil, approximately equivalent to gringo.

martelo: Hammer kick.

martelo de estalo: Crack of the hammer.

martelo de estalo pulava: Crack of the hammer with a jump.

martelo giratório: Turning hammer kick.

mascate: Peddler of wares.

massapé: Fertile, dark, rich, clay soil suitable for growing sugar cane.

mate: Paraguayan tea.

matuto: Backwoodsman.

mazombo: A Brazilian born of white European parents. Derogatory term.

Mbundu: The Bantu people living in the area of highland bordering Congo, and the area drained by the Kwanza River.

médio: Medium sized (as in medium sized cabaça). Also berimbau de centro.

meia-lua de compasso: A turning kick delivered with the heel; literally, half moon in a compass.

meia-lua de frente: A front kick; literally, half moon to the front.

melado: 19th-century malta slang meaning blood (literally, honey).

Menininha do Gantois: Menininha was the legendary mãe ("mother") of the Candomblé terreiro of Gantois in the early part of the 20th century (the 1930s). In her youth she had been a talented seamstress and had made a living from that profession. She was the foremost priestess of Bahia after the death of another famous mãe, Aninha, in 1937. Mães Aninha and Menininha were said by some to represent the last generation of the orthodox classical Yoruban Candomblé priestesses of Bahia.

mestizo: Part white (Caucasian) and part Indian person. Again became a generic term for mixed-race parentage.

mestre: Master.

mestre de açúcar: Sugar master in an engenho.

mestre de campo: The leader of a colonial militia.

meter o andante: "To stick the thing that walks," as with a chapa de frente.

mina: Mine. Slave from the Mina coast of Ghana, sometimes known as the Gold Coast.

mineiro: A miner or an inhabitant of Mina Gerais.

mocambo: Originally a dwelling inside a quilombo, then another name for a quilombo. A hideout in the forest.

moço: Young; often used to describe young slaves.

modinha: A popular urban song deriving from drawing room ballads originally.

moeda: A coin used to play the berimbau.

moedira: A female slave who fed sugar into rollers.

moenda: Mill rollers. A capoeira technique performed close to the ground, reminiscent of the Angola style.

mola: Flip from the shoulders to the feet.

mole: 19th-century malta slang meaning coward.

moquette: 19th-century malta slang meaning to strike with a wooden club.

morador: Resident or squatter given leave to settle under certain strict conditions.

morena: A brown-skinned girl.

mortais: Mortal, or deadly, as in salto mortais somersault.

mucamba: House slave.

mulatto: A person born of white (Caucasian) and African-Brazilian parents.

muleque/moleque: Word of Bantu origin, meaning a young African. In Brazil, it means child or kid.

muxilingoes: Bandits.

mwene puto: Kongolese and Central African term for Portuguese colonial administration.

nagô: Yorubans from Nigeria; the name given to them in Bahia.

nagoas: Powerful 19th-century capoeira gang in Rio de Janeiro.

navalha: Barber's straight razor.

ndembu: Title for warlords and slave traders in southern Kongo.

ndende: Kimbundu term for palm trees; basis for dendê, the palm oil.

ndongo: Sometimes said to be the alternative collective name for all Mbundu people. In the 16th century, the ndongo was a sub-group of the mbundu, along with other sub-groups which would have included the lenge, the songo, the mbondo, the pende, the hungu, and the libolo.

Ndongo: The Kingdom of Ndongo was a tributary to the Kingdom of Kongo, and its king, the Ngola a Kiluanje, was a vassal of the ManiKongo. Ndongo became independent from Kongo after war in the 1550s. Its subjects were Mbundu Kimbundu speakers.

negaça: To deny.

negativa: Said by Mestre Pastinha to mean "positive black." A capoeira ground technique, literally meaning denial.

negativa de fundo: Deep negativa.

negativa de frente: Negativa to the front.

negativa de solo: Negativa on the floor.

negativa lateral: An Angola negativa to the side.

negro de ganho: A working slave who gave a set portion of his earnings to the master.

nenem: A baby.

ngola: A peice of iron held by most Mbundu lineages as an important lineage authority emblem; associated with the samba people.

Ngola a Kiluanje: One of the new types of political structure that evolved from the ngola as an authority emblem; this was a title that began as a subordinate one to the Kiluanje kya Samba, and then in the early 16th century became the most important title among the Mbundu people.

ngolo: Zebra dance, in Angola. Said by some to be the root of capoeira.

nigé: Nigeria's people.

nome de guerra: War name (capoeira nickname).

Nossa Senhora: Our Lady

novena: Slave punishments that were continued for a nine-day period.

nzimbu: Marine shell fished from Luanda Bay and used as currency in colonial Angola.

Nzinga: The famous Angolan queen (Ana de Sousa) who occupied Matamba in the early 17th century and brought a degree of political unity to the Ndongo. Queen Nzinga claimed the ngola a kiluanje title in Matamba, on the Wamba River, as she led one of the most powerful Mbundu states in the1640s, at the time when the Portuguese had attempted to create puppet ngolas to replace authentic Ndongo rulers.

ogan: Male layman in Candomblé.

Ogum/Ogún: God of War in African Brazilian pantheon.

Olórun: Supreme creator god of the Yoruba people. Also known as Zambi.

Olódùmarè: Supreme being in Yoruban religion, which was the origin of Candomblé in Brazil.

orixá: A god or goddess of the African Brazilian pantheon.

ouvidor: Judge in colonial Brazil and Luanda.

Ovimbundu: The people living on the Ovimundu highlands, or the Benguela plateau, who differed more from the Mbundu than did the people of Kongo, and from whom came many Imbangala.

Oxalá/Orixalá: The foremost masculine divinity in Brazil. In Africa, called Obatalá. Represents divinity of the divinities, creation, and sexual reproduction.

Oyó: The region and city of Nigeria that was the capital of the ancient Yoruban empire, as in "the old Oyo empire."

palácio de cristal: 19th-century malta slang for an urban prison.

Palmares: The region in Pernambuco that served as the site of the most famous of all Brazilian quilombos, dated from the 17th century.

palmatoada: A stroke inflicted on the hand as a punisment.

palmatória: Hand claps that accompany capoeira music. Also a wooden paddle used to punish slaves by striking the hand.

pandeiro: Small frame hand-held drum affixed with cymbals (a tambourine). One of the traditional instruments in the ensemble of Capoeira Angola and Regional.

parafuso: Literally, screw. Jumping screw kick.

pardo/parda: A brown-skinned person.

parnahyba: A long bladed weapon used by cangaçeiros in Pernambuco and Paraíba.

passada: Footwork

passage: See passo a dois and chamada.

passo a dois: Literally, stepping in tandem. The same as a chamada, a ritualized movement between the two players that acts as a break in the game or a game within the game.

patrão: Master, as in senhor de engenho or slave master.

patúa: An amulet blessed by magical ritual and often worn around the neck or on the body for psychic and physical protection.

pau Brasil: Dye wood after which Brazil was named.

paulista: Inhabitant of São Paulo.

pé: Foot (as in pé da cruz or pé do berimbau).

peça: Literally, piece; in the days of slavery, a term used to denote a slave.

pegada: 19th-century malta slang for a pitched battle between rival gangs.

pelourinho: Stone pillar (signifying municipal status), where also whippings and public punishments were carried out against slaves and others.

peneiração: A type of ginga, or swaying.

pernada: A combative style of capoeira taught in Rio in the '50s; also a name for the batuque game.

petrópolis: A club carried by 19th-century capociristas, possibly because of their association with the "Black Guard," monarchists who acted as bodyguards for Princess Isabel, whose home was in the palace in Petropolis.

piaba: Literally, small fish; 19th-century malta slang for useless capoeirista.

pião de cabeça: Headspin.

pião de mão: Handspin

pipa: Cask in colonial times of 500-liter capacity.

pisão: "Big step," side kick.

platinelas: The small metal discs on a pandeiro.

poeira: "Dustbin." A jail. Dusted.

pokwe: A fighting knife associated with 19th-century Lunda people of Angola.

pombagiras: Feminine aspect of the orixá Exú in Candomblé.5

pombeiro: A caravan leader in colonial Africa. In Brazil, a mining prospector.

ponte: Bridge

ponteira: Front kick delivered with the ball of the foot.

positivo: Early 18th-century phrase for comrade or partner.

povo da rua: Street people.

prêto de ganho: See negro de ganho.

prêto velho: An ancestral spirit of an old black slave.

pulava: "Jumping." Can be added to other technique names when they are a flying technique, such as armada pulava.

pulo do macaco: Monkey jump.

quadra: A song type in capoeira, with four verses, sung call and response between soloist and chorus.

quebra: To smash, as in au quebrada, a cartwheel with a smash.

quebra de braço: Amerindian arm-breaking fighting game.

quebra pescoço: A choke hold in Capoeira Regional.

queda de quatro: Falling on four, an esquiva in capoeira.

queda de rins: "Fall on the kidneys," a capoeira technique.

queixada: "Chin strike," a capoeira kick.

quilombo: "Maroon town." Runaway slave colony.

quilombola: An inhabitant of a quilombo.

Quimbanda: A variation of Umbanda, and sometimes said to be the "dark side" of that religion. It is heavily influenced by African traditions.

quingingo: Tasks given to slaves over and above the daily quota.

quintal: A slave pen or barracoon.

quinto: The "fifth" tax in the colonial era, which involved paying a fifth of the value of goods to the Portuguese Crown.

rabo de arraia: Literally, stingray's tail. A capoeira kick like mea lua de compasso, and various other capoeira techniques according to region.

rasteira: Capoeira foot sweep.

razzia: A raid against a quilombo or mocambo.

reco reco: Percussive instrument used in capoeira. Often a bamboo scraper.

reconcavo: The area bordering All Saints Bay outside Salvador.

recuo: A capoeira escape technique.

Reconquista: Spanish war of reconquest.

reduções: "Reductions," the villages where Amerindians were sometimes forced or coerced to live by the Jesuit missionaries.

Regional: Capoeira Regional, the style developed by Mestre Bimba.

reinado africano: Coronation of an African king and queen in Brazil.

réis: Currency unit.

relógio: A capoeira technique; literally, clock.

resgate: Enslavement of Amerindians who'd been saved from capture by other Amerindians.

resistencia: A capoeira defensive ground technique.

reza: Prayer, ladainha.

risco dos escravos: Literally, slave risk, or the financial risk involved in high slave mortality.

roça: Forest clearing, often resulting from slash-and-burn techniques.

roda: The circle of capoeira. 19th-century malta slang meaning "let's run away."

roda de bamba: A roda where only the best capoeiristas play.

rolé: "Roll," a capoeira floor technique.

rondas: In the early 19th century, special patrols that were employed in particular Recôncavo districts to enforce curfews, check passes carried by slaves, and arrest both slaves and freedmen suspected of committing crimes.

rujão: 19th-century malta slang for a battalion or group.

S dobrado: Double "s," a capoeira technique, the same as chapéu de couro.

sabiá: A type of bird.

sacarolha: "Corkscrew," a capoeira technique.

safra: Sugar cane harvest.

saída: "Exit," or "exiting" from the pé da cruz to enter the roda.

salve: Salute or greetings (often said at the beginning or end of capoeira classes by certain groups.

samba: A musical and dance style in Brazil.

Samba: "The people who brought the jingola to the Mbundu are remembered as 'Samba,' obviously the 'Samba a Ngola' of the ngola aetiological legend. Matamba, the sixteenth-century Kikongo name for the ancient province lying near [the highland regions near the headwaters of the Lukala river] ... identifies the source of both the Samba and the ngola since the Portuguese form of the name 'Matamba' was the same word as the Kimbundo term 'Samba.'"[6]

samba de roda: A berimbau rhythm, an early form of samba in northeast Brazil, which takes place in a ring.

samba duro: Hard samba, a type of batuque.

santa maria: A berimbau rhythm.

Santidade: A religious cult in Brazil that fought against Portuguese rule.

santo: Patron saint or Orixá.

santo christo: A straight razor used by capoeiras. Like the petrópolis wooden club, this weapon appears to get its name from São Cristóvão Palace, signifying its association with the monarchist capoeira players of the "Black Guard," who used it.

são bento grande: A berimbau rhythm.

são bento grande de Angola: The rhythm as stated to distinguish it from Regional style.

são bento grande de Regional: The rhythm specific for Regional capoeira.

sapé: Grass used for thatching.

sarandage: 19th-century malta slang for small-fry capoeiristas.

sardinha: 19th-century malta slang for straight razor.

saudade: Sentimental nostalgia for somebody, someplace, or a thing.

senhor de engenho: The owner of a sugar mill, a plantation owner.

senhor de terras: A large-scale landowner.

senzala: Slave quarters on Brazilian plantations. The name of Mestre Sombra's academy in Santos. The name of the influential group formed in Rio de Janeiro in the 1960s.

seqüência: "Sequence." Mestre Bimba popularized sequences in capoeira instruction and they became a mainstream method for teaching capoeira in academies.

sertanejo: One who lives in the backlands.

sertanista: One who knows the backlands well.

sertão: The backlands of Brazil.

seu: Colloquial shortening of senhor.

sinal: Sign.

sinhá/sinhô: Corrupted forms of the words senhor and senhora, used by slaves to describe the landowning class.

soba: Kimbundu word for a local chief.

sobrados: Colonial two-story townhouses found in Angola and Brazil.

sovelão: A stiletto dagger, shaped like a larger version of an awl, popular with 19th-century capoeiristas.

tembanza: A Cokwe term referring to the kilombo leader's principle wife.

terreiro: The place where magical and religious rituals take place.

tesoura: "Scissors," a capoeira technique.

tico-tico: Bird.

tocar: To play music.

topete a cheirar: 19th-century malta slang meaning a head-butt to the nose.

toque: Term for berimbau rhythms, as in toque do berimbau.

tronco: Wooden or metal stocks used as punisment in Brazil.

tumbeiro: "Floating tomb." A slave ship. A slave hunter in African interior.

tungar: 19th-century malta slang meaning to wound a foe.

Tupinambá: Generic term given many Tupi tribes in 16th-century colonial Brazil.

Tupi-Guaraní: An Amerindian language. An Amerindian people or tribe.

Umbanda: A Brazilian religion that contains varied elements from spiritism, Candomblé, positivism, Amerindian religion, and Roman Catholicism.

urubú: Vulture.

vadia: Vagrancy, idleness.

vadiacão: Hanging around, unemployed on specific work.

valentão: A brave man, or slang for a bad guy.

valente: Valiant.

Valongo (Rua do): The main street where slaves were penned and sold in colonial Rio de Janeiro.

vaqueiro: Cowboy from northeastern Brazil.

vaqueta: Stick used to play the berimbau.

vara, vêrga: The main body of the berimbau instrument. Vara also means measure of length 1.10 meters, corresponding to an English or American yard.

vingativa: Vengeful, vicious. Like a banda, a leg swipe behind an opponent.

vintém: Old Brazilian coin that can be used to play berimbau.

viola: The berimbau with the small cabaça that plays the most variations in the capoeira ensemble.

virada: Doubling on the berimbau, a variation of the rhythm on the berimbau.

violinha: Equivalent to the viola.

Vodun: African religion of Benin, practiced by Gegês in Brazil.

volantes: Police forces and special squadrons that emerged in Brazil in 1920; primarily military police and rapid-response squadrons. For the next two decades they were deployed especially in the rural, feudal regions in northeastern Brazil, and were active against the bandits called cangaceiros.

volta do mundo: Circling in capoeira. Taking a turn around the world within the roda.

Xangô: God of thunder, lightning, and justice. Also an African and Amerindian religion in northeast Brazil.

xique-xique: A plant of the cactus family.

Zambi: The supreme God of Bantu and Umbanda cults. A different name for Olórun. Sometimes used in Portuguese texts by commanders referring to Zumbi, as in "great lord," although probably this is from Nzambi Mpungu, which is the Kikongo term for God.

zuavos: A special African-Brazilian battalion during the Paraguayan War (the

War of the Triple Alliance), made up of capoeiristas usually pressed into front-line service after prison sentences or being caught in raids by press gangs. The zuavos were often without guns and attacked Paraguayan positions, fighting only with knives, swords, and other weapons used by capoeiristas of the period.[7]

Zumbi: The famous leader of the 17th-century Quilombo dos Palmares. Also an apparition or ghost of the dead that wanders in the night.

BIBLIOGRAPHY

A vital source of information for the workings of Brazilian sugar plantations was Stuart B. Schwartz's excellent book, *Sugar Plantations in the Formation of Brazilian Society Bahia, 1550-1835*. The early history of Amerindians in Brazil is best told by John Hemmings in *Red Gold: The Conquest of the Brazilian Indians*. For translated documents of the colonial and slave era in Brazil, the best source is *Children of God's Fire: A Documentary History of Black Slavery in Brazil*, edited and translated by Robert Edgar Conrad. For information about quilombos and translations of primary sources, an informative book is *Maroon Societies: Rebel Slave Communities in the Americas*, edited by Richard Price. Also very useful in this regard is *The Brazil Reader: History, Culture, Politics*, edited by Levine & Crocitti.

For an overall picture of the Atlantic slave trade, Hugh Thomas's *The Slave Trade: The Story of The Atlantic Slave Trade, 1440–1870* is a reliable beginning. Walter Rodney's books, *How Europe Underdeveloped Africa* and *A History of the Upper Guinea Coast* are also valuable histories which deal extensively with the slave trade and colonial period. For information on the slave trade between Angola and Brazil, Miller's *Way Of Death: Merchant Capitalism and the Angolan Slave Trade, 1730 –1830* is indispensable, as is Miller's *Kings and Kinsmen* for a description of early states in central Africa.

For a better understanding of African military strategy and fighting techniques, the works of John K. Thornton are very rewarding. Of particular interest are *The Art of War in Angola: 1575-1680* and *Warfare in Atlantic Africa: 1500-1800*. For a fuller understanding of police networks in Empire period Rio de Janeiro, Thomas Holloway's "'A Healthy Terror': Police Repression of Capoeiras in Nineteenth Century Rio de Janeiro" is very useful.

Central African influences on Brazilian percussive music in Brazil are thoroughly explored in Gerhard Kubik's *Angolan Traits in Black Music, Games and Dances of Brazil: A study of African cultural extensions overseas*. Kubik has also provided further interesting information in the first volume of *The Garland Encyclopedia of World Music*, which deals with Africa.

In Portuguese, Waldeloir Rego's *Capoeira Angola Ensaio Socio-Etnografico* has sometimes been referred to as the "Bible" of capoeira history, and for an interesting anthropological glimpse of early twentieth-century Bahian candomblé, Ruth Landes's *The City of Women* is recommended. Gilberto Freyre's *Casa grande e senzala (Mansion and the Shanties)* is well worth reading, as is his classic, *The Masters and the Slaves: A Study in the Development of Brazilian Civilization*. The handbooks of *Capoeira Angola* and *Curso de Capoeira Regional* are both available in Portuguese, ghost written with the supervision of mestres Pastinha and Bimba, and are a useful source of information about the main techniques in these capoeira styles.

Abreu, Plácido. *Os Capoeiras*. Rio De Janeiro: Livraria Serafim, 1880.

Abshire, D. M, and M.A. Samuels, eds. *Portuguese Africa*. London: Pall Mall Press, 1969.

Ajayi Ade, J. F. and Michael Crowder, eds. *History of West Africa*. New York: Columbia University Press, 1972.

Alexander, Sonya. "Top Gun." *Brazzil* (May 25, 1999), www.brazzillog.com/pages/p25may99.htm.

Almeida, Bira. *Capoeira: A Brazilian Art Form*. Berkeley, Calif.: North Atlantic Books, 1983.

Almeida, Manuel Antônio de. *Memórias de um sargento de milícias*. Rio de Janeiro: Ediouro, n.d. 1855.

Amado, Jorge. *Gilberto Freyre: Sua ciência, sua filosofia, sua arte*. Rio de Janeiro: José Olympio, 1962.

Anderson, Robert Nelson III. "The Slave King." *Brazzil* (October 1995), www.brazil-brasil.com/cvroct95.htm.

A.P.D.G., *Sketches of Portuguese Life, Manners, Costume, and Character*. London, 1826.

Awolalu, J. Omosade. *Yoruba Beliefs and Sacrificial Rites*. Brooklyn: Athelia Henrietta Press, 1996.

BBC World Service. *The Story of Africa: Early History*. www.bbc.co.uk/worldservice/africa/features/storyofafrica/2chapter 5.shtml.

Bales, Kevin. *Disposable People: New Slavery in the Global Economy*. Berkeley, Calif.: University of California Press, 1999.

Bamaguje, Mallam. *The "Mistake" of 1914*. Katsina State, Nigeria, 2001. www.nigerdeltacongress.com/articles/mistake_of_1914.htm.

Bastos, Augusto. "Traços gerais sobre e etnografia do distrito de Benguela." *Boletim da Sociedade Geográfica de Lisboa*, 26a Série, 198 (1908).

Barman. Roderick J. *Citizen Emperor: Pedro II and the Making of Brazil, 1825–91*. Palo Alto, Calif.: Stanford University Press, 1999.

Bernal, Martin. *Black Athena: The Afroasiatic Roots of Classical Civilization*. New York: Vintage, 1991.

Bethell. Leslie, ed. *Colonial Brazil*. Cambridge: Cambridge University Press, 1987.

Birmingham, David and Phyllis M. Martin, eds. *History of Central Africa*, vol. 1. New York: Longman, 1983.

Blum, William. *Rogue State: A Guide to the World's Only Superpower.* London: Zed Books, 2000.

Boles, John B. *Black Southerners: 1619–1869.* Lexington: University Press of Kentucky, 1983.

Brittain, Victoria. *Death of Dignity: Angola's Civil War.* London: Pluto Press, 1998.

Burke, Ray. "The Bee, the Reed, the Root: the History of Sugar." Academic Alliances: Southeast Georgia Collaborative. http://class.georgiasouthern.edu/fl/sugar/sugar-b.htm .

Burlamáqui, Aníbal. *Ginástica nacional (capoeiragem) metodisada e regrada.* Rio de Janeiro, 1928.

Burns, E. Bradford. *A History of Brazil.* New York: Columbia University Press, 1980.

Campbell, Dugald. *In the Heart of Bantuland.* Philadelphia and London: Seeley, Services and Co. Ltd, 1922.

Capello, Hermenegildo Carlos Brito and Roberto Ivens. *From Benguela to the Territory of Yacca.* Vol I. London: Sampson Low, Marston, Searle and Rivington, 1882.

Capoeira, Nestor. *Capoeira: Roots of the Fight-Dance-Game.* Berkeley, Calif.: North Atlantic Books. 2002.

Capoeira, Nestor. *The Little Capoeira Book.* Berkeley, Calif.: North Atlantic Books, 1995.

Carmichael, John. *African Eldorado.* London: Duckworth, 1993.

Carneiro, Edison. *Religiõs Negras. Negros Bantus.* 2nd ed. Rio de Janeiro: Civilização Brasileira (orig. published separately in 1936 and 1937).

Cavazzi da Montecuccolo, Giovanni Antonio. *Istorica Descrizione de tre regni Congo, Matamba ed Angola.* Bologna, 1687.

Chomsky, Aviva, Barry Carr, and Pamela Maria Smorkaloff, eds. *The Cuba Reader: History, Culture, Politics.* Durham, N.C.: Duke University Press, 2003.

Conrad, Robert Edgar, ed. *Children of God's Fire: A Documentary History of Black Slavery in Brazil.* University Park: The Pennsylvania State University Press, 1995.

Cooper, Carol. *The Gospel Box. Writing the Song of Songs: An Evolutionary History of Black Gospel Music.* Burbank, Calif.: Rhino Entertainment Company, 1999.

Da Costa, Emilia Viotti. *The Brazilian Empire: Myths and Histories.* Chicago: The University of Chicago Press, 1985.

Da Cunha, Euclides. *Rebellion in the Backlands.* Samuel Putnam, trans. New York: Picador, 1995.

Davidson, Basil. *In the Eye of the Storm.* New York: Doubleday, 1972.

Davies, Glyn. *A History of Money from Ancient Times to the Present Day.* 3rd ed. Cardiff: University of Wales Press, 2002.

Dayan, Joan. *Haiti, History, and the Gods.* Berkeley, Calif.: University of California Press, 1996.

De Azevedo, Kathleen. *Tales on a String.* www.brazzilmag.com, 2002.

Debret, Jean Baptiste. *Viagem Pitorêsca e Histórica ao Brasil.* São Paulo: Livraria Martins Editôra, 3a. Edição, 1954.

De Oliveira, Valdemoir. *Frevo, Passo e Capoeira.* Recife, Brasil: Companhia Editora de Pernambuco, 1971.

Dias, Luiz Sergio. *Quem Tem Medo Da Capoeira? Rio de Janeiro, 1890–1904.* Rio de Janeiro: Prefeitura da Cidade do Rio de Janeiro, 2001.

Dow, George Francis. *Slave Ships and Slaving.* Minneola, New York: Dover Publications, Inc, 2002.

Downey, Greg. *Capoeira Angola from Salvador, Brazil.* Washington, D.C.: Smithsonian Folkways Records, 1996.

Ennes, Ernesto. *As guerras nos Palmares (subsidios para sua historia).* São Paulo: Edições de Companhia Editora Nacional, 1938.

Ennes, Ernesto. "The Palmares 'Republic' of Pernambuco: Its Final Destruction, 1697." *The Americas,* 5:200–216, 1948.

Fage, J. D. and Roland Oliver. *A Short History of Africa.* New York: Penguin Books, 1995.

Falola, Toyin and G. O. Oguntomisin. *Yoruba Warlords of the 19th Century.* Trenton, N.J.: Africa World Press, Inc, 2001.

Fausto, Boris. *A Concise History of Brazil.* Cambridge: Cambridge University Press, 1999.

Ferreira, Augusto. "Historia da Capoeira." *Jornal da Capoeira*. São Paulo: Editora Cordão de Ouro, Ano 1, no. 3, p. 2.

Freyre, Gilberto. *The Mansions and the Shanties*. New York: Alfred A. Knopf, 1956.

Freyre, Gilberto. *The Masters and the Slaves*. New York: Alfred A.Knopf, 1946.

Freyre, Gilberto. *Order and Progress—Brazil from Monarchy to Republic*. New York: Alfred A. Knopf, 1970.

Fryer, Peter. *Rhythms of Resistance: African Musical Heritage in Brazil*. London: Pluto Press, 2000.

Gaines, Charles and George Butler. *Pumping Iron: The Art and Sport of Bodybuilding*. London: Sphere Books Ltd, 1974.

The Garland Encyclopedia of World Music. Volume 1: Africa. Stone, Ruth, James Porter, and Timothy Rice (editors). New York: Garland Publishing, The Taylor and Francis Group, 1998. (See Part 2: Issues and Processes in African Music. Chapter by Gerhard Kubik: "Intra-African Streams of Influence." Also Part 3: Regional Case Studies. Chapter by Gerhard Kubik: "Central Africa: An Introduction.")

The Garland Encyclopedia of World Music. Volume 2: South America, Mexico, Central America and the Caribbean. Olsen, Dale A. and Daniel E.Sheehy (editors). New York: Garland Publishing, The Taylor and Francis Group, 1998. (See Part 2: Issues and Processes in the Music of South America, Mexico, Central America and the Caribbean. Chapter by Charles A. Perrone: "Popular Music of Brazil." Also Part 3: Nations and Musical Traditions. Section 2: Countries and Peoples of South America and Their Music. Chapter by Larry Cook: "Brazil: North East Area." Also chapter by Gerard Béhague: "Afro-Brazilian Traditions.")

Giblin, James. "Issues in African History." Art and Life in Africa Online. www.uiowa.edu/~africart/toc/history/giblinhistory.html.

Gobineau, Joseph-Arthur (Comte de). *Essai sur l'inégalité des races humaines*. Paris: Éditions Pierre Belfond, 1967.

Gonçalves, A. "Capoeiragem: rebeldia e habilidade negra no Rio." *Jornal da Tarde*. São Paulo, June 10, 2001.

Goulart, José Alípio. *Da palmatória ao patíbulo: Castigos de escravos no Brasil.* Rio de Janeiro, 1971.

Gray, William G. *Western Inner Workings.* York Beach, Maine: Samuel Weiser, 1983.

Hancock, H. Irving, *Educacão Fisica Japanesa.* Rio de Janeiro, 1906.

Hemming, John. *Red Gold: The Conquest of the Brazilian Indians.* London: Papermac, 1995.

Henderson, Lawrence W. *Angola: Five Centuries of Conflict.* Syracuse: Cornell University Press, 1979.

Heywood. Linda. M., ed. *Central Africans and Cultural Transformations in the American Diaspora.* Cambridge: Cambridge University Press, 2002.

Hilton, Anne. *The Kingdom of Kongo.* Oxford: Oxford University Press, 1978.

Hobsbawm, Eric. *Bandits.* London: Weidenfeld & Nicholson, 2000.

Hochschild, Adam. *King Leopold's Ghost: A Story of Greed, Terror and Heroism in Colonial Africa.* Boston: Mariner Books, 1998.

Holloway, Thomas H. "A 'Healthy Terror': Police Repression of Capoeiras in Nineteenth-Century Rio de Janeiro." *Hispanic American Historical Review* 69:4. Durham, N.C.: Duke University Press, 1989.

Howell, John Lloyd. *Capoeira: Martial Art of Brazil.* London: Warrior Dreams Publications, 1998.

James, C. L. R. *The Black Jacobins.* New York: Penguin, 2001.

Kapuscinski, Ryszard. *Another Day of Life.* New York: Penguin Books, 2001.

Kraay, Henrik and Thomas L. Whigham, eds. *I Die with My Country: Perspectives on the Paraguayan War, 1864–1870.* Lincoln: University of Nebraska Press, 2004.

Kubik, Gerhard. "Angolan Traits in Black Music, Games and Dances of Brazil: A study of African Cultural Extensions Overseas." *Estudos De Antropologia Cultural.* N.10. Lisboa, 1979.

Landes, Ruth. *The City of Women.* Albuquerque: University of New Mexico Press, 1994.

Laquer, Walter. *A History of Zionism.* 1st ed. London: Taurisparke Paperbacks, 1972.

Levine, Robert M. and John J. Crocitti, eds. *The Brazil Reader: History, Culture, Politics*. London: Latin American Bureau, 1999.

Lewis, J. Lowell. *Ring of Liberation*. Chicago: University of Chicago Press, 1992.

Library of Congress Federal Research Division. "Gold Mining Displaces Cane Farming." Library of Congress Country Studies: Brazil. http://lcweb2.loc.gov/frd/cs/brtoc.html#br0016.

Lovejoy, Paul E. "The African Diaspora: Revisionist Interpretations of Ethnicity, Culture and Religion under Slavery." *Studies in the World History of Slavery, Abolition and Emancipation*, II, 1 (1997). www.geocities.com/CapitolHill/Lobby/2897/diaspora.html.

MacDonald, N. P. *The Making of Brazil*. Lewes, East Sussex: The Book Guild Ltd, 1996.

McIntosh, Roderick J. www.archaeology.org/9807/abstracts/africa.html. The Archaeological Institute of America, 1998.

de Macedo, J. M. *Memórias da Rua do Ouvidor*. Brasília: Editora da UnB, 1978. http://www.biblio.com.br/templates/joaquim-manueldemacedo/mmemoriasdarua.html

Mannix, Daniel P. *The History of Torture*. London: New English Library, 1964.

Mathews, Caitlin and John. *The Western Way. A Practical Guide to the Western Mystery Tradition*. London: Arkana, Routledge and Kegan Paul, 1986.

Miller, Joseph C. *Kings and Kinsmen: Early Mbundu States in Angola*. Oxford: Clarendon Press, 1976.

Miller, Joseph C. *Way of Death: Merchant Capitalism and the Angolan Slave Trade 1730–1830*. Madison: University of Wisconsin Press, 1988.

Monteiro, J. *Angola and the River Congo*, vol 1. London: MacMillan, 1875.

Moraes Filho, A. J. M. *Capoeiragem e Capoeiras Célebres, Festas e Tradições Populares do Brasil*. Rio de Janeiro, 1901.

Moraes Filho, A. J. M. *Festas e Tradicões Populares do Brasil*. Rio de Janeiro: H Garnier, 1888.

Morgan, Philip D. *Slave Counterpoint: Black Culture in the Eighteenth Century*

Chesapeake & Low Country. Chapel Hill: University of North Carolina Press, 1998.

Morwyn. *Magic from Brazil.* St. Paul, Minn.: Llewellyn Publications, 2001.

Needell, Jeffrey D. "The Abolition of the Brazilian Slave Trade in 1850: Historiography, Slave Agency and Statesmanship." *Journal of Latin American Studies* 33:4 (November 2001): 681–711. Cambridge: Cambridge University Press.

Needell, Jeffrey D. *A Tropical Belle Epoque.* Cambridge: Cambridge University Press, 1987.

Newsome, Dennis. "Interview with Contra-Mestre Preto-Velho, Group Malandros-Touros." *Planet Capoeira Magazine* (May 24, 2002). www.capoeira.com/planetcapoeira/view.jsp?section=Features&view Article=116.

Newsome, Dennis. *Kalenda.* www.osmalandrosdemestretouro.bigstep.com/homepage.html.

Nieuhof, Johan. "Voyage and Travels into Brazil and the East Indies," 1704, in Churchill, Awnsham, and John Churchill, eds., *A Collection of Voyages and Travels: Some Now First Printed ...,* vol. II. London, 1732.

Nina Rodrigues, Raymundo. *O animismo fetichista dos negros bahianos.* Rio de Janeiro: Civilização Brasileira, 1935.

Nina Rodrigues, Raymundo. *Os africanos no Brasil.* São Paulo: Companhia Editora Nacional, 4th edition, 1932. Reprint, 1976.

Nzongola-Ntalaja, Georges. *The Congo from Leopold to Kabila.* London: Zed Books, 2002.

Okpewho, Isidore, Carole Boyce Davies, and Ali A. Mazrui, eds. *The African Diaspora: African Origins and New World Identities.* Bloomington: Indiana University Press, 2001.

Parfitt, Tudor. *Journey to the Vanished City.* New York: Vintage Books, 2000.

Pastinha, Vicente Ferreira (Mestre Pastinha). *Capoeira Angola.* Salvador: Escola Gráfica Nossa Senhora de Loreto, 1964.

Pastinha, Vincente Ferreira (Mestre Pastinha). "Capoeira: Brazilian Karate." *Black Belt Magazine.* Valencia, Calif., Black Belt Communications, March 1964, p. 22.

Pitta, Sebastião da Rocha. *Historia da America Portuguêza*. (1st ed., 1730). Lisbon: F. A. da Silva, 1880.

Pelissier, Rene and Douglas L. Wheeler. *Angola*. London: Pall Mall Press, 1971.

Penna Marinho, Inezil. *Subsídios para o Estudo da Metodologia do Treinemento da Capoeiragem*. Rio de Janeiro: Imprensa Nacional, 1945.

Pereira da Silva, J. M. *Segundo Período do Reinado de Dom Pedro I no Brazil. Narrativa Histórica*. Rio de Janeiro: B. L. Garnier, Livreiro-Editor, 1871.

Pope-Hennessey, James. *Sins of the Fathers*. London: Sphere Books, 1970.

Price, Richard, ed. *Maroon Societies*. Baltimore: Johns Hopkins University Press, 1996.

Ramos, Artur. *O folk-lore negro do Brasil*. Rio de Janeiro: Civilização Brasileira, 1935.

Rath, Richard Cullen. "Drums and Power: Ways of Creolizing Music in Coastal South Carolina and Georgia, 1730–1790." Way Net. http://way.net/creole/drumsandpower.html.

Rego, Waldeloir. *Capoeira Angola Ensaio Socio-Etnografico*. Salvador: Secretaria de Educação e Cultura do Governo do Estado da Bahia, 1968.

Reichmann, Rebecca, ed. *Race in Contemporary Brazil*. University Park: Penn State University Press, 1999.

Reis, João Jose. *Slave Rebellion in Brazil*. Baltimore: Johns Hopkins University Press, 1995.

Revista do Serviço Público (Brazilian periodical of Estado Novo era).

Rideau, Wilbert and Ron Wikberg. *Life Sentences: Rage and Survival Behind Bars*. 1st ed. New York: Three Rivers Press, 1992.

Robinson, Randall. "Haiti—A Call for Global Action: Honor Haiti, Honor Ourselves; Forget Haiti, Forget Ourselves. *The Black Commentator* 71 (January 1, 2004). http://blackcommentator.net/71/71_robinson_haiti_pf.html.

Rodney, Walter. *A History of the Upper Guinea Coast*. Oxford: Clarendon Press, 1970.

Rodney, Walter. *How Europe Underdeveloped Africa*. London: Bogle-L'Ouverture Publications, 1983.

Röhrig Assunção, Matthias. *Capoeira: The History of an Afro-Brazilian Martial Art*. Sport in the Global Society, 45. Oxon: Routledge, 2005.

Salvatore, Ricardo D., Carlos Aguirre, and Gilbert M. Josephs, eds. *Crime and Punishment in Latin America*. Durham, N.C.: Duke University Press, 2001.

Salway, Lance. *Gold and Gold Hunters*. London: Kestrel Books (Penguin Books), 1978.

Sandler, Dido. *Capoeira, Rio Past and Present*. Dissertation for the Department of Hispanic Studies. Liverpool University, 1987. Translation by Gerard Taylor.

Schneider, Donald M. *Order and Progress: A Political History of Brazil*. New York: Queens College City University of New York, 1991.

Schwartz, Stuart B. *Slaves, Peasants and Rebels. Reconsidering Brazilian Slavery*. Champaign: University of Illinois Press, 1996.

Schwartz, Stuart B. *Sugar Plantations in the Formation of Brazilian Society*. Cambridge: Cambridge University Press, 1998.

Schultz, Kirsten. *Tropical Versailles: Empire, Monarchy and the Portuguese Royal Court in Rio De Janeiro, 1808–1821*. New York: Routledge, 2001.

Segal, Ronald. *Islam's Black Slaves: A History of Africa's Other Black Diaspora*. London: Atlantic Books, 2002.

Smith, Joseph. *A History of Brazil*. London: Longman, 2002.

Stedman, John Gabriel. *Stedman's Surinam: Life in an Eighteenth-Century Slave Society*. Richard Price and Sally Price, eds. Baltimore: Johns Hopkins University Press, 1992.

Stein, Stanley J. *Vassouras, A Brazilian Coffee County, 1850–1900: The Roles of Planter and Slave in a Plantation Society*. Princeton, N.J.: Princeton University Press, 1985.

Steinberg, Rafael. *The Cooking of Japan*. New York: Time Life Books, 1985.

Stuckey, Sterling. *Slave Culture: Nationalistic Theory and the Foundations of Black America*. New York: Oxford University Press, 1987.

Suret-Canale, Jean. *Essays on African History.* Trenton, N.J.: Africa World Press, 1988.

Thomas, Hugh. *The Slave Trade: The Story of the Atlantic Slave Trade, 1440–1870.* London: Papermac, 1998.

Thomson, Jim. "The Haitian Revolution and the Forging of America." *The History Teacher* 34, no. 1 (November 2000). www.historycooperative.org/journals/ht/34.1/thomson.html.

Thornton, John K. *The Art of War in Angola: 1575–1680.* Cambridge: Comparative Studies in Society and History, Cambridge University Press, 1998.

Thornton, John K. *The Kingdom of Kongo: Civil War and Transition, 1641–1718.* Madison: University of Wisconsin Press, 1983.

Thornton, John K. *The Kongolese Saint Anthony.* Cambridge: Cambridge University Press, 1998.

Thornton, John K. *Warfare in Atlantic Africa: 1500–1800.* London: UCL Press, 1999.

Toop, David. *Rap Attack: African Rap to Global Hip Hop.* Edition 3. London: Serpents Tail, 2000.

Vandevort, Bruce. *Wars of Imperial Conquest in Africa, 1830–1914.* London: UCL Press, 1998.

Vianna, Hermano. *The Mystery of Samba. Music and National Identitiy in Brazil.* Chapel Hill: University of North Carolina Press, 1999.

Vogt, John. *Portuguese Rule on the Gold Coast, 1469–1682.* Athens: University of Georgia Press, 1979.

Walsh, Robert. *Notices of Brazil in 1828 and 1829.* 1st ed. London: Frederick Westley and A. H. Davis, 1830.

Wheeler, Douglas L. and Rene Pelissier. *Angola.* London: Pall Mall Press, 1971.

Williams, Daryle. *Culture Wars in Brazil: The First Vargas Regime, 1930–1945.* Durham, N.C.: Duke University Press, 2001.

X, Malcolm. *Malcolm X on Afro-American History.* Atlanta: Pathfinder, 1992.

Xavier, Arnaldo. "The Greatest Poet That God Creole." *Callaloo* (Johns Hopkins University Press) 18:4 (1995): 777–795.

INDEX

A

Afonso V, 11, 12, 39, 464

Agogô, 240–241, 321, 322, 323, 324, 325, 330, 331, 355, 493, 505

Aimoré Amerindians, 17, 199, 493

Aleixo, Prof. Mário, 28, 238, 444

Amotinado, 23, 173, 177, 184, 185, 457

Antonio I, King, 20

Aruak Amerindians, 13

Ashanti, 21, 24, 25, 27, 176, 177, 178, 179, 180, 181, 195, 250, 251, 252, 253, 254, 256, 259, 326, 495

Atabaque, 289, 321, 322, 323, 325–327, 330, 335, 337, 355, 497

Azores, 10, 37, 40, 53, 175

B

Bandeirantes, 18, 19, 89, 135–138, 141, 150, 175, 187, 188, 190, 195, 198, 199, 200, 463, 494, 496

Bantu, 7, 46, 90, 219–243

Berimbau, 240, 282, 283, 289, 321–355, 431, 434, 494, 495, 496, 497, 498, 500, 502, 506, 510, 511, 514, 517, 518, 519

Bight of Benin cycle, 23

Bimba, Mestre, 27, 322, 426, 452, 453, 499, 500, 506, 516, 518, 522. See also Machado, Manoel dos Reis

Book of Knowledge, 9, 10

Burlamáqui, Aníbal, 28, 29, 445, 450, 524

C

Cabral, Pedro Alvares, 13, 46, 47, 48, 49, 53, 54

Candomblé, 26, 208, 209, 213, 214, 215, 216, 217, 279, 288, 290, 291, 323, 324, 325, 327, 328, 329, 331, 332, 333, 334, 335, 337, 342, 419, 427, 430, 449, 453, 493, 494, 495, 497, 499, 500, 507, 510, 513, 515, 518, 522

Cão, Diogo, 13, 39, 40, 46, 48, 86, 139

capuuera, 13

Caravel, 10, 14, 38, 47

Carib Amerindians, 13, 50

Casa da Mina, 12, 40

Ceuta, 10, 37

Chocalho, 341

Columbus, Christopher, 13, 33, 36, 48, 58

Cresques, Abraham, 9

Cuba, 4, 50, 208, 223, 224, 226, 266, 271, 316, 326, 338, 340, 342, 350, 478, 509, 524

D

da Fonseca, Deodoro, 5, 396, 407, 409, 411, 412, 415, 419, 421, 461

da Gama, Vasco, 13

da Nóbrega, Manoel, 15, 49

da Sousa, Tomé, 15, 470

Dahomey, 18, 45, 62, 71, 125, 156, 176, 177, 178, 179, 213, 253, 254, 259, 260, 262, 263, 266, 267, 271, 274, 280, 303, 325, 505, 508

Dan Fodio, Uthman, 22

de Moura, Alexandre, 17

de Vasconcelos, Luis Mendes, 17

Dias, Bartolomeu, 40, 46, 47, 48

Dias, Paulo, 16

Disease, 15, 16, 24, 50, 65, 140, 173, 202, 228, 230, 305, 325, 335, 368, 405, 416, 420

Drums, 25, 65, 91, 104, 120–122, 178, 214, 224, 264, 282, 285–288, 290, 291, 319, 323–327, 335, 336,

337, 344, 348, 349, 350, 355, 473, 495, 497, 513, 530

Dutch East India Company, 17, 112

Dutch West India Company, 18, 94, 95, 96, 107, 110, 112, 163

E

Eanes, Gil, 10

Eu Sei Tudo (Aleixo), 28

F

Fante, 24, 25, 108, 179, 253

Feitiçaria, 290, 428

Ferdinand V, 11, 50

G

Games
  kicking game, 311, 312
  wrestling game, 186, 342, 343

Ganga Zumba, 19, 88, 97, 98, 99, 103, 105, 117, 130, 131, 132, 133, 134, 141, 145, 155, 208

Gé Amerindians, 13

Ghana, 7, 8, 10, 21, 24, 32–34, 62, 154, 155, 175, 179, 180, 252, 256, 259, 267, 325, 326, 495, 511

Gidigbo, 186, 342, 343

Ginástica (Capoeiragem) Metodizada e Regrada (Burlamáqui), 28, 29, 445, 450, 524

Gold Coast, 14, 19, 20, 21, 39, 53, 84, 108, 155, 156, 162, 176, 180, 181, 190, 250, 251, 252, 495, 511, 532

Gold mining, 31–55, 149–217

Gomes, Fernão, 12, 39

Gordo, Eddie, 5

"Guinea," 20

H

Haiti. *See* St. Domingue

Henry the Navigator, 10, 21, 31, 36, 37

I

Imbangala, 16, 17, 18, 68, 90, 91, 95–98, 100, 102, 104, 105, 108, 109, 110, 111, 114, 115, 116, 117, 120, 121, 124, 125, 146, 178, 198, 212, 213, 232, 331, 351, 506, 513

Inconfidência Mineira, 23, 24

Inquisition, 12, 41, 71, 86, 203, 211, 290, 506

Isabella I, 11, 12

Islam, 31, 34, 34–35, 63, 64, 236, 245, 249, 254, 255, 256, 257, 258, 259, 262, 264, 291, 427, 469

Islamic jihad, 22, 245–267, 479

J

Jejes, 257, 265, 266, 267, 279, 291, 428

Jesuits, 14, 15, 41, 49, 52, 57, 62, 63, 70, 118, 136, 137, 141, 170, 171, 188, 202, 208, 280, 494, 516

K

Kiluvia, 95, 96

L

Lovejoy, Paul, 3, 257, 270, 428, 479, 480, 528

Luther, Martin, 14

M

Machado, Manoel dos Reis, 27, 399, 423, 426. *See also* Bimba, Mestre

Madeira, 10, 37, 40, 41, 53, 58, 60

Magic, 91, 93, 121, 152, 178, 207, 226, 248, 249, 290, 352, 419, 427, 428, 429, 431, 434, 477, 484, 499, 509, 514, 518

Mali empire, 8, 9, 15, 32, 33, 34, 35, 37, 245, 246, 259

Manganga, Besouro, 27, 28, 354, 426, 427, 430, 431, 434, 435, 441, 509

ManiKongo, 13, 15, 43, 46, 55, 241, 242, 512

Mansa Musa, 8, 9

Mbwila, Battle of, 20

Mina coast cycle, 21, 62

Mondo, 91

Muhammad, 7, 256, 258

Music, 40, 67, 120, 195, 196, 214, 226, 278, 282, 283, 286, 287, 292, 317, 319, 322, 323, 324, 325, 327, 328, 331, 336, 337, 339, 340, 341, 343, 345, 347, 348, 349, 354, 355, 386, 400, 401, 419, 423, 424, 444, 445, 449, 462, 476, 481, 483

N

Nagos, 257, 266, 267, 295

Ndongo, 13, 15, 16, 17, 18, 19, 102, 116, 118, 119, 121, 242, 512, 513

Ngola a kiluanje, 13, 15, 16, 44, 68, 94, 96, 110, 117, 233, 512, 513

Ngolo, 221–224, 351, 352, 353, 453, 454, 512

Ngoma ya mukamba, 91

Nzinga, Queen, 18, 19, 45, 46, 47, 68, 70, 104, 110, 111, 125, 212, 213, 286, 331, 513

O

Ogum, 335, 513

Oyo, 20, 23, 26, 125, 242, 254, 256, 257, 259–267, 271–273, 513

P

Pandeiro, 321, 322, 331, 341, 355, 513, 514

Paraquayan War, 26, 348, 376, 378, 380, 390, 393–396, 399, 407, 413

Pastinha, Vincent Ferreira, 27, 216, 222, 321, 322, 333, 334, 418, 426, 442, 452, 453, 483, 484, 489, 490, 502, 512, 522, 529

Pereira, Manoel Henrique, 27, 426, 430, 431

Plague, 15, 20, 89, 161, 173

Porto, Lt. Santo, 28

Q

Quilombo dos Palmares, 17, 19, 20, 21, 83, 85–89, 91, 93, 95–103, 105–107, 109, 111–115, 117, 119, 121, 123–135, 137–147, 190, 199, 208, 209, 461, 463, 465

R

Rebellion, 26, 64, 75, 99, 123, 134, 135, 162, 163, 165, 166, 176, 177, 189, 252, 257, 264, 270, 271, 273–275, 278, 280, 291, 292, 294, 295, 300, 312, 354, 357, 361, 398, 400, 427, 428, 437, 472, 477, 480, 482, 490, 525

Domingue rebellion, 23, 270, 274

Stono rebellion, 22, 122, 123, 124, 275

Reco-reco, 321, 322

Revolt of the Tailors, 24

Rousseau, Jean-Jacques, 22

S

Santidade, 15, 202, 203, 204, 517

Sarakole, 7

Sextus IV, 12

Sierra Leone, 11, 12, 39, 260

Silvino, Antonio, 435, 437

Siozinho, Mestre, 27

Sokoto Caliphate, 22, 255–259, 262, 267, 337

Songhai, 11, 15, 32–35, 44, 63, 259

Songhai empire, 11

St. Domingue, 10, 125, 269, 270–301, 316, 326, 357, 369, 480

Sugar plantations, 57–81

Suriname, 4, 126, 149, 223, 225, 226, 311, 326

T

Teixeira, Pedro, 198

Treaty of Tordesillas, 13

Triangular trade, 52, 156

Tupi Amerindians, 13, 15, 49, 52, 57, 58, 62, 86, 100, 136, 139, 146, 198, 202, 498, 499, 506, 508, 518

V

Velho, Macaco, 28

Vita, Dona Beatriz Kimpa, 21, 123, 124

W

Weapons, 88, 103, 109, 115, 117, 118, 121, 122, 128, 146, 177, 178, 185, 186, 187, 200, 201, 227, 231, 235, 247, 287, 295, 297, 360, 370, 373, 374, 392, 395, 431, 438, 443, 499

Witchcraft, 71, 83, 97, 225, 249, 290, 387, 419, 428, 429

Women, 51, 61, 65, 66, 71, 73, 78, 80, 85, 88, 100, 104, 115, 126, 129, 136, 138, 154, 165, 171, 175,

178, 190, 191, 195, 196, 199, 208–217, 221, 225, 281, 285, 291, 333, 387, 391, 397, 400, 429, 442, 477, 484, 527

Y

Yoruba, 8, 21, 22, 26, 55, 64, 186–187, 202, 214, 216, 254–267, 272, 280, 323, 324–337, 342–343, 346–347, 427–429, 480, 490, 499, 505, 510–513, 523, 525

Z

Zumbi, 19–21, 97, 105–107, 113, 114, 117, 127–129, 133, 134, 135, 139, 142–147, 441, 519, 520

ABOUT THE AUTHOR

Gerard Taylor is one of the first generation of non-Brazilian students who have benefited from capoeira's establishment in Europe. After having been totally sold on the fitness and marathon running boom of the late 1970s, he first heard of capoeira in the mid 1980's and began training in Britain's first capoeira school, The London School of Capoeira, in 1989. He trained three to four times a week with Master Sylvia Bazzarelli and Contra Master Marcos Dos Santos for the next seven years, before moving to Oslo, Norway, where he co-founded the Oslo Capoeira Klubb with Agnes Folkestad, another of the LSC's students.

Since the late 1970s Gerard has worked in various fields of journalism and copywriting, including for the Foundation for African Arts, and as Northern Ireland editor for the *Black Voice* newspaper. More recently he has written text for theatre companies in London and for Apple Records on the Beatles1 official website. At the present time Gerard has numerous capoeira writing projects underway, including *Capoeira Conditioning,* a whole-body training manual based on capoeira movements, to be published by Blue Snake Books in 2005. He is also finalizing work on a vegetarian and vegan cookbook, and has recently finished an encyclopedic history of Los Angeles and San Francisco punk rock music.